Home Is Where My Earrings Are

Life in the slow lane where
'no froblem' is the modus operandi
and Insha'Allah, God willing,
is the way of life.

Best Wishes, Uganda!

Dannie Russell

Dannie Russell.

the Peppertree Press
Sarasota, Florida

ISBN: 978-1-61493-049-5

Library of Congress Number: 2012939414

Printed in the U.S.A.

Printed May 2012

Dedication

My family first and foremost,

My professional colleagues in schools around the world,

My writing colleagues in countries around the world,

My ethnic acquaintances around the world,

My American neighbours around the cul-de-sac.

To authors who taught me the trade and craft and
the art of storytelling.

In a sense, we're all global nomads.

Thank you all for being part of my life.

Contents

Prologue

Writing and Fishing

They say couples who have been together for some time become as one. I'm not so sure about that. They say couples start to look alike. Someone help us both. They say couples can complete each other's sentences. In our case, I'm pretty sure opposites attract. Daryle, my husband of over 50 years, is the smart one. I'm the cute one.

Over the years, I realized that we enjoy more similarities than differences. Yes, I'm talking of his love of fly-fishing. No, I never loved fishing. I love the rivers and streams and quiet riverbanks, clear, cool water and scenery that defies description. At the same time, I couldn't avoid my obsession with words; with putting thoughts, ideas on paper trying to figure out what was happening, trying to figure out what I was thinking.

Sitting on riverbanks in Africa, New Zealand, the Black Forest, I noticed a parallel between fishing and writing. Daryle digs around in his little tackle box for the perfect feather, he calls it a nymph, I search in my thesaurus for the perfect word, I call it word-smithing. "Writing, like fly-fishing, is an elaborate conspiracy to make lyrical an activity that is inherently a business of barbs and worms." I wish I had said that. Wayne Fields said it in *What the River Knows*, his story of fishing in Michigan.

So I wrote some of my stories down. The characters we met while living and working internationally made the imprint. The story, while written in first person, is not my story as much as it is their story; a chronicle of remarkably diverse personalities. Tamene, the Priest, Seyoum, Sister Katryn, even Mai Thai; Mirwaz, Imelda and Ronny; Bernie, Asha and Mouna taught me about their ethnicity and customs. Attempting to understand cultures through characters is what this book is about. Ultimately, of course, it's about understanding myself.

Our international life started at a time when we were idealistic, newly married, adventuresome and young. We were ready to save the world, whatever that meant. America was appreciated, respected, feared, invited to assist. That was then.

This is a story of perceptions. My perceptions of how it seemed. It reflects a life of growth; a life which began as a desire for us to get outside of ourselves: A chance to ask not what our country could do for us, but what we might contribute to the world. Well that was naive.

In the beginning, it was a time that was like living the pages of a textbook. Experiences seemed surreal, like I was living outside of myself, walking in the ruins of Athens, meeting the Emperor in the palace, hearing the lions from the royal grounds roar at night, observing the country in mourning. I must be reading these experiences from *National Geographic* or *Sociology 101*. It couldn't be me.

It was before instant information, before internet technology, before touch phones and messaging. It was after TV, but most information came from then called 'wireless' shortwave news services, certainly in Africa. It was a time when a hardship post was one without CNN. In America, it was a time of civil rights unrest. It was a time when marches, shootings and riots, notoriously the Los Angeles Watts riots, confounded northerners and southerners, easterners and westerners. It was a time when the American President was assassinated.

I hoped to teach, though I was not trained. I was 22 years old and ready to go. The first year in Addis I was frustrated. I planned carefully, but when I tried to wing-it, my classes of 40-75 students were chaotic. Cause and effect. I was frustrated then worn down by the constant touching and mauling in crowded places, and everyplace was crowded. We enjoyed a great advantage of being married. Little frustrations multiplied if allowed to fester; we saw the contagion in colleagues. We encouraged each other; pulled each other up with humour and support. If we could find any wine, that helped too.

It took years to process. I went through the motions, lived through it, but the measure of it all came much later. I'm still processing; still learning from our global life. Seeking out cultures gave depth to our work. For us, life was more than the corporate cul-de-sac, company compound or any army base. Taking risks gave me opportunities and I lost my innocence, my naïveté.

Instead of peeling away the layers of the onion, experientially we built scaffolding upon which each successive event added a new layer. From the mud walls of Africa, to Bamboo of Asia, to the dunes of the Middle East; from the eye-popping wonder of Addis Ababa to reflective analysis of unfolding international events in New York, from Ethiopian riots to Iraqi rockets, the characters along the way told the story. Told my story; told our story.

Bias? Of course. Personal agenda? Of course. Perspective? Of course. This book is about reflection.

The Title

I am often asked, "Where do you consider home? You've lived in so many places." And now you know the answer. Home is where my earrings are. This impetus to learn about cultures, to be of service perhaps began at age sixteen when I traveled with a small group to Hermosillo, Sonora, Mexico. We volunteered to build a couple of adobe buildings. I fell in love with an 18 year old Mexican boy who showed me how to stack mud bricks then how to paint the new construction a bright *azul y amarillo.* Juan Miguel told me, "You have beautiful eyes." *Que romantico!* Fortunately, I had to finish eleventh grade. We did correspond for some time, in Spanish, but of course I never saw him again.

Each time the green aerogram arrived from Mexico, my mother couldn't wait to learn what Juan Miguel wrote. Her Spanish was not very good so I made up the translation and she loved it. She wanted me to apply to American Field Service as an exchange student but I wasn't ready. She was the one who wanted to travel.

Years later as I moved around working the cocktail circuit, family and non-traveling acquaintances urged me to write a book. I was not sure where to start. I tentatively carried my earrings to Ethiopia and took a few notes. I drug my earrings to the Philippines. I packed my earrings for Saudi Arabia not knowing what to expect. I was determined to write a book after leaving Saudi and the Gulf War. That book never got written. We went to New Zealand then to Pakistan for three years. I hauled my earrings along. The notion of writing it down always drew me back.

I should have written a book when I went to Afghanistan after the fall the Soviet Union at the start of the Taliban when discussion centred on the legitimacy of the young talibs. By that time I knew the title before I formatted any chapters.

We spent more years in Dubai. A book should have been forthcoming but was interrupted by two years of cancer and treatment. Could of, would of, should of… done. I submit my reflections with immense appreciation and gratitude to my family because home is where my earrings are.

Foreword

By Jessica Russell
Ob-La-Di, Ob-La-Da, Life Goes On

I'm not sure when it happened. It was a prolonged process, a metamorphosis, which began slowly and gradually progressed until they emerged, retired and renewed.

The changes were subtle at first. About the time we moved out, they started to upgrade their camping equipment. First there were lounge chairs, then cots and caviar. They began roughing it in style. They started to stay in hotels, which had star ratings. Their hotel rooms had sofas and beds and came with telephones and hair dryers in the bathrooms. They began to eat dinner at restaurants instead of saving bread rolls from the airplane. Sure, they often traveled economy and still visited exotic locales, but now they made pit stops, ordered room service and didn't have to share beds. They check their luggage in and now pack in bags with wheels.

There was a time, back when we still traveled together, when we crammed into minuscule cars and drove across the country with our faces pressed to the rear windows as we gave up our seats to make room for the bags. We used to stop by creeks, on the side of the road to eat the crackers we had hoarded from airplanes. We traveled through Europe sleeping in single rooms; the four of us packed like sardines into a single bed. The trick was to sleep by the wall so you wouldn't be knocked out of bed; of course, if you were in the middle you had a better chance of getting some covers. We never used to check our bags; we carried everything and then used our bags to sleep on as we waited in airports at exotic locales for 10 or 11 hours for our next flight. It goes without saying, there were no up-grades, we traveled cattle car wherever we went.

I wouldn't change the adventures we had; it is just that we have noticed, my brother and I, that things are not the same. My parents, who used to cherish peace and tranquility – quiet lakes with canoes, empty beaches with waves quietly lapping, forests and jungles where the only noise was the persistent droning of mosquitoes, my parents, who used to cherish vast desert expanses where the silence was heavy in the air, have changed.

Now they attend rallies for motorcycles and four wheel drive vehicles, with a high noise level being the norm. When they head back to

Florida, I expect that we will find them at Daytona or camping in the wetlands which surround the space shuttle launch pad. They may even buy a "hog" and tour the back roads of America down Route 66. Their belt buckles will grow in size and they will both be sporting bare skin under little black leather vests. "Out of character?" one might wonder. I don't think so, not anymore. It seems they are spreading their wings and leaving the nest more often to take to the dangerous and noisy skies. The first time they retired, they went fishing in New Zealand for three months. The next time I expect we will find that they have been bungee jumping from Victoria Falls.

Masai Sisters

Give Peace A Chance

Chance

United States Peace Corps

1963-1965

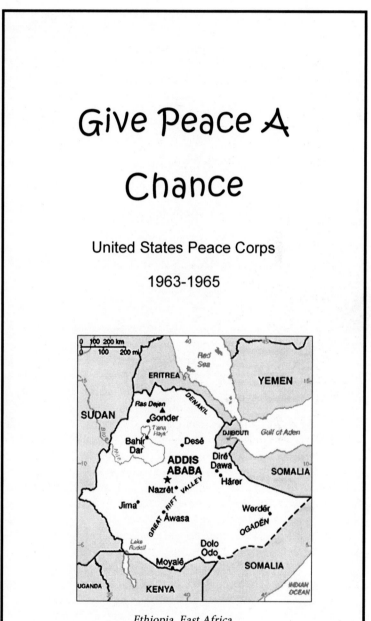

Ethiopia, East Africa

Culture Shock

"Marry me and I'll take you around the world." I did and he did. I was thinking Paris, London, Rome. We went to Ethiopia. E-thi-o-pi-a. I had to look it up.

"Why do you want to do a thing like that?

"You're throwing your life away," from my father. Then, from Daryle's grandmother,

"Why you goin' over there with all them pickaninnies?

"They're Neeegroes, you know.

"They're coloured; heeethens.

"In the Geographic Magazine they show them nasty pitchers; they're naked!"

Then with finality,

"They don't know Jeeesus."

No comment from my mother. She always wanted me to travel; she was thinking Paris, London, Rome.

Nothing prepared me for what I saw and experienced in that first forty-minute ride from the airport into Addis Ababa. At UCLA we read the history of the ancient Coptic culture and studied the language. It was not enough. I was not prepared for the first-hand sensory assault.

From the airport, the coaster-bus splashed through muddy potholes as we swerved and slid along the violent roads amongst throngs of milling city-dwellers. I was struck by the drab lack of colour. The men wore khaki jackets and trousers. Small boys, urchins, wore khaki shorts and torn tee-shirts or handed down, outgrown and tattered khaki jackets. The women wore white. Along the road, small shops displayed big black hunks of meat which hung from hooks in the open air. On closer look, I realized hundreds of swarming black flies sucked at each bloody carcass. We swerved in the mud and slid through throngs of milling pedestrians.

I looked to the left. Pyramids of oranges perched precariously on tables, provided a splash of colour. To the right, sacks of rice and sugar in bulging burlap bags sprawled in patches of dry dirt; but the mounds of meat covered with a host of adhering flies made the imprint.

As I looked out the window of the van, boys hobbled on thickened knees alongside us and banged at the window with their fists. Women thrust their upturned begging palms at my face. Lepers with missing fingers and stubbed feet forced their wounds at my whole being.

Others limped along with a wooden crutch, a twisted bent leg, some with stubs of arms and legs, and unimaginable deformities. It was my first time to see the ugly effects of leprosy: raw fingers, exposed bones and diminished cartilage. I tried not to be sick. I tried not to look away in disgust. I tried not to stare in disbelief. I did not read about this in California.

The stench assaulted my pores; the air smelled putrid. Rank urine, uncontained, permeated crevices of stone walls; the fetor hovered in corners, drifted in the breeze, in each intake of breath. Butter substance, used as hair-oil, embedded in scalps and tight braids, turned rancid in the African sun. The mephitis hung fuming in the air. Would these people be my neighbours?

Then I recognized it.

This was culture shock.

I didn't expect it to be so in-my-face.

Hints of housing along the route made me wonder where we would live. Reminiscent of *adobe* homes in Mexico, huts made of mud, covered with thatch or corrugated aluminum roofs, peeked between open lots and leaned against each other for support. I watched ladies come out of those mud huts, walk in the rutted, muddy lanes of the rainy season wearing spotless white *shammas*.

To my husband of two years I whispered, "Where do you think we will live?" I continued to wonder: how do ladies keep their *shammas* so white? They can't have washing machines? Will we have electric power? Indoor plumbing? Plumbing at all? As the coaster bounced on, I wondered who my students would be. Would they come from these dirt paths and mud huts? Would they carry disease and disabilities? Would I ever know their families? Would I be able to teach English and literature to them? Did it matter? Did they need these skills in the depths of Africa?

Later that week, I tried to write to my parents. I knew they worried, especially my father, his young daughter, 'throwing her life away' somewhere in the African bush. Sensitive to becoming the two-week expert, I analyzed nothing, just observed. I wanted to tell them everything that I saw and experienced. I knew to be cautious. I did not want my observations to be misinterpreted or offensive to anyone who might intercept the thin blue aerogramme.

I wanted nothing quoted in the American press or home town news. I knew my mother, an enthusiastic, proud and socially involved community member, would be tempted, even though I was not in Paris, London or Rome.

I wanted no headlines about world conditions usurped from my notes, thank you. I decided to gloss over the details, writing in very general terms, using Spanish as some secret code that only my parents understood, oblivious to the fact that Ethiopia had once been an Italian colony, and anyone who spoke Italian would know Spanish. I wrote,

September 27, 1963

"*The mail-service no esta muy bien, es muy malo. Mom, in spite of all we have read and all we have learned, es imposible to believe. Todo es imposible escribir a usted.*" Then I wrote, "*After a few days rest, I don't know; we have begun to adjust, or accept, or maybe just realize where we really are.*"

The House

"**W**hoa! Did you try that *wot*?"
"What's *wot*?"
"That fire-pit they served for lunch."
While we looked for a house, we stayed at University College eating in the dining hall. Predictable, non-threatening; that's how we viewed

breakfast: hard rolls, marmalade and sweet tea, supplemented with fresh fruit. We were told over and over, "If you can't Wash it, Peel it, or Boil it, don't eat it;" the WPB mantra. Bananas and oranges were a big hit.

Dinner was, however, another issue. The University served the national dish every night. We started right out eating traditional Ethiopian stew, known as *wot*, served with fermented, spongy *injera* bread used to scoop up the *wot*. We ate without utensils; chunky red-pepper stew pinched-up with sour crepes eaten with our fingers. After a life of 'Don't put your hands in your mouth, Dannie.' And 'Dannie, use your fork,' the rules were suddenly irrelevant. The trick to successful eating, involved delving-in up to the first knuckles of your right hand. This would be a useful skill when we moved to Saudi Arabia years later. The red pepper, paprika and bebere mixture of spices, burned all the way through. It burned the lips, blazed on the tongue, scorched the throat and seared the stomach. We loved these pungent dishes of beef, goat, chicken or vegetables.

"Oh-m-god! Look at my bed! Look at me. Fer sure, I'm eaten alive."

Those few nights at the University we slept on one-inch thick pallets tossed over cots. Invisible bed bugs feasted as we slumbered. Our sheets were splattered with blood spots like a Picasso painting and our bodies swelled with welts. I didn't tell my mother. She was thinking London, Paris, Rome.

The showers at the University dribbled cool, brown water. The toilets consisted of bowls with no seats or covers, which we visited regularly, sometimes hourly, during those first few red-hot, chili-pepper days. The tissue, a cross between sandpaper and pink crepe paper, seemed more suited to decorate the gym than scrape our pepper-paprika-chili sensitive bottom-sides.

We found a new duplex down a small muddy lane not far from our schools. It was built of *tsjika* We wrapped our tongues around the word to pronounce it as close to the explosive T sound as we could and came out with chica. The *tsjika* in our muddy lane was the same *tsjika* that mixed with straw to form the *adobe* for our small house. Although only a few hundred square meters, we boasted two bedrooms, a tiny living-room-dining-room-fireplace, an indoor bath and outdoor kitchen. The fireplace divided the units and weeks later provided salacious entertainment; better than TV since there was none. The dwelling included a generous yard and servant's quarters, electricity and even a small tank of hot water. I thought we found a real gem, and wrote to my parents, "It's just darling."

Darling, perhaps; dysfunctional 'fer sure.' The indoor bathroom presented a developing-world challenge. I asked the housekeeper/cook, who lasted less than a month, if he knew how to use or fill the toilet paper holder.

"Francis," he had a Christian name, "do you know how to use this paper-holder?"

"Oh yes, madam. That is for holding-on when getting up from seat."

The small crowded water-closet, emphasis on closet, accommodated the fixtures like the packed aisle of a home improvement store. The bathroom housed a toilet bowl, a narrow, short, porcelain tub, a *bidet* (what's that thing?) and a sink, and left no room for maneuvering in the tiny closet. We learned from a year of dysentery that it was possible to sit on the loo and throw-up in the *bidet* without moving. The pipes to the loo measured ½ inch diameter and clogged-up. The only way to remedy the problem involved digging inside the pipes to scoop it all out every few months. There was no plumber to call, because no one in the village had these *farenj* porcelain pieces. They were strictly for show, and were non-functional.

For one month, on my knees, bent over the narrow bathtub, I sloshed the sheets in the tub, trying to agitate suds with my arms whirling around like the spindle of a Whirlpool. The heavy sheets seemed impossible to manipulate. I twisted the wet bedding, wringing out the water. The tangled soaked fabrics writhed like serpents back and forth in conflict as I manipulated the laundry to the outdoor line. I replaced the housekeeper with a couple of healthy students who managed the soaked sheets just fine, in exchange for a room.

October 12, 1963

"We just love our house. It's just darling. We thought we would be living in a mud hut, but we have, like, this great little house. Actually, it izz a mud house, but it is painted white and, would you believe, it has hardwood floors. But we face quite a challenge. You know, like, it takes so long for charcoal to get hot for eggs in the morning. But meat is inexpensive. I can't identify the cut, I just point. I do know what a chicken looks like. They're the ones with all the feathers. Nothing is packaged, of course. I'm lucky. I found a small shop where the meat is inside. So we have steaks, or something red, on an open fire every night...Mom, have you ever tried to wash your sheets in a bath tub? What a pain. I don't mind the work, but it takes so much time every week."

The open *Mercado*, the largest in Africa, became our Museum of Modern Art, our Pier One, our Home Depot and IKEA all in one. Deep in the heart of the old city, we sauntered up and down muddy, irregular aisles between stalls of ancient string instruments, wooden drums stretched with taut zebra skin, tables of Coptic crosses, juxtaposed against plastic jewelry, black pottery bowls, containers and *bunna* pots for coffee. "Madam. You come. You look. You like my things? You buy something. How much?"

That was supposed to be my question: 'How much?' I started off with *"Konjo new,"* it's beautiful. *Konjo* was one of those Amharic words you had to spit out; it started with an explosive K. The word was easy to remember from Amharic classes, but exorcising the explosive from the back of the roof of the mouth was not natural in English. I practiced at every stall. Then, of course, I had to deal with whatever I claimed was so beautiful. I haggled for hours, always drawing a crowd. I was good at it from my practice at Mexican border towns. I was fearless. Sometimes I feigned insult. Sometimes I pleaded poverty. Sometimes I walked away. I thought I got great prices. At least I never paid the starting price which was insanely overpriced because of my nationality, assumed wealth and perceived naiveté.

"Sint new? How much?"

"Yelem, Yelem. No, no. That's too much."

My market-Amharic was brilliant. I honed my negotiating skills early but I didn't then know this would be a life-long skill and essential tool for my future.

One of the men from the market nailed-together a sofa, a bench with a back and arm rests. At the sugar stall I found burlap bags, stuffed them with recently slashed grass from the garden and stitched them up. I don't believe I did that, but I did. Using heavy, coloured yarn from the *Piazza* I stitched huge pink, orange, red and purple wild-flowers across the cushions. I evolved from some sort-of Beatnik sans black, to a Hippy sans tie-dye. I neglected the poetry; I overlooked the granola. I was in Africa, but it was still the sixties.

Goats clip-clopped and chickens fluttered at our ankles. No longer riding in the van observing the view, I now walked amongst fresh-slaughtered goats hung from hooks, as black flies swarmed and clustered. I never got used to it; and always the smell of rancid butter and urine. Beggars hobbled and tugged at my skirt, constantly touching me. I never got used to that either. Children followed us and hovered like the flies on the bloody meat.

At the end of the day we jumped into a shared cab then walked down our lane, toting our possessions. The cook/housekeeper expressed disappointment with our treasures. He expected us to purchase gold, appliances, and imported items. We were not like other Americans. We hung, draped and placed the Mercado treasures on the walls, floors and tables. We were *Yeselm Guad:* we were Peace Corps.

Psychologically, we were prepared to live in a hut, deep in the African bush. However, we were assigned teaching positions in Addis Ababa, the capital city. Its façade was sophisticated, a holdover from the Italian occupation.

Just down the road from the school, I discovered frothy *cappuccino* and warm *croissants* at the *piazza*. Every week I sampled new varieties of *formaggio* from the little shop next to the Italian ice cream parlor. I never faced Velveeta again. Italian cheese arrived in round wheels covered in wax. No long, yellow box. I found several shops where the meat was at least under glass. I never got very good at identifying the cuts, except for chickens purchased whole and dead. I learned that pizza and pastas are served as a first course, and most evening meals featured seven courses served one by one. The Ras Hotel employed an Italian violinist, a remnant of the occupation, who strolled gingerly between tables playing familiar Italian arias during dinner. This was not living in the bush, and I never looked back.

The Village

To get to the main road, I walked along the dirt lane through our small village in the heart of Addis Ababa. The path cobbled together uneven rocks and during the rainy season I hopped from stone to stone, avoiding mud crevices. The mud from the rainy season squished like the sound of its Amharic name: *tsjika*; it stuck to shoes. It stuck to my shoes. Students never seemed muddy. Maybe that's because the rains seemed to come in the afternoon, after class. I often got caught on my way home. *Tsjika, tsjika, tsjika,* squish, squish, squish.

I learned to dodge the men who, with no warning, stepped only slightly aside to relieve themselves. The ladies squatted along the side of the lane, their beautiful white shammas surrounding them like the skirts of a whirling dervish.

Our village harboured the lame and disfigured, as well as energized kids who laughed, ran and screamed in and out of their huts, up and down the lane. I saw the same neighbours every day. The children, not able to attend public school, ran after me in daily pursuit.

"*Farenj, farenj.*"

I waved back, "*Tenaisteleen,*" Hey there.

"Hey, *lijjoch!*" Hey kids. I sometimes paused to shake their little hands.

"Hey, Joe!" loosely translated, 'Hi foreigner.'

"*Carmella*?? You give me *carmella*."

"*Yelem, Yelem, Yelem.*" No, no, no.

You can always tell when the army has been in town; the children never forget. I never gave them candy, but for two years, every day they asked.

Under the base of the big tree at their *Ha-Hu-He beit*, village kids shouted out their ABCs with the discipline of an army platoon. Amharic instruction energizes the senses. Learning my *Ha-Hu-Hes* always seemed like the opening warm-ups for choral practice. All I retained is the first letter, *ha, hu, hi, he, heh, huh, ho*. Okay, I remember a few more, like *ba, bu, bi, be, beh, buh, bo*, and *ma, mu, mi, me, meh, muh, mo*. Thirty-three symbols make up the Amharic alphabet and each letter expands to seven vowel forms; the number of characters equates to 276 including explosives. The children knew them all and every day shouted them out. I envied them.

A woman with a leprous black hole in the centre of her face wandered across the lane. The first time I saw her, I was aghast. I never saw anything like that in California. Where once a nose sniffed the pungent aromas of bubbling chicken *doro wot*, there was now an open vacuous hole. The next time I saw her I realized she was a neighbour. Her leathery weathered skin probably belied her age. She looked craggy and old, sorrowful and resigned. Every day she wore the same permanently stained brown dress which hung on her thin frame. She leaned on a stick, negotiating the lane with cracked and callused bare feet.

I looked away the first time I saw her. She was ugly and deformed. The hole in her face was large and black. No one else seemed to notice. The next time, I forced myself to nod as we passed. Over the weeks, I learned to look into her tired eyes, avoiding the hole in the centre of her face, as we spoke simple salutations each day.

Author and the village Priest.
embroidered burlap sugar bags and drapes.

The kid on the corner in scruffy khaki shorts and jacket could not walk and hobbled along on his knees until he got to the highway, where he rolled along on a skateboard contraption. I knew them all.

Eventually, I met the holy man of the village. No one introduced us, but he seemed to take as much interest in me as I did in him. His demeanor personified royalty. The priest seemed perhaps 80 years old, and walked slowly with great decorum. I suspected he could muster up a sprightly jig, but his bearing embodied dignity. He dressed in white jodhpurs; a loose top with fitted sleeves peeked out from under a heavy, elegant black and purple cape. He wandered the lane with an intricate, silver, Coptic cross, mounted atop his tall wooden staff. A thin, white, wiry beard spread across his face and neck, down to his chest, and a spotless white turban wrapped his head in religious elegance.

"*Shai, yifelegalu?*" One day the priest asked to come to tea; not at his place, at mine. I met him in the lane on the way home from school. He indicated he wanted to come for *shai*. I invited him in. He sat on my bench-sofa, the one with hippy-embroidered cushions. It was the best piece of furniture in the house, certainly the most colourful. Solomon, the student, boiled water for the tea. In the outdoor kitchen, he picked-out strings and wee bugs from the crass, course sugar, emptied from the burlap bags which now adorned the sofa with embroidered psychedelic poppies.

In retrospect, I have no idea what we discussed for two hours. He knew no English. In Amharic, I knew verbs and nouns, and probably three adjectives. I felt special that he visited my home; I never before entertained a missionary, Mormon or Baptist, or anyone else, for two hours of tea in my home. Never. What did we discuss? Not religion; I knew no religious words in Amharic except *Xabier (Igziabiher)* which I assumed meant savior. The discussion was non-threatening, non-religious and comfortable, just getting to know each other, by families and indirectly, by cultures. After that day, we often shook hands, a double hand clasp, a long prolonged handholding of warmth and affection. Solomon, years later told me the priest visits houses requesting a donation to the church. If he asked that day, I didn't know the word for tithe.

Within weeks, I accepted my village as, perhaps, they had accepted me. I was the one out of sync, the one who didn't belong. I was the *farenj*. Perhaps I was the one with the ugly face, the one on the corner lot, the woman with the too-white skin; the teacher at the Menelik II School.

The Goat Goes Through The Gate

His Imperial Majesty Emperor Haile Selassie I

The Palace

The palace grounds. Imagine. Soon after we arrived, we attended opening ceremonies on the palace grounds for Little Mescal a festival to commemorate two things: the ending of the small rains, which bombarded us daily since our arrival, and to celebrate the annual crowning of His Majesty Emperor Haile Selassie. There was also symbolism of the finding of the true cross upon which Jesus died.

The ritual started with prayers, religious canons and chants. Hundreds of priests from the villages paraded in regal red, royal purple, imperial indigo embroidered and beaded capes and robes. They carried velvet, sequined parasols, magenta and teal, that sent sparkles bouncing off the sequins like the facets of well-cut diamonds. With their right hands the priests gripped ornate, silver Coptic crosses that glistened as the sun caught the sharp corners of the cutout metal. I looked for my village priest. The palace lawn was green and lush from the rainy season and the ceremony, preformed for His Majesty, seemed magical, if not religious, in the late afternoon.

I had never been invited inside a palace. I had not seen the crown jewels in London. I did watch the television tour of the White House hosted by Jackie Kennedy. I pinched myself. Could it be true that a twenty-two year old could be invited to the palace of an African Emperor?

A small group of twenty-five westerners walked through the reception line. I practiced a short Amharic speech. I learned all those words in language instruction, but now, the only sentence I remembered declared, *"The goat goes through the gate."*

My nerves took over. What was protocol? Should I curtsey? Bow? Give a firm handshake or a limp-wrist knuckle-up? My knees weakened, my palms dripped. As my turn came, I curtsied and gave my four-line speech about the beauty of the country, how pleased I was to be working in Ethiopia, and what an honour to meet His Majesty, His Royal Highness.

"Your country is beautiful.

"I like to work in Ethiopia.

"I am a teacher.

"I am pleased to meet you, Your Royal Highness."

All present tense: subject, verb, object.

I tried not to giggle from nerves or to sweat down the front of my dress.

What a tiny, slight man, unlike other large African leaders who suffer from too much opulence. Kindly, he made no corrections to my attempt at the language and while still wondering at the success or failure of my faltering speech, the curtains of the reception room broke apart like the start of a Broadway review as a parade of white-jacket waiters promenaded forward with trays of champagne and hors d'oeuvres. I wrote home,

September 23, 1963

"It was just fantastic! I just played like I was Jackie. I wore a little black velveteen dress (glad I threw it in at the last minute) and spoke small-talk in my breathiest voice."

I liked this. I loved this. Whoa. This was the career for me. Palaces, parties, pretty people. The glamour of government work caught my imagination. From inside the carpeted, chandeliered, golden palace, who guessed that one block away my lame and disfigured neighbours sat on dirt floors ready to greet me when I walked home?

Wodajo

We hired a *zabana* who provided twenty-four hour security. We didn't think we needed him, but the embassy believed the absence of visible security provided an open invitation to crime. Wodajo spoke no English, but this did not hinder his jovial attempt at communication. He stood at the front gate of our small compound in his army-green pea-coat, layered with an army-green blanket during the winter months. The whole ensemble, oversized, hung to the ground on his wiry frame.

"Hey Wo!" He didn't know what we were talking about.

"Hey Wodajo. *Tenaisteleen.*" How goes it? Anything to report today?

"Tenaisteleen," how are you? He smiled, nodded, picking his teeth with a stick. He walked around the compound at night; during the day, he wandered about the yard, pulling a weed or two, finding some minor project. I'm sure he slept during day and most of the night, but when we were around he was alert, coherent and helpful. Doubtful he prevented anything at all; it never came to that. He carried a rusty, World War I rifle over his shoulder and usually opened the gate for us. Over the years, safety issues increased and Wodajo taught us, as our first security guard. In Ethiopia, security was an issue because poverty was an issue.

Thievery ran rampant and unrestrained in the disadvantaged capitol. Amber and shimmering jade shards protruded from the tops of compound walls as a deterrent, even for our mud house. One ploy: robbers loitered outside the wall, hunkered down in the tall grass. Executing critical timing, the thieves extended a long bamboo pole over the wall to the clothesline to hook and steal clothing. Razorblades laced the bamboo. If the *zabana* grabbed the pole to save the clothing, his hands throbbed from the effort, sliced and bloodied, as the thieves yanked the pole in a tug-of-war to the outside of the wall. Only once did robbers attempt to remove clothing from our outdoor line of clothes. Wodajo foiled the attempt without sliced fingers by yelling and yanking the pole. Most of the time, Solomon and Daniel were there paying attention to their after school chores.

Wodajo tried to be useful around the house and garden. The problem of clean food remained a constant concern. I suffered with dysentery every day for a month until we fired the cook and still I lived with dysentery most of the first year. Not just any dysentery. This was dysentery without a proper bathroom. The *shinte beit* at school was too filthy to use. Years later I read that teachers have a high rate of kidney infection because they never get a break to use the toilets. The one time I looked into the school *shinte beit* I was aghast at the communal filth and stench. I avoided the building the remainder of my contract. This meant that many days I surged out the gate of the old school, up the hill sprinting into the house for relief, usually just in time. The embassy said over and over, if you can't wash it, boil it or peel it, don't eat it. We were careful, but not pedantic. We boiled our water; we did not peel our lettuce.

We decided to try our luck at growing our own lettuce and tomatoes. Wodajo, Daniel and Solomon, helped with this project since I didn't know a weed from a carrot top, a tomato vine from a grape vine. Wo watered the garden and pulled weeds. He took great pride in our little plot. The *zabana* was a proud Amhara.

I came back from classes one afternoon and pushed open the gate. Wodajo stood in the garden watering the lettuce. He held the hose to the side of the vegetables and urinated with accurate precision directly on each head of lettuce. Maybe we would peel our romaine.

Our British neighbour, who shared the fireplace, invited us for a dinner party. We did not eat salad. Sandra entertained an older, Italian sugar-daddy left over from the Italian occupation of Ethiopia. He was not a live-in; too old for that but Sandra and Mr. Pintinelli included us in several provincial trips and evening soirées during her stay as clerical assistant with the United Nations. I wrote:

September 30, 1963

"Mom, it was just a dinner party, but it was served in courses, and for us it was much more. Getting to know some British points of view, we discussed British politics, the Profumo scandal, the Alabama-Governor-Wallace-crisis, the building civil rights movement, Martin Luther King, Jackie Kennedy, pop music, Ertha Kitt, whom they all love and Anthony Newley. It was a grand evening for us; you would have loved it."

I thought everyone passed the chicken, served themselves and ate salad at the same time, family style, just like my family in the California Valley, like fer sure. I didn't know about serving meals in courses. It astonished me that our British and Italian neighbours recognized our problems in the southern United States. It never occurred to me that American issues would be of concern around the world. That night I learned about global awareness, though it remained undefined for some time.

Wadajo slept soundly as we walked home. Swaddled in his army blanket, he slumped against the shard-studded wall, the rusty gun propped against his sagging body. A small fire of eucalyptus branches burned near his feet. We walked by him, still animated from the evening. He never stirred. He needed to care for the garden in the morning.

Bye-Bye American Pie

Daryle played basketball with the Olympiacos team. He thrived, the team thrived and everything was *bene*. Towards the middle of the basketball season, I started to get the hang of it, culturally. Italians express emotions visually. They hang their passions right out-there in the middle of the court. They talk with their hands; they bellow from their throats; they articulate bilingual messages with their bodies. At basketball, they shout collectively in groups. If they resent a referee decision, simultaneously they leap out of the stands, onto the floor, yelling at the official with fists raised into the air. That's how this crowd behaved.

Saturday night, the refs threw several players out of the game, but there were no major fights, no one received serious injuries, no concussions and none of the fans was arrested. The emotional ups and downs infused the crowd, but the game ended with relative calm. To top it all off, *bravo!* Olympiacos won by eight points.

We headed for the Patrice Lumumba Bar. The lot was empty. We arrived before the crowds. *Bene*! We'd get a decent table. The bar was dark and the owner came to the door.

"We're closed." What was this?

"Why?" We hovered around the door like zebra milling about the watering hole.

"I'm sorry, Sir. We are closed."

"Why are you closed?"

"It's only 11pm?" We found this strange and felt insulted. Why didn't they want our business?

"Out of respect, Sir."

"Come on…. What are you talking about?"

"We just want a few drinks and some good music."

"We always come here. You've never been closed before."

"Your President's been shot, Sir."

"What?! What president? Come on…"

"President Kennedy has been shot. We are very sorry for you.

"We're closed out of respect."

We walked back to our cars, not pretending to comprehend the African sense of humour, but trying to understand this bizarre circumstance. Still parched, we drove to another bar where they presented a similar story from the darkened interior. Now thoroughly baffled, we decided to go back to the house to listen to the short-wave. We rattled down the dirt track amongst the straw and mud huts to our small western-looking dirt house.

The athletes sat cross-legged on the floor hunched around our new Grundig short-wave radio. Its rounded corners bevelled the mesh-covered speaker. I dialed the spindle through waves of static and heavy, somber music. I rotated the fine-tune dial through the sing-song cadence of Chinese, the punctuated rhythm of Russian, the guttural gravel of German and the rolling sounds of Spanish and Italian; the rhetoric jolted us with occasional Americanisms like 'Dallas' and 'Kennedy' before we stumbled into an English language report from the British Broadcasting Company.

Around the radio, the Italians and Americans listened with apprehension as the static cut in and out at critical points in the story. Between French, German and Italian, the dreaded fact emerged. American president, John Fitzgerald Kennedy, was dead. The details came slowly; the reality even slower. No one slept.

In the morning we made our way to the American Embassy looking for information, instructions and support. At the embassy we received no instructions and no support. A two-line typed statement confirmed the assassination of President John Fitzgerald Kennedy. The memo taped to the security guardhouse curled in the sun. The embassy closed for the day. We went home and tried to learn what we could from the *Ethiopian Herald*, the English language paper, other expatriates and the short-wave radio.

The following day, we stood in line with hundreds of others: peasant crop-farmers and international diplomats, young college students, old women with walking sticks, weathered men whose cheeks bulged with chat, young women balancing one child on a hip and another tied to their back, all stood in line to sign the embassy Book of Condolences. Emperor Haile Selassie flew out immediately to attend services in Washington D.C.

Grief overwhelmed everyone. Ethiopians stopped us in the road to express their sorrow for us and for our president. Our village neighbours, wrapped in *shammas* and heavy blanket shawls came up to touch me on the arm or walk with me. The children ran out to the lane and stared. They said nothing; they knew. The mothers, offering sympathy, clicked their tongues in pity and disbelief, sometimes ululating in grief as we walked by. The elders told us,

"Mr. Kennedy great man.

"Too young die.

"America sad today.

"World sad today."

My gentle priest stopped me in the lane, responsive to our pain. He clutched my hands in his and held them for some time shaking his head back and forth.

Ethiopia closed down for official mourning, as did much of Africa. Merchants padlocked shutters on every little shop; the thriving Mercado, the largest outdoor market in Africa, emptied. Schools closed. Streets, except for stray goats and chickens, were deserted. We felt alone. We felt far away. For the first time, we sensed the isolation and geographical distance and the chasm of the communication-information gap. We depended on whatever short-wave programming we could find and rushed for the *Ethiopian Herald* each morning.

On the third day after the assassination, the stress and tension merged into depression. The men, including some of the Italians, headed for an empty basketball court to shoot hoops for emotional release. After a few minutes of vigorous running up and down the blacktop shooting free-throws, the small crowd which gathered on the fringe, hooted them off the court with insults and jeers. How could they be so disrespectful to their country, to the death of their president? How could they go out and play games at such a time? We failed to anticipate this cultural response.

In our minds, a secure America prevailed. A stable government prevailed. A new president prevailed, quickly sworn in. We knew little about the mentality of a developing country, their fear, apprehension or dread of impending chaos. It seemed ironic. We knew to fill our tub with water at the first rumour of a coup should it occur in Addis. We once expressed interest, from a sociological perspective, in living in a developing country during a coup d'état. We never, ever considered the possibility of disruption of government in the United States. The small crowd understood nothing of our confidence in the American modus operandi.

Nor could we explain stress management. We grieved. Oh how we grieved, wept, tried to understand; we needed to run it off, but never questioned the stability of our own country. We viewed no body, attended no funeral, felt no closure, though we attended a memorial at the U.S. Embassy. We clearly, unintentionally offended. They saw us as ugly Americans, hooting up and down the court, disrespectful and loud.

All the cultural training and orientation courses still left us unprepared for this American tragedy and its international implications. The

Emperor, diminutive in full military dress, attended the funeral alongside French President Charles de Gaulle, German Chancellor Erhard, Philippine President Macapagal, South Korean President Chung Hee Park and hundreds of world leaders. Who could forget those images? Who could forget the imprint of Jackie, the children decorous in their grief, standing throughout the procession, three year old John-John in salute to the cortège?

Weeks passed before Olympiacos played another competition, and by that time Ethiopia was back to business as usual. Everything was *bene*.

The Goat

When Tamene came back from his village one weekend, he brought a goat; a beautiful white goat. Hmm. Tamene was one of the older students. He went home to see his ill father and came back with a goat. For me. At last, I could use the brilliant Amharic I learned at UCLA, "The goat goes through the gate."

What did this mean: A student brought me a goat. What should I do with it? Was it a pet? A meal? A gift? Now, several cultures removed, I'm wondering, a proposal? Culturally, how did this work? I never thought about culture or race except when I put my hand on a student's desk. Touching the paper, the exam, the essay, my hand next to their hand, I was white. Chalk white.

When Queen Elizabeth came to Ethiopia we were instructed to march our students to the parade route and wave little British flags. Of course it was orchestrated, but in a way, it was okay. Lessons were on hold for the day and the kids loved it. They missed the instruction, but they got a front row view of Queen Elizabeth and the Duke of Edinburgh riding in an open burgundy Rolls-Royce. More selfishly, I got a front row view. It gave us an opportunity to discuss the monarchy with the students.

"Madame, she's so white," Tamene.

"She is too white," Abebech

"Her skin is too white. It's like chalk," Solomon.

"Is she sick?" Tesfay.

"My skin is white," I said in defense, I guess.

"Oh no, Madame. You're not that white," they all agreed.

I felt white when I put my hand on their desks next to their dark brown hands. Otherwise, I saw myself in a student-teacher relationship void of racial differences. In reality, cultural and racial differences played-out every day.

"Why do you always smell so, so like a store, so sweet, or something?" they were frank, if not tactful. I never voiced my thoughts about body odor. It was just something to endure, especially in afternoon classes. I came to realize that my artificial scents of deodorant, even perfume were offensive, not natural. Body odor was in, deodorant was out. Rancid butter was in, scented hair spray, out.

We stood on the splintered wooden floor at the front of the classroom. Tamene towered over me leaning on one leg, then the other. He grinned a very shy, tentative smile. "Tamene, you brought me a goat? For me? You brought it from your village? Thank you. Tamene, thank you. Shall I take it home?"

No one ever brought me a goat. I got a goldfish as a party favour when I was 10. My mother was not thrilled because of course it came in a water-filled plastic bag and it was our job to feed and house the golden fish. I sensed the same responsibility with the white goat.

I thanked him profusely for the beautiful albino. I liked this young man. He was a responsible student. Tamene sat in the back of the class. He wore a dark suit jacket. His thin black moustache enhanced his handsome face. He bore a Harry Belafonte look and remained shyly hushed.

We rushed the goat back to the house before classes. *"The goat goes through the gate."* I laughed to myself, feeling rather smug. He tied the animal to the fence with a long lead. As we still maintained the vegetable plot, I didn't want the lettuce munched or watered by the goat; I still employed Wodajo.

Plenty of grass grew near the fence but when I returned from class that day, the goat was dead. The dog, a gentle puppy, attacked the tied-up goat, and gutted the throat.

I pushed open the gate and was horrified. The goat lay on its side. Burgundy blood pooled in the dirt and stained the pure white pelt. A gaping neck cavity exposed ripped-apart tendons juxtaposed against the lifeless pelt, once the colour of snow.

"Wishsha!" Amharic for dog, we pronounced it Wusha.

"Wusha! Bad dog." The bilingual mutt came a running, confused, tail wagging between his legs. I couldn't punish the dog. I knew some primal instinct provoked the pup, which didn't have a mean bone in its body. We long ago decided he probably wouldn't protect us, beyond barking at an intruder, though this was never challenged.

Wodajo was nowhere to be found.

My mind raced. What was I supposed to do? Culturally. How would I present this to Tameme? How would he respond? What would be the repercussion? Would it mean I didn't care for him? Would it mean I didn't respect the gift? Would it prove my incompetence, lack of respect? I didn't know what to tell him. Someone butchered the goat.

In the morning I told him what happened; it sickened me. He seemed resigned, disappointed. He never gave me any idea of what it was all about. We connected in a very intimate way, but I could not explain it; I could not understand it. I was too white.

Thinking of You

Queuing is not an Ethiopian concept. Inside the old building pedestrians pushed their way toward wooden window cubicles and demanded stamps, aerogrammes, letters and packages. Of all the things the Italians did contribute to the country, standing in orderly lines was not one of them. Shoved and jostled toward the front of the crowd, I presented the now much wrinkled, stamped paper. "Third and Final Notice." That's what the crumpled slip of paper threatened. It was covered with ink stamps: purple ovals, red triangles, and blue rectangles, proof that this was the final notice.

The man behind the window turned the paper several directions before looking up blankly. I tried several Amharic words; nothing clicked. People behind me shoved, breathing *bebere* chicken down my neck. I bet they were sorry they were behind the *farenj*. The clerk walked away to an inner room. He did not come back.

I pushed my way to another window. I became an animal. I had my paper. I wanted my package, or whatever it was. They were not going to send me another notice. This was the final notice. I got this far, I would go the full route. I stuck my elbows out, gaining my space, if nothing else. With herd mentality I shoved my crushed pink paper at the next clerk.

He reached for it. He held the paper upside down and looked back at me. I could lose my composure here. I tried the Amharic again; still no clue of comprehension. In desperation, I took out a pencil and drew a square, added what I remembered of perspective, and a pencil line representing twine, with a knotted bow on the top. Picasso it was not, but the man recognized the sketch of brown paper packages tied up in string. Then we began the charade of how big I thought the package was. I guessed it might be an audio reel and assumed, correctly, it was a small, flat square box.

It was March, 1964, when we received the holiday tape from our Portland relatives. Excited, we looked forward to hearing the voices of our distant family. Was Mom Bertine involved in orchestral performances? What activities were the kids taking up? How was Grandpa Beebe's health? Was he still driving backward on the freeway?

We set up the tape machine, placed the large plastic reel on the spindle, carefully threaded the fragile tape through the adjacent empty spool, and turned the dial. Sipping cups of hot Kenya coffee, we settled-in for sixty minutes of family news and gossip. Mom Bertine, Daryle's mother, put forward the first voice.

"Hi Daryle and Dan," she started. "I hope I've got it right this time. I sent you a long message and then when I played it back, it was on the wrong speed and I couldn't understand a word of it. I sounded like Donald Duck in super speed. At first I laughed at myself; I could just imagine you two trying to figure out what I was saying. I started again and tried to remember everything that I did before," she said, "but I don't remember everything I said the first time." She sounded exasperated.

At that time, she worked for Portland Natural Gas. She got the job during World War Two, as it was called. As a single parent of a toddler and a preschooler she gratefully accepted the position as a way to support her family. It was not easy work.

Her job entailed traversing the city reading gas meters, recording data, submitting daily reports to the billing office. The diminutive young woman leaped up to the running board of the Plymouth, swung into the car and peered through the steering wheel every morning, six days a week. She battled severe weather elements, fought-off wild deer, frothing dogs, and crotchety landlords. The ugly grey meters hid under bushes in back yards, behind wrought iron gates of mansions, in dark, damp basements, and in kitchens of both fine hotels and ghetto apartments. She sleuthed them out.

On the tape, for forty-five minutes she apologized and explained about the various speeds, the forward button, the rewind function, and twice she erased everything. With fifteen minutes left on the reel, she hid the microphone behind the Christmas tree to record everyone's conversation as they came in to decorate the tree.

During the difficult years, Mom Bertine ran circles around her male counterparts. She fought for upgrades in women's regulation shoes and safety glasses, and fought for equal pay for equal work. It took her years to get an audience, to get support, to get action, but she persevered. Her accomplishments preceded women's rights advocate Gloria Steinem by decades. She was a 'libber' before there was vocabulary for it.

"Don't put the candy cane there, no one can see it."

"Who put these lights on, anyway?"

"I'm going to bed."

"Give me that."

"She took my icicles."

"Did not."

"Did too."

"Now this whole string is out."

"Stop it, girls."

"I'm going to bed."

Grandma and Grandpa Beebe came in at just the right time for the final few minutes of the tape. They were nervous and wrote out their speech. It began, "Hello our little Africans..."

Mom Bertine played violin throughout her physically draining work schedule, maintaining a rehearsal agenda for sometimes three orchestras each season while sustaining Daryle and his sister at day care, summer camps and after school.

She ended the holiday tape by playing her own violin arrangement of "Silent Night," and Grandma Beebe concluded, "Merry Christmas to you out there with all those heeethen Neeegroes. We're proud of you way down there in Africa, and want you to know, we're so very proud of you, Merry Christmas and, we're thinking of you."

T'ej

In the afternoon, at the end of the school day, 4,000 students swarmed out of school like bees out of a hive. I buzzed across the street following Seyoum, pushing through the crowd, as he flagged a Fiat *Cinquecento* taxi. Seyoum's father owned a winery-brewery and one week Seyoum offered to take me there after class. His family brewed *t'ej*, a sweet, yellowish wine, made from honey and honeycomb and also *tella*, a thick beer brewed from the dregs of the wine. We crowded into the tiny taxi with five other passengers, riding as far as Seyoum's village, then walked down his cobbled lane. They produced and bottled the wine from the house.

I hoped I was doing the right thing; I hoped I had not made a mistake going to his home. The afternoon daylight gave me confidence. Seyoum was one of the older students in my tenth grade class. I trusted him. To verify, I asked if I could meet his father, and if his father would explain the *t'ej*-making process to me through Seyoum's translation. English practice, of course.

The *Cinquecento*, an undersized Italian people's-car, even smaller than the German folk's-wagon, rolled into Ethiopia with the Italian occupation. The small taxi started off empty and picked up passengers along the way. By the time we reached Seyoum's village, there were four of us crammed together in the back seat and three in the front plus the driver. I sat as far forward as possible, my knees pushed into the front seat. At Seyoum's signal, I bolted with him and followed down the lane to his place. I smelled it before I saw it.

The *t'ej*, pronounced t-edge, explosive T, fermented in a state of agitation, emitting a pungent odor, strong, bitter, and unmistakable. The process takes months, up to a year, to complete each batch before it is bottled; at least that's the way I remember it.* Maybe it was the honey that produced the distinct smell. It was not sweet; it did not produce a 'bouquet' or 'aroma' but a smell. The *t'ej* smelled acidic and strong, not sugary. I didn't notice how the honeycomb or the honey fermented into the cloudy liquor. I expected to see swarms of bees, or boxes of beehives, or honeycomb hanging in chunks. Instead, a few innocent bees floated on the surface.

Seyoum's father presented his *t'ej* in the form of thick mead. At home, all women made *t'ej* and *tella* for their families. Seyoum's family *t'ejery* business produced *t'ej* for public consumption at *t'ej-beits*, wine houses, located throughout villages and cities, not unlike *bunna-beits*, coffee houses and pubs.

T'ej is said to be the oldest beverage known to mankind, the oldest prepared beverage known. For 5000 years this ancient drink has been produced in Abyssinia and was said to be the wine of toasts between the Queen of Sheba and King Solomon in 950 BC.

I wasn't thinking about Solomon and Sheba. I looked in the vats of wine with small bees floating on top, their wings spread apart and drenched. I thought, this student invited me to see this process of *t'ej*-making. I reflected even at the time: this young man and his father are sharing their lives with me.

"Seyoum, what is this?" I asked peering into a huge yellowish vat.

"This *t'ej* is not yet ready in this place (vat)."

"Do you drink *t'ej* with dinner every night?"

He laughed, lifting the back of his hand to his mouth in embarrassment. His father looked for translation.

"No, I don't even like *t'ej*."

"But your family is producing *t'ej* for the *t'ej-beits* and for your family."

"We only drink *t'ej* on the weekends, or for special family gatherings. I like *tella* better." I guessed that Seyoum was between 23 and 25 years old.

Much was lost in translation because Seyoum didn't know English words for the procedure his father was describing. I nodded often. With my middle class, very Protestant background, I barely knew the difference between red wine and white wine. I had no experience with a winery or brewery so I couldn't help with vocabulary. The words were lost on me. I got the idea that the sediment was strained from the vats and was drunk as *tella*, Ethiopian *bira*. Fermented honey and honeycomb were added to sweeten the bitter taste of the hops. Or, maybe it was the other way around. I should have paid more attention for future use in other countries when I wanted to know how to covertly turn the water into wine.

The three of us walked through the winery up and down hard-pack dirt aisles, as Seyoum and his father showed me various stages of the *t'ej*-making process. Even in the final phase of *t'ej* production, the wine, as well as the process, seemed cloudy. I should have paid a lot more attention.

Tej comes from local hops, water, fermented honey and honeycomb, and compliments the spicy wot. The sediment becomes very thick, is strained and can be drunk as tella, Ethiopian beer. The winemaker adds honey and honeycomb to sweeten the bitter taste. As the process continues, the wine ferments, bubbles and grows and the sediment sinks to the bottom.

Do You Know Nat King Cole?

Outside the winery a small peep of chickens pecked at invisible grain and unseen bugs. Seyoum shooed them aside with his foot. They scattered and clucked in protest but allowed us to transition across the lane to his home.

I sat on the edge of a bench in the central room of the house. Whitewashed walls displayed a framed, glassless picture of Emperor Haile Selassie standing with the palace lions and, more notably, fixed to the wall with thumbtacks, magazine pictures of movie stars.

Seyoum's mother was more beautiful than the divas push-pinned to the wall. She radiated pride, that day wearing a spotless white *shamma* as she brewed tea on a hotplate. His sisters sat side by side, modest and shy, sharing a folding chair. They also attended Menelik II School in the lower grades. Sipping the sweet *shai* I asked about their interests, what they liked about school, what they dreamed. They didn't yet know English and never once mentioned going to America. Did they have boyfriends, I teased? They were Coptic Christians, so I could ask. They giggle, covered their mouths, and turned toward each other still giggling. Seyoum's father beamed as they timidly lifted their eyes to express their thoughts. Seyoum translated. The girls idolized their older brother.

"I want to finish school."

"I," her sister boldly interjected, "want to be a cut-sewer to make dresses for parties.

"I like to draw dresses.

"Do you want to see my drawings?" She reached for a dog-eared, lined schoolbook.

"We must stay in school if our parents will help us."

"Seyoum helps us sometimes with our studies.

"We can study just like our brother, and help our parents." They interrupted each other as Seyoum attempted to translate, or maybe left some of it out. I understood the drift, but his translation impressed equally his parents and his teacher.

Nat King Cole died in February, 1965, three months after my visit with Seyoum's family. The crooner captured the hearts and souls of the Ethiopians including my young adult students. Although he was not known for singing African music, or for reaching out to find his African roots, his sense of jazz, big band and ballads resonated with Ethiopians and his music preserved on vinyl, reverberated in bars, t'ej-beits and hotels

"Sometimes Seyoum buys us notebooks." He was shy and embarrassed to translate this, but the girls insisted, nudging his shoulder, "Seyoum, tell her."

"I want to work so I can help my family."

"I want to work in the bakery. Someday I want my own family."

"Working in a bakery, we will always have food."

They asked me questions too. Was I married? How many children did I have? Why no children? Everyone asked. I learned to answer this with "Not yet," and they seemed satisfied. Why did I come to Africa? Did I like Ethiopia? Was Seyoum a good student? Did I live in Hollywood? Did I know Nat King Cole?* What movie stars did I know?

I knew a few 'stars' and threw out their names and told stories; this validated my status as an American. I knew Natalie Wood** from junior high school days. She never talked to us; she was too good for us. We didn't think so, but she did. That's how school girls can be, even in California; especially in California. Even in Ethiopia, in Pakistan, in Saudi Arabia. We girls can be catty and mean in third grade and again about seventh grade, and god help the cheerleader group. I later spent much time working with preadolescent girls, working through she-said/ she-said disputes with mediation skills and conflict resolution. Natalie, something of a prima donna, never had much time for any of us. Maybe I was jealous. And I noticed she had skinny legs when we dressed-down for sports. The girls loved that story. Seyoum's sisters were the right age for movie star gossip.

In the San Fernando Valley I went to school with Martha Dickenson, whose parents performed with the Modernaires, a vocal group who sang with Glen Miller, Artie Shaw and Tex Beneke. They were from the big-band era recording "Chattanuga Choo Choo" and "Ive Got a Gal In Kalamazoo." Martha and I, from the next generation, oh-m-god, we sang, like, fer sure at the top of our lungs, like in gym class, like down the halls, while digging through our lockers, like always at the top of our lungs, "Sh Boom, Sh Boom, Life could be a dream, if only I could...." In PE we sprinted to the courts screaming our own version of "Blue Suede Shoes."

"Well, its one for the money,

"Two for the show,

"Three to get ready,

"Now go, (girls) go.

"But don't you...

"Step on my (old gym) shoes."

We never got in trouble; the teachers endured our enthusiasm. We stood in formation doing warm-up exercises. Jumping-jacks, sit-ups, and the worst of all, while stretching our elbows, shoulder-height behind our backs, Mrs. Adams made us yell, "I must, I must, increase my bust." We were mortified. "I can't hear you," from Mrs. Adams. I did not share that memory with Seyoum. Martha was a wonderful person and brought her parents' vinyl records to class. She lived in a big house in the Val with several sisters. I loved going there. Seyoum's mother was interested in the house and asked if everyone in America was rich.

No, I never met John Wayne. I knew Debbie Reynolds from yet another school. Debbie was a down-to-earth person whom everyone loved. With red hair and freckles she enamored her peers as well as adults. She twirled a baton and I remember she rode a horse, maybe in a parade. She was fun, athletic, and never talked about herself. Hey. I was a California girl. For once, my California background served me well in this Ethiopian home.

Before dark I headed back. *"Ameseghinallehu."* I thanked Seyoum's father for showing me around his winery and I thanked his mother for the *shai*. I told her she had a beautiful family, in basic Amharic, all in present tense, same pattern as the-goat-is-beautiful, the-goat-goes-through-the-gate: subject, verb, object, that I learned at UCLA.

"Your family is beautiful

"Seyoum is beautiful

"Your girls are beautiful.

"Thank you for tea; it was good.

"I like to see *t'ej-ery*; thank you." Not very fluent, not very pretty, but I tried.

Seyoum and his sisters walked with me to the main road where he flagged a Fiat. The girls, one on each side, laced their fingers between mine. *"Dehna hunu."* We said goodbye as I eased into the crowded blue and white cab like a bee easing back into the hive.

** In1981, 17 years later, Natalie Wood disappeared and drowned off her boat near Catalina Island in Southern California. It was a big story locally. The body disappeared and there were many questions when it washed ashore the following day. Was it suicide, murder, drugs, alcohol? Some reporting suggested that she had always been insecure and unhappy in life. Reflecting back, I wonder if she was too shy to talk to us. We didn't see it that way at the time. She was already famous. Insecurity never occurred to us.

Finger Food

A one-string *masenqo* resonated as someone plucked a lyre and another hammered a drum. Berhanu beamed when he spotted us. With long strides he made his way across the grass. This gangly student invited me to his sister's wedding saying his family would be honoured if we attended. We scooted out of the small taxi and headed toward the large canopy and the sound of traditional music.

His beautiful sister, Mariam, married a tall, intelligent, nervous looking young man named Bekele; she radiated. Her mocha skin, narrow straight nose and high cheekbones enhanced her slight frame. She wore a small tiara and her black hair curled around it. They made a striking couple. Berhanu took me by the hand to meet the wedding guests introducing me as his teacher. He and his parents made us feel as though we enhanced the occasion; as if we were dignitaries.

We sat at long tables under a huge white tent awning. White plates rested on white linen. Stemless wine glasses sat to the right of each plate and white cloth napkins framed the setting. The white napkins were meant to dab the red *berbere* pepper spice, not to mop up. Ladies and their spouses dressed in white: the women in *shammas* with wide colourful boarders, as was the fashion, and men in white tunics and jodhpurs. Waiters hovered in white dinner jackets and white pants. The evening was white and pure and innocent.

A few months before the wedding my teaching colleagues decided I needed a *shamma* for special occasions. I hesitated. Going native was not my style, though I appreciated the beautiful elegant cotton dresses from the first day on the minivan from the airport. They took me to a tailor.

Shammas are hand made, often at home, often including the hand woven unique colourful border for the hemline and the accent on the shawl. Some years the style featured wide, five inch borders, other seasons the trim featured narrow bands of woven design. The tailor took my measurements, length of sleeve, waist, length of skirt. My teaching sisters insisted I wear my new *shamma* to a holiday staff luncheon. They raved and made a huge fuss over my new white cotton dress.

Mrs. Thomas dressed me in a silk sari one afternoon and chatted on with tedious instructions for wrapping meters and meters of silk, pleating it in the front in elegant folds. The sari did not work like a beach towel or a wraparound sarong at the beach. The sari was meant to flow and flatter. I never mastered the technique. I wore it only one time to her home for dinner. There is something about other cultures that appreciates dressing an outsider in its native dress. I have never understood this idea; never felt a desire to dress a non-American colleague in cowboy boots and jeans or a pioneer dress and bonnet. I wore my *shamma* to the wedding.

Food culture in Ethiopia dictated that food must be taken from the communal plate with the right hand. We knew the drill; knew how to eat with our fingers, but it was seldom stress-free. Finger food in California meant carrot strips and celery sticks. The basis of most Ethiopian food is stew. I worked at carefully removing the food from the shared platter to my own plate without dripping on the table or spilling on my bleached white *shamma*, and then to my mouth. Further, it is considered very bad taste to indulge too much of your fingers into the succulent stew. The science of eating with your hands is really the art of eating with your fingers. The science is further defined as dipping into the communal platter only to the first knuckles of the fingers of your right hand.

As soon as we sat down waiters came to each guest pouring warm water over our hands before we started the meal. The hand-washers were followed by waiters pouring *t'ej,* honey wine into the provincial stubby glasses that looked more like Libby juice glasses than French stemware, and then came around with sliver platters lined with grey grain fermented *injera* crepes. They served individual servings of *injera,* cut in strips and rolled to look, we said, like ace bandages.

Waiters ladled out the first stew, *doro wot,* the popular, favourite chicken red pepper stew onto *injera* covered platters. The pieces of chicken often gave me trouble in a formal setting. The idea was to tear off a piece of *injera,* hold it in your right hand then scoop up the chicken using the crepe as a tool, without getting your fingers stained by the red pepper. I usually misjudged the size of the *injera,* tearing it too big or too small to encase the fragment of fowl. It was easy to mop up the stew juices, but more difficult to grasp a chicken leg or the slippery hardboiled egg that accompanied the *doro wot.* I did not tackle the egg.

As they ladled it out, the aroma of garlic, ginger, nutmeg and peppers preceded the next *injera*-lined platter filled with *siga wot,* beef stew. I asked for a Fanta orange drink, knowing I dare not drink the unboiled water. I was leery of the *t'ej* although the *berbere* burned my tongue, throat and stomach. I loved it and couldn't resist. I should have known better.

At one end of the tent the trio of *azmari* musicians played lively folk music on the lyre, drum and *masenqo,* a one string instrument played with a bow. Guests enjoyed the music, based on a five tone scale* and at various times during the meal joined in the dance.

Dancing with a partner or in groups, wedding guests clapped, sometimes ululating and shuffling to the rhythms.

The white-coats encircled the tables bearing silver platters, this time offering sharp silver knives. I took a knife and looked around for an indication of what to do. With no clue forthcoming, I watched the dancers and clapped along to the music. When the waiters returned they came in pairs. One man held a raw carcass from a hook while the other rotated the beef toward the guest. We were expected to slice off chunks of flesh to place on our plates to eat with *injera* and sauces, like steak tartar. Visions of meat hanging in markets, fly infested, rotting in the noonday sun flooded my memory.

I was in trouble. I had no choice as a special guest. This was the main course, the highlight of the evening menu. I couldn't push it around on my plate.

Several years before, fraternity guys in some macho ritual, swallowed live goldfish or whole raw eggs. The concept made me ill. I prayed this trend would not infiltrate the women's residences. Just-in-case, I predetermined my strategy: I would squeeze my eyes shut and swallow fast. The visual of a goldfish flopping 'round in my stomach stuck with me. Never mind issues of animal rights.

"If you can't wash it, boil it or peel it, don't eat it." Oh-m-god. I needed a strategy. I looked at Daryle on my left and at other guests at the table. As the cow came my way and was presented as an offering, I took my razor-sharp knife and sliced a thin sliver. The second waiter took my blade and hacked several more thick slices and placed them on my plate.

"*Tinish, tinish, betam ameseghinalleuh, kilil new,*" just a little, thank you very much.

"*Betam tiru new,*" it's very good, I bluffed.

The condiments saved the evening. My quick and spontaneous strategy: I prepared to masticate small bites of meat between my jaws, and quickly swallow, without squeezing my eyes. I made an *injera* wrap and popped the morsel of raw beef into my mouth. It was more tender than I expected and went down easily. The next bite I dredged the meat, after cutting it bite-size, in *mit'mita*, a dry red chili blend-of-fire

---

"The pentatonic scale (5 tone scale) uses the same notes as the diatonic scale, but two of the notes have been removed so there are no half-step intervals. Do-re-me... sol-la...do. You can see that these notes make the same patterns as black notes on a piano: a cluster of three, a space, a cluster of two, a space. If you start on Do and play the next 5 notes up on this pattern you have the next pentatonic scale. If you start on La and play the next 5 notes up, i.e. going around the pattern for a second time, you have the minor pentatonic scale. One scale breathes both hot and cold!" Mark Haldoway, Kalimba Magic.

and doused it in lime juice. The merger of bitter *injera*, fiery pepper and tart lime gave the *tere siga*, raw meat, a gourmet taste. I ate my share. The damage was done. I anticipated the worst.

After additional courses of vegetable stews, waiters served fresh roasted *bunna* coffee, served in tiny cups to signal the end of the meal. It is believed that coffee originated in Ethiopia.** The beans are the essence of the country: rich, authentic, strong, and flavourful, the antithesis of anemic American brews.

The music wound up as the meal wound down. The trio played and the guests danced and clapped, sometimes surrounding the newlyweds. Of course, I danced; mandatory. I knew the shoulder dance, that's what I called it, pretty well; at least I thought I had the hang of it. It had a name, Eskista. Moving with the edgy beat of the drum to the five notes of the scale and the jumpiness of the measures, I loved it. Finally we left for home while the honeymooners and peers danced on as we waved *Dehna hunu*, goodbye.

"See you in class Berhanu."

"But Madame,"

"See you on Monday; it's not your honeymoon."

"Thank you for coming Madame," from Berhanu's parents.

"Is Berhanu a good boy?"

"Of course he is. Thank you for including us in this wonderful celebration."

"Dehna hunu. Ciao."

Cramps, seizures in my stomach, the awful clue; what was I thinking? At two in the morning, right on cue, Daryle and I padded around the little house back and forth to the efficient bathroom. Why did I do that? Why did I eat so much *berbere*? Why the raw meat? I knew the drill. I knew the routine. Out to dinner, don't offend, come home and rotate between sitting on the loo and retching in the bidet. There were decided advantages to the small bathroom.

Once the wild foods passed through my body, I was fine; a free woman. I knew every time, after the fact. Sometimes, even at the time I indulged. I couldn't resist the wonderful food nor could I risk offending our gracious hosts or my students. So, up at 2am, predictable. This time it was a weekend and I had no morning classes.

** *"More than 1,000 years ago, a goat herder in Ethiopia's south-western highlands plucked a few red berries from some young green trees growing there in the forest and tasted them. He liked the flavour – and the feel-good effect that followed. Today those self-same berries, dried, roasted and ground, have become the world's second most popular non-alcoholic beverage after tea. The Ethiopian province where they first blossomed – Kaffa – gave its name to coffee." Selamta, In-Flight Magazine of ETHIOPIAN AIRLINES. Volume 13, Number 2. April – June 1996*

Homework

What was wrong with these kids? Antsy, hyper like preschoolers on a rainy day, they squirmed with nervous energy. I didn't have their full attention, unusual for these twenty-year-olds. I knew them well. I worked with the class daily for the past two years and today I wanted to practice and talk about using idioms. Even when we diagramed sentences, not thrilling, they gave me polite attention. But today, the young men in class fidgeted. They twisted around on splintered, hardwood classroom benches, looking over their shoulders through the cracked and broken windows.

"Seyoum, turn around," the *t'ej* student was twenty-three or twenty-four, he was not sure.

"Abebech, try this idiom 'Sitting on the fence,'" one of four girls in this tenth grade class.

"Madam, I think it means it is better to sit on a fence than on a wall."

"You could get cut sitting on the top of a wall with all the broken glasses."

"Twolde, please turn around.

"What do I mean when I say 'He's sitting on the fence'?" Twolde was lean and fit; a track star for the school, a barefoot runner.

"I know, Madam," attempted Afework.

"I think it means resting too much."

"Madam, I know 'raining cats and dogs.' That's an idiom," replied Bayene, totally off track.

Sporadic rumours hinted that the university students up the road planned to go on strike. My students sat bunched together sometimes leaning their elbows on their wooden desks. I stood ineffectually at the front of the room. The blackboard shined from years of classroom instruction written, rubbed out and erased until the chalk no longer adhered.

The students sat like rows of floor fans swiveling back and forth, focusing one minute on the front of the class, then pivoting to the side to peer through the broken windows, then back to the blackboard, then back to the windows. From a distance we heard the procession on its way down the road, building momentum as it pulsed toward the Parliament.

The air crackled with tension.

From Haile Selassie I University campus, where Daryle worked, riot police lined King George Street, the main road through the centre of town, one of the few paved roads in Addis. The blacktop road started at the Coptic Church on the hill, passed the university, passed Menelik II School and on to the Parliament buildings. In shoddy uniforms and worn-down loafers the police waited in readiness. We heard the students before we saw them.

I put the chalk down.

I didn't know what was coming but the kids knew. Their brothers and cousins talked about it at home. The mob came closer, spilling down the road like lava rumbling down the side of the mountain. The noise level intensified like the climax of Tchaikovsky's *1812 Overture*.

The drumming and chanting deafened until the sound took the shape and form of the university student procession. They marched down the boulevard, picking up energy. The students defied everyone. Their anger festered into indignant shouts.

The young militants clamoured for freedom, barked for economic reform and land reform, all pork barrel for their chanted-out cadence demanding a decrease in tuition fees.

My twenty-year old students wanted to be out there too, on the edge, cutting classes, making a statement; much cooler than learning English idioms. I saw the tension in their eyes. I saw it in their backs as they twisted around hoping to get a glimpse of the action, any indication of the turbulence outside.

Overeducated and young, the university students took to the streets protesting what they saw to be shameless corruption of the Haile Selassie government. However, plans failed to go according to their strategy. My students told me that their brothers and cousins intended to march to the Parliament; it was well envisioned. They planned to present their demands regarding tuition fees to whoever would receive them.

The scholars antagonized the police, who were undereducated and untrained for such events. The demonstration went very wrong and out of control. What happened next, I would never have imagined. The riot police on both sides of the road lunged toward the university students swinging clubs in all directions, attempting to disperse the noisy crowd.

College students pushed through the animated barricade of police. Once through the police barrier, they crawled through the hedges of Menelik II School and barged through the huge iron gate. Police followed, hanging on to their riot gear and to their image. Their bare feet slipped inside rundown leather-like loafers and they ran forward panting. Salty droplets ran down the red faces of the bloated police. Awkward and out of shape, they huffed and puffed swinging bats and clubbing any students they could reach.

Once on campus, in a frantic attempt to merge with the secondary students, the college men charged though the open schoolyard. They lurched into my classroom pushing aside the unpainted door that hung on one rusty hinge. Outside the room, other demonstrators pushed-up the broken wooden window frames and climbed into the classroom like daddy-long-leg spiders. In their anxiety, they yelled at my students and pushed me toward the dusty blackboard.

They hid in the classroom hunched under desks like lions crouched in the grass; others crowded onto the benches feigning classroom attention and interest in idioms. They hoped to mingle with the high school students, all the same age.

As the adrenalin kicked-in I yelled, "Stay in your seats; stay in the room; do not go outside." Some of the boys willingly went along with the college guys but others resented paying the price for their older academic siblings. They worried for their brothers and sisters; they were afraid for themselves and caught-up in the escalating emotion of the moment.

Everyone seemed to lose control. College men yelled for support, my students yelled back and I hoped they would not beat each other to death. With the rage they mustered, one ill-fated blow to the head might have been fatal. Maybe I should let them run to escape. As I struggled to choreograph calm, it occurred to me that I could be setting us all up for a brutal disaster.

With no let-up, the police, the thin ones, ran like a platoon of dancing cranes, lifting their knees to their chins in an effort to go faster. If it hadn't been traumatic, it might have been great comedy. They burst into the classroom shouting, asking for the university students, then pushed forward seizing the largest boys.

Students grabbed the desks and began hurling them toward the police. Everyone shouted. The girls hovered in the corner whimpering, the boys ripped apart strips of wood from the desks and timber from the old wooden window frames, using anything for a weapon.

Adding to the bedlam, a mounted rider galloped into the crowded classroom. The horse frothed in panic, its large black eyes flashed back and forth. Prancing in place, stomping loudly on the fragile wooden floor, there was no place for the pitiful creature to go. The room emoted pandemonium.

Others on horseback harassed from atop their scrawny mounts. They galloped into the courtyard toward the children and teenagers who emptied from their classrooms like agitated herds of wildebeest in migration. Four thousand children screamed in chaos and confusion.

"What do you think you are doing?

"Get out of here. Get that horse out of here.

"You have no right to be in here with these students. Get out.

"This is a classroom. Get out!" I screamed.

Then, in Amharic,

"You bastard. Leave. Who's your mother? You don't even know.

"You Mother F***er. Get out." Where did that come from? I used all the profanity I knew in Amharic. I never talk like that in English. Why do we learn rude phrases in foreign languages? I know some zingers in Spanish, too.

"Please Madam, don't say anything. It's okay."

"Please don't say any more," Abebech begged, tugging my arm.

"Leave them alone, Madam," Tesfaye warned.

"You'll only make it worse, Madam; please don't say anything," pleaded Bekele.

The shocked and insulted horseman glared. I was shocked myself. The students urged, pleaded with me to refrain, afraid that I could make things worse for them. They were right, of course. I was angry. I was protective. I was the authority figure and in the end, I was culturally out of sync. It was their problem, their government, their university but they were my students.

The girls came home with me. Frightened and concerned, they weren't ready to go home. I cleaned them up, made hot shai with milk and sugar and washed the blood from their school dresses and from their bruised arms. We did not talk too much about who or why or what. We just sat together comfortably until they were ready to leave.

I spent the next week going between the jail and the hospital. The police incarcerated several of my older, assertive students. Tesfaye, a studious young man, Seyoum the maker of t'ej, Twolde the runner and gentle Tamene giver of the goat, stayed in several quarters of the dirt-floor jail. I must have seemed self-assured, maybe pushy, as I paraded into the jail to see the prisoners. I hardly felt like parading; I was frightened of what I might see. But I feigned confidence and the warden took me to their prison quarters.

This was not a full-service-jail. They provided no food. I sat on the edge of Twolde's mat and we talked. Twolde was very bright. Today he projected defiance and anger. Tesfaye sat on the dirt while we talked. Tamene remained sweet, his innocence disrupted; Seyoum paced. For several days I brought baskets of *injera*, the fermented unleavened bread and aluminum containers of red-pepper fire-chicken *wot*. Those young men became uncharacteristically shy at my presence, touched that I was there in that horrible place, perhaps embarrassed to be seen in such surroundings. I don't know how it sorted out but days later they came back to class.

Several of my girls were beaten. Abebech took a board across her face, a weapon forged from a dismembered bench; it flattened her nose.

Zara endured a broken arm. Mohamed returned to class with a cast on his arm. A pregnant teacher, beaten down the stairs in the panic, miscarried, a young child died and an elementary teacher died in the stampede down the stairs. The US Embassy wanted a full report.

When school resumed I knew they must write. This wasn't about diagramming sentences. It was not about writing process. This was about getting it on paper. This was about thinking through the events; figuring things out.

I asked them to write a letter to a friend or relative in another village to describe what happened *The Day the Students Went on Strike.* As I recall, I did not give them much of a prompt. We all did just fine after that. Nothing needed explanation, we were all there. No one sat on the fence. We all got on with our lives and homework was due on Wednesday.

Post Script

First Week ... Last Week

After the riots, I reflected on my first week of classes, my first week in Africa, in Addis Ababa two years before. In some ways, it seemed like just days ago that we bounced and slipped on the mud passing the open markets, finding our little house, eating the local foods. In other ways it seemed like years ago that I entered my first class.

The eighth grade class terrified me that first week of school; fifty-two kids in one room, most of them between 14 and 22 years old. Most of them with no paper, no pencils and no one owned a book of any kind. I met Solomon and Daniel in that class, two of the brightest. The bonus with those two was that they were so much fun; spontaneous and fresh and energized, intelligent and quick. I would miss Ethiopia, the rancid aromas, the pungent flavours, the untamed and diverse personalities of the students. I didn't realize how much.

My studies endowed me with a double major in English and art; my minor, economics. I read books and sketched. No wonder my father thought I was throwing my life away. I guess I thought teachers read the book, shared it with students and the students learned. At UCLA I picked up tricks for teaching oral English, especially repetition of sentence patterns. It went like this:

Teacher: This is a book. That is a book, pointing to objects near and far.
Students: Theez eez a buk. That eez a buk.

Teacher: This is a pencil. That is a pencil.
Students: Theez eez a penceel. That eez a penceel.
Teacher: What is this? It's a pencil.
Students: Wot eez theez? Eeetz a penceel.
Teacher: What is that? It's a pencil.
Students: Wot eez that? Eeetz a penceel.

The UCLA professors also taught us about role-playing. This should be scripted around daily-life scenarios to practice vocabulary. The example was "Going to the movies." More appropriate would have been, "The goat goes through the gate."

The postscript to the riots left a level of unease on the part of the School administration and staff. The concern was to pursue the offenders, who by all observations were the police. In my country it would be difficult to fight city hall, but it could be done. Nobody likes a bad cop. In this country, Ethiopia, it would seem impossible.

Mr. Blake boldly directed the school. Irreverently, amongst ourselves, we called him Twiddle Thumbs. He settled in Ethiopia 30 years before and had the good luck symbol of having three thumbs. On the thumb of his right hand, a second thumb sprouted from just below the knuckle. His nails were manicured, all eleven of them. He hustled across campus, waddling as fast as his stubby legs would go; his shoulders rocked from side to side. He walked briskly, with purpose, and rubbed his chubby hands together in a perpetual state of anxiety.

Mr. Blake made his way across the front of the staff room. He pontificated and opined over the Official Riot Report which he presented to staff the first day back after the mêlée.

Every month we assembled in the dingy staffroom where we met for teacher meetings and also gathered to receive salaries. The last day of each month we waited in line after school, while two men, who sat behind a small table with flour sacks of cash, searched for our names on a hand-written employee list which included tea-boys, disciplinarians and teachers. They painfully counted out the cash, *birr* by *birr* including the remaining coins.

"The students resisted the authority of the police. This caused the police to have an 'accident'," Mr. Blake read from the badly translated Report.

The first Tuesday of the month we discussed school issues with Mr. Blake administering the monthly agenda. The dark-skinned man from Madras was empowered with a huge responsibility: Discipline and Order. Judy, my American colleague the first year, hated the meetings, but attended dutifully. One month she took her knitting project. As

Mr. Blake droned on in his fuddy-duddy way, Judy knitted and pearled row after row. I took notes to stay focused.

"Miss Woods." She looked up at Mr. Blake resting her needles on the ugly wooden table.

"Miss Woods, please put down your sewing." I restrained myself. Judy didn't miss a stitch.

"Mr. Blake. My brains are not in my fingers," and she continued 'sewing.' He shuffled his papers and continued as well.

We listened to the badly translated Report and discussed our responsibilities to the students and the concerned parent community. Fact: the university students demonstrated. Fact: the police rioted.

In my first teaching job, there was no curriculum guide, just the course title, Eighth Grade English, Ninth Grade English, First Grade English. No teaching aids, no books, no paper or pencils for students, no student store, not even a library. I caught myself stealing stubs of chalk from classrooms.

You must help students to not have revengeful attitudes," Mr. Blake advised.

Teachers must guard against a future happening," he continued.

It is the teachers' responsibility to get things back into order." Asefa, the assistant, who usually wore a khaki safari suit, emphasized teachers' as if absolving the administration of this responsibility.

The first week of classes my first year, I brightened-up the classroom walls with pictures and vocabulary words using the whitewashed walls as bulletin boards. Everything disappeared. It disturbed me. As with any robbery, I felt violated. I admit to being disappointed. I later understood that the visuals I added to the room, thoughtfully prepared at home, were probably hanging, push-pined to someone's *tsjika* hut. Poverty was an issue; education was not.

Mr. Blake taught me the value of planning, even if there were no curriculum guides; especially as there were no guides.

In the post-riot staff meeting we listed our concerns. Asefa, wrote on the cracked black board using a shard of white chalk.

"Whoever ordered the police must be penalized." He meant: whoever directed, whoever was in charge of the police must be penalized.

"This brutality was intentional," was the feeling among many.

"Our students showed their Menelik ID and were beaten anyway," according to one father.

"There were seen five police on one student." This was observed as unjust.

One day during the first month, Mr. Blake visited my large eighth grade class. My thinking catapulted to another level. When I returned to our *tjika* house that night I tried to think about how to channel my rambunctious students. They were great kids and I laughed with them; still, something had to change. Mr. Blake was not confrontational nor did he offer any mentoring or clue about curriculum expectations. There was no curriculum guide. I had to figure out how to engage them all and still expect them to perform and retain. I had to figure out what I wanted to teach and develop some strategy to connect the dots.

"Oh. Well. I see you are here, Mrs. Russell," Mr. Blake said clear enough for the entire class, rubbing his chubby hands and thumbs together. The kindly man from Madras had a huge responsibility: Discipline and Order.

"Yes, Mr. Blake," what could I say? "I guess the students are a little loud."

I was mortified. It did not occur to me that they were so loud the noise reverberated down the hallway of the grimy, rundown building. They were out of control; the roll playing scenario was not working. He left, returning, waddling, oblivious to the ugly hallway, though he heard the noisy roll-play of conversational English.

Mr. Blake inadvertently, unwittingly mentored by compelling me to figure things out for myself. He forced me to work through lessons. He forced me to think. I considered splitting the class into small groups. Where fifty-two seemed unfathomable, I learned that the smaller groups could work, practice, drill, even write together, freeing me to walk between the groups, to set up lessons, to give examples and work with the large group and the smaller groups.

Mr. Arukian, the displaced Armenian science teacher was a kind man; the students never mucked about in his class. Mr. Zaki, short, stout, Egyptian, sporting a black beret, never laughed in class; nor did his students. They were terrified of Mr. Zaki. I had to find my groove. Mr. Blake, Twiddle Thumbs, forced me to do so. His job was Discipline and Order.

We continued to list our concerns on the wobbly blackboard:

- *What about future demonstrations?*
- *A student and a teacher died.*
- *The security of the students, teachers and the school was at stake.*
- *Finally, lost books and notebooks was a major issue.*
- *It was time for exams.*
- *Books and all school supplies were very expensive.*
- *How would we handle the final reviews for leaving exams?*

I looked around the room. Mr. Arukian, an elderly man, sat with his hands folded on top of the splintered table, concerned for the safety of all. Mrs. Arukian who taught me to prepare baklava with Ethiopian honey and walnuts and very thin pastry sat next to her

*husband. Mr. Zaki paced in the back of the room in his trade mark
black beret offering many comments. Violet Zaki was in my ninth
grade class that year and gave her father her teenage perspective on
the riots. Mrs. Thomas sat up straight afraid the serrated wooden
furniture would snag her silk sari.*

We formed committees. The student council, executive council,
administration, teachers and staff all participated. In the end, it came
down to us, the teachers, to counsel, advise and prepare students for
the end of the year, and for following years.

I knew my students well by the end of two years. We connected
from the first week. I knew they were stable, were not overly stressed
from the riots. I knew they were ready to review for exams. They knew
about idioms, sentence diagramming and subject/verb agreement.
They were writers with expanding vocabularies. These kids were remarkable, wonderful, brilliant, but not because of my efforts. Their
pronunciation was American while I was there. That was my doing, I
suppose. They could write a paragraph with a topic sentence, though
they never figured out fragments.

The little ones, still memorizing their ha-hu-he's, learned to read
the ABCs and short words; could chat away in simple sentences about
the goat, the chicken and potatoes in the market. They knew "The
Little, Little Spider Went Up the Water Spout" and "I'm a Little Tea
Pot" complete with choreography.

For many years after we left, I heard from students via thin blue
aerograms. Life in Addis became difficult as the government collapsed
into anarchy. Student demonstrations escalated causing disruption
and the closing of the universities for months at a time until it became
impossible to continue advanced education. My students transferred
to other schools, even dropped out, but they continued to correspond
in five sentence paragraphs with occasional idioms interspersed.

They were thrilled to know that I was expecting a baby when I left
Ethiopia. They went on and on with adoration over the birth of my
first child, baby Jessica. It surprised me that they were so involved in
the birth. They seemed to have some pride of ownership, as if every
student was an auntie or uncle to my first child. It surprised me, this
genuine concern for my health and the health of my baby daughter.

From the first week to the last, I was the learner. I learned how to
make *t'ej*, I learned to make baklava, I learned to wrap a silk sari. I ate
formaggio, and drank *cappuccino*. I learned to receive a goat, to receive handmade baskets. I appreciated their birthdays and weddings. I
learned discipline and order. I learned I was white.

Orchids,

Stone Fish

and the

CIA

Manila via Taipei

The interim years in the United States served our needs, but not our desires. There was a gap to bridge; an empty hole to fill. One doctoral diploma and two children later, we headed out. We accepted a position in Manila, tossed our possessions in bags, grabbed the kids and flew to the Philippines, making our way back to international employment. I missed it from the day we left our work in Addis Ababa.

At the time, we could not describe it; the need to return. Relatives could not define it, much less understand it.

"Why are you going so far?"

"You're taking your children?"

"We have so many needs in America," from my aunt Evelyn, whom I loved and respected.

"Why don't you stay here and help your fellow Americans?"

"We wish we could do what you're doing, but we have our house."

"We wish we could do what you're doing, but the kids are in school."

"We wish we could do what you're doing, but we have a dog."

Friends and neighbours envied or misunderstood. Relatives lacked empathy. We packed our bags and never looked back.

"What cha doin' Dannie?"

"Diggin'."

"If you dig deep enough, you can dig all the way to China."

The little girl played in the back yard, scooping a hole in the dirt with the kitchen serving spoons.

A strong typhoon raged with furious agitation. We gripped the arm rests as the plane dipped and climbed, tossed about like a leaf in the wind. Jessica and Ian squealed in delight. My palms dripped with fear. The typhoon interrupted our flight into Manila. The plane diverted to Taipei. All flights in the region were grounded. We waited-out the typhoon for three days in Taiwan at the beautiful Grand Palace, a hotel rich in culture, history and Chinese beauty.

If she succeeded at this apparently plausible notion, a 'Chinaman' would pop his head up through the hole. She learned very early that the world was round like a California beach ball, and that

49

other cultures lived on the other side of the ball. Her father encouraged her to dig while he raked leaves.

Howard Wire, then head of the Taipei American School, directed us to the magnificent National Palace Museum with treasures dating back many centuries. The new museum opened in Taipei in 1965, the year we left Addis Ababa.

She pictured a man in a pointed 'coolie' hat wearing a long-sleeved shirt, with slit eyes and a long braid down his back. She wore braids too. She didn't like hers; sometimes her braids pulled too tight. In her mind, as she dug deeper, he was always a little dirty when he popped his head out of the hole. She was dirty too. They would be friends, and then she expected that she would visit where he lived by crawling through her dirt tunnel. Maybe it was her mom, the romantic dreamer, who gave her the serving spoons for digging; she, the one who wanted to travel, who planted the seed.

The angry, ranting typhoon facilitated our first introduction to China. That is, after her father introduced the subject in the back yard when she was four, the age of her own son on this flight. Now in Taipei, albeit by accident, we thrived on the overture to Taiwan and to greater China.

We learned that "The Committee for the Disposition of the Ch'ing Imperial Possessions" formed in China to organize a complete inventory of the 'Objects of the Palaces.' These objects shaped the basis for the collection now housed in Taipei.*

Jessica thrust out her little arm sprinkled with pink welts and watched with wide-open eyes. We were not prepared for mosquitoes. At the hotel Mrs. Wire said,

"When you have a very itchy mosquito bite, take your thumb, and press your nail into the centre of the bite two times.

"Like this, forming an X in the centre of the bite.

"May I show you?" Jessica nodded.

"Is the itching gone? Has it stopped?" Jessica nodded again.

Mrs. Wire generously offered to keep the children a few hours

---

* With sensitivity and forethought the Chinese took great effort to preserve and protect the 'Objects of the Palaces.' Conflict between Japan and China led to Chinese concern about the art treasures located in the palaces. In 1933, seven years before my birth, quiet arrangements directed the entire collection of art works and treasures to the south of China, out of the Forbidden City. The treasures went first to Shanghai, then to Nanking at the end of that War, in 1945. Fighting continued, however, between the Nationalists and Communists; they shipped the collection of the Imperial Court off-shore this time, to Taipei. This extraordinary exhibit contained ceramic celadon, blue and white, lucent, scalloped eggshell ceramic, jade, silks and ivory sculptures among other relics.

for naps while the typhoon whirred like a blender on frappe, enabling us to revisit the museum a second time in as many days.

The displays presented breathtaking selections offering pure pleasure to the senses. Infatuated with a Sung Dynasty hanging scroll, *Children at Play in an Autumnal Garden*, I purchased a copy in the museum shop. The silk painting portrayed two children, gently bent over a table concentrating over the intricacies of the game.

The girl appears to be older than her brother and about the age of Jessica and her brother, Ian. They wear robes typical of the Sung period, mid-12th century. The flowers in the garden are blossoms of hibiscus and chrysanthemums, symbols of autumn. The artist, Su Han-ch'en specialized in human figures, and earned praise for his ability to represent children in their naïveté.

I later learned the piece was one of Su's surviving masterpieces. It whetted my appetite for things Chinese and beautiful. The young woman looked for the man in the coolie hat. No one in the Taipei museum wore a long black braid. She knew she would dig deeper into this stunning culture continuing her mission of international inquiry.

Culture Shock

Arrival and Indignation

Jessica's View

For me, moving overseas with my family was a natural continuation of my life. I remember being on the swings, pumping my legs so that I would go as high as possible to experience the exhilarating feeling of my stomach plummeting to the back of my body, as the swing plunged downwards from the highest of pinnacles. I was on the swings when I boasted to a fellow preschooler that I was moving to the Philippines. Naturally, neither of us had a clue what a "Philippines" was, but at six I remember being aware that I was about to begin a different life.

After a 3 day weather delay in Taipei, we arrived at the Manila International Airport amidst the torrential downpour of the 'legendary' typhoon of 1972. The stewardesses shuttled passengers under jumbo umbrellas across the tarmac and into the smoldering shell of what had once been the airport, now a bombed-out jolt to the senses. The memories that my mind recorded as a six year old were of sloshing

51

through water that was knee-deep while my brother, who only came to my knees, was carried across the tarmac by one of the stewardesses. My indignation was immense at what seemed to be a slight. He was four; he could have walked.

As a kindergartner in the Philippines, my assimilation into the expatriate community of peers was easy. Although I didn't realize it then, kindergarten was just the launch-pad to what would become a life of global experiences, education and career. I now have two children of my own and I wonder what my four year old thinks as he swings at the park in Dhahran, Saudi Arabia. I just heard him boast to a fellow preschooler, "I'm going to visit America." And I'm sure he has little idea what an "America" is.

—Circa 1996

Martial Law

September 1972

M oving can be a challenge for spouses left at home with no contacts, no friends. I was careful of the trap. I worked at establishing the house while Daryle jumped into projects and duties at school. I sat at the kitchen table trying to learn the culture with Natty, newly hired domestic help, as my tutor.

"How do you say potato?"

"*Patatas.*"

"So, banana is ba-na-nahs ?"

"Hee hee. Aye, no, Madame, *naku naman!* Oh my goodness! Banana is *ang saging.*"

"Oh.

"Chicken?"

"*Manok.*"

"Good morning, how are you?"

"*Magandang umaga po. Kamusta po kayo?*

"Fine?"

"*Mabute po.*"

Her English was good enough.* I asked for vocabulary translations. I asked her about Pilipino foods and customs in her province. I asked about the markets. I entrusted her with my queries. She answered at her level of ability.

One can be tempted to be a best friend, a sister, to a domestic helper. Natty and Perla were the only women I talked to for some time until I established friendships. There is a fine line between employer and employee but the line becomes blurred when they 'borrow' your sweater; when your hand cream disappears. You have allowed it to happen. Domestic helpers are employees, not sisters. I learned to be cautious, to the point of being aloof. But this attitude developed slowly over the years.

School opened late, after Labour Day. Jessica and Ian met classmates. Ian attended a smaller preschool and fell in love with Miss Tan, his bubbly, young pre-kinder teacher. He whipped the playground into shape within days; king of the play yard at 4 years old. Then he attacked the classroom to become master of glitter and glue. Jessica attended the big school with her father. She was more reserved than her brother but quickly became friends with Miko, Mia, Heidi, Gretchen, Jonathon and Julie. Miko's dad was married to the former Miss Sweden and the owner of the Gilarmi Apartments where we stayed while workers painted the mildew that covered our new home. Mia's father was Manuel Elizalde, anthropologist who 'discovered' the Tasaday tribe, Heidi's dad worked for Leyland Motors, and Gretch, Jona and Julie's dad worked with Crocker Bank. The kids remained friends for many years.

Within weeks of unpacking, we awoke to marching music.** We twirled the dial. No morning news, no rock 'n roll, not even the monotonous Vietnam anthem, "Tie A Yellow Ribbon 'Round The Old Oak Tree." All stations played military marching music. The phone rang.

"The country is under Martial Law."

"What does that mean?"

"We're not sure yet, but the embassy is telling us not to open school.

"Stay off the streets.

"Stay by the phone for further information.

"If parents phone, we are just taking precautionary measures.

"We will reopen as soon as we get clearance from the embassy."

What did it mean? Tanks in the streets? I peeked out the windows. We knew what to do: fill the tubs with water. Our Philippine home, upgraded from the mud house in Addis, included five bathrooms, four tubs; we hoarded water. Natty filled two tubs and I opened water taps for the other two. We had no power most of the day, but we had water stashed in our tubs. A coup d'etat seemed eminent if not already in progress. In fact, however, President Ferdinand Marcos declared Martial Law; no tanks. No coup; not yet.

The bombed-out Manila airport symbolized the beginning of our awareness to the disruption, dissatisfaction and frustration of the population. Random bombings escalated in markets and cinemas. Strikes and student demonstrations occurred on a regular basis.

We continued to twist the dial. We only heard marching music; a total news blackout. We depended on our radio during the first thirty days and thirty nights for updates on incoming typhoons and weather information, for the announcements of school closures, and political news. Without information, without a news program, even once a day, tension swelled like a balloon ready to burst.

We knew nothing; marching music, brassy, drumming, patriotic music and no information; no instructions, no warnings, no explanations. Our imaginations ran wild. But we had water.

We swapped our table-top Grundig shortwave from Ethiopia for a more manageable, newer, smaller, battery operated radio. Without it we were cut off. The shortwave preempted the marching music for the Voice of America and announced: *"Martial Law has been declared in the Philippines by President Ferdinand Marcos, as a result of an assassination attempt on Secretary of Defense, Juan Ponce Enrile."**** We said nothing to the kids, but continued to peek out the front windows. No tanks in the streets. The children were four and six. We explained nothing about the political situation because we knew nothing.

Inside our secure village gates Natty and Perla prepared thick slices of fresh fruit from the Dole pineapple farms and hot scrambled eggs, ignorant of any political change. Daryle and the administration closed the school for several days. The Marcos government, like college administrators, set a country-wide curfew at 10pm and everyone scurried through meals and parties to rush home. The novelty wore off and there were many evenings when adults stayed over because they couldn't make it home in time. The VOA and BBC reported no deaths, no violence. We trusted these external sources over the days while the local radio played strident Souza.

---

*The country, colonized by Spain for 333 years, was later colonized by America for 48 years. In the city, most Pilipinos are bilingual. Tagalog, a blend of languages beyond its Austronesian roots, includes recognizable chunks of Spanish and English. Taglish, is popular in Manila.

**September 21, 1972

***Enrile himself admitted after Marcos's downfall in 1986, his unoccupied car had been riddled by machinegun bullets fired by his own men on the night that Proclamation 1081 was signed (Martial Law). Ronald E. Dolan, ed. Philippines: A Country Study. Washington: GPO for the Library of Congress, 1991.

Wild West

The night Martial Law was declared the government of Ferdinand Marcos arrested Benigno Aquino, popular leader of the opposition. Marcos shut down the newspapers and mass media. Journalists, critics and activists were slammed behind bars along with 30,000 opposition politicians. We learned this first through rumours, then through orchestrated editorials of the Philippine *Daily Tribune* and finally confirmed by the BBC.

Around town, everyone waited. What would happen? The embassies buzzed with speculation. Would the opposition fight back with gun battles in the streets? Would the army rise against the President? The U.S. wanted this to blow over without incident, without international intervention.

The administration of Richard Nixon supported Marcos during his announcement of Martial Law but on the ground, on site, we wondered how this would play out. How would this Declaration be made manifest. So far, no tanks. We drained two bath tubs littered with floating winged things and kept two tubs full of water, just-in-case. The power continued to cut out regularly; this meant no running water, no air conditioning, no overhead fans to push the stifling wet air. It meant no washing, ironing, cooking. But we had our battery-pack radio. There were no street riots as in Addis Ababa, no city-wide mayhem. We waited; amateur sociologists observing change.

City residents tried to conduct business-as-usual without power. Everyone carried guns. It was cowboy territory. Taxi drivers, pedestrians, businessmen, bankers, workers, the common *tao*, everyone carried guns. Restaurants and hotels reminded guests to "Please Check Your Guns at the Door." Posted in one restaurant window, "You are welcome. Your gun is not."

Schools reopened. The brownouts continued, occurring way too often. During the day, elevators stopped mid-floor, lights went out, fans stopped, refrigerators melted, water, dependent on electric pumps did not flow, air conditioners sparked and popped. Brownout schedules were listed in the paper like prayer times, like tide tables, but the schedule fluctuated like the power.

It seems all Filipinos garner nicknames, even the politicians. The son of Marcos was called Bong-Bong. Baby was a popular nickname as was Boy. The Aquino family was known to all by their affectionate nicknames. Everyone loved the Aquino's. The children of Aquino's brother, Agapito Aquino, called Butz, attended the International School. While Ninoy, as he was known, sat in prison, Corazon*, Ninoy's wife, hosted birthday parties for all the Aquino cousins and included Jessica and Ian. Cory was a humble person, a common *tao*, and an unpretentious housewife, but birthdays mushroomed into family celebrations-of-life including puppet shows, *calesa* rides around the village and always long-life pasta noodles served as spaghetti.

No one had electric power. In our *barrio*, people converged at the Intercontinental Hotel to conduct meetings or do business with the assistance of giant hotel generators. In the black hole of evening darkness, the Intercon provided a beacon of florescence; a cool respite; a hub of normalcy.

Kids appeared in the evening with bulging backpacks and sat in groups at tables, or sat sometimes on the thick carpet to complete homework in the lighted, air-conditioned hotel lobby, not because of Martial Law but because of continuing brownouts. Our teachers at the International School were heartless. No excuses. Homework was due, power or not.

Each night Makati Mayor Nemesio Yabut held court, his own *majlis*, in the lobby of the Intercontinental Hotel. We walked over to the hotel during frequent brown outs. Everywhere the hot, sticky air hovered throughout homes and hovels. Romantic candle light deferred to muggy frustration. The Mayor sported an 'old society' black dyed, well slicked pompadour and sat centre-stage, in his white *pina* cloth *barong tagalog*. He, his cronies and body guards occupied the sofas in the centre of the lobby facing the revolving doors.

"Hey! Doc!" to Daryle. He always called us over. This was flattering on one hand; intimidating on the other. Several times he made space for us to join his *majlis* inner circle. I always watched over my shoulder. Though guns were checked, I never trusted this around the Mayor. His body guards maintained plenty of munitions. If anyone was a target, it would be the Mayor. Gang rivalry continued to thrive as hotel soirées flourish. His son, Ricky, studied at the International School Manila.

"Hey, Doc! How's my boy doing?" then a round of introductions.

"You keep Ricky in line. He's a lazy kid."

"He's a good kid, but he has no appreciation for education; kids!" he said in mock distain.

---

*After her husband's death, Corazon Aquino became leader of the opposition and president of the Philippines, 1986.

Distracted, the Mayor looked to the side, then back.

"These kids, now-a-days, have it too good.

"They don't know how hard we've worked to get them a good education.

"You're running a fine school. You keep it up, Doc," and we were dismissed.

"Thank you Mr. Mayor. I plan to; I appreciate your support."

The Halloween Affair
October 1972

In our gated Golden Ghetto in Makati we received fliers printed on pink paper regarding this year's 'Halloween Affair,' a direct reference to the American 'Watergate Affair'* which even in Manila, we were beginning to hear about on a daily basis.

The United States involved in election scandals? The United States, promoter of democratic ideals? The United States, champion of democracy and free elections? The break-in by employees of President Nixon's reelection committee astounded the world. America squirmed in a series of scandals involving the administration of President Richard Nixon. The intrigue progressed daily with arrests, accusations and trials. The international press thrived on the antics, the dirty tricks, as they became known.

The pink neighborhood memo instructed: "For the Halloween Affair the Compound Gates Will Open At Exactly 6pm." Residents knew to prepare baskets of sweet treats for the annual ritual. We carved a squash, closest we could find to a pumpkin shape, lit a candle and were ready to celebrate.

Jessica dressed in an itchy Hawaiian grass skirt atop her swim suit and a lei of frangi pangi strung together in the afternoon. Ian dressed as a handsome cowboy with a penciled-on mustache, a scarf tied around his neck and a little cowboy hat perched atop his head. At the pumpkin hour, they went with Natty and Perla. Daryle and I stayed home to dispense the treats.

At 6pm sharp, the security guards opened the gates. I didn't understand the implications to the memo until 6.05pm.

Tattered, barefoot children, maids, even adults burst through the barrier down the streets of our Ghetto, like water gushing from a broken main. The surge forced us to close our own gate and hand out candies through the bars. No cute or scary costumes; no costumes, no masks; no shoes.

"You give me candy," demanded the chorus at the gate.

No "Trick-or-Treat;" no "Thank you, *salamat po*." No eye contact, but lots of giggling as the pack darted off to the next house.

At first this shocked me. Jessica and Ian were reminded to say 'thank you' at every house. I wondered if they remembered. These giggly barefoot urchins and the gaggle of housemaids and other assorted adults urged the children to use their four words of English to scoop up the sweets to fill their crumpled paper bags: You Give Me Candy.

The custom of the Halloween Affair, introduced to Pilipinos during the American colonial period, was well known in the *barrios* as a time for handouts, begging without shame. Maids and domestic workers reverted to giggly childish personas. They ran from house to house to get as much fodder as possible before the gate closed at 8pm. I'm sure Natty and Perla contained their lust only because they were responsible for our two candy snatchers. The cousins wanted to be there racing from door to door like the children they no longer were. Nonetheless, their own stash of loot was impressive. The community was generous.

I found the whole affair disturbing. Poverty scaled the walls behind my house like a wave of army ants driven and focused to come to the gate for Halloween giveaways. Tattered, barefoot children, maids, entire families came running down the streets at 6pm.

One Sunday, on a day-trip to México, a young girl and her family wandered about a small plaza just outside Tijuana. Well-wisher gathered in front of the church to applaud a wedding procession. Pigeons fluttered about like doves of peace, occasionally pecking at the dirt. Vicariously, the California girl watched.

A mariachi band standing beneath a shady tree played festive brassy aye-ay-ay tunes while the bride, resplendent in white, skipped down the steps of the church, clutching her new esposo with one hand and steadying her tiara with the other. Friends and relatives tossed rice over the couple to wish them fertility, prosperity and a lifetime of blessings. On cue, it seemed, church bells rang as the bright young bride and handsome groom left the church.

"What are they doing?" the teenager asked her brother.

The burglarization of the Democratic Party headquarters, located in the Watergate apartment complex in Washington, DC gave rise to juicy headlines internationally; a journalist's dream and welcome diversion from local stories, in our case Martial Law.

"What are those people doing?" she whispered to her mother, though she knew the answer.

To her horror, waifs and others mingling about the plaza, along the peripheral near the church, scrambled to scoop up the rice, grain by grain, before the pigeons grabbed the granules.

Natty and Perla returned, each holding the hand of a cowboy and a hula dancer; the cousins clutching their own crumpled paper bag of goodies. The poverty gap reflected México and Addis Ababa. We lived on the other side of the wall.

EARCOS

November 1972

In my mind's eye, I saw it clearly, though I was not there, but at home, just across the highway. In November of that first year, shortly after the Halloween Affair, the International School hosted the East Asia Regional Conference of Overseas Schools, EARCOS. Daryle's experience in choreographing conferences made him the designated driver for organizing the huge event.

"Will delegates come to Manila?" from the superintendent.

"Will the city remain stable if they do come?" from a staff member.

"I've been here three months.

"You have a better feel for the region and especially for Manila.

"What do you think?" from Daryle.

"Martial Law should make people comfortable; you think?"

"We can't cancel the hotel at this point."

"What assurances do we have that the situation will remain calm?"

"Well, Mayor Yabut has agreed to give the welcome remarks. He has a reputation here. "He wants it to work," again Daryle

Three hundred delegates registered to attend the EARCOS meetings. At the time, the region included Hong Kong, Korea, Taipei, Thailand, Malaysia, Japan, Singapore and Indonesia, as well as the Philippine Islands. Although the country remained under Martial Law, a sense of lawlessness still prevailed. The conference would go on.

I saw it clearly. Three days before the delegates arrived, a shoot-out occurred in the lobby of the five-star Intercontinental Hotel. The Mayor, our Mayor Yabut, and cronies, entered into an apparent face saving opportunity with rival politicos. Five gangsters, good guys or bad guys, were shot dead. The Mayor survived but the event received front page publicity across the region.

It wasn't a premonition, but I saw it clearly. The Mayor, surrounded by cronies, sits in the lobby in his usual place facing the revolving doors. Around three in the morning, others swagger in one at a time through the rotating doors. The Mayor and his men exchange glances and stand. In crisp white barongs they adjust their shoulders. They exchange words. They fire guns. Five battered bodies lie in pools of blood; the cadavers ooze. The barongs stain scarlet. The Mayor leaves. Mayors don't observe curfew.

There was no question of canceling the conference. It was too late. In the luxurious hotel lobby, workers mopped-up blood which covered the carpets like a thick oil spill, even as delegates from the region arrived. The show would go on.

It was show-time. Opening day and delegates filed into the grand salon for the plenary session like kids on the first day of school. Some meandered like gazelle on an open plane, meeting and greeting colleagues and renewing friendships. Others hurried in, coffee in hand like rush-hour commuters heading for a front-of-the-room seat. Mayor Yabut arrived on time.

Daryle introduced the Mayor who walked across the stage with great confidence and only a slight limp. The impeccable crease in his black pants, the elegant *barong tagalog* embroidered white on white exuded class, wealth and leadership. Honouring his commitment for opening ceremonies, the Mayor, at Daryle's prior invitation, arrived, took his place on stage and delivered judicious and appropriate Welcome Remarks. The conference was off to a flourishing start.

I was not, however, the only one looking over my shoulder.

Imelda

December 1972

By all accounts the conference was proclaimed a major success. For the final evening delegates rode from the blood-stained

Intercontinental Hotel for a twenty-minute jaunt in decorated *cale-sas* through the traffic, down the boulevard, to the prestigious Manila Polo Club. From the opening remarks to the culminating gala, the critiques were generous and enthusiastic.

Eleven days later, in early December, Daryle received a call from Malacanang Palace. In broad daylight, an assassin stabbed and slashed Imelda Marcos in a murder attempt. She survived, brought her children back from international schools in Europe and asked that Imee be enrolled at the International School Manila.

When she returned from Europe Imee, a twelfth grade senior, arrived at school with a flotilla of body guards, rifles, pistols, and escorts; escorts in the parking lot, in the hallways, in the cafeteria, in the locker room. She attended classes for several weeks trying to resume a normal high school life. It was not normal; nor was it normal for all the other kids at school; nor was it normal for staff needing to accommodate the guards in the classrooms.

Between classes, for six minutes the hallways pulsed with the energy of 400 high school students rushing, shouting greetings, exchanging high-fives, quiz notes and urgent messages making their way to lockers, and classrooms. The interludes energized everyone.

The platoon of sentinels charged with the protection of the First Lady's daughter added an element of suspense to the mix as well as more bodies; with weapons. The armed entourage secured passage, surrounding Imee like a school of fish all going the same direction darting one way, then the other.

The novelty turned into nuisance. It was difficult for everyone. Daryle decided that Imee would study at the Palace and the teachers take the assignments to her. To accommodate, he went to Malacanang on a weekly basis like a groupie following a rock star.

Although not privy to the shoe closets, he made note of elaborately framed oils and pastels standing on the floors propped against the walls of the entry and living areas. Mrs. Marcos recently returned from a buying spree in Paris and London. These paintings were later labeled as frauds, copies, faux. Was she duped? We all suspected so.

Imelda and Daryle became friendly on an almost first-name basis except that they both kept the relationship professional, using titles. What is protocol around first ladies?

"Good morning, Doctor Russell. How pleasant to see you again," nodding as she spoke.

"Good morning, Madam Marcos. This morning, I would like you to meet Imee's math and science instructors," then, turning to Imee,

"Hey, Imee! Good morning. How've you been this week? Lessons going okay?"

"Hi Dok! Sorry: Doctor Russell!" Imee demonstrated discipline and maturity as a student. In front of her mother, she knew not to call Daryle, 'Dok,' and apologized. In her final year of secondary education she prepared with diligence for her future university work at Harvard.

Imee's mother dropped infamous pearls for the local press, outrageous one-liners; shimmering sound bites. So lustrous, the international press snatched them one by one and strung them out.

"If you know how reech you are, you are not reech. But me, I am not aware of da extent off my wealth. Dat's how reech we are," once quoted in the *Philippine Daily Inquirer*, March, 1998.

"I was born ostentatious. Dey will list my name in da dictionary someday. Dey will use *Imeldific* to mean ostentatious extravagance," quoted by *Associated Press* in April of the same year.

Imelda loved to shop. Bloomingdale's, New York, was a favourite Mecca for her. It was reported that she asked for the store to be shut down to avoid the media and crowds while she and her jet-setting friends shopped. Media reported that she owned 3,000 pairs of shoes.

"I did not hap tree-tousand pairs off shoes; I hap one-tousand and sixty." I read that she once saw a New York poster in a shoe store which claimed, "There's a little Imelda in all of us."

I sat on the rain-soaked cement floor of a huge warehouse with a group of students; we sacked rice for a *barrio* wiped-out from a typhoon. Imelda Marcos showed up in a too-small tee-shirt which pulled across her ample breasts and conformed to her rolls of opulence which lopped over her waistband. The message on the shirt was something like Imelda Cares. Her long, heavy legs and chubby feet sported open-toed, high-heeled sandals as she stepped above and over the crowd of volunteers. Her off-hand remarks remained painfully callous and insensitive to the common *tao* and the have-nots, of whom there were so many.

"When dey see me holding up a piss prom da sea," she said, "dey can see I am comportable wit kings as well as wit paupers."

"The problem wit First Ladies," she also said, "is dat you have to set da standard. My role is to be boat star and slave."

When Andrew Lloyd Webber's brilliant musical *Evita* opened in London 1978, a play loosely based on the life of Eva Peron, the Philippine press had a field day. They made obvious comparisons between the two first ladies. Imelda was said to be furious. I'm paraphrasing, but I remember the quote well, "I am no-ting like Eba Peron. No-ting. I am not a prostitute."

Graduation

June 1973

As the school year came to an end Daryle somewhat casually asked Imee if her dad would be interested in being the graduation speaker, the polite, protocol, political thing to do. "I don't know, Dok, I'll ask him." Of course he would not fit this mundane exercise into his schedule. But he did.

Would he show up? Who would be prepared with the back-up speech? President Marcos was famous for not showing up. Or, and this would be equally difficult, he was notorious for arriving hours late while everyone waited, often in sweltering sun.

Graduation day approached; no cancellation. Daryle rehearsed the backup remarks and met with security forces; a nightmare. Our own security staff swept through the halls, bathrooms, classrooms, libraries and labs. Each floral arrangement, each bouquet was scrutinized. Custodians set up chairs, checking each one, and verified the working condition of the public address system. The podium perched in its place centre stage; extra rotating fans sat on the platform. The big, old gym promised to be muggy-hot at the start of summer. We arrived early to assure that everything was in order.

With both kids tagging along, I checked the library where the PTA arranged the post graduation reception and beseeched the moms to pray fervently for no brown-outs. It was early. As we wandered back to Dad's office I noticed shiny, black security cars in the parking lot.

The security men from the Palace meticulously fondled all the floral arrangements, the bouquet of roses for the First Lady and, as dictated by custom, the extravagant leis for the First Lady and the President. Palace security re-checked each chair in the gym, the vents, and the podium. Everything percolated along, still on schedule; we were prepared for the long wait. Parents arrived, abuzz with the security stimulation and excitement of celebrity attendance.

Daryle's phone rang: "The President is entering the school, Sir." He came. He came early. Now what? Nobody anticipated this turn of events. What do we do with him? Imee went directly to her assembly point with other soon-to-be graduates. Imelda and Ferdinand Marcos walked, escorted, to Daryle's office. We introduced the children; Daryle was now definitely first name. It was my turn to escort and I took Jessica and Ian for a walkabout. Presidential conversations were not for children, though they would have been fine.

Pomp and Circumstance played from the sound system. The President and First Lady joined the processional, followed by the faculty and graduating seniors, and took their places on the stage. Following student speakers, and introductions, "A man who needs no introduction...." the President commenced his address. He spoke and talked and pontificated in a plethora of monotone.

Overhead fans barely pushed the air. On stage, graduates sweltered in halter tops and shorts under traditional gowns and caps. Fathers, too proud to wear the practical and elegant *barong tagalog*, dripped in suits and ties, mothers fanned and dabbed at their made-up faces; siblings squirmed.

Parents crossed their legs, then shifted them back again. The president droned on. Students fidgeted with their gowns, the girls picked at their nails, the guys tried to spot people they knew in the crowd. At one point the rotating fan swooped upon the President's speech, catching several pages, tossing them into the air before they fluttered one-by-one to the stage. An administrator gathered the pages and the President droned on as if on automatic pilot.

When he finally concluded his remarks, a staff member prepared to escort the President and entourage to their cars, but Marcos sat down and waited for the diplomas to be conferred. Daryle prided himself in pronouncing all the names, Marcos being one of the easy pronunciations, and as the graduates tossed their caps to the rafters, the recessional led to the PTA reception.

We made it; no security issues, no brown-outs, no no-shows or delays. We thanked the President and First Lady and congratulated them on Imee's graduation. Still they stayed. They went to the reception and wandered amongst other proud parents. Imelda, joviality personified, giggled and joked with other parents,

"I was so delighted when da pan blew dose papers off da podium.

"God knows, we would still be in dere listening to dat spitch."

They asked for a plate of sandwiches and cakes to be served in Daryle's office. I circulated with the rest of the parents. And the President stayed. Although the headmaster was "Daryle," she remained, Madame Marcos, and her husband was always Mr. President, Sir.

Dreams

"**C**'mon! Let's go. Hurry up. We need to get down stairs."
"Why? What's wrong? Where are we going?"

I grabbed Jessica by the hand; she grabbed Pippi Longstockings. I swooped-up Ian who slept clutching his Tonka truck, the wheels embedded in his chest, and we padded down the stairs. The plate glass windows, the entire back side of the house, tinkled to the floor in chards. Barefoot and night-gowned, in the street with neighbours, we watched the glowing fire behind our homes. Black smoke billowed and swelled forming round balls of orange and red flames. Just like the dream.

I knew what it was in the predawn, that early time before prayers. Kicking the covers aside, I heard the blast then the clinking glass. I knew from a late-night dream and rushed for the children. I dreamed of a deafening explosion. Simultaneously: a massive blast, red and orange flames extending above the trees, to the clouds, replacing the clouds. The dream was real. The explosion was loud and the inferno brilliant. I could feel the heat from the ball of fire. It took time to fall back to sleep. The vivid details seared an imprint: a loud, bright image.

Now, I don't recall which part was the dream; which was fiction, which was non-fiction. A rutilant globe of fire blasted us out of bed in the early morning. I rushed to get the children, mindful of the scurrying cockroaches at my feet. The kids were dazed and confused; they seemed so vulnerable.

We huddled in the street with other residents. The fire escalated. Would there be another explosion? Which way would the fire spread? The oil bunkers; Meralco, the power company. It had to be the worn oil bunkers. Was it sabotage? An accident? Maybe a plane was down? Fear manifested itself in the early hours, in that time of morning before light but after the dark; the time when Muslims wait to begin the fast. The time before the cock crows; before the thread becomes visible.

Impatiently, Daryle strode behind the house and around the block to determine the damage, the cause or at least the problem. Huge oil storage tanks of Meralco electric company, burned out of control behind our house. He didn't get very near. We stayed close to the house, peering over the rooftop at the huge flames and black clouds. We milled about the street with our affluent neighbours for some time in the approaching dawn, until we felt safe to return to the house to dress and assess. Daylight helped.

Three houses behind us burned to the ground, instantly leveled, left smoldering. Gutted cars and trucks on the street blazed, until they became charred carcasses of twisted steel. Daryle came back murmuring of many lives lost.

We played-at the breakfast. Natty and Perla, afraid and nervous, prepared the meal in unusual silence: fresh pineapple from the Dole farms sliced in big uneven chunks, scrambled eggs and bread toasted in another new toaster. The young women were on edge, didn't speak, didn't ask questions, anxious about the blazing fire behind the house. I knew they wanted to bolt, but stayed because we stayed. I pushed the eggs around my plate. Daryle inhaled the meal, his thoughts elsewhere. I nagged at the kids.

"Chop! Chop! Let's go. Scoop up those eggs.

"Take another bite of pineapple. Chop Suey!

"Do you have your spelling list?

"Let's go!"

Calm was required; calm is contagious; an antidote to panic. At the time, I felt calm. The kids went off with their father and the driver to school. I stayed at the house. How did I have this dream? How did I know about this? I did have the dream. I did see it all before it happened. What would I do with this information? Had it helped me? Why was it revealed to me? I really didn't want to think about it, the depth of it, what it meant. But I did think about it.

The back side of the house, now wide open, made us vulnerable to *shiftas, lebas,* opportunists, and thieves in the night, those without, those on the other side of the wall. I asked Natty to brush up the chards on the terrazzo floors. Our shiny six foot Christmas tree suffered a mini meltdown. On one side of the tree, plastic pine needles melded to each other in some demented bliss. Ornaments merged together from the meld.

Business as usual; keep up the calm front. I phoned several window companies to come out immediately with new panels of glass for the sliders. The fire continued to burn and crackle throughout the day.

"Sorry madame. Der's a pire der. We can't bring in our fruck.

"Maybe we come tomorrow. No froblem."

By early afternoon, the fire fiercely intensified, building and escalating. It was not contained. Another explosion as loud and ferocious as the first rattled the house. I learned from embassy neighbours that the U.S. government offered chemicals to drop on the fires, but could not do so without an official request by the Philippine government. Marcos would not call upon another country. Cultural face-saving prohibited the government from requesting assistance or especially, accepting assistance.

Fire frucks screamed in and out behind the house replenishing water supplies, yet the fire raged. Water pressure was low; fire hoses drooped like overcooked long-life noodles. To myself I screamed, "Do something Mr. Marcos, Mr. President, Sir. Get out of your palace and do something."

No let-up all day. The fire department did not contain the blaze. I paced from room to room. I wandered outside, checked the flames then wandered back. I dusted then re-dusted. I pulled food from the fridge then put it back. I tried to read a book and was too distracted. Daryle came home early, mid-afternoon. My nerves frayed, my head pounded from the tension. I lashed-out, as if it was his fault.

"What is going on?

"Why didn't you call me?

"What's happening at school?

"What are you doing with students and parents?

"Who is in charge?

"Why didn't you call me?

"Why doesn't the government do something?

"Can you see the fire from campus?

"Do you want something to eat? Get it yourself.

"Did you hear the second explosion?

"Why didn't you call me?!

Late afternoon, after swim practice when Jessica and Ian returned, we went for a walk around Bel Air Village. I needed to get out; get perspective. Daryle was there. That helped. As we reached the park, a third explosion detonated and reverberated loudly through the air. The bulging black clouds over the oil containers again intensified behind the house. We waited at the park trying to calm the kids, and ourselves, deep breathing, trying to make a rational decision on what to do. We had our lives, our children. What else was there?

What Else

Well.
There were passports, paintings, appliances, gold investments, papers from the safe and jewelry. There were the items for resale on the black market if we left the house open: TVs, refrigerators, stove, air cons, iron, and kitchen appliances. Clothes were marketable. If looters came in, everything was free-game.

The four of us sat on the grass of a small knoll in the park like ceramic gnomes in a Norwegian garden, eyes riveted in the direction of the house. The fire blazed out of control. The flames reached over the top of the roofs.

I sat on my haunches ready to catapult to safety, wherever that might be. The rigid muscles in my back gave me a backache. My throbbing head gave me a headache. I could not relax though I felt better to be out of the house with my family at my side. I thought the air itself might burst. It felt electric, crackling like the flames of the fire. What would happen? When would it happen: and how would we cope?

Sitting at home, waiting, helpless and frustrated I paced from room to room, walking outside then back indoors. I now sat in the grass, my family at my side, and watched the escalating inferno. As the oil flames ascended and soared into heavy bulging orange and black clouds, the anxiety and nervous tension continued to build. The negative energy infiltrated the heavy black balloons and orange orbs of concern which permeated the psyche of the residents. I was only moderately appeased by the afternoon walk to the park.

I wanted to get out of the house, but now staring at the escalating flames I watched almost as an out of body observation, detached from myself. I felt my anxiety, the nervous tension, manifest itself in stress verging on trauma as I hung on to reason by a thread.

The third explosion rocked the ground. We clutched each other's hands like members of a new-age spiritual sect. All around us panic ensued. Kids and adults ran in all directions back and forth in the park, screaming and crying. We sat taking it all in, perhaps trying again to instill calm. Maybe it was religious as I practiced deep breathing techniques. We needed clear heads while all around us others seemed to be losing theirs.

"You're squeezing my hand."

"Am I? Sorry. Just want to hang on to you."

"Mommy, your hands are wet."

"You're right. Let me swipe them on your shirt."

"Mommy!"

Residents and domestic workers stampeded to the compound gate like evacuees from a war zone. Fear attempted to conquer the mind. It embedded itself in the faces, in the eyes of our neighbours as they tried to flee. Should I be fleeing with my family? My own workers fled early in the day.

Parents, children, *lolas* and domestic helpers crowded into the front and back seats of the family car cradling possessions like bargain hunters the day after Christmas. They screeched through the streets swerving and dodging other escapees heading toward the gate. Vehicles filled with televisions and air conditioners raced to the exit; neighbours strapped stoves and refrigerators to the roofs of their automobiles like *hajjis* hauling their wares on a pilgrimage. A sedan screeched by, dragging a bicycle. The child still attached to the bike, scraped and screamed along the blacktop of the road as sparks flew, unbeknownst to the driver.

At dusk, Daryle returned to the house while we waited at the park. The oil storage tanks no longer tolerated the intense temperature caused by the explosions. They broke apart from top to bottom like eggs cracked on the side of a bowl. The contents oozed down the road like thick glycerin. The huge, cylindrical tanks split, tearing the iron bunkers, peeling back the edges liberating the thick, burning, boiling crude to escape down the street past the skeletal remains of houses burned out and smoldering.

. What was of value; true value? Suddenly nothing seemed significant. We had our lives; we had our children. We forced ourselves to focus on the materialistic. Daryle grabbed the passports, the gold, a few paintings, papers from the safe. I returned with the kids to quickly pick up their pajamas and their homework notebooks. Natty and Perla were nowhere in sight and Rudy, the driver, long gone.

Diversion

"Wow! Are you okay? Man, you poor people," from Mark the teenager.

"You must be worried sick," from Shirley.

"Come in, come in! Shower if you want. Try to relax," she offered.

"I bet you could use a G&T," John, always practical.

"Never knew a situation that wasn't made better by a healthy gin and tonic."

We drove to the home of Shirley and John Britt and after a couple of drinks, light on tonic, and a comforting meal of chicken curry and rice, John and Daryle decided to spend the night at our house, back at the fire scene; the fire that continued to rage out of control. They slept downstairs on sofas, with bolo knives, next to the void left from the former plate glass.

Shirley and John Britt were always a great diversion. They cultivated a menagerie in their garden including an eight foot boa constrictor housed in a six foot terrarium on their tropical patio. They fed the snake every seven or eight days and often invited us for the ritual, followed by drinks in the garden. John and Shirley were British and John offered gin-and-tonics all day, any time after 10 am, before if he had any takers.

The snake-feeding ceremony started with Mark and John or Daryle and John seizing the reptile while the third cleaned the terrarium. The snake writhed and it took two, sometimes three adults to keep it from squeezing any one of them to their death. When the enclosure was clean, two of them uncoiled the constrictor from the arm and body of the third to help the reptile slither back into the sterile terrarium. This accomplished, they tossed in a couple of white mice. The kids, indeed all of us, watched in morbid fascination. We all knew the outcome, yet thrived on the suspense, the buildup and the climax of the final scene. The ending never disappointed. The mice never escaped. We did not clean the terrarium that night, but the familiarity of their home brought a bizarre sense of familiarity and security.

Life always looks better in the morning. Following an uneventful night, the men joined us for a hot breakfast. I returned to the house and others went off to their jobs and school, homework in hand. I tried again to get someone to repair the sliding glass doors and a reputable company agreed to come within the week. Natty and Perla did not return for days. The women were so afraid they simply ran away. It made me wonder how they might react if we left the children at home under their care.

Family

Larry Cojuangco was one of the first of our neighbours and friends to stop by to inquire about our shell collection. No one asked how we were, how were we getting along. They asked,

"How are your shells, how is your beautiful collection of shells?"

"Fine, fine. Please come in."

Over the years we became avid shell collectors. The magnificent mollusks of 'one hundred million years of inspired design' seemed an extension of my California life. I remained a water baby, a beach bum at heart.

I studied the families of shells, joined the local Malacological Society and learned that the best specimens were taken alive, scooped up while snorkeling or diving. Other people dived. I was snorkeling. No way was I going to breathe underwater. I was, like, fer sure, like, totally, like freaked out by the idea. I was nearly claustrophobic with a rubber mask over my nose and a tube sticking in the air to help me breathe. I was not a fish. I was meant to breathe with my feet on the ground. I had arms, not fins. I would breathe from the atmosphere, not from a tank.

Dead shells washed up in the surf tended to be faded, chipped and damaged: beautiful but not collector quality; better used for shell craft or buttons. We learned to bring up living cowries, cones and olives. We learned to clean them quickly before the soft body specimen rotted the shell and destroyed the commercial value. But before I leaned all of that I sometimes left bits of the soft body, rotting flesh, in the shell. I hid shoe boxes of shells clandestinely under the beds. No one talked about ecology, of saving the environment or of raping the sea.

We kept an aquarium at the house and watched to see who lived with whom and who ate whom. Sometimes we brought live shells and nudibranch back from the beach in a small aerated tank which I straddled between my feet for the winding drive home. The hermit crabs climbed out of the aquarium like multi-legged turtles wearing

their colourful houses on their backs and we often found them clack-
ing across the terrazzo floors.

The sometimes stinky shoe boxes of shells hid under our beds. It
was time to design a display table. I knew exactly what I wanted. I
went to Habitat Furnishings, a domestic shop featuring Scandinavian,
minimalistic design utilizing Philippine Nara, a form of mahogany.
Based on a Spanish design, I commissioned a low coffee table 4'x4'
with a glass top. Habitat suggested a black felt lining to highlight
the shells. The result enhanced the shells and fit in well with our
furnishings.

Friends sat on the sofas, sipping tea, nibbling fresh, baked cookies, always on hand, and looked at tibias, cones, cowries and olives
displayed in the table, in wonder that the explosions and fires had
not destroyed the collection. Although the Christmas tree melted,
the shells remained works of art, 'inspired design.'

"Look at that tibia. What a beauty."

"It looks perfect."

"Where did you find it?"

"Actually, it was off Matabungkay; not too deep they told me."

"Live?"

"Yep."

I was touched that they came. The malacologists were family.

No Froblem

Employees from the glass company arrived the following week.
They jumped off the fruck toting tool bags over their shoulders.

"Aye, Madam. You have a froblem?"

"Yes, thank you for coming."

"Ah. Da glass ees broken, no?"

"Yes. Can you please replace the glass?"

"You want new glasses? Your glasses are broken, no?"

Yes, that is why I called you."

"Aye, Madam. We'll just go now and get da glass. No froblem."

"You didn't bring any glass? When will you return?"

"Aye, we'll come bak soon, *naman*."

"Today? Are you coming back today?"

""No froblem."

"Yes, you must come back today. Thank you."

"We'll just place our tings der, in da back, no?"

The workers returned two days later. Off the truck, they carried large sheets of glass around the side of the house to the back.

"Aye, Madam. You have a froblem, no?

"Yes, thank you for coming back."

"Ah. Da glass ees broken, no?

"Yessss. Can you please replace the glass?"

"We'll just place our tings der, in da back wit our tools, no?" was this déjà vu?

They set up wooden saw-horses on the back deck, propped the panes on top and plugged in an electric glass-cutting saw. The men meticulously measured the window openings from top to bottom, height and width; the entire back side of the house.

The electric power was on at that hour. They cut the glass to precise size. The glass-cutters carefully lifted the heavy pane and positioned it in the window frame.

"Da glass ees no fitting, Madam.

"Berry sorry, Madam.

"No froblem. We bring new glasses tomorrow."

The glass was centimeters short. It did not fit; cut too small. It wouldn't keep out mosquitoes, let alone scurrying or flying cockroaches. They loaded the wasted glass onto the fruck and made their way back to the factory. I asked Natty, recently returned, to brush up the shards from the deck. No froblem.

Rumours

The fires burned for five days. Rumours around town suggested and strongly inferred sabotage.* The international press condemned the Marcos government for resisting international assistance. After five days of continuous burning, the government invited US helicopters from the military bases to drop chemicals on the flames. The fires stopped. Abruptly. Immediately.

In the end, we never knew what caused the explosions; whether sabotage was involved or deterioration of the containers, dysfunctional equipment or politics or who wanted to destroy whom. In the end it was the common *tao* who suffered from the constant black outs and suffered from the high electric rates.

President Marcos accused Meralco Company** of cutting the power when he attempted to address the nation regarding the striking jeepney drivers or when making any national announcements. The conflict continued the entire time we lived in the Philippines. The Lopez family, owners of Meralco, fought Marcos and other political parties for years. The Lopez family was part of the 'old society.' Did the government blow up the oil bunkers? We never knew.

Dreams

Sometimes I do have dreams. Most seem to announce a serious pending situation. I never talked to anyone about my dreams. I know what I would think of my friend if she told me she 'had dreams.' I'm not clairvoyant, though I think if I cultivated the sensitivity, I would know more than I want to know. This dream came to me several nights in a row; the explosion, the fire and the confusion. The morning I realized it to be true, I felt less terrified because I knew what was happening. I heard the explosion; I saw the flames night after night.

The same year, one morning I woke up to check the children. As I shuffled across the bedroom wearing *chinellas*; aware of scurrying cockroaches, I clutched at my chest, groping to be sure I was all there. Cancer. I have breast cancer. No, it's a dream. I don't have cancer. I'm still in one piece. The image, the reality was as clear as the explosion dreams.

Who was sabotaging whom? According to the press, the power cuts caused great conflict between the palace and the electric company. The power cuts caused great stress to the customers. I carried a small flashlight in my handbag. Every time I entered an elevator in one of the high-rise offices, I looked around to assess who also hoped to ascend a few floors. Sometimes the outage times were printed in the paper but there was no guarantee anyone stuck to the schedule. We coped during the day but evenings were especially uncomfortable.

**Brothers Eugenio and Fernando Lopez acquired Meralco, the power company, from American owners in 1962. Hostilities between Meralco and Malacanang intensifies or weakened depending on the political flavour-of-the-month.*

You Never Know

Bombs permeated our daily culture: bombs in the supermarket; bombs in the theatre; bombs in the shopping malls; bombs on the public busses. Armed guards were expected in front of the banks. They became accepted in all business offices, and were highly visible in hotels, malls, Cineplex, markets, everywhere the public frequented. Armed guards did not prevent the explosion of bombs.

Every day, gate guards searched students coming onto campus. You never know. It made for a new homework excuse, "The guards destroyed my homework. I had it, but..." Most of us tolerated the search procedures. At school we prepared a mini security plan. Essentially, it revolved around the existing fire-drill plan; at the signal, everyone proceeded to the parking lot, play-fields and designated areas to line up by classrooms; no talking. Administrators made a full school sweep checking lockers and classrooms while students and remaining staff waited in the baking sun. They never found anything but, you never know.

Then came the hoax phone calls. The hoaxes frustrated and tested the staff. The kids know you have to honour a threat, because, you never know. The very time the administration dismissed a bomb threat, it just might be a reality. Kids know the ropes.

We learned how to answer a bomb threat made over the phone.

1. Keep the caller on the line to allow the call to be traced or monitored.
2. Gather as much information as possible; where was the bomb, when would it go off?
3. Listen for background noises to help determine the location of the caller: on a busy street, in a mall, at home with other background voices?
4. Listen for national identity. What accent did the caller have? What was the level of English proficiency?
5. What age group was the caller? Student, adult, young adult?
6. Why was there a bomb at the school? (Was there a political statement being made?)

I only answered a bomb threat once. I tried to remember everything. I struggled to keep the caller on the line and simultaneously communicate like a circus mime with my office mates across the room. "I have a bomb threat on the line," I mouthed. My colleagues looked at me as I waved my free arm like a traffic cop in the plaza. I mouthed:

BOMB. Then B-O-M-B, my lips exaggerated the pantomime as I continued to gather background information.

Of course, by the time I figured it all out, the caller hung up on me and I called Daryle and security with the information. Ring the bells, everyone to their designated area, you never know. A full search; nothing found, but it provided another chance to miss class.

One day, during after-school activities, a security guard walked anxiously to Daryle's office.

"Doktor, der seems to be some-ting suspicious in da boy's bat-room. Tink you should check it out?"

"Like what, Ramon?" It was four in the afternoon and nearly time for the after-school busses to load for the final run of the day.

"Some kids, dey say, dey say, dey heard, well, you know, dey tink dere's a bomb in da boy's bat-room."

"Did you check it out?"

"Well, Dok, I am tinking you would want to know about eet."

"You did the right thing, Ramon. Let's check it out."

The men walked to the bathroom at the back of the campus near the afternoon busses. Ramon held open the door and Daryle walked in. They pointed to the second stall. 'Dok' went instead to the third booth, stood on the toilet bowl and peered over the divider. There seemed to be wires attached to the door. He stepped down, got on all fours, then rolled on his back and slid under the door of the suspect toilet stall. He saw just enough to slide back out, his tie mopping the floor, and called the police.

Within the hour the Makati Bomb Squad stormed the campus like a team of commandos and headed directly to the back toilets; the boy's bat-room. They caringly removed the small box affixed to the door of the stall as if untying a fragile parcel. The contraption was wired to detonate when the toilet door was urgently pushed open. They brought the device into 'Dok's' office and tentatively placed it on his desk. Oh great. The Bomb Squad took close range photos of the wires viewing each side of the box, the top of the box and the bottom. They dusted it for fingerprints before meticulously dismantling each wire. My palms sweated as Daryle retold the tale at home over a neat scotch.

The investigation determined that a new transfer student designed the device. No motive seemed apparent except some insignificant student gripes; attention getting. No national plot, no international anti-American plot. He was expelled. The story was big in the parent community, especially after it made *Time* and *Newsweek* international editions. Everyone was on edge. You never know.

We started searches of all persons coming onto the campus including students, parents, staff, and vendors. Jessica and Ian went to school at 5am for before-school swim workouts. They staggered out of the car, tossed their book-bags on the table at the gate and waited for security to paw through their pencils, *Hello Kitty* erasers, homework, text books, local M&Ms, swim suits and towels. Parents gave up the privacy of their hand bags and briefcases. "Terrorism" was not in the vocabulary. I think we called it violence, but the scenario was a prelude to what would become routine in the 21st century.

Playboy Club

With no day-job, I joined the American Women's Association and became active on the board in various positions. When I took the role as program chair, I ran on the platform that I wanted to bring substance to the meetings. I hope I didn't say it quite like that, though I probably did, but that was my intent and I was elected to the position. No more cooking sessions, no local ethnic dress programs, no lessons on tropical gardening. I invited authors, professors, journalists, ambassadors. But there was still one tradition I couldn't escape: the annual Spring Fashion Show. I had to think out of the box for this apparently must-have, traditional, by-popular-demand program.

EZ Black the charismatic bachelor from mid-America was manager of the Elks Club where we took the kids for swim lessons and competition. People gravitated toward EZ's personality and welcoming mannerisms. He was a first-rate club manager. He was 'easy' to be around. EZ's next job, he considered a plum. He became the manager of the new Manila Playboy Club.

"Dannie, you have to come down some weekend. It's a real family atmosphere."

"What?! EZ, since when did the Playboy Club become a family playground?"

"No, you know, husbands and wives. Bring Daryle and come to the Club.

"It's not what you might think, not like other clubs on Roxas Boulevard or Mabini Street."

There were some sleazy places in downtown Manila. The Hobbit House was run by dwarfs. When they came to your table to get your drink order, their chins rested on the table tops and their stubby fingers, clutching a damp cloth, reached across the table to wipe it off; a novelty, a side show. I went once.

A block down the street was the Daktari Bar. After a few drinks, one could purchase a bucket of slops and get inside the cage with a huge Bengali tiger for a photo-op. The bar was run by Hans, a Bamboo German who never returned to Germany. In between these bars, girls stood in the shadows, not really hidden, soliciting business.

Nobody went to a Playboy Club. Nobody I knew. My friends didn't go in bars. By the time I was old enough to drink, I was on my way to Ethiopia to save the world. There were plenty of cocktail parties at my parent's home, but I had no experience in bars. I attended a college where alcohol was forbidden; there were no sororities or fraternities, just dorms and clubs. It sounds boring. We didn't do bars. I didn't even drink wine at the Italian restaurant. The Playboy Club was a reach, a party scene out of my comfort zone. I learned to drink slowly, in homes. Never in bars.

My father wanted me to go to Texas Christian University and marry a rich rancher. I wanted to go to a small school, major in Christian education and marry a pastor. I saw myself hosting church events, meeting with teens, leading women's bible studies. It didn't happen. I hated what I saw in the missionary students at my conservative college. They were fat, acned and simplistic. Their idea of fun was singing hymns where they clapped their hands.

"Thanks, EZ." I tried to visualize the high school principal coming out of the Playboy Club. It didn't work with the educator image or the role model.

How would I make the traditional, annual fashion show a program of substance? I wanted to create something beyond the dots; outside the box. I selected a small boutique with upscale clothes at reasonable prices. Nothing came to me. I was uninspired.

"Hey, EZ." I piped one night at a reception.

"Hey, Dan. When you coming down to have a look at the Club?

"Why don't you come on Monday? Let me show you around."

"I thought you were closed on Mondays."

"We're closed to the public, so I can show you around. You'll love it."

The new driver took me to the Club. I considered getting out a block away. Instead I mumbled something about a meeting. I felt conspicuous. Like a big-time party girl who was about to do something naughty. I looked around before entering the large doors. No one was watching. EZ greeted me with a gregarious noisy welcome. I looked around again. The Club was palace-like; elegant, large, carpeted and tasteful. He gave me a tour of the kitchen, the bar areas, the band stand, the dance floors. *Tres chic.*

"EZ," I started from nowhere, then couldn't stop the thought.

"I'm planning a fashion show for AWA. What would be the chances of having the show here, in the morning, before the Club opens to the public?"

He paused, then, "We could do it. What'd you have in mind?"

"I want a great venue. I found fabulous clothes, the members will model, Linda Bernardo will choreograph the show to disco music." He leaned forward in his leather swivel chair.

"Why don't we do lunch for you?

"You can have the whole floor.

"We can have the Bunnies here in full 'uniform.'" That meant cinched-in and pushed-up; rabbit ears, black bowties, mesh stockings, fluffy tails and little else. He started to get excited with the concept. I tried not to be prudish at this suggestion. Would this be cool, or tacky?

"You can bring all your women here; we will do a formal lunch with linen and flowers on the tables. You and your committee can select the menu and I will arrange a tasting session before you select. It would be wonderful to have AWA here." EZ was no fool. He saw the marketing potential. "Let's talk about the fashion show. I need a platform and a runway.

"C'm on, Dannie. Let's go down stairs. I'll show you the band stand and stage. We can set up lighting and a full sound system. How 'bout a revolving mirrored disco ball?"

"EZ, what's this going to cost? You know American women. They want a bargain."

"I will give you the luncheon menu at cost, no charge for the Bunnies in their uniforms, no cost for the set-up, no cost for opening up on a non-work day. You will pay a 5% service charge. What do you think? We can add wine to the menu, if you like."

I liked it very much. I walked out in the sunlight, my head high. The Playboy Club was awesome and we were going to be part of it.

I staged my own coup d'état. The women went wild. We sold out in one week. There was something naughty, something titillating about going to the Playboy Club. EZ arranged for additional tables. We sold out again. We felt a bit wicked, and knew it was acceptable. For three weeks the buzz was giddy. The food committee sampled several entrée choices. We rehearsed at the Club, then presented on the day of the Spring Fashion Show. The models, energized by Linda's choreography, swished and twirled down the runway between nearly nude bunnies.

Of all the brilliant speakers and interesting programs of the year, the Spring Fashion Show was probably the most inspired and memorable. So much for substance.

Fam-Tours

I pushed into the scrum of clinking glasses with faux confidence. I got better at it, but still found it difficult to introduce myself and begin a conversation with unknown guests. Cocktail parties and receptions provided the venue for peripheral business and networking. This occasion was held at Pietro's residence in the Golden Ghetto of Makati, the garden decorated to perfection by Ronny of course, with bird of paradise and orchids.

"Good evening, Mrs. Russell," 'Ms' was not yet an option. It never even occurred to me that I might one day have my own prefix identity. We all wanted our independence, but in fact, many countries would not expedite visas to expatriate couples with separate names. We fought our battles quietly. I was not offended; much of my life and work were in fact, closely linked to my partner, the good Doctor, as he was to become known in India.

"Good evening, Mr. Marshall." Don Marshall, expatriate magnate, owned a shipping line and other ventures including the local franchise for Northwest Orient Airlines. He served on the school board and was the father of four teenagers.

We mingled between the guests, I just learning to work the crowd, Don an established pro. Working the crowd meant having a conversation with party A while discretely surveying the room to target your next exchange with party B. Making that transition seem flawless required adroitness and a bit of dexterity dancing through the cocktail glasses of the invitees. I learned to segue like a dancing crane. With nimbleness and deftness I waltzed my way around the room seeking new and familiar partners; but not at the beginning.

There's no such thing as a free drink; everyone worked the crowd. My mission was to talk with parents, try to remember their kids, and listen for potential concerns. I learned to escape to a bathroom to jot quick notes on the back of cards, sometimes on squares of toilet paper, to remember names and ages of students. If I had an idea who might be on the guest list, I flipped through the yearbook at home, in a background check of sons and daughters, the way a dealer flips through the deck before doling out the cards. I was not employed by the school, but I knew many of the kids and wanted to meet their parents.

Working the crowd required great skill and I never really mastered it. I tended to be engaged with party A. When I remembered to zero-in on party B, my transitions weren't very smooth. I later learned that cocktail receptions facilitated anecdotal conversation; one-liners; sound bites. In-depth discussions blossomed at small dinner parties, not vast affairs. My most common segue: "I need to freshen my drink, excuse me." Don Marshall was a pro. I later became rather abrupt, "I see someone I need to speak with, excuse me."

In the beginning those soirees were painfully difficult. The first year in Manila, Pat Bruce, the superintendent's wife, the only person in the room I knew, left me standing alone in the corner of the cafeteria. It was open house, the third week of classes. "Okay, Dannie. Can't talk with you now. I've got to meet these parents." I was terrified. I retreated further to the corner and reached for a chocolate chip cookie. Second rule: you can't talk to people with food in your mouth. I remembered an article about Jackie Kennedy who always ate a small sandwich before going downstairs to host a cocktail reception: the definitive hostess, a model of grace, and class.

"Dannie, I've noticed you seem to know much of the expatriate community here in Manila. "Why don't you work for us at Northwest Orient?" from Don.

"I'm listening," I paused.

"I have no experience in the travel industry." Don surveyed the room.

"No, no, you don't need any of that background. You just need to see people at affairs like this. Mention to CEOs about Northwest for their business travel and for their family travel.

"Make contacts, document it once a week and submit your report. You would be great. You know everyone in this room."

I decided why not, and reported-in the following week. The hours were flexible so I could be home when the kids were home, or be at school for swim practice or track meets. I could still do the lunch scene, the women's groups, and if I mentioned the airlines, I could document it. The pay was minimal, but the perks were travel benefits. I learned everything I could about the routes, stopovers, special offers, various fares, VUSA fares, round-the-world fares and memorized the new brochures every week. Two months later, they sent me on a "Fam-Tour."

"What's a Fam-Tour?"

"Northwest sends employees to meetings at various NW destinations; next month there's a meeting in Chiang Mai. Everything is laid on. You'll love it. You'll visit the hotels in Thailand, get to know the restaurants, sample the foods. Sound good?" The manager laid it on thick.

"As part of the trip you'll go on several side excursions in order to sell these packages to your clients. Fam-Tour is: Familiarization Tour."

I flew to Bangkok like a canary flying loose around the house. We went as a group to dinners, visited hotels and took-in the nightclubs. Well. Lots of music and no clothes; the clubs showcased different genre: a musical revue, cabaret, chorus line. Unlike Las Vegas, these shows lacked class. They verged on crude and rude and I was the prude. That's how it was at the time. Bangkok's reputation did not disappoint.

Tiny Thai, nearly nude female dancers cavorted on stage with snakes and lascivious creatures to the delight of the audience. Any other place, there might have been a drum pulse as the dancers removed outer layers of clothing. In this case there was nothing left but strings and strategic stars. The highlight of the late show was the climatic banana dance.

The later the hour, the more provocative the gyrations. It was nothing like a strip tease. There was nothing left to strip. All manner of props proved evocative; snakes, anything cylindrical. The evening culminated with the lead dancer heaving up and down on a mat like a yogi relaxing the pelvis.

With suggestive bumps and grinds the dancers hugged and danced and rolled on the floor as singles, as partners, and with snakes writhing between their legs. The music rose in crescendo like the final measures of Ravel's Bolero. Glistening men also sporting strings ambled lustily across the stage like waiters at a tropical café, carrying silver trays of bananas. Slowly, peel by peel, the virgin fruit, exposed and firm, was mouthed and accepted by the writhing dancers on the mat.

Each female dancer began to shoot the bananas from between their thighs; a competition for distance. The crowd roared with each expulsion as the dancing waiters attempted to catch the bananas on their silver trays.

Amazing how far she shot that banana. How did she do that? Where was my veil? Who goes to these shows? I never saw anything like this anywhere. I never knew there were such shows. I looked around. The audience was mostly Thai men, but there were many western couples as well. So this was a fam-tour. Others seemed to be having a great time. Admittedly, when we got back to the hotel, I laughed my head off with everyone else like hyenas enjoying a good joke.

We traveled by coach to the dense jungle and verdant mountains of Chiang Mai; the Golden Triangle of illicit opium production at the confluence of Thailand, Laos, and Myanmar, previously Burma. We checked into an elegant five-star hotel. Orchids dripped from vaulted ceilings to the floor, cascading in purple, pink and white over balconies and indoor galleries like the waterfalls of the jungle. No chocolates on the pillows; no single orchid blossom. Rather, a full stem of orchids decorated each pillow like a salacious suggestion. The travel agents met in a private room overburdened with more orchids, tropical plants and enormous staghorn ferns for briefings before we wandered about Chiang Mai.

The charm of ethnic Thailand stimulated all of my senses as I wandered through the village of Chiang Mai. Smaller villages in the hills showcased the colourful, simple life as the scent of incense drifted through the air like a dancing butterfly. Earthy aromas of cooking fires brought me back to the reality of daily life. Children dashed between shops that displayed local crafts, or baskets or antiques. The villages seemed unsullied, more pure; more naive than their sister city, Bangkok.

Back in the elegance of the five-star hotel, the manager informed us of the features of the hotel; lavish pools, room service, privacy suites, three dining areas, ballroom facilities for conferences and gala events. The seventh floor was reserved for families.

I questioned that,

"Could families with children stay on the first floor, for example closer to the pool?"

"We prefer they stay on the seventh floor.

"We will reserve those rooms when you indicate you are booking a family." I looked around the room at my colleagues. Then the great aha!

These were sex tours.

Mom and the Third Floor

One morning at the Northwest office I received a call from Bob. He asked if we could talk.

"Sure Bob. Would you like to come to the office here, or can I meet you at your office at the embassy?"

"Maybe I could meet you at your house after the lunch hour today." Bob worked on the third floor of the US Embassy and he and Sue had kids at the high school.

"Sure, that would be fine, say 3.00pm?"

"Fine. I will meet you there."

I called the house and asked Perla to prepare limonada and cookies for afternoon merienda. A man from the embassy would be stopping by.

I offered him a seat gesturing widely like a preacher welcoming the congregation. He selected the table and chairs on the screened-in lanai. Overhead fans pushed the air aside while we talked. Condensation dripped down the side of the iced *limonada*.

"Dannie, I understand you do some private tutoring of ESL," he began.

"Yes, I do."

"And you work with adults."

"Yes."

"The North Vietnamese have just opened an embassy here, in Manila.

"It's small, but they are here now."

"Yes, I read that."

"Would you be interested in teaching English to their staff?"

What was he getting at? Did the Vietnamese need flights on Northwest? Was Bob the conduit? Was this a political gesture between the US Embassy and the North Vietnamese Embassy? Would the US State Department be funding flights for the North Vietnamese? My head swirled. This could be a big sale; a big plumb for NWA.

I thought about this as he took a sip of limonada. I could certainly teach English to Vietnamese. I already worked with Japanese women. I had worked with several Chinese adults. Each culture has its own dialect issues when learning English as a second or third language. I guess Bob knew I worked with parents and community members.

"What kind of English do they want? Need?" He didn't really have any idea. Why was he approaching me with this opportunity? I did have a full plate since I worked for the airlines. The overhead fan cooled us as we sat on the screened outdoor veranda. The two Labradors were lazy in the afternoon heat.

"Business English? Vocabulary enrichment, casual conversation?" I suggested.

"Something like that. They will pay you, but we will pay you additional fees to write up reports after each lesson." It sounded routine. And yes, I would expect remuneration.

"I could do that. What kind of reports?" thinking lesson plans.

Curious that he would want copies of the lesson plans. Maybe he planned to take his family to North Vietnam. The rest of us could not get into the communist North; Bob carried a diplomatic passport. Most probably he could get his family into the country. Embassy employees seldom travel first class, I thought as I listened to his request, so that would not be a big ticked sale, and the distance was not that great from Manila. And there was a war going on. He would not be taking his family I quickly realized. Still, a sale was a sale.

"Well, anything of interest." I came back to the conversation. "Everything would be of interest to us, even the smallest detail, whatever information you can obtain. Of course everything will be confidential. No one will know, and the reports will be private."

"I see," I said. In fact, I didn't see at all. No one will know. Why not?

"This will be a wonderful opportunity for you to go to the North Vietnamese Embassy, meet with some of their staff for lessons, and through casual conversation, learn as much as possible. Look around, tell us what you see."

Years later, when the country started to heal I traveled to the unified Vietnam, in the north and in the south. It was then that I realized the necessity of vocabulary enhancement and pronunciation drills. The Vietnamese needed me. Apparently the US Embassy needed me as well.

"I think I need to discuss this with Daryle."

"Yes, of course. You can call me at my office." He pulled out his card emblazoned with a spread eagle, olive branch and arrows clutched in its claws and handed it to me as he left. Now I knew; his cover was blown. He worked on the third floor. He was Central Intelligence and wanted me to do casual work; a stringer for the CIA.

After he left, I decided not to go back to the office; I needed time to process and reflect. What was he really asking me to do? And why me? Okay, I was glamourous, intelligent, well connected in the international community.

Maybe not. I'm a swimming mum. I don't work at school because of the prevailing 'no couples' hiring policy. I work flex-hours with the airlines for travel benefits. Bob wants me to work for the US Embassy as a stringer for the CIA. A spy. A spy for the USA. I need more time; more time to process this. It was the stuff of summer beach reading.

It was a perfect cover: housewife, swimming mum, community volunteer. Not really cloak-and-dagger stuff, but covert; a quasi legitimate position teaching English and gathering information. That's what it was about. I walked around the house. I walked outside, around the garden. I talked to Pepe, the golden lab. He looked at me, tilting his head from side to side as I talked out loud.

I would do it in a minute. When Daryle came home Perla served drinks and we discussed our day. I wanted to do it. I loved teaching ESL. I didn't know anyone from North Vietnam. Many American families stayed in Manila to wait-out their husband's and dad's tour of duty in Vietnam. Kids attended classes and fathers flew in for TDY or R&R. All toys in the Manila shops reflected war. GI Joe was big. Toy guns were big. The Vietnam War was big. Jane Fonda was big with rhetoric. I already tutored several Japanese women, and one hopeless Japanese man. He wanted a geisha. I didn't dance, sing or make tea. Just English; he was not very bright, or maybe he just wanted to extend the lessons.

"I had a chat with Ricky Yabut today," Daryle started. I listened patiently.

"Any problem?"

"I just wanted to encourage him a bit. I really like him."

"He's a good kid, easily distracted." He reached for some peanuts and took a drink.

"I met with Bob after lunch," I ventured.

"From the Embassy? Are they planning their summer vacation?"

"Not exactly. He came to the house to talk to me."

"That was convenient for him," he said, not comprehending.

"Yeah. He told me about the North Vietnamese setting up an Embassy in Manila," now I took a drink and fingered a few peanuts.

"Bob wants me to teach English and submit reports to his office; on the third floor."

I wanted to do this. I could work at the North Vietnamese Embassy. Bob was offering me a job to work inside the embassy. Not the American Embassy, the North Vietnamese Embassy. The adult students I currently worked with came to the house for lessons. The Asian language needs for English were different from European language background and needs. I understood this.

It was easy to work around my Northwest Airline hours because of my flexible schedule. I was sure I could still do this and have lots of time afterschool for the kids and their swim practice, drama, and track and field training.

If I was turned-in however, I would be deported; have to leave the country. I would have to leave immediately, persona non grata stamped in my passport. Daryle would leave as well with the kids. I wanted to do this. How could I make this work? Daryle wasn't much help. Maybe he never took it seriously. I allowed myself to think about the contribution I could make, to say nothing of the intrigue of it all. Movie plots roared through my head.

I envisioned driving up to the embassy, entering a vast hall with beautiful vases and art work. In fact, the building was very 'low-rent.' I'm very sure there were no huge murals. Just functional concrete rooms. I allowed myself the indulgence of fantasy for a day or two.

I sat on it. Finally, I decided it was not worth the risk. I was not a single female. Not a 'Ms' after all. I was very connected to my husband and my kids. If anything became suspect, under question, my husband's career would come under scrutiny. We would all be deported.

I called Bob several days later.

INTERNATIONAL
SCHOOL OF UGANDA LTD
P. O. BOX 4200, KAMPALA
TEL: 200374

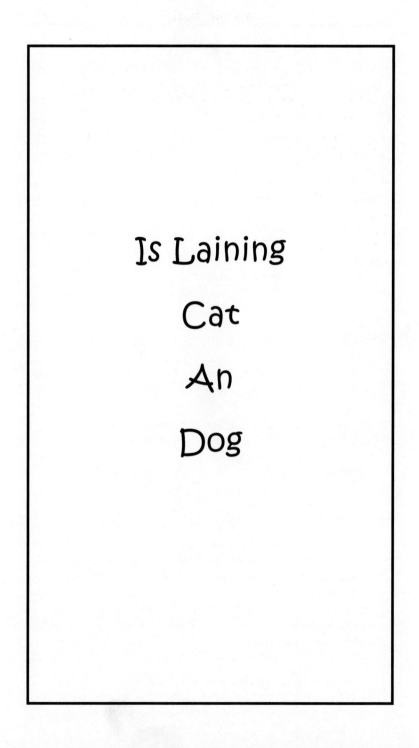

Is Laining

Cat

An

Dog

Invited for Tea

nvited for Tea at the Residence of the Chinese Ambassador; I pinched myself. This was not a party for hundreds of guests. There were eight of us. What was protocol? The invitation read:

> *Ambassador and Mrs. Ke Hua*
> *Cordially Invite You*
> *For Tea*
> *August 01, 1977*
> *Three O'clock In the Afternoon*
> *The Residence*
> *Forbes Park, Makati*

The driver swung into the circular driveway and slowed at the front; security guards opened car doors like valets at a Hollywood premier and we walked up the steps of the residency. The butler waited at the open door of the opulent embassy home. I felt like Yeh-Shen the Chinese Cinderella going to the ball to meet the prince. I clicked my slippers.

Our unexpected, typhoon-driven stopover in Taipei was my first introduction to China. Although the US travel ban to the communist country was partially lifted, only the American Ping-Pong Team was invited as a sort-of soft-opening of diplomatic relations; it could not even be termed a cultural exchange because the Cultural Revolution took on a very different dimension in China.

After the successful exchange of ping-pong matches, President Richard Nixon visited China in a formal State Visit in 1972, the year we touched down in Taipei; the same Richard Nixon who was later forced to resign the presidency after the scandalous Watergate break-in. However, the ever opportunistic Imelda Marcos in 1974 made her first official State Visit and signed an important trade agreement. China sold crude oil to Manila and the Philippines sold coconut oil, lumber and copper to China. The following year, 1975, the first Chinese Embassy opened in Manila.

Trade started and bilateral talks began, but tourism was not encouraged. Although no longer looking for the man in the coolie hat, I longed for things Chinese. I wanted to continue digging into this culture.

What to wear? I admit it. I spent hours, well not hours, but some time considering this event. Fashion statement or conservative? Long skirt, mini skirt, spaghetti straps or beaded top; cotton or silk, sandals or open-toe, high heels or flats. It seemed so important. I was getting a feel for the cocktail scene with the little-black-dress, a throw-back to champagne at the palace with Emperor Haile Selasse. But this was afternoon, not an evening affair. Afternoon Tea at the Chinese Embassy was like attending a wedding and an interview at the same time. If I salted my chicken before tasting, I might be denied a visa. I chose a conservative suit.

I knew nothing about tea culture. My British friends made a production out of preparing tea, boiling, steeping and straining as did my Japanese students who constructed an entire ceremony over a little cup of tea. I usually grabbed a teabag and dunked it up and down in the cup a couple of times until it turned the right colour. And, God forbid, I zapped it in the microwave. I didn't know Lipton from Earl Grey, Green Tea from Oolong. Well, the Chinese were not the British or the Japanese and I would just observe and follow; go with my instincts.

American tourists were still not granted visas to China. Our supervisor parenthetically asked why we even wanted to visit that pinko, communist country. Well sir, if you have to ask the question, you won't understand the answer. If the meeting went well, we would be issued invitations to visit the People's Republic of China. I did not feel on edge, or nervous, just excited. The whole experience struck me as surreal; an out of body experience, like I was watching from the outside. I didn't know it then, but this scene would play out again twenty years later in an equally unlikely scenario during a dinner interview, interrogation, before entering Afghanistan.

In our case, Yeh-Shen's ball symbolized going to Shanghai and 'Peking,' as it was then spelled. Ambassador and Mrs. Ke Hua greeted us in a living area. Madame Ke Hua stood straight, elbows at her side as she held her right hand, palm up, in her left. She gestured with her right palm and slightly nodded in the direction of the sitting room. Her smile was kind. Mine was effervescent, and too much for the occasion, too toothy, too Western. I couldn't help it.

We sat on black lacquered chairs swathed in silk cushions of reds and golds; large tassels hung from tufted corners. I took it all in. I wanted those chairs. They framed low, lacquered tables grouped in conversation areas. Black and red, black and burgundy, hints of gold, the look was minimalist, clean, and elegant. Nothing overstuffed. Blue and white ginger jars perched on shelves alongside celadon platters like birds on a crowded wire. Long scrolls garlanded the walls like breath taking waterfalls. Pale Tai Ping carpets luxuriated over terrazzo floors. Mr. Lee introduced himself. He was there to talk to us about our proposed trip to China and served as translator.

He presented a typed itinerary: palaces, government buildings, parks and gardens and the Great Wall. We presented a counter agenda. We wanted to see schools. These were not on the schedule. "It is difficult to make changes." Daryle and I wanted to see the site of early man, Peking Man. Roger wanted to visit a factory of Armor-Dial; he was Philippine country director for Dial Soap. Everyone wanted to visit the beer factory of Tsingtao. These were not on the agenda. "These ideas are difficult. You will greatly enjoy Gate of Heavenly Peace. Other things may not be possible."

Maybe we wouldn't be invited, after all.

White-coated embassy staff elaborately poured and served tea from small pots and offered diminutive savories then sweets on silver platters. Mrs. Ke Hua wore an uninspired, dark suit. I wondered, instinctively knew, that she wore a similar suit to Malacanang Palace with the extravagant Imelda Marcos who always wore butterfly sleeves, long gowns and exciting shoes.

"Your residence is very beautiful," to Mrs. Ke Hua.

"*Xie-xie,*" Thank you, she responded, dipping her head slightly; it sounded 'shey shey.'

"Thank you for having us here today, I enjoyed meeting you."

"*Xie-xie,* thank you, Madame," she said `extending a limp hand. I knew to give a gentle squeeze to her fingers rather than a firm, assertive American grip.

We were dismissed. At home we waited, went on with our activities; I dared not hope we would be accepted to travel. But within weeks we were invited to travel to the People's Republic of China. August 1977. We had little time to prepare. The invitation was offered: take it or leave it, now or never. The date and itinerary were fixed. We took it and accepted with gratitude.

Maybe is Difficult to Make Special Allangement

The swim coach agreed to stay at the house with Jessica and Ian while we traveled to China. We had only been separated one other weekend. There were many logistics to arrange and I agonized over being away. Both children enjoyed swim practice before and after school.

There was homework to monitor from the summer program, weekend sleep-overs to plan, play dates to choreograph, and play practice to coordinate. Their lives were more complicated than ours. The school administered a full summer program, a brilliant after-school program and Ruth Butler directed children's theatre with a production of Rip Van Winkle.

We flew to Hong Kong and took the train to the Lo Wu border-crossing at Canton. Mr. Li, of the China Travel Service, Peking Branch, met us. "Maybe it ees difficult to make special allangements." Still, we pursued our agenda. As we sat in the lounge of the train depot we discussed the itinerary.

The Gang of Four was on everyone's mind. Their arrest in 1976, several months before our arrival, signaled something new in China; a crackdown perhaps; progress perhaps. We did not know what to anticipate. When the Great Leap Forward took China economically a great leap backward, Chairman Mao revved-up his Cultural Revolution. But the Revolution remained controversial internationally. In its final years, Jiang Qing, wife of Mao Zedong, was appointed special emissary for the Revolution. However as popular sentiment shifted, she and three of her colleagues became known as the Gang of Four. One month after Mao's death, the Gang of Four was arrested.

It was in this context that we arrived in China. We accepted whatever itinerary they planned; we were invited guests.

We wanted to see schools so Mr. Li arranged a visit to a special school for deaf students; not exactly what we had in mind. We were thinking local public schools. This, however, was what they showed us: deaf students treated by acupuncture, some daily, some three times a week. With extraordinary acupuncture treatment, they claimed 70% recovery. I realized the uniqueness of the school, the government's show-and-tell, a show-case school. Still, it was impressive.

We stood at the back of the classroom, staring at the board covered with math equations. Each child sat at a wooden desk. Simple school supplies included a small slate, a shard of chalk and a book. Mr. Li translated:

> "Eight men
> "Were going to town.
> "Along the way
> "They met 9 others...."

The young teacher read the lesson phrase by phrase. She held the book in front of her mouth to prevent the students from lip reading, to aid listening skills.

During the lesson a young girl lowered her head to her desk and rested a cheek on her outstretched arm. The acupuncture treatment intrigued me. A teacher-assistant applied a needle at a pressure point or acupoint near the child's ear. Several students participated in this routine, placing their heads on their wooden desks. The needle remained in the child's head, just below the temple, for some time. When the assistant returned, she removed the needle and the child resumed class work. After some time, each child turned their head and the treatment began on the opposite ear.

The students seemed very brave to me. This may have been put on for our benefit. I was skeptical, but the kids took it routinely. No screaming as the needle person approached, no fighting, no resistance. They accepted the needles as part of the morning routine, part of their treatment. Perhaps much as a diabetic child pricks their finger to read the blood-sugar count, or inserts a critical insulin needle. Very brave indeed.

I thought of my two children at home in Manila. Would they endure such treatment? While waiting in line for inevitable shots for the health card requirements, Jessica screamed and howled; hysterical carrying on; she kicked up a horrible fuss; one of those times you want to stand aside and pretend it is someone else's child. Recently, I asked her why she had been so afraid, so hysterical. She remembered the incident, all right. She told me she screamed so much because she always had 98 inoculations at one time. Maybe she had two.

Banter on the van fluctuated between serious and silly. This day Mr. Li and Mr. Lee wanted to talk about American idioms.

"We must impluve hour Engrish.

"We hear, 'laining cat and dog,'" Mr. Li started. "What means this?"

Indeed, what does mean this? Someone ventured an answer. Everyone laughed.

Then the other Mr. Lee, said, "Amelican's rike hot dog," continuing, "Why you rike dog to be hot? How you get a dog hot? Chinese people we eat dogs; vely big dericacy." Moans from the Amelicans.

"You mean you eat dog meat?" Kathy, Roger's wife, asked incredulously. Not unlike in the Philippines, I wanted to add, but did not. She continued, "When Americans talk about 'hot dogs,' we are talking about a kind of sausage." It did sound stupid. "We eat them at baseball games; sausages, not dogs. Hot dogs."

Mr. Li or Mr. Lee said, "We know good Amelican idiom."

"What's that?"

"Paint the town led. Ha, Ha, Ha."

"Ha, Ha, Ha. Yes, that's good."

"We Chinese, we rike that idiom. Vely good, Ha, Ha. Paint town led." Then to explain,

"Led, like Led Guard, like Chinese Communists." More laughter, "You una-stan?"

"You mean like Chinese Reds?"

"Yes, yes. You know it?" Ha, Ha, Ha.

"Vely good 'Melican idiom."

From then on, every day we asked Li and Lee to help us 'Paint the town led.'

We were on a roll. "Ely-one name Lee in China. Ely-one name Smith in 'Melica, Ha, Ha, Ha." Mr. Li, or was it Mr. Lee, arranged for us to visit another school.

Killing of Flies Ballet

We rode in the van through throngs of black bicycles. Though the volume of vehicles was minimal, bicycle transportation reigned with lanes of traffic six across, going both directions. Mr. Li took us to a School for the Performing Arts, another special school. The teenagers, members of the Red Guard, wore bright red scarves, tied more like scouts than cowboys.

The social studies lesson, which could well have been a science lesson, in fact a morals and values lesson, emphasized the life of Marx and represented integrated curriculum. The teacher instructed:

"Marx was from Germany; a great leader of the proletariat." The teacher continued, "He is a good thinker of each problem. Modesty is learned from others. If there is complaining, there is no progress in science, but with effort and diligence we will make progress in the field of science. Learn from Marx to execute pure science. When we grow up we can make a greater contribution to our country." Mr. Lee translated.

The younger students, well coached, performed a dance program. We stood at the back of the classroom as the informal dance program began:

Chairman Mao is the One, Ballet.
Flowers and Banners, Warmly Welcome Dance
Killing of the Flies Dance
Lower middle school wearing headbands of big ugly flies to emphasize the campaign to eradicate flies.
Silver Ball of Friendship

A dance illustrating Table Tennis Ballet. In this dance the students wore white PE shorts, blue golf shirts for the boys, red for the girls. White tennis shoes and ping pong paddles added the final props.

Lastly, a traditional string instrument played with mallets by a red-scarfed, young man of the Red Guard.

The children took the dances seriously. The Welcome Dance and Silver Ball of Friendship were steeped in symbolism. More than that, the dances were choreographed with a measure of sophistication. Chairman Mao is the One, Ballet, was a beautiful little ballet. I laughed at the Killing of the Flies Dance, similar to any first grade performance. They were not silly, but serious as classmates waved their fly swatters in perfect syncopation and wore their ugly fly headbands with great pride. I liked what I saw. I didn't yet know what was taught when we were not observing, or if this approach, this curriculum, would ever work in our own system of education, but I was thrilled that we were given this glimpse and found myself intrigued. I needed to sort it out.

The children of these two schools received special attention. The school for the deaf performed a medical service embedded in the educational curriculum. The school for the arts provided specialized training for talented children and catered to their academic needs. Are these schools, the school for the deaf, the school for performing arts, meant to illustrate the new, Revolutionary China? The idea that deaf students be given an equal opportunity to learn, the idea that gifted children be cultivated and directed to bringing the arts to the masses seemed to confirm the original philosophy of the Cultural Revolution. I wondered, knew instinctively, these were special schools, to be shown and shared around the world.

Boys and girls wearing school uniforms and red scarves of the Red Guard.

What about the rest of China's children? What were the rural children learning? What kind of education were they receiving? I suspected we would not be shown those typical schools; they were not for show-and-tell. And could a whole population have changed its way? Why are they showing us these schools? Why did I doubt this? We did request to see schools, but these were exceptional schools, model schools, lab schools. Jiang Qing and the Gang of Four had just been arrested. Yet these children performed dances confirming Jiang's agenda of bringing culture to the masses on issues related to the peasants. One day *Killing of the Flies Ballet* might be compared to *Madame Butterfly*. One day.

After School Activities

W ater dripped down my neck, down my chest, to my stomach, it ran down my arms; my legs felt wet. Any breeze might have cooled my drenched body, but there was no movement of the air. August in Shanghai stifles energy; stifles thought. The air hangs sodden; it heaves a wet blanket of air at your face. The heat and humidity so dense we saw water in the air, not rain, not even fog; just wet air, even inside the huge Number One Department Store. Like all places in Shanghai, the vast superstore proved crowded and congested. I elbowed my way in slowly, as the foreign person, foreign friend, and leaned across the counter to purchase two small towels to drape around our necks in the sopping, wet humidity of August in Shanghai.

From our hotel room we looked down on the street. In the evening, men stripped down to their sleeveless undershirts, sat on stools in front of their shops. They fanned the evening air like lifeless butterflies unable to lift a wing. Women walked slowly, shuffling along, as if defying the need to move. Others, slowly lifted chopsticks, slurped noodles and played chess over boards balanced between their stools. The air did not move by itself; it barely moved when pushed by paper fans. In our hotel room, a creaky overhead fan slowly cranked like a vinyl record on the wrong speed.

In the morning, after a restless night tossing and turning, tangled in sheets, Daryle headed for a cold shower. I looked out the still open windows beyond the street, to the park. Rows of people stood on the grass performing the silent movements of Tai Chi. Adults stood holding out their arms, legs separated, going through the soundless, deliberate movements, a slow physical and mental exercise. Others, on the street walked slowly, pushing their fans, nudging, begging the air to move. No one slept. The time was 5am and the outdoor temperature measured 120 degrees Fahrenheit. What would it be by afternoon?

The Revolutionary Travel Committee made magic. Every day we visited a different school. One afternoon in Shanghai we visited a high school. The students engaged in after-school activities; some kids were intense, some giggling, some snickering. I was thinking afterschool ballet, ping pong, basketball.

The kids practiced afterschool acupuncture.

We walked into the first classroom. The teenagers, some fit, some gangly, all with shiny lacquer-ware-black hair, sat around tables hunched over small clear plastic human figures the size of GI Joe and Barbie. A small electric fan rested at the end of one table like a prop plane waiting to take off.

Students studied the figures, resting their arms on the plastic swathe which covered the tables. Narrow aluminum medical trays, long tweezers, and jars of needles speckled the tables. Human anatomy posters illustrated the location of arteries, veins, muscles and bones.

The plastic figures, dotted and marked with points and pathways, similar to the pointillism on the posters, showed pressure points for acupuncture and acupressure. Otherwise the dolls looked just like naked Barbie and G.I.Joe. The students studied the points on the dolls, occasionally looking up at the posters then tried to locate the same points on each other stabbing the needles in various acupoints. The instructor said something to Mr. Lee. He translated.

"Anyone here has any probrem?"

"You rike student que you probrem?"

"Sore muscle, any headrake?"

Daryle volunteered. "What's you probrem?"

I have a slight headache."

"You seet here."

"Good afta noon, sa," from one of the girls.

Several girls gathered around the patient. He placed his arm on the table. The schoolgirls enjoyed practicing on their foreign friend. One girl with shiny black pony tails took his hand. She held his large hand palm down, then with her own small thumb, supported by her delicate fingers, pressed and squeezed the space between his thumb and index finger. The pain began to subside. She held the pressure point for a minute or so. What a great trick to remember. We used it several times while in China; I still use it when I remember. The headache vanished. I tried to imagine if Jessica or Ian would ever take an acupuncture after-school activity class. I could only imagine Jessica with acupressure, never with needles. Ian, on the other hand would really get into jabbing needles all over the place.

On the asphalt field across from afterschool acupuncture class, cadets in neat lines practiced marching to commands. They carried out routines like a marching band. They carried rifles and twirled them like shiny silver batons. Boys and girls stood in straight rows to fire at targets. They kneeled on one knee and fired. I thought for a minute they might fire over their shoulders like a military Globe

Trotters exhibition game. We walked across the blacktop where they marched. They held their rifles proudly like ROTC cadets. After the show-n-tell routines, the cadet leader offered me a rifle.

"Here, Madame, you can shoot."

"Oh," pause. "Thank you; I don't know how to use a rifle."

He looked at me with incredulous disbelief. Then, "You ah teachah, yes?"

"Well, yes.

"We don't teach this in our schools." We don't teach ping pong or acupuncture either.

Under a shaded area, rows of tables hosted the table tennis activity. Singles, doubles, girls, boys batted that little ball back and forth like professional athletes.

He slammed it like he was killing flies.

His colleague patted that little ball back as if it was made of crystal.

She scooped it like it was a game of jai alai.

He swung at it like a game of baseball.

Her opponent used one hand.

He played with two hands gripping the paddle.

Or they played ambidextrous.

Back and forth.

Table after table.

Ping and pong.

Yin and Yang.

The strategy engaged us. If they employed this strategy to political diplomacy, we could see effective potential for dialogue. Ping Pong Diplomacy: all sides must employ a tactical approach to all issues.

The students offered their foreign friends a challenge to play a match or two with them. The teenagers slaughtered everyone. Not even close.

Then the students tried to give their foreign friends a chance; still pathetic.

Students played with one hand behind their back.

They played blindfolded with their eyes closed.

They played like it was a Chinese-fire-drill, running around the table between swipes.

We were still hopeless. We conceded finally to great applause and slinked, laughing, back to the van.

The Party Line

Although "maybe it is difficult to make changes," the Revolutionary Travel Committee came through with most of our initial requests made at the Chinese Ambassador's residence in Manila. They took us to a soap factory, a brewery, the cave site of early man, the Great Wall, a carpet factory, an ivory workshop, as well as gardens and beautiful palaces and of all things, a circus and Chinese opera.

One morning Mr. Lee told us we were going to visit a soap factory. Who really cares how soap is made? This was for Roger, CEO of Dial-Armor soap in the Philippines. We visited the Shanghai Number One Soap Making Factory. For Roger visiting the factory was a big deal, so we tried to get into it. Student workers, perhaps part of the reeducation, members of the Red Guard, stirred the mix of laundry soap and we watched the process of molding the bars. It reminded me of third grade soap-making for mum on Mother's Day.

"Shanghai now an industrial city under the leadership of our Chairman Hua."

We accepted the soap samples and surreptitiously passed them to Roger. Who really wants a lump of soap in the bottom of their backpack? The rest of the day we chanted, "Aren't you glad you use Dial? Don't you wish everyone did?" He would take them back to the main office in Manila; perhaps make the trip a business write-off.

Then, to our delirious glee, in the stifling summer heat, we visited the Tsingtao beer factory built by the Germans on the eastern coast of China in a small fishing village. This was on no one's list. Must have been something Mr. Li and Mr. Lee wanted to see.

The last time I visited a brewery was in Addis Ababa. This time the brew was yeasty. I peered over the tops searching for floating bees, but this was not honey beer. A yellow malted mixture swirled around in huge sanitized vats. The mixture was then bottled via conveyer belts and capped in time for our consumption. The production and assembly lines were not dissimilar to those of the soap factory, and the party line was exactly the same.

Even the brewery was subject to party line under the great Chairman Mao who suggested,

"Plant our own hops." And later we learned, "The Wall is also seen as an agricultural aid by protecting hops from devastating north winds."

I should have paid more attention. The brewery vats, though on a larger scale, worked the same way as Seyoum's t'ejery in Addis. These breweries could have taught me a great deal for my future life in the Middle East. It never occurred to me to pay attention, to consider the steps to the process and query the ingredients and measurements of the yeasty, malty substance.

"Thanks for the soap samples. How 'bout handing over your beer samples?"

"Get outa here. No way, Roger."

"Don't think so, Rog."

"You never drink beer."

"Well, today's different."

No one gave away their beer sample. I don't even drink beer, but the weather was wet, hot, humid and the beer refreshing.

The biggest surprise was the side trip to visit the site of Peking Man. "Maybe it is difficult to make changes," but they did. For Daryle and for me, Mr. Li and Mr. Lee arranged a drive to the caves of the Peking Man. After listening to the party line since our arrival, we realized this was a special concession.

Early Man has nothing to do with progressive man; nothing to do with the Cultural Revolution, Chinese progressivism and the propaganda machine, the re-education of the peasants or the re-education of western Foreign Friends. I'm not sure why they added this to the itinerary, but we were thrilled to visit the site of the discovery of Homo erectus who lived 500,000-300,000 years ago during the early Paleolithic age. The new China 'under the leadership of Chairman Hua' was not about the discovery of Homo erectus of the early Paleolithic age.

The site was simple; disappointing in a way. The skeletal remains were significant but the site simplistic: a cave, the skull, a few bones; nothing more. I was thinking how a diorama would work wonders. It was not developed in a Smithsonian way; just there. The bare bones in a cave off the side of the road. Still, the area, the cave, was of great interest: a strange place for these bones, for this relevant, important discovery.

And that was it. All we could really say was that we were there. We tried to place it in context, especially over the years as we visited other sites of early man in East Africa and Saudi Arabia.

Later that day we climbed huffing and puffing along the Great Wall of China, walking along its wide swath. Like walking through the pages of National Geographic, I walked along the top of Great Wall, pinching myself. At some stretches along the Wall, the incline of the path was so steep I couldn't stand up straight. I leaned forward to make my way leaning into the Wall, nearly parallel to the ground;

a most unusual sensation. The guide's information about the Wall was delivered in mono-tonous phrases; informative, and dull.

"For two hundred years the Wall repaired and extended.
For three, four centuries after that,
Many sections collapse for lack of maintain.
One early concern of Ming emperors was restoration for defense.
After liberation Wall repair again to accommodate visitors.
Forty-five degree incline provide excellent training for soldiers."

When Imelda Marcos feigned dizziness two years before, I laughed out loud. The First Lady was quoted in the paper and we saw her and heard for ourselves on the evening news reports. Television cameras continued the story in Manila, filming Imelda's response.

"I am haping bertigo," she whined.

"Ay! I peel so deezy. Naku Naman. Oh My Goodness." She abruptly left China and went home to Manila, during her first lavish official state visit.

"I am suppering prom bertigo. Naku Naman."

"I was porced to leeb China bepore I plant," she regretted in Ilocano dialect.

She could not walk along the wall with its steep incline. We laughed about that especially after our own experience. It was a steep wall; steep and wide and impressive; one of the few landmarks easily identified from the moon. From some vantage points on the Wall, one can see for hundreds of kilometers across the land. "Chin Shih Huang-ti is dead, but the Wall still stands," the Chinese proverb said.

We wanted to see schools. We got the circus. Culturally, it was more interesting than I expected. Everyone knows about Chinese acrobats. I just didn't fancy going around the world to watch a circus; especially without my kids.

The opening act featured five acrobats riding around on one bi-cycle. One-by-one they took a running jump toward the moving cycle to leap on the shoulders of the man peddling. Although it was not a unicycle, the performer peddled around the circus pavilion with his arms outstretched for balance. He propelled around the tent several times until the next acrobat cart wheeled and leaped onto the second man's shoulders.

Each man balanced on the shoulders of the previous stuntman. As the cyclist peddled around the perimeter of the tent, the next artist leaped and somersaulted his way to the top of the human pillar until five men soared around the tent, arms stretched out, 'look ma, no hands.'

No roaring lions or dancing bears as I recall, but the next act featured a goat. A goat walked a tight-wire eight feet off the ground. A goat with funny feet; hooves or something. A goat, like *Three Billy Goats Gruff* clomping along a wooden bridge; that was feasible. Trip-tromping along a tight-wire was not. This was a Chinese circus, a Chinese goat.

We began to understand the Chinese message. We talked about it in the evening, during dinner and after dinner. What were they telling us every day? Our individual privately arranged invitational tour served the Chinese well. We attempted to understand each lecture, each discussion from our hosts. The guides, translators, school directors even factory workers always encouraged questions: the mentors were good. Foreign Friends were welcome and encouraged to ask questions. As a result of cadre schools of reeducation, they had the FAQs down pat. We queried with naiveté.

Their answers reflected the new philosophy of the country: reeducation, again, just after the death of Mao and the arrest of the Gang of Four. I felt like the cyclist balancing the information as if riding round and round adding more weight on my shoulders at each stop, several times a day. Processing the information was as overwhelming as trying to decide where to focus at a three ring circus hoping to take it all in, not wanting to miss a thing. What I thought I understood at the time became fodder for continued reflection years later.

Gang of Four

I didn't concentrate all afternoon. Mr. Lee advised there might be a demonstration after dinner. Who would demonstrate? What was the issue? Would it be dangerous? We spent the day in Beijing. Mr. Lee was vague; didn't tell us what it was about. People would be bused in from the villages to demonstrate in front of our hotel and on down the main road toward Tiananmen Square. We should stay inside. Would it be dangerous, we asked again? He remained vague. He said we should not get involved but we could watch upstairs from our hotel room windows.

He told us this in the afternoon.

What-if scenarios played out in my mind all day. We wondered among ourselves what this could mean. We asked Mr. Lee if this had anything to do with the Gang of Four, or with Jiang Qing, the arrested wife of Mao Tse-tung. Mr. Lee did not comment. I thought of posters; remembered what we had been told about Jiang Qing and her work with the youth and Red Guard. My palms were wet from nerves. At dinner we slurped-up our noodles and speculated at what, if anything, would happen.

"So what do you think will happen tonight?"

"What did Mr. Lee say to you? Any indication of what's going on?"

"Why is he so vague?"

"What is going on? Will there be violence?"

"Man, I want to see it, but you know, if there is a crowd,"

"What? What's the worst that could happen?"

"If anyone shows up, you know, emotions are contagious."

"Yeah, but do you think the Gang of Four will be paraded, maybe even executed here?"

"Oh my god. I don't want to be the round-eye in the crowd if that happens."

Peasants gathered in the street. The crowds grew. All were equal: peasants, workers, residents. Men and women wandered about in unisex navy or grey pants, wide-legged and calf-length. They wore dark 'Mao' jackets with 'mandarin' collars. Everyone wore black cotton shoes. The women's shoes looked like Mary Jane's with straps; the men's simple shoes lacked the strap.

As the crowd grew, we ran upstairs to watch out our windows. Thousands of men and women wandered in the street below. We ran from room to room to see who had the best view. When we could stand it no longer we cautiously went downstairs, looked around and ventured outside.

The evening was balmy, much nicer than the stifling heat of Shanghai. Cautiously we wandered down the street to observe. Who knew what this enormous crowd demanded? Perhaps they would parade the Gang of Four in some public viewing. Mr. Lee hinted at that. Perhaps there would be a hanging. Were we ghoulish? Ambulance chasers? We were bystanders, amateur sociologists eager to observe change as it happened.

The throng was polite. It was noisy, but nonthreatening. Of course we did not know what was being said from the loud speakers along the road in front of the rally platform. Huge posters and banners screamed out the message in geometric characters. It was not brilliant to be there as part of this massive demonstration. We did not blend in with our very round eyes and light hair. I kept a grip on Daryle's shirt, not holding hands, or walking arm in arm, but grasping his shirt, just to feel grounded. The crowd pressed in. No one touched me, but soon it would be impossible to avoid contact and the inevitable pushing and shoving or maneuvering for a better view of the platform.

Cognizant that the anger could turn on us at any moment, we watched with some reservation trying to figure out what was going on and what might happen. Why were all these people gathered at Tiananmen Square? Whatever it was, it seemed all of China was out to witness. The Square was packed body to body and everyone looked alike; equal.

The line between demonstration and riot is fine. An inappropriate remark, overzealous police, passionate leadership can twist the emotional outcome and change the turn of events. What happens when a well-intended demonstration turns into devastating riots?

I saw this in Ethiopia. I knew the fine line between involvement, demonstration and passionate chaos. Emotions are vulnerable and contagious. Still, we watched, secretly hoping for something exciting, even fanatic, the chance to observe history-in-the-making. Academically we also knew better. It was not the time to be a foreigner in someone else's country, with someone else's issues.

We started back to the hotel and ran into Mr. Lee and his friend from the China Travel Service. We were surprised to see each other. I was shocked to see anyone we knew amongst the hundreds of thousands of demonstrators. We asked again what was going on. Again, ambiguous deflection. Perhaps it was something as benign as wage increases for the masses. Perhaps it was serious, more somber. They did not inform us. We watched from our hotel windows. No riots, no disturbance, just masses of people demonstrating. At least that night, there was no hanging and the Gang of Four remained in prison.

Peking Duck

B efore traveling to China, most of what I knew about Peking, besides elegant pieces of art, consisted of Peking Man, Peking Duck and the Great Wall of China. We walked the Wall and as Richard Nixon remarked infamously, "It's really great." We visited the cave of Peking Man, "It's really old."

As if to complete this popular depiction we visited a duck farm. Oh great. Well, I knew about rabbits and chickens from my dad.

I even had a duck, a mallard, when we lived in 'fer shur' the San Fernando Valley. I called him Gregory Peck. He didn't know any tricks, but Gregory was noisy and followed me all over the property, right at my heels. If I ran, Gregory shuffled his stubby legs as fast as they would go, and if that didn't work, he flapped his brown wings to catch up. We had no pond, but Gregory thrived on grains and grasses and a few unsuspecting insects. As Mr. Peck matured, we realized he was not a drake. Gregorie Peck was a hen.

Seven hundred egg-laying Peking ducks lay 185 eggs per duck, per year. It sounded like a math problem. In a way, it was. We walked through several acres of the well kept farm. The ducks, separated by age, stayed mostly in free-range areas.

The formula was precise. The ducks fed on grains and bugs and ate on their own for 50 days. Then for 14 days the ducks were force fed. The farmers shoved a hose down their throats and shot the ducks with extra feed. At that point, the last two weeks, they stayed in smaller pens becoming fat and ready for market. When the ducks reach 2.5 kilos, they are ready to sell. The quota on the farm was 60,000 per year and any extra the commune kept.

Chop sticks were cool and easy to use. I felt a bit smug. In our group finger flexibility with the little sticks denoted status. I picked up peas, even peanuts with my chopsticks. I ate poached eggs with chopsticks, which of course was not necessary, just being cheeky. In the beginning my colleagues struggled with the unfamiliar sticks. There was no choice for us: figure it out or starve.

"Like this," I tried to assist.

"Balance the first stick on your ring finger holding it in place with your thumb.

"Place the second stick at a parallel angle holding it in place between your pointer and

middle finger. It's easy."

"Dannie, it's not easy," from Don.

"Ok," Polly, a bit encouraged, "now what?"

"Scoop and pinch," I suggested.

"I can't keep anything between the chopsticks long enough to get it from my plate to my mouth," from Roger.

"Give me a Tsingtao beer. I know how to swallow."

"I am wasting away to nothing in this country," again Don.

"Don, no one will notice."

"You have to hold the chop sticks more in the middle, like this," Daryle had his own style.

For three weeks we never saw a fork. Don lost 22 pounds, Kathy lost 12 pounds, others lost 6-8 pounds. I enjoyed every course of every meal. Even ten course meals did not leave one feeling bloated or feeling full. The combination of vegetables, meats, fish, soup and rice seemed to endorse healthy meals, though the sweet/sour sauces caused high sodium and sugar count.

These days, they say Peking Duck should be served in three

courses. In Peking, at the Peking Duck Restaurant, Peking Duck courses included each duckling body part. Our meal, I counted, contained twelve courses.

For the first course, waiters brought out sliced gizzards. They placed the platters on the round spindle. Li and Lee joined us to translate and enjoy. As the centre platter rotated, Mr. Li, sitting to my right, helped himself. I followed jabbing my sticks into the gizzards, pinching a pair, depositing them on my small plate. I poured some soy and mixed it with pepper spices. I dragged my gizzards through the mix.

Next came a dish of kidneys, then hearts, then sliced livers. These phenomenal dishes were followed by platters of tongue, webs and jellied wings, all parts of our duck. Each course was dredged in soy or hoi-sin.

What was this? Eggs. Black eggs. Century old eggs. These wonderful eggs seemed to be fermented, at least marinated in soy. Not just overnight, but maybe also not 100 years. Not large duck eggs but smaller eggs. They appeared crackled, the veins permeated with dark soy. With our chop sticks we pinched the slippery eggs or as last resort, stabbed them. This was much easier than plucking whole eggs out of a pot of Ethiopian doro wot with a swatch of *injera* between the tips of our fingers.

"Mr. Li," I leaned toward our host.

"What can possibly come next? This is a wonderful meal."

"You rike it?"

"I rike it very much." No, I didn't say that.

The soup came in the middle of the meal. The terrine contained duck soup, mostly broth with bits of duck and flavoured with herbs and five-spice which consisted of cinnamon, fennel, anise, cloves and pepper, a combination of sour, bitter, sweet, pungent, salty. Sometimes ginger, nutmeg and licorice are added. Served in deep bowls we used ceramic spoons or grasped the bowls with two hands to drink from the crockery. This was a sign that the carcass had been stripped and sliced to perfection for the following, final courses.

Kitchen staff brought fried liver served with small dishes of seasoned salt, then hearts and green pepper served with peanuts, pepper, ginger, soy, water chestnuts and mushrooms. And finally, the last course: crepes of steamed thin lumpia wraps to be filled with strips of spring onion, thin slices of cucumber, and precisely sliced bits of roasted duck; more *hoi-sin*.

"This is best part, coming now," predicted Mr. Li.

He demonstrated the exact structure for each mini-wrap:

1) spread the small crepe with hoi-sin,

2) add a spring onion strip,

3) add a thin slice of cucumber and

4) add a morsel of roast duck.

Carefully wrap and enjoy. You could use your fingers. No one would starve. Throughout the courses small cups of tea were replenished again and again.

Okay. I did the math: 700 ducks at 185 eggs each, per year, equals 129,500 eggs per year. The government quota required 60,000 ducks per year. One hundred twenty nine thousand, five hundred minus 60,000 ducks to the government left a potential of 69,500 eggs if they all survived. Those would be used as eggs or hatched as ducks and sold at market after supplying the needs of the commune. I didn't learn how many went to the restaurant or if the restaurant was run by the government or the commune.

As evidenced by the meal, the duck farm did well. As a group, we did quite well with the chopsticks. We were told somewhere along the way that a soiled table was the sign of a well appreciated meal. The cloth was a mess. We dribbled hoi-sin, cilantro, peppercorns, webs and livers. The table confirmed: our best meal in China.

What Did It All Mean?

In Shanghai, we were told over and over of the great progress since liberation under the leadership of Chairman Hua. Mao's wife, Jiang Qing, became leader of the Gang of Four in the final stage of the Cultural Revolution. At the same time the United States was defeated in Vietnam in 1975 and in September 1976 Mao Zedong died leaving Hua Guofeng as head of state. He promptly arrested Mao's wife and the Gang of Four.

During the Cultural Revolution, the Red Guard was incited to destroy all forms of perceived self-indulgence. Thank god they did not destroy the Peking Duck Restaurant. The mandate was to destroy all things related to free enterprise, to capitalism, to widening the economic gap. Ah, spared from the throes of the Red Guard, the Peking Duck Restaurant survived. The Restaurant was about supporting the commune and to some extent supporting the government. One goal of the Revolution was to bring all citizens together. The point of the Red

Guard was to spread the word of the new philosophy through large posters and to purge those who thought differently, the educated, the wealthy and the artistic.

Students of the Red Guard were ordered to destroy ancient relics, monuments, statues; admonished to destroy anything connected to the development of the mind: libraries, books, university buildings, art and traditional musical instruments; instructed to destroy Confucian customs, symbols, philosophy and education.

The idea to involve youth was brilliant, to form a Red Guard. Yes! My kind of thinking! My kind of leadership. Get those kids involved. But what was the thinking behind closing the schools if the intent was to reeducate? Closing the schools served two purposes, it seems, but I didn't ask: to criticize the professors and teachers, it was said, and to permit the student Red Guards the independence to attack, harass and reeducate citizens; all designed to stop the emergence of a privileged class in China.

Yet some of the students went too far. Did she, Madam Jiang Qing, ever acknowledge this? Was she thought to be ahead of her time, in wanting all citizens to be equal; to stifle creativity for the sake of personal pleasure, in favour of creativity for the masses? Or did they see it that way?

At the time, I did not understand the passion that was behind the Cultural Revolution or the relief of the post revolution which we were currently experiencing. I didn't understand the part played by the leaders, by Jiang Qing, Chairman Mao's third, and most beautiful wife.

At the time we visited China, students of the Red Guard were back in school. In the end, when the Guards factionalized and fought each other, the army stepped in and regained control. Old educational ideals were transformed. The educational philosophy changed enrollment procedures to include workers, peasants and soldiers. The idea was to strengthen the leadership of the working class in schools and colleges.

Mao was dead and the Gang of Four arrested. Factories, industry and agriculture could flourish again. The Red Guard no longer interfered; no longer interrupted production with rallies.

'Education must serve the proletariat and the soldiers; must combine the students with the masses and combine theory with practice,'

So we were told. No person left behind.

Interview with Madam Jiang Qing

*"In the world today all culture, all literature and art belong to defi-
nite classes and are geared to definite political lines. There is in fact
no such thing as art for art's sake, art that stands above classes, or
art that is detached from or independent of politics."*

*Mao Tsetung, 1942 Talks at the
Yenan Forum on Literature and Art*

What? No art for art's sake? What kind of Cultural Revolution was
this?

My final reflections on our visit to Mainland China rattled around
in my brain for months, for years. When we were permitted, encouraged, to ask questions of our guides I was ill prepared. There are now
questions for which I have formed my own answers over the years.
Over years of continued research and reflection, I fabricated an interview with Madam Jiang Qing. In my head it went something like this.

"Madam Jiang Qing, you are a beautiful actress. How did you
change your thinking about art? About drama? How did you come to
relate drama to culture and to the Revolution?

"Madam, please tell me, why did you decide to destroy all known
art? You are a beautiful and successful artist. How did you come to
resolve that art must be destroyed?

"Is it true that you and Mao Tsetung fell in love due to your mutual
interest of art to serve the people?

"I have read that Chairman Mao believed that there is no such
thing as art for art's sake.

"Did you agree with that in the beginning?

"And Madam Jiang Qing, the Chairman was an intellectual. What
was Chairman Mao's reaction to obliterating culture, literature, even
drama and art? What was his thinking about destroying anything connected to the development of the mind, like libraries, books, university
buildings, to destroying Confucian customs, symbols, philosophy and
education?

"Was he difficult to persuade? Was it his idea?

"I suspect this came from you. Can you talk to me about this?

"It is said that because of you, Madam, the Chairman understood the role of women, especially in the dramatic arts; that women actors were elevated from prostitute status to dramatic artists.

"Did you also encourage women to work in the agricultural fields; to supplement the great struggle?

"And finally, Madam Jiang Qing, I now want to know what happened to the concept of the valuable role of Chinese women. Why today, are thousands and thousands of Chinese girls abandoned at birth? How did this corruption come about?"

A Palace For The Pope

Ronny

I first became aware of *Ronny's* in the early seventies. Ronny ran a flower shop in the old Ermita district of Manila. He prepared extravagant, elegant arrange ments for large homes in Forbes Park, in the golden ghetto of Manila. He arranged the flowers for chic dinner parties of the upper classes; huge white, floppy magnolias and regal bird of paradise, or delicate branches of orchids of copious varieties, colours and shapes.

A trip to *Ronny's* was at once therapeutic and exhausting. Beautiful objects hung from the walls, from the ceilings, from indoor trees. Ancient Chinese bowls and decanters enhanced narrow tables between cut flowers and potted plants. Striking pieces from San Francisco and London were one-of-a-kind. If you saw something at *Ronny's* and had the presence of mind and the financial means, you snatched-up a beautiful treasure, for it surely would not be there the next time. Ronny traveled to San Francisco, Hong Kong and London. It was said he had a home in San Francisco.

After some time, he opened a second, larger store in a newer renovated area of Manila. The new shop, in Makati, while offering-up the same tasteful fare, to me, never had the panache or the ambience of *Ronny's* in Ermita; I preferred the congested chaos and the new shop always seemed clinical with wide aisles and orderly display shelves.

Ronny, everyone called him by his first name, often choreographed the décor for state dinners at Malacanang Palace. When Imelda traveled to China, Ronny accompanied the first lady on the first official visit to Beijing; the start of open relations. I was quite interested in that trip, as I hoped to travel to Beijing, although China was not open to western visitors.

Thousands of orchids and tropical flowers were flown in for the reciprocal dinner hosted by the Philippine first lady at a Chinese palace. I devoured the details reported in the local news. The descriptions took my breath away. Ingredients for each course, each Philippine delicacy, were flown in for the evening, each entrée accompanied by individual floral presentations. It represented an elegant extravagance of two struggling countries hosting and toasting each other.

In circles of the wealthy, the socially and aristocratically class-conscious, Ronny was a household name. It was said, a well known hypothetical truth, that Ronny was the reason for a party's success. People liked to name-drop that 'Ronny was doing' their party. We women can be so affected about what we perceive others expect.

The men got caught up in it too, dropping comments like, "Oh you know Grace, she won't be satisfied unless Ronny is decorating the garden." He choreographed décor for dinner parties of the business community and political senators. These social events included hundreds of guests and were often held outside in lush garden settings of private homes, enhanced by his artful touch: expressive, controlled chic.

He embellished garden walls as if to conceal the cavernous gap between the upper class and the impoverished masses living on the other side of the walls, in the slums of Tondo. At intimate indoor parties, sit-down affairs, silver sliders, caught in twinkling candlelight, glistened under plates. Tools of cutlery, lined up in marching order, bordered platters that served as individual place settings. Ronny enhanced each table with balance: candles and flowers which discretely augmented the hostesses theme or menu. We attended these dinners, Daryle as the smart one, I was the cute one.

Strength and Flexibility. Watercolour by Ian Russell

A Table for the Pope

It Was Said

R onny opened a hair salon just blocks from our home. The shop
nurtured ladies needs through pure luxury. When you walked into
Ronny's Hair Salon you were treated like a princess, offered coffee or
tea and draped in an elegant cape. The beautician stood behind your
chair and luxuriously tied the bow in front, around your neck as you
watched in the mural of mirrors.

Ronny didn't wash your hair; he lathered and massaged your scalp.
"We never use brushes or nails which damage your scalp or hair, only
the balls of our fingers to massage and stimulate." Oh my god. Do it to
me: massage and stimulate my weary scalp. Reclining chairs made of
natural rattan waited at the sinks and tall-back rattan chairs beckoned
at the bank of mirrors. All of the appointments were Philippine décor, the tasteful décor, not the tacky patio furniture so often associated
with bamboo; not the sort sold on the highway.

It came as no surprise then that soon after the opening of the salon
Ronny opened a small Furniture Showroom next door. His designs were
unique and tropical. Where others favoured light and white, Ronny often used dark and heavy, though the materials themselves were light.
The counter-effect, the juxtaposition was startling. He was a genius, it
was said; perhaps of the brilliance of Dali, without the madness.

For several years we looked for a formal dining table. I had no pre-
conceived idea of what I wanted. I was thinking maybe heavy Spanish,
perhaps something from the era of the Spanish occupation of the
Philippines, but even in the provinces, I never found exactly the right
piece. I expected that it would jump out at me and beg to be taken to
my home. It never happened so I continued to search. I stopped by the
new Furniture Showroom.

From the back room, the manager brought out the catalogue, a
scrapbook of photos. As I turned the pages of the thick photo album, I
found *The Table*, the perfect table, it cried out to me, beseeching me to
take it home, but they would not sell it to me.

Ronny was not selling to residents, but only producing for export,
by request and by special order. Why in the world did he have this
beautiful showroom, if he wasn't selling? I didn't figure this out. The
table was not for sale to foreigners. Ronny was under contract with
Bloomingdale's.

I had only a superficial knowledge of Imelda's shopping obsession with shoes, paintings and jewelry and of her trips to Bloomingdale's. I should have guessed she might have entered into some business dealings. Because Ronny enjoyed an exclusive contractual agreement with Bloomingdale's in New York, he would not be able to sell to me in country because in theory, I would eventually export the furniture to America.

I loved that table.

I fell in love with the size of the rattan. The Chinese revere bamboo for its strength and flexibility. Rattan projects strength and power. Rattan, usually used for better furniture does not split and break as easily as bamboo. It was the size and strength that got to me, the boldness which called out.

"When are you returning to the US?"

"We have no immediate plans to leave. We have been here for seven years."

Then in a more chatty way, "Our children are growing up here and our work is here. This table represents the best of the Philippines; Ronny and his designers add to our love and appreciation of the country." Then I brought out photos of Jessica and Ian their arms draped over the shoulders of their Pilipino classmates and swim mates.

This seemed to be the disclaimer that worked for them. They agreed that they could make an exception if we planned to stay in the country. They would not be violating any export agreement. There was one table of this design in the country, it was said, and it was ordered by the First Lady for the Bamboo Palace, later renamed the Coconut Palace, which she was building for the visit of Pope John Paul II.

Pope John Paul II visited the Philippines several times. When the Pope announced a visit in 1978 the First Lady commissioned a new and opulent palace along the waterfront on Roxas Boulevard especially for the Pope. Each of seven suites featured a different Philippine product and region. Décor included pineapple fiber, banana fiber, pearls, capiz shell work, rattan, bamboo, and coconut lumber. The Coconut Palace became the Presidential Guest House built at an outrageous cost at the time of US$10,000,000 it was said. The table in the photo album was being built for the Pope's Palace.

My table, as opposed to the Pope's, at Ronny's suggestion, would be stained deep burgundy. The thick glass tabletop, which rested on those powerful cylinders of rattan, would be smoke-tinted. The Pope's glass tabletop was clear. Bamboo branches and leaves etched the corners of his table. The Pope's table seated twenty-four, mine seated eight. The Pope's seat covers were raw silk. I had children.

No one would have taken much note of the outrageous philandering, the too typical abuse of funds, the characteristic squandering that had come to be expected, had it not been for the fact that the Pope refused to stay in such opulence. Once the Pope expressed his humility, the common became incensed and outraged at the extravagant spending.

The Table, my table, made it through several moves. From Manila we eventually moved to Saudi Arabia; The Table came with us filling the small dining room. The Table spent time in storage then came to its final resting place in Florida after a fight with the interior decorator.

"We don't do dark furniture here. This is Florida," Teresa patiently explained.

"I'm sorry, but your rattan won't work here."

How could I have trusted anyone with long, wavy, public-school hair? Of course The Table works here. It is the central focus of our small Florida home and everyone asks, "Where did you find that beautiful Table?"

"Ronny designed it for me.

"He works for Bloomingdale's." I'm such a name dropper.

Ronny spent less time in Manila, more and more time in San Francisco, it was said. Years later, it was said he was murdered there, in San Francisco, rumored in a life-style triangle. This was never printed in the Manila papers, but at cocktail parties and dinner soirées, it was said.

Zambales
Negritos
and
Tasaday

Pigs

"**P**igs!

"Oh my god, they're getting our food. Bring your flashlights. Hurry!

"Get out! Out! Out!" I screamed at no one, while stumbling forward in the dark.

I heard the snorting. What was going on? I peeked out of the tent looking toward the noise and saw in the darkened night, the silhouetted loathsome beasts; pigs foraging about in the tent. The food tent.

"Help me! Pigs are everywhere!

"Someone! Everyone, get out here. Help me!"

Flashlights in hand, running about in bed clothes, we lunged toward the snorts. Wild pigs rummaged through the rice, the tubers, the lentils, canned goods, sugar, powered milk, pastas, and drinks. Everything seemed fair game.

We came at the pigs like a swat team from the forest. Startled teenagers stumbled out of their tents with pillows as weapons, yelling and hollering like cowboys on a round-up.

"Yeee haaaw! Get outa here!

"You idiot pigs! Get outa our fooood!" Donny galloped toward the pigs, his usually floppy hair matted to his head.

Well, of course, it was too late. The pigs rooted through everything, eating much of it, soiling and redistributing the rest. Sacks, bins ripped open, eaten through, even tins were uprooted. In the dark we saw our rice strewn across the canvas flooring of the tent. We beat the pigs with pebbles and sticks and pillows until they squealed and snorted on their way to less frenzied foraging.

"Man, that was the best pillow fight ever!" Tim confessed.

"*Pangit,* Ugly, Man. Stupid pigs." Luis was disgusted.

"Can we do that again?"

"Get outa here. Go back to bed." Teenagers, I thought.

"We have to clean up this mess in the morning."

I agreed to accompany the twelve gnarly high school students, college bound in June; all American students from the International School of Manila. We spent 10 days and nights within the Negrito community at the base of the Zambales Mountains in the Philippines. Luis and Rick were Filipino-American. Don Mead towered over everyone with a curly flaxen mop that hung over his ears. Twelve involved dedicated, energetic and committed students; seven strapping guys and five brilliant girls. Dick Leon, a young visionary pastor, organized the work camp and gave the gang its dimension and cohesion.

The Negritos of Zambales, like other minority tribes of the Philippines, lacked formal education. As a semi-nomadic culture, they moved constantly utilizing slash and burn agriculture practices. While they did not amble far, they were not rooted. The government lacked jurisdiction. One strategy was to build schools providing a structure, a fixed place where children would report on a daily basis; a place and a reason to ground families.

We drove hours, bouncing along horrible pitted dirt roads, winding along the foothills of the mountains, laughing, singing, telling terrible jokes, each one dumber than the previous.

"Why don't cannibals eat divorced women?"

"Because they're too bitter." Arg. Then Ricky offered,

"The teacher asked the ESL students to make a sentence using pink, green, yellow. The boy in the back row raised his hand. 'I know,' he whispered waving his hand in the air. The teacher called on him. 'Yes, Miguel?' He replied, 'I hear green, green, green, and I pink up the phone and say yellow?'"

"Man, that's terrible. Don't start on chicken jokes. I can't stand it."

"Are we there yet?"

The kids from the International School volunteered for the service project. The Rev, as they called Dick Leon, engaged the kids in a community project they couldn't resist. I went along to help with the girls and to assist with the meals.

The project was a ten day undertaking to build a school. Dick pursued a second agenda as well. He instilled the concept of community service, not charity. He endorsed working hand in hand with local Negritos. After dinner, he chatted with the kids about their issues, elevating evening discussions centred on political events, world and local issues, their lives and international connections as global nomads. Dick treated everyone as an adult peer and they responded in kind. All would attend universities in the US.

What did I know about engineering, building construction? In the interest of full exposure and transparency, I admit: I knew nothing about building construction. Well, I would be the foodie. I would feed these strapping teenagers, sit-in as the mother-figure, chat with the teenage girls and be the surrogate parent for the crazy boys. And so it began. We set up tents, one for the girls another for the guys. We started construction of the school; we had 10 days.

The guys gathered-up and accumulated bamboo trees from the woods and quickly lashed them together to make a cooking station for our teen-team. To construct the school, they cut and split the poles under the guidance of village builders. Squatting in the dirt, the muscular small men from the community deftly split the long bamboo shafts wielding huge bolo knives. They resembled other Negritos we met in the forest on family weekend outings with John Britt.

Nana Nana Nana Nana .... Bat Man

Friday night we attended the ballet at the Cultural Centre and Saturday morning, only two hours away, we poked around in the jungles and forests just outside Manila.

"Mr. Britt is forcing uuusss," whined Kimberly as she trudged along a narrow path.

"How much farther?" The seven year old chubby cherub was soaked in her own sweat.

"Mr. Briiittt? I can't go on," she panted in the thick jungle.

We all felt the heat but delighted in discovering the Philippine Islands one by one, path by path, weekend by weekend. John Britt was a once-a-week explorer and took every chance to infiltrate new territory. We were three families. With John in the lead, we never hiked more than an hour without stopping for a G&T. John believed that a gin and tonic was the elixir of all things. We often ran across nimble Negritos inside the forest.

No doubt we were too loud traipsing along the path looking for orchids and ferns for our own gardens. We found the Negritos friendly and curious. They raced circles around us dashing up and down the trail, telling us about the orchids and trees and sharing their own names. They spoke in dialect, but understood Tagalog.

That day, as we came around the corner, three men sat squatting around a small fire roasting meat.

"Oh ho ho!" said John as he saw the men cooking their lunch.

"What do you have here?" Friendly and gregarious, everyone loved John. The Negritos trusted him immediately and everyone laughed before they had a chance to answer. John was well over six feet tall, the men, barely over a meter, like The Jolly Green Giant and the forest elves.

"Eeeuw," from Kimmy.

"What is that?" The small man rotated the meat, stretched over small sticks like kebabs.

"Is he going to eat that? Eeeuw.

"What is it?"

We all wanted to know. I speculated it might be a large frog or small bird. Nope. They were roasting bats. They invited us to join them. We sat in the dirt with the men. They squatted on their haunches. How do they do that? I never mastered that position. I sat cross-legged in what my kinder teacher used to call 'Indian' style. The inevitable was next.

"Eeeuw. Mr. Britt is forcing us.

"I'm not eating that.

"It's bat-meat. Eeeuw." Kimberly always voiced what the rest of us thought.

"It tastes like chicken, Kim."

"How do you know?"

"It's okay Kimmy. Don't make it a public issue," her mum hissed from between her teeth.

They shared their meat; we shared our sandwiches and gave them our water while we poured ourselves another G&T. Every weekend we enjoyed some sociological encounter.

The next weekend as we came from the forest, a group of wiry little men, all slightly bow-legged, appeared from the river. They seemed animated and we quickly noticed why.

At the centre of the group men danced around a large deer. With enthusiasm they reenacted the stoning. The men worked together. They chased the deer from the clearing toward the

river. As the deer reached the narrow riverbed, the hunters threw stones to further confuse the creature, stunning the mammal. They aimed their small bows, pulled the string taut and injected the startled deer with handmade metal arrowheads to bring it down.

They tied the legs together and lashed the beast to bamboo poles. Slinging the poles over their shoulders they shuffled through the dust to bring the meat to the village. On one occasion Daryle traded his Timex for several arrows and a small handmade bow. Everyone was happy.

Back to the Future

In the golden ghetto of Makati, far from the foothills of Zambales where the teenagers wrestled a Negrito school into existence, and equally far from the forests and caves of southern Mindanao, we enjoyed the late afternoon with friends.

"Manuel Elizalde is taking a group into the forest."

"Yes?"

"You know the cave dwellers?"

"You mean to see the Stone Age tribe, the Tasaday?"

"Yes! Come with us!"

"What are you talking about?" I asked incredulously.

"He's taking the helicopter in," they all chimed in as we sat in the generous, back-yard garden drinking afternoon tea under the shade of aged eucalyptus.

Manuel Elizalde was Mia's dad. Jessica had been to Mia's house after school. Mia's hair hung below her waist and her maids brushed it after class while the girls drank ice cold calamansi juice. Jessica loved that. Her own hair hung to her shoulders and she brushed it herself. Secretary Elizalde was the head of PANAMIN, the agency created in 1968 to protect cultural minorities. His father was of Spanish lineage and his mother American. A controversial figure on several levels, a socialite and interested in primitives of the islands, he took credit for discovering the Tasaday, a Stone Age tribe located in the forests of Mindanao.

"John Nance is going."

"John the journalist from Oregon?" I knew John from the cocktail circuit. John Nance, covered the war in Vietnam from 1965-1967 and moved to Manila as Bureau Chief with *Associated Press* in 1968. As news broke on the discovery of the Stone Age tribe, he quit his position with AP to report exclusively on the Tasaday. At receptions we talked about life in the Great Northwest. His presence with Elizalde validated the trip.

"Carol Maloney's coming. She's going as a linguistic anthropologist. She's dying to study the language." Carol's husband, Reg, worked with Daryle at the International School.

"We can take one more. Come with us!"

"This tribe is from the Stone Age."

"We will fly to Mindanao."

"Manda's chopper will drop us into the cave where they live." They all talked at once.

"The cave dwellers have had no communication with the outside world.

"None.

"They don't wear clothes. Well, okay.

"If they wear any covering, they wear leaves.

"They forage fruit and roots.

"It's a brilliant opportunity."

It was too fast; too much to absorb. The crowd was fast. My friends lounging around the garden that afternoon were seemingly carefree. Off to the caves, off to the coffee house, off to the discos. My kids were young and at home. Perhaps a weekend, but during the week, I paused.

In some ways, it seemed like a fast-lane junket back to the future. Our weekend forays enabling sociological casual encounters with Negritos and my ten day work camp with Zambales Negritos led me to question the legitimacy of this helicopter ride to the caves.

I declined the offer.

The Whole World Watched

C arol Maloney, John Nance, Manuel Elizalde, several anthropologists and sociologists flew into a clearing near the caves. John took his camera to begin documentation of the small tribe. Over the days and visits he became the spokesperson for the Tasaday documenting his observations of the small tribe based on seventy-two days of field work over a three year period. His book, *The Gentle Tasaday*, told the story of the cave dwellers.

Carol Maloney spent 14 days in observation, making recordings of speech patterns and vocabulary. She noted the language, recording their words and sounds and claimed the Tasaday had no words for bad, enemy, war, kill. She further documented that they had no word for agriculture, inferring they did not plant or harvest any crops.

The Tasaday were known to be living in Paleolithic conditions. They used stone tools and stone scrapers to create bamboo tools for piercing and sawing. They were not thought to be hunters but gatherers and trappers.

Of course I should have gone. It was the story of the Philippines for several years. I didn't appreciate the impact of the narrative in the garden. We met interesting Negritos on the weekends; villagers who stoned deer, who roasted frogs and bats in the forest. At the time, it seemed like one more 'adventure' with a very fast Manila crowd. Elizalde's reputation was well documented as a wealthy socialite, rumoured playboy.

As the Tasaday story proliferated around the world, scientists descended on the country like lions round a kill wanting a snatch of the best meat before the vultures descended. Like a burgeoning potential for a Nobel Prize for science, the Tasaday story flourished as the story of the century. Scientists climbed all over each other to be the first to observe the newly located Stone Age tribe thought to be living in caves in the southern Philippines. Each wanted to be on the early research team.

All the media wanted to report a scoop. A full crew from National Geographic flew in to document the newly discovered tribe. The whole world watched. Twenty-seven people formed the small group of Tasaday including seven men, six women and 14 children. It bothered me that there was so much attention to the small group, yet I was as interested as everyone else. Once the outside world infringed on the Tasaday world, they would never again be isolated. Whatever the reporters documented would be tainted from that point on.

Flash Floods

In Manila the story absorbed us. It consumed the world. The narrative presented a different perspective of the low-keyed events in Zambales where American students toiled with skilled Negritos; different also from our laughing weekend encounters with villagers who stoned deer and roasted bats in the forest.

In Zambales, everywhere I went around the campsite, the building site, a gaggle of wild-haired Negrito kids followed, floating around me like flies in the buttermilk. In the afternoons as I sat down, the swarm sat at my side. Sometimes we played hand games, sometimes we played word games. We started English lessons just outside the almost new school. It could have been Addis. It could have been Kampuchea. On occasion, Freddy assisted with Tagalog translation; great to have Freddy along, the only eleventh grader.

And then it happened: a flash flood.

A torrent of brown water, pounding down from the sky, surged through our campsite. In the dark night the rains beat down, unrelenting. One moment it was raining. The next moment we were ankle deep, then calf deep in dirty flood water. The strong rain flattened the tents as simultaneously water gushed through the canvas in a violent flow of mud and water. No one found any problem with the rain storm until the water surged over and through the tents leaving little doubt the force of nature was in charge.

We crawled out of our tents and gathered under the canopy of the big tree. We staggered around in the dark, skimming our flashlights over the ground. There was nothing to do but wait-out the storm. Waterlogged, soaked through to the skin, sleeping bags soaked and soggy, we waited. As the storm passed, we pushed up one tent and all crawled inside until dawn. No one slept, but in great resilience, the kids started telling ghost stories attempting to further terrify each other until daybreak.

At dawn, without sleep, we assessed the damage. The tents would dry. The sleeping bags would dry. Eventually our clothes would dry. Once again, the food stores were in trouble. The rice was soaked and washed away; a feast for the chickens perhaps. Like on a scavenger hunt, we wandered about salvaging the canned goods washed down road in the flood. As all the labels washed off, we engage in 'Name that Can.'

The villagers were no better off. We could not purchase anything from the local village. They were equally hit and at a loss. They were devastated. We, at great psychological advantage, had homes in the golden ghettos. This was a temporary assignment for us.

The flash flood affected everyone. We sent a couple of men with the boys to the local market two hours away to see what they might find that we could cook up. There was not much to purchase. The guys came back with rice, eggs and mystery meat.

The teenagers were great sports. They never complained about the inconvenience, and it was inconvenient. They never complained about their clothes being soaked through. They never griped about the food or lack of it. Everything was taken in stride in the spirit of adventure.

"Ok guys. What is this?"

"Hey man. It's meat."

"Right. What kind of meat?"

"Hey. It's meat."

"Ricky, you know Tagalog. What is it? How do you call it?"

"Hey man. I know Tagalog. Pero I don't know cooking stuff."

"It's not cooking stuff, it's some kind of animal, Ricky."

Since no one could identify the meat, Luis volunteered to, if not marinate, then pulverize the slabs. He grabbed a hammer and took each chunk of meat and began pounding it to a flattened state, a still unrecognizable slab of protein. Perhaps it was goat, or I didn't want to make the suggestion, dog. Actually, the dog meat or rabbit would be more tender. The beef, horse, goat meat was impossible to recognize and difficult to digest. Luis did his best to pulverize it before I cooked it to death.

It was not gourmet, but then, they probably wouldn't have jumped up and down for goose pate or escargot either. Teenagers will eat anything if you serve it with Tabasco. They joined in the meal prep and if they hated the food, they sure ate every morsel with committed zeal. They were starved by the end of the day.

"Hey Man, you sure this is dead?"

"Yeah, what is this?"

"You cooked it."

"Pass the Tabasco."

"Say 'please' you illiterate."

"Gimme that Tabasco, puleeeeze."

"Yeah, Man, your plate is heaped."

"Hey, like it's good; I'm starved. I like it."

"Me too. So bug off, Man. You're cooking tomorrow. Remember?"

"This stuff's a lot better than what my maid used to cook.

"Maaaan, she was awful. My mom finally told her it wasn't working out.

"Me and my dad thought she was trying to poison us."

"My dad and I. You can't speak English, Man, let alone Tagalog."

Pounding mystery meat

Cookin' it up

Friend or Faux

Fifteen years after the discovery of the Tasaday, a hoax theory took precedence as the new story of the Philippines. In my mind, the indisputable resemblance of the Negritos of Zambales, the Negritos of the woods outside Manila, and the aboriginal indigenous inhabitants of the caves remained irrefutable. Saying the Tasaday tribe was a hoax was like saying there was no Nessie, no creature of the Loch Ness. I didn't want to believe it.

Friend or faux? The critics pointed out legitimate reasons to question the Tasaday 'discovery' of Manual Elizalde. The length of time devoted to the study of the tribe was limited. The number of the group was too small to represent a viable Stone Age group. There was no indication of any long term life in the caves, no rubbish, no bones of the deceased. Some scientists claimed the tribe could not maintain their weight and dietary needs with only the foods of the region.

Why Elizalde wanted to concoct such a fabrication was open to speculation. Did he have interests in the mahogany of the forests? What other desires fed his ego? How much recognition did he seek? Photos corroborate Elizalde's needs to be respected, even deified some said; to be seen as a god-form descending from the helicopter, clutched and loved by the Negritos of the caves; seen holding and nurturing the exposed cave dwellers.

John Nance confirmed the existence and personalities of the tribesmen, women and children with photos and compelling narrative. The plausible notion is that the 27 members of the cave clan were simple, common *tao*, existing in Paleolithic conditions with stone tools. Nance describes each member by name, giving them personalities through photo documentation and translated conversations. After reading his book we knew and loved each member of the clan.

Evidence suggests that for whatever reason, the Tasaday were separated from the Manubo clan. The details of how long they were separated and why are for the anthropologists and social scientists to determine. Some have suggested 2000 years, which would put the separation at the time of Christ; others 500 years, 100 years, 2 years.

When Martial Law was declared in 1972, all press reports came under censorship. Local media reported nothing on the Tasaday. The next year Marcos declared a national preserve for the Tasaday and the area was closed to all outsiders for 13 years, devastating researchers. When Marcos fled the country in 1986, Swiss journalist Oswald Iten made an unannounced visit to the Tasaday area.

The caves were deserted.

There were many questions. He found the Tasaday living in houses, wearing clothes. The scientific community posed queries. The public was enraged. Were the Tasaday friend or faux? Authentic Stone Age cave dwellers or frauds? We felt duped.

Politically, it went something like this: When Benigno Aquino was assassinated in 1983, Elizalde left the country, rumored over conflict with Imelda Marcos, who was alleged to have masterminded Aquino's assassination. Elizalde, with PANAMIN funds it was said, fled to Costa Rica to live on a coffee plantation. He answered no questions, gathered up a group of young girls and remained silent, according to tsismis gossip. Eventually he was expelled from Costa Rica.* Marcos was forced out of the Philippines in 1986 after which time Elizalde returned spending the next three years defending the legitimacy of the Tasaday.

Pigs, floods and teenage labour-camp: working with the Negritos represented a living text book experience. Our village colleagues could have wandered up from Mindanao, as Tasaday, to live in Zambales. The social structure of the villagers could have been that of cave dwellers. Physically, they mimicked each other. I found it plausible that the Negritos of Zambales were of the same tribe as the Tasaday, who now experienced exposure to village life. The Tasaday family evolved year by year through trading and marriage; year by year by communication with others of the race; the human race.

The Tasaday in the caves of southern Mindanao, the Negritos in the woods outside Manila, and those at the mountains of Zambales seemed of the same clan and they taught us much. I wanted to believe they were of the same tribe.

Though we were not anthropologists, sociologists, linguists or reporters, we did build a school. When we packed our tents in Zambales the only remaining project was to assemble bamboo benches and tables. The walls, roof and main structure were up and ready for the new teacher who would arrive after the rains.

The New York Times obituary, "Manuel Elizalde, 60, Dies; Defender of Primitive Tribe,"

Robert McG. Thomas Jr. Published: May 08, 1997.

Scuba

Kathy knew the thought of diving made me break out in a cold sweat, even in the humid islands of the Philippines, of which there were 7,000 at high tide.

"Hi Dannie. I'm giving a SCUBA course next month. Wanna join?"

"No." She presented the opportunity every once in a while. I always said No.

She called anyway to ask if I would like to take a SCUBA course with the US ambassador's wife, Marie Sullivan. Every other expatriate loved to spend weekends diving in the beautiful waters of the Philippines. The idea scared me. The idea terrified me. I was phobic; irrational perhaps. Kathy Taylor belonged to the Professional Association of Diving Instructors, PADI.

Her kids studied at school and I liked them as young high school Third Culture Kids. She never pushed; never pressed me to dive. She offered courses regularly and offered an open invitation, 'Dannie, whenever you are ready.' I never accepted. Yet this time, she called and asked again. She presented the proposal as a one-on-one; an opportunity, in her mind. For some reason, this time I was okay with the idea.

A water-baby from birth, I grew up on the beaches of California. Water provided therapy; sun demanded worship. I was a California Girl and the Beach Boys were my ambassadors. We all loved the beaches. My own children grew up on the beaches of the Philippines to the tune of 'Tie a Yellow Ribbon.' It was a different era.

Swimming about in the depths of the sea, under the water, was of no interest. I was terrified of being under the water with no air. I should go under the sea, freezing, teeth chattering, my small frame turning blue, with no air and nasty creatures all about? Why?

Goggles, no problem; I enjoyed swimming with goggles observing beautiful blue and yellow and orange fish and multi-textured coral reefs. It was the mask that put me off. A wetsuit covering my arms, legs, torso fine, no problem, but don't cover my nose. Don't restrict my breathing.

Even with the snorkel, I could not relax. I couldn't get the rhythm. I thought if I took in the air with my mouth from plastic tube, ostensibly on the surface above the water, I would suck-up salt water. I just didn't get it. I couldn't make it happen. I panicked every time I tried, ripping the constrictor off my face like an octopus ripping lichen off a rock as if fighting for my life, fighting for oxygen.

I learned to snorkel just like I learned to swim. One day when I was about 8, while flapping my arms about in the public pool, the plunge, I realized I was swimming. Nothing was touching the bottom of the pool. I was dog-paddling, thrashing across the water. They closed the pool early that day due to a red-alert for smog. It was a hot summer day and the air hung heavy with pollution. As we walked home, it hurt to breathe. The California smog hurt all the way down the centre of my chest.

It was the same summer of a polio outbreak in southern California and another young girl rested in a green iron lung at the shopping centre. She was my age, living in a metallic green iron cylinder. I was impressionable. Now I wonder what my parents were thinking taking me to see her; what the community was thinking placing that girl on exhibition for the city to see. Gawk, pity, whatever the aim, I remember it clearly. I was claustrophobic even then.

I floated with a snorkel and mask, just holding the glass over my eyes, lifting my head and releasing the mask to breathe. All of a sudden it worked; I could do it, like learning to swim. I could use the snorkel and that was it. I breathed through that plastic tube.

I cruised with fins and mask and snorkel for hours, until my back blistered. The fish of the Philippine South China Sea sparkled in the shallow warm waters. I gathered shells, observed coral and ogled over tropical fish. I was never the same. I inadvertently mastered the mask; not by design, not by academic studious pursuit or from Kathy's class, but by accident. That was it.

Mrs. Sullivan wanted to take the SCUBA course and wanted to take it in her private pool at the residence. Kathy wanted me to take the course with Marie Sullivan. ' Would be better if she had a partner and Kathy thought I would be the perfect person. For some reason, this sounded reasonable to me. I sometimes still felt claustrophobic underwater and the diving tanks did nothing to eliminate this angst. Being in Marie's back-yard pool at the residence made sense. Just the two of us with Kathy.

I went to the Sullivan's every day for pool instruction, clearing minimal security at the gate. We also studied the physics and math segments of the diving. Kathy walked us through the instruction. Which was more difficult: the physics lessons or the instruction in the pool with the tanks? I did not study physics in school, so these concepts were new to me. I was nervous and still not comfortable with the deep sea but the lessons progressed and my confidence started to grow.

Marie Sullivan exhibited as much grace at the pool as she did at official functions. While her husband, Ambassador William Sullivan, explored diplomatic issues especially extending the land lease on US military bases, Marie pursued her own interests.

"We're living in a region which hosts the most beautiful water in the world.

"I want to be in it; I want to see what's there

"I want to explore the coral, swim with the fish.

"I want to learn everything. I have to do this while we're here."

I was not so sure.

Several times during the course, Jessica and Ian joined me at Marie's for water instruction. She graciously invited them to come along if they were not at school or working-out with the school age-group swim team. They loved the ice cold calamansi juice and cookies served on silver with linen cocktail napkins when we emerged for a break, dripping.

One session reviewed life saving instruction. Ian got excited about Resuscitator Annie who was twice his size. He was seven. He blew into her mouth and punched her chest until she breathed again. I knew I wanted Ian with me if I had any trouble in the water.

The kids were naturals with the equipment and gear. They learned how to put on the tanks, how to clear the regulators and suck up air from yellow tanks of oxygen. They both used junior tanks.

Jessica figured out how to waddle in flippers by lifting her knees and prancing to the water's edge. Big into image, she thought the best part was spitting into her mask and smearing it around the glass like a real diver; way cool. We learned that this coated the mask and prepared a clear vision through the glass. She could do that; it was awesome.

One day we put aluminium foil inside our masks to obstruct vision; we were to swim across the pool. Again my fears of claustrophobia emerged. Jessica floundered too. Academically, I knew I was in Marie's pool. Physically, I couldn't see anything. I flailed my arms, disoriented. Emotionally, I was a wreck. I soared to the surface like a flying fish. The pool was only 10 feet deep; had I soared to the surface in the ocean, I would have contracted the bends emerging at that panic pace. Jessica thought it was cool though scary and disorienting. She was nine.

Marie was ready. Bring it on. I was not that confident.

On The Beach
Just Us Girls

It was the weekend of the open water check-out dive. All of our training consisted of paddling around the luxurious embassy residence pool, cautious of chipping the tiles with our tanks.

This was the big test: the open water check-out dive required for certification.

We reserved *nipa* huts on the beach and drove to the water on Friday afternoon. Just us girls. Kathy's driver drove through village after village as we three chatted with great animation in the back seat. We piled our backpacks in the front so we could squeeze together in the back like college women on spring break.

We yakked all the way to the beach, mostly from nerves. Imelda was great fodder for discussion. That week, she invited multinational CEOs to Malacanang Palace including City Bank, Bank America, Firestone, Armor-Dial, Colgate, Mobile, Shell, Caltex, Intel and scores of others. Of course it was mandatory attendance. The CEOs hated those invitations. It took all day. The 'invitation' was for 9am. They arrived, and she showed up between 11am and 12 noon. Hurry up and wait.

The gist of the meetings involved quarterly reports of corporate earnings. Once reported, taxes were imposed and mandatory donations were requested for the personal projects of the First Lady. Imelda left no international corporation off the list. Corporate bosses in Ohio and New York, enraged, inferred that their country managers were not minding the store. Americans were not officially allowed to pay bribes, which was the only way to conduct international business with the Philippine government. And on it went.

"They say Imelda is in the mining business" Kathy offered.

"I never knew that," I said.

"When the CEOs, or worse, landowners, meet her she says, pointing dramatically,

'Dat's mine, dat's mine and dat's mine.'"

Marie rolled her eyes and we all laughed.

Bill Sullivan, Marie's husband, was ambassador to Laos before taking the post in Manila. We discussed the intricacies of Asia including the region of Cambodia and the new leadership of Pol Pot, of whom we knew very little, the crazy ways of the Marcos duo and the fabulous treasures in the Taipei Museum. We did not know it then; the Sullivan's would next be posted to Iran, not Asia.

As we drove to the beach through the villages, we named them all. Poinsettia Village was a riot in full bloom with double poinsettias that burst like exploding pyrotechnics. The heavy blooms heaved regally toward each side of the narrow road, their thick stalks awkwardly entwined. Chicken Village was famous for the proliferation of poultry; chickens that milled back and forth across the road, a confused collection, aimlessly pecking for insects; roosters and hens we artfully dodged at slow speed.

"So, why did the chicken cross the road?" It started.

"Duh. To get to the other side."

"OK. Why did the chicken cross the park?"

"Again?"

"To get to the other SLIDE."

"Arg.

"That's the world's dumbest joke. Third grade playground humour."

The driver looked in the mirror. Did he speak English?

"My turn. What did the chicken say to the bully?"

"Peck on someone your own size."

We drove on. Fingernail Village was known for a resident whom we often saw on the way home from the beach. She was an older woman with long flowing gray hair which hung down to her waist. Her claim to fame, as we saw it, was her finger nails. They were so long they curled under, all the way to her palms even when her fingers were extended. I'm not sure how we noticed this as we passed through the village; we never stopped. Yet this woman was often alongside the road. She was so striking that we always noticed her.

"Did you see that woman?"

"Her hair is so long."

"Did you see her nails?"

"They were so long. They were curled around, curled under. Did you see that?"

"She's the same woman we saw last time."

"How do you think she can peel a banana with those nails?"

"How can she do anything with those nails?"

We all looked at our own polished, manicured nails.

"Wonder what her toenails are like."

"No, I never noticed, but she had on rubber flip-flop *chinellas*.

"What size? How long were they? How long were her toenails?"

The driver looked straight ahead.

At the beach, I picked at the tepid rice and fish-heads for dinner then crashed before our morning checkout dive. Marie and I were way too nervous to enjoy a girl's night out. After dinner, in my small room, on a cot, I fell asleep anxious about the morning dive. I tumbled back and forth on the flimsy bed. At two in the morning the wind picked up and howled through the thin palm branches of the thatch. The sea slapped against the shore, like a scene in an angry movie; a slap across the face again and again. Whack, whack, whack.

I was wide awake. The storm built to a furious howl as it whistled through the small hut and the waves pounded with finality against the shore. They pummeled the beach until I wondered what would be left of the shoreline.

I tossed and turned as the force of the wind lashed through the hut. I thought of the pending morning dive. Suddenly, I saw the dive in reverse. What if I went down with my partner and was forced to bring her up because of the storm? What if I had to bring Kathy up? What if she was dependent on me, rather than my total dependence upon her expertise? What would I do?

Methodically, step by step, I went through the entire process of the dive: How to resurface from various depths and how to administer or share air, buddy-breathe with my dive partner. My pulse raced. It was an agonizing dive review. I did not sleep.

In the morning the wind whipped the whitecaps like staccatoed pointillism. My stomach heaved in nauseous maneuvers. The weather was not bad enough to cancel the dive. My head throbbed. I had to do it. I had to go through the routine of the open water dive.

We didn't talk much; even nervous giggles eluded us. The serrated water accentuated the whitecaps which danced on the surface of the sea. I did not feel cool; my palms were wet, my temples pounded like a tympani solo at the concert. I checked the buoyancy compensator, regulator, cylinder, pressure gauge, then put on the weight belt.

Marie and I walked into the sea from the shore, laden with greasy, cold fried eggs; our fins flapped ahead of us as we walked into the water. In we went. And down we went. For that dive, our first open-water dive, we walked into the water from the shore like gangly intergalactic creatures in black suits with long extended webbed feet. We lifted our knees high to thrust the creature-fins forward.

Kathy took the lead. She led us to the deep drop down the side of the underwater escarpment. Although it was churned and white-capped on the surface, we enjoyed the deep water somewhat. I was way too stressed to fully enjoy the beautiful fish, the urchins, the eels or the beauty of the escarpment edge. I concentrated on the maneuvers of dropping deep, and especially of doing the maneuvers to get safely back to the surface without the bends.

It was true. The deeper we dropped, the fewer colours we enjoyed. Closer to the surface the colours were bright with yellows, blues, reds and greens; all the primary and secondary colours. As we descended, the variety diminished until the only colours were dark and scary. Deep blues and blacks were visible but not the brilliant orange clown fish, black and white angel fish, striped lion fish and tiger fish, blue and green nudibranch that were spotlighted by the sunlight in the more shallow water. Everything magnified in the mask. An aquarium fish took on the size of a predator, exaggerated and magnified by the face-mask.

I was very happy to rise to the surface with my partner. We enjoyed good visibility and gave each other practiced hand signals during the dive, mostly thumbs up. I did not suck-up all my air on the first dive. We saw barracuda, which I identified and other tropical fish which I did not. I did have the presence of mind to acknowledge their beauty as they undulated in the deep.

That first dive was traumatic, partly because I had been up all night. It was all so serious, and rightly so. I never took diving for granted. I never took it lightly. If my family was going to be underwater, I sure as heck was not going to sit on the sand wondering if they were all right. I would be down in the water with them. And that's how it all played out.

After a sandwich, we went out in a boat and dropped over the edge for a second and third dive with more confidence each time. I can't say I was overjoyed with the whole experience. Weightlessness in water is a sensation of freedom, perhaps like they describe in space; still I never relaxed on any dive. I always felt tension; pressure to be aware, to be vigilant at all times. I felt like there was a big yellow proceed-with-caution sign just in front of me, around each shelf of coral.

Big fish scared the bejabbers out of me and I swallowed most of my air in several gulps when I encountered a barracuda, sleeping shark, anything larger than a gold fish.

Boy did we celebrate. That night really was our girl's night out. The three of us hooted like college coeds on a Saturday night. We congratulated each other, toasted Kathy, our brilliant instructor who got us through the certification process. We enjoyed bad local wine and toasted the owners of the huts and the cook who prepared terrible food. We toasted Ferdinand Marcos and Imelda. We toasted Nixon and Watergate. I slept like a princess that night. If there was a storm, I never heard a thing. Whoo Hoo! I was a certified SCUBA diver.

Black Gold

We never saw it coming; how could we? We snorkeled around Sombrero Island flipping our separate ways. It was not in the water; then it was. Though the kids played in the sand gathering crabs and building forts, most of the time we floated face-down in the sea, suction-cupped to our masks. We never saw it coming.

We drove to the beach, through all the familiar villages, hired a bangka and headed for Sombrero. Sombrero Island, named for the way the rock protruded from the water, was a great place to dive. Bangkeros took us to the island where we sometimes dived, sometimes snorkeled. We pushed our gear into the narrow hull of the bangka; towels, snorkels, masks, flippers, lotion, water, juice-boxes and sandwiches. The thirty minute boat ride was usually uneventful. If the water was calm, the kids balanced on the outriggers playing their own version of chicken. But sometimes the water was rough and we bounced about like popcorn dancing in the pan. Everyone knew about Sombrero, but no one was ever there when we went. It was our own island.

The kids played in the sand for a while but the relentless sun drove us into the water. We were all scavengers; at first we just collected pretty shells and coral bits. Later I studied the shells. I learned the categories of each class and phylum. I learned that collector-quality shells were not old, faded or tossed about in the ocean, washed up on the shore. Collector shells, the most beautiful shells, came from the sea alive or recently dead. In the beginning we brought home bags of cones, conches, cowries, olives, pecten and pieces of the above. I sat in the school library looking up shells and taking notes. Then I bought my own books to further classify and identify mollusks.

We decided to specialize. I collected and studied cowries. I looked for Asellus, Guttata, and Helvola. My favourite was the illusive pink based Mappa and everyone loved the small Cyprea Cribraria with its white polka dots on brown. Jessica looked for cones and Ian collected olives. Daryle picked up anything interesting, including several varieties of poisonous cones. He stuffed them into his Speedo-stretch-bikini, one generation removed from the thong: great potential for disaster there. It's hard to remember that those skimpy Speedo suits seemed appropriate beach attire; it was the 70's.

While visiting a shell dealer one year, I wandered about the back yard between mountains and pyramids of shells; not even pretty shells: shells to be exported for buttons and shell craft; for house and hotel décor; tacky mirrors and coffee tables embellished with shells and glitter. It turned my stomach.

I was part of the problem. Daryle tried to tell me that our little bags of shells on the weekend amounted to nothing; not in comparison to the systematic dredging of the ocean floors. The way it worked professionally, and we saw it all over the islands, local fishers gathered all the shells and took them to dealers who paid several *centavos* for each shell. It was the start of my ecological awareness of raping the environment. I learned to leave shells in the ocean and only take specimens that were unique or better quality than what I already had in my collection.

It developed into a serious hobby for us. The new learning consumed me. We attended shell meetings and shell auctions. I joined the Philippine Malacological Society and soon joined the Hawaiian Malacological Society.

"Hey, Ian. Look at this.

"I found a black olive, want it?"

"Um, le' me see it," he mumbled through his snorkel tube and flipped his way over to his sister.

"Cool. Thanks." He admired the beautiful black cylinder and dropped it into his mesh dive-bag. It looked like a purple black Greek Calamata.

We snorkeled most of the morning then took a break for sandwiches and drinks.

"Luuunch," I called over the lapping surf.

"Time to take a break.

"Get out of the water and have something to drink," I called out again.

"I'm starved."

"Me too. What do we have?"

"Drink some water and juice."

We dumped our bags of loot on the mats to pick and sort the good stuff. Jessica found a beautiful Textile cone, the best find of the day, plus broken coral bits and various specimens of pecten and cypraea. Daryle staggered out of the water, reached into his crotch and pulled out several interesting cones: Striated, Geograhpus, Leopardus. Hard to think of those cones, some of them poisonous, popped into his skin tight Speedo.

The simple packed lunch tasted like a feast. The liquid re-hydrated our souls and energized us before we headed back into the clear water that housed colourful schools of orange clown fish, black and white angelfish and electric blue aquarium fish. We never saw it coming.

The black wave of thick lubricant washed over us as we drifted in the calm water. We each noticed it at the same time. I rubbed my hands together, but the spot grew bigger. The slippery black covered my arms as I kicked toward shore. It permeated our skin and bikinis.

We surfaced from the sea, black and covered in crude oil, saturated in black grease. It covered our arms, clung to our legs and matted our hair like permanent greasy pomade.

I felt like a pelican drenched and covered by an oil slick. I wanted an ecology-volunteer to capture me, place me in a large plastic tub and mop off the oil with a soapy environmental solution. Our swim for the day was over. We ran to the other side of the island, but the slick was already there. We had no way to clean off with unpolluted water.

"Eeuw. Gross."

"Look at your hair."

"Don't touch me."

With towels, I mopped-down the kids as much as possible. The crude washed ashore from a huge tanker-spill like hot fudge over ice cream.

Sombrero was uninhabited. No trees, little vegetation; the bird life minimal. We felt like submerged water birds, drenched, overwhelmed, unable to fly. It was only us. The birds were not affected by this spill, at least on Sombrero. The oil leak suffocated the sea life below. By morning much would be dead without oxygen.

I tried to protect the car seats, but we had used the towels to scrub the lubricant off our bodies. Still we sat on the towels; I would throw them out anyway. *Bangkeros* took us back to the mainland where we slid into our car and silently returned home. I threw out all the swim suits; they were ruined. We showered and shampooed for days to get the tar-like bunker oil out of our pores, our skin, our hair. We left the island covered in Black Gold. Gold for somebody; a disaster for the environment.

Whar Be Yor Loot, Mai-ty

Pancakes with flavoured syrups, French toast, cheesy omelets, a full range of cereals and piping hot coffee greeted us each morning. The chef made magic in the galley, smaller than a master bath. Don Marshall, owner of Northwest Orient Airlines franchise and shipping tycoon, on several occasions most generously offered us his boat and crew to cruise the islands. The crew included a chef and a dive master. No detail was unattended. Meals, snacks and hors d'oeuvres, satisfied our needs and stimulated our palate.

We climbed over the side of the boat for a morning dive, came aboard for mid-morning *merienda* of grapes and cheese, juicy fresh-sliced mangoes, pineapple wedges or cookies and milk and another steaming pot of coffee. We rested, read books and identified coral with the kids before plunging in for the afternoon of more diving, snorkeling and shelling. The dive master kept the tanks filled, regulators clean and clear, organized the weight belts, and cleaned the salt off our fins and masks after every dive. Faulty equipment could mean a fatality. We were spoiled to have the luxury of a personal dive master.

In the heat of the day, we slid into the café-style benches to enjoy a lazy lunch inside the cabin.

"Pasta! I love this! Thank you!" from Jessica.

"How do you always know what we like?" Ian, to the chef.

"I'm glad you like it, Bibi. Are you hungry?"

"I'm really hungry."

Hot pasta, salads and soups, sometimes thick, layered sandwiches; we seemed to be voracious eaters after each water session. We rested and sort-of dressed for dinner, enjoying cocktails as the sun set.

Every night we watched for the Green Line or Green Flash as the sun dropped into the sea, but we never saw it there. I did see it once in the Philippines, but what I saw may have been another phenomenon. As the huge red ball of fire slid into the sea, the whole horizon line streaked green, a fine thin line where the water meets the sky at the edge of the earth, brilliant green. The photos I have since seen

---

* Red Sunset, M. M. Dworetsky, Department of Physics and Astronomy, University College London.(Originally published in Gnomon, Newsletter of the Association for Astronomy Education, December 1995)

indicate the Green Flash is but a small image over the red sun as it slips beyond observation. Jules Verne wrote in *Le Rayon Vert*. The Green Ray (1882).

> "...a green which no artist could ever obtain on his palette, a green of which neither the varied tints of vegetation nor the shades of the most limpid sea could ever produce the like! If there is a green in Paradise, it cannot be but of this shade, which most surely is the true green of Hope."*

At night we often slept on the deck because it was cooler than in the state rooms. The fresh air, the feeling of freedom, the oneness with the sky, the stars and sea was like camping on a waterbed. The stars glittered like handfuls of newly cut multifaceted diamonds rolled across a jeweler's cloth of black velvet. We lay on our backs identifying the constellations, nearly able to touch the Dippers and Orion's Belt. We watched for falling stars which streaked overhead as if they might land on deck.

What was that?

I stirred, not sure if I was awake. Nothing. I listened again. I listened toward a slight sound, not something I could identify. Some indication; a feeling, not really a sound, on my side of the boat: security guards. Instantly wide awake, I heard a muffled commotion. I shifted my eyes, not wanting to make a sound, to see what was trivial at first, then more pronounced as the guards pointed big green weapons at the water, whisper-shouting barely audible commands in Tagalog. I dared not breathe. I made out silhouettes in the night. Shapes in the water hovered next to the yacht. The boaters paddled silently, approaching the vessel. I never heard one splash; I never heard them approach. I never heard one ripple, one cough or whisper.

Up to that time, I was unaware of any night security. The men I saw on-board, I assumed were part of the crew, the maintenance, the sailors, the boatmen. I certainly never realized there were guns on board. Throughout the night, security guards maintained a rigorous vigil for our protection and the protection of the yacht.

The guards on watch confronted the bandits and prevented their entry on-board; prevented the confiscation of cameras, binoculars, alcohol, dive equipment, the boat itself, and kidnap abductions of the expatriates on board, aka our family. No one fired a shot. As silently as they arrived, they soundlessly paddled away, our security guns pointed directly as their heads; their own automated weapons confiscated. No one on deck spoke of it until morning. At sunrise we rolled off our cots and all talked at once in animated discussion.

"Did you see that last night? Did you see them?" to each other.

"What exactly happened last night?" to the guards.

"When did you see them?"

"Were you up all night?"

"Wow. Thank you for being there. So what did they want?"

"You're kidding? Pirates? Pirates here at this boat?"

"Eat your breakfast," to the kids.

"I think I'll sleep below deck."

Piracy was a known problem in Philippine waters. We were naïve, but fully aware after that night.

Stonefish

The weekend was unmercifully hot. We spent most of the hours during the day loafing in the warm shallow water or flipping about collecting ooh-ah shells and bits and pieces, even dead stuff that washed up on the shore. The gaggle of kids followed Ian back to where we sat in the shade.

"Ian, put it down.

"Drop it right now and wash your hands in the sea."

"Mom, it's cool."

"Ian, it's dead. Yes, I'm sorry it died, but we can't help it now." He reluctantly dropped the dead seagull. I wanted to talk about it in some way, make it an educational experience more edu-babble, but the decaying body put me off any discussion.

"Hey, we could bury it," said the curly-headed girl, then, "Why did it die?"

Thinking quickly and not wanting this to be a religious rite, I suggested,

"I think this is an old bird. Maybe an old grandpa seagull. Maybe he was tired after he helped raise all the grand-chicks. That's a nice idea to dig a hole and cover him up."

The project was on and the kids all helped dig the hole.

"Dig it right here, nice and deep, then just shove ol' grampa seagull into the hole. You won't have to touch him. You can just cover him with the dirt. Good idea you had."

The kids were never at a loss to discover new treasure: a rotten fish head, a dead crab or a gnarly piece of driftwood. I put my foot down when someone wanted to drag home the dead seagull.

We were a long *bangka*-ride away from any other islands and hours away from home; great to be out of the city. We found a beautiful stretch of sand and pitched our tents to enjoy snorkeling and camping with our like-minded friends and their kids.

We sat on low beach chairs partially submerged in the water reading trivia and trite beach-books in moderate comfort; a reprieve from the sun which covered us like a heavy blanket. The folks-back-home shivered in northern countries.

A few palm trees provided relief for lunches and breaks under the leafy coconut palms, and as a generous gift, the evenings were cool. Thinking back, we loved those searing weekends at the beach. For some reason, no one got sun stroke, no one's skin blistered and the kids always got along well. Water therapy; you can't beat it.

The camping meals were simple, and seemed gourmet. We thrived on lots of juice for breakfast and throughout the day; fruit and non-meat sandwiches for lunch and pastas for dinner. Sometimes someone brought steaks and charcoal, but usually it was too much to pack into a *bangka*. We started out with ice for afternoon beers and the cocktail hour, but the ice never lasted.

We usually made a small fire; not for warmth but for ambience. We sat up solving the problems of the world. Sometimes we listened to the BBC or VOA, for even though we relished being away-from-it-all, the news of the world was always on our minds. Our colleagues were out-there, possibly where the news was being made while we escaped at the beach. An earthquake, a coup d'état, everything had a ripple effect to our international lives.

By Sunday afternoon we packed up; time to take down the tents and bundle everything into the outriggers to head back to the cars, then Manila. Everyone pitched-in breaking camp. I helped take down the tent then headed to the water to cool off again before gathering up the other gear.

"I'll be right back; just gotta cool off a minute.

"It's sooo-- eeee!

"I stepped on something; a piece of ...oh!

"Man, I have to sit down."

I waded in, then stepped on a sharp piece of glass. It went right through the side of my rubber thong *chinellas*. It must have been a pop bottle shard. I hobbled back on shore as my foot started to throb. I couldn't walk and sat in the sand as the waves lapped against my legs. The pain shot up my ankle, then my calf. Someone carried me under the palm where I sat unable to continue.

I wanted to scream; to howl and moan. I couldn't make a scene; my kids were there. I couldn't control my response. The pain was excruciating. Man oh man. It hurt so much and, I don't know where this idea came from, I grabbed someone's towel, twisted it and placed it between my teeth so I wouldn't shout out. I did moan; I couldn't control it. I hoped it was muffled.

What was this pain? I felt the throbbing, somehow accentuated by the unforgiving sun. The sensation pounded like a constriction-expansion pulsing faster and harder toward the epicenter of my circulation.

I tried to see where the glass was. Maybe I could pull it out. There was no blood. It was not a shard. I stepped on something else, but what? Daryle went back to the edge of the water. There was nothing there. No sharp metal object, no sharp piece of shell. There was only one answer. I stepped on a perfectly camouflaged stonefish. I already knew this was the most poisonous fish in the world and deadly.

The venom is in the dorsal spines. It is part of the lionfish and scorpion-fish family. I had seen them before while hovering over a spot and always carefully avoided them, especially if there was any current in the water. They are difficult to see because of their grey mottled colour. They look like the sand or stony bottom of the sea.

We often spotted zebrafish, tigerfish, turkeyfish, especially the beautiful lionfish. They seemed to float by gently waving their fins like large Spanish fans. I have read that the lionfish can be aggressive, lunging toward your mask, but I never experienced that. Stonefish, by contrast, rest on the sand or stony bottom, not swimming about, but shuffling along like a slow-moving snow plow gently fanning the water and the sand.

Others managed the tents as my foot swelled to double size. By the time the *bangkas* were loaded, my leg was swollen past my knee to the diameter of an elephant leg. Not sure how my skin stretched so much, like my leg was pregnant. There was nothing to do. Some injuries can be cleaned by using vinegar or urine on the wound. No one offered. Someone rummaged up an aspirin. The pain continued for hours. When we returned to the house there was no power; no water.

"Arg. Again. There's no power."

"Yeah, there's no water, either."

"Okay, let's go to the club and shower there. They will have power."

We were salty, sticky and tired. Daryle grabbed clean, dry clothes for everyone and we proceeded to the Manila Polo Club where I hobbled into the locker rooms to clean up. Jessica helped me sit on a shower stool while I ran hot water over my beleaguered foot and leg, while still in my swim attire. It seemed too much effort. I didn't know it then, but the hot water was excellent therapy for the venom. It seems the hot water cooks the poison destroying or dissolving it.

"Are you alright?" from a friend at the club.

"Yeah, I will be," I mustered up a smile.

"What happened? Did you do that here at the club?"

"No, it's from a stonefish."

"When did you do that? Where were you? Your leg is huge."

"This afternoon; we just got back.

"No power at the house, so we came up for a swim and shower."

"Oh, good idea. We didn't have power this morning either, but it came back about noon."

"We'll just wait it out."

"I hope you feel better. That's a nasty looking leg."

"Thanks. I'll be fine."

And of course I was.

Echinoids

I enjoy a love-hate respect for sea urchins. I've eaten them once or twice but not as a first choice; never 'let's go out for sea urchin tonight.' Nope. Today, however, I would be more inclined toward the roe with a dollop of wasabi on the side or minced onion. I love the beauty and variety of the urchins. I don't love when I get stung. Urchins, from the sea, are part of the Echinoidea class, the echinoderm phylum. I know this now because of our search for the fossilized echnoids years later in the dunes of Saudi Arabia.

One weekend as we snorkeled outside of Manila, we came upon a shoreline of sea urchins. They weren't there when we pranced into the sea with our flipper fins. However, as we returned to our towels on shore, we swam up to a black field of spines.

The spikes spread across a swath of several meters with hundreds of sea urchins of numerous varieties. The scary ones exhibited long three inch black spines which we attempted to avoid as we glided along on our bellies. The long dark needles spiked up like poisonous pin cushions glimmering in the afternoon sun. In the shallow water, the spines brushed our stomachs as we drifted glass-eyed over the sand. The dilemma was to avoid standing up, smashing the urchins as they simultaneously spiked us, or to back-pedal away farther down the beach to make an alternative landing on shore. These urchin spines break off in your skin and are painful reminders of who's in charge in the water. While not particularly harmful, they are a literal pain until they dissolve.

Others of the echinoid family exhibited colourful red spines or porcupine striped spines which swayed in the slow surf. I spied a beautiful urchin and reached down to scoop it up to examine more closely. The perfectly round, pinkish globe looked like an offering on a cocktail tray. Each tiny spine held a different miniature shape. It looked like a cocktail hors d'oeuvre offering of circle, diamond, spade shapes, like treats on the end of toothpicks. Each spear supported a different shape on its tip. As I balanced the sphere on the palm of my hand, it projected poison from the tips of the mini javelins into my fingertips. Shocked and in denial, I continued to observe the beauty of the form. Unlike the pencil urchin, whose thick spines served as wind chimes, the delicate spears shot through my fingertips. As I observed in innocence, in naiveté, that cocktail oval harpooned me. Where's the justice.

Wonder Woman in Rubber

Whatever possessed me to make a night dive is beyond my comprehension. What was I thinking? Why did it seem like a good idea?

Others.

It always comes down to someone else's idea of a brilliant experience. There was no divarication. Everyone was into it. I wondered if sharks can smell fear, as they say dogs can. Sharks do register frenzy sometimes caused from fear and panic. Okay, there are fish swimming about in the night. Why disturb them? I made my first and only night dive with my family. Don Marshall again offered us the use of one of his boats, the Stiggins, with a full crew and dive equipment for a three day weekend.

I looked over the edge of the boat.

The water was black.

I leaned over further, closer to the water's edge; still black. It was nine o'clock at night. I could see nothing but undulating black water. My mind raced. I imagined octopi gargantuana waiting for me with ten meter tentacles ready to wrap around my legs and my wet-suited body. I envisioned twenty meter sharks and long black eels the diameter of my head.

We were leagues from any land and anchored in the middle of the South China Sea.

The cabin was abuzz. Everyone else was excited. I helped the kids with their wet suits, then slipped into my own and zipped up tight from my crotch to my neck, wonder-woman in rubber.

The crew readied the equipment. We check our regulators, weights and paraphernalia and spit in our masks. The only additional gear included a torch. A torch: a tiny-beamed underwater torch; a torch to light the way, this little light of mine, oh–my–god, to illuminate a narrow swath of formidable, opaque marine.

We climbed over the edge of the boat, unable to utilize the ladder due to the awkward length of the fins. I breathed out slowly as I descended into the ebony sea. I stayed under on sheer adrenalin, though I wore lots of weights on my belt. We each carried our light.

I wanted to see where I was going and what was out there. I wanted to be there; I hated being there. I needed to see what was in the beam of my light. I did not want to know what was in the beam of my light. Nocturnal fish are huge. I could only see what was in the narrow corridor of the beam.

Swinging the torch in a wide circumference, I looked to one side then to the other, afraid of what I might see. I swung around sure that something huge was preying on me, behind me. I swiveled from side to side, causing whiplash from my huge yellow tank as I fanned my torch in all directions. Small schools of fish scurried by in the beam of my light, this way, then back again, as if triggered by some remote control. Big fish came at me, then moved on as I swallowed up cubic kilos of air.

Jessica and Ian ebbed and flowed between their father and me, seemingly loving it all, taking it all in, gesticulating in gregarious hand gestures of underwater sign. A sea turtle hovered; strange that it was deep and so far out to sea, possibly migrating; reassuring, somehow, the Chinese symbol of stability. Most beautiful of all, a manta ray floated by, like a magic carpet.

Who could relax? Who could enjoy this? I felt stressed and tense the entire dive. No doubt I ate my air way too fast because I gulped it in fear. I did it. I made the night dive qualifying me to babble away at the next cocktail party.

I thought of other night excursions.

If you want to observe nocturnal life, you have to go out in the dark. Even as a kid I didn't like the dark. I wanted my bedroom door left open so I could see a light somewhere. I wanted the closet doors shut because I didn't know what might be lurking in the dark space. My monsters were the unknown.

On night safari anywhere in Africa, searching for lion or leopard, there is at least the protection of a vehicle. When you are in the water diving there is no protection unless you carry a spear gun and that wouldn't help in most circumstances.

I experienced a similar rush of trepidation when boating in the dark in the Okavango swamp. Never mind the crescent moon shining on the water. It was not a moonlight cruise. Hippos, one of the most dangerous African animals, loiter in the water before lumbering on land to graze during the night. At any moment, if disturbed, the rounded mound might emerge, splitting the canoe and submerging the victim.

I felt the same terror from this night dive. A thrill a minute, an exhilarating experience, a brilliant opportunity some called it. I wasn't that brave. I always went along and have lived to tell the story, but always as the reluctant adventurer.

I like being a risk taker; thinking outside the box, taking thoughtful chances. I'm not so courageous when it comes to my life, especially after dark.

I was not the first one back in the boat; after all, Jessica and Ian, the children, went on that dive with junior tanks. I was not the last one either. As soon as someone made a move back toward the boat, I made an abrupt u-turn, gently kicking my fins, so as not to generate a frenzy. We quickly, cautiously, made our way back on board. This time we staggered up the starboard ladder. We clutched the railings and heaved ourselves up the rungs, the fins a great hindrance.

I was out of that wetsuit at warp-speed. As we surfaced, aromas of a four-course meal surrounded our senses. We ate like predatory sharks in a ravenous frenzy. The night dive, diving with the monsters, injected a kinetic energy. We all slept a sleep as deep as the sea we invaded, like huge sea turtles sprawled on our beds in Asian stability; stable in a tranquil sea.

I missed Marie, my first diving partner. She probably would have thrived on the night dive, if she could have found any security men to go with her. She and her husband transferred to Iran where William Sullivan served as US Ambassador in Teheran often meeting with Shah Mohammed Riza Pahlevi. Ambassador Sullivan was responsible for 35,000 Americans living in Iran.

I never dived in the dark again.

Soup

Soap

unt

Souls

INTERNATIONAL
SCHOOL OF UGANDA LTD
P. O. BOX 4200, KAMPALA
TEL: 200374

Sister Katryn

Lasers beamed through the screened porch drenching wild orchids; burgundy, white and yellow, all collected during trips to the rainforest. It was early, not yet humid, not yet searing; still fresh and unscented from the pollution of the day. The time of day when heads are clear, minds are sharp. I sat outside at breakfast with my family.

While we ate, thousands of refugees pressed across the border from the Killing Fields of Kampuchea into Thailand. The torrent of devastated souls, presented a crisis of international dimension.

The world community however, was not yet aware. In Manila, we read sketchy reports that indicated an enormous disaster. The story wrapped itself around my head; I didn't sleep. I had no plan, no personal expectation of my contribution, but this time I felt I could not just choreograph a gala fund raiser, or write a check.

Friends with World Vision filled me in on unreported details. A UNHCR refugee camp opened on a few day's notice at the border of Kampuchea and Thailand. They waited for staff to run it. I wanted to go. The more I considered the idea, the more I obsessed.

At breakfast I tried to articulate my thoughts as much for myself as for my family. Was this a knee-jerk bleeding-heart response? What could I actually do in a refugee camp? Would I be in the way? My senses stirred, I felt confident I could make a contribution. I discussed it with my family, the need there, the plight of the refugees and the implications of Mom being gone for a period of time.

"Sure Mom. Why not? Noooo problem. Can I have some syrup?"

"Please; say please." The reminders never ended.

"That's my shirt, ya know?" The disputes never ended.

"So, what do you think?"

"About what, Mom? Oh yeah."

"We'll be ok. They neeeed you," all conversation seemed overly dramatic.

"And besides, it's not that big a deal, ya know, you being gone." Hmm.

"You should go. Dad's still here, soooo?"

"Can Perla bring more mangos? PULEEZE?"

To my surprise I guess, my family supported my concerns. I wasn't as indispensable as I wanted to think.

Ka-chink. Ka-chink. A grimy overhead fan pushed the wet, humid air. Two days later, I sat in the neglected, under-funded office of World Vision, Bangkok. I waited for a driver to take me to the frontier. Earlier that morning, at my desk in Manila, I systematically scheduled first class airline tickets for multi-national corporations.

As an international "local-hire" for the airlines, I used the opportunity to catch a quick flight to Bangkok. I knew the Thai capitol somewhat. I attended education meetings in Bangkok over the years and went on the infamous, never-to-be-forgotten 'Fam-Tour' culminating in the erotic banana dance. The city was not new to me. The Manila station manager, a large American man, promoted from within the organization, up-from-the-ranks, incorrectly assumed the only reason women travel is to shop. He approved the pass request and asked me to bring back "a little something for his wife." I accepted the pass without comment.

I jumped in the open jeep with the Thai driver. We jinked along. Traffic was slow and horrific, bumper to bumper, from downtown Bangkok directly east, straight to the border of Cambodia. Once through the traffic, the pace picked up; my hair raged and slapped me in the face as we flew down the road. The driver said,

"If the Cambodians invade Thailand, they will be at the border in less than an hour."

He paused for effect, then looked at me in the rear-view mirror.

"But it will take three days to get through the Bangkok traffic."

"Ha, ha. I make big Bangkok joke," he attempted. "Ha, ha. Funny joke."

Khow-I-Dang camp-site came into view. I stared at the sight of sprawling disjointed tents: small tents, large tents, tents with the sides rolled up for ventilation, army green and hospital white; they represented a mishmash of a temporary city. Thousands of Cambodian and Vietnamese refugees milled aimlessly about the area and hundreds remained listless on the ground under the branches of lethargic trees.

Khow-I-Dang opened on four day's notice on November 21, 1979 as waves of refugees fled the communist government of Kampuchea. In four days UNHCR mapped out the overall design of the camp and developed a simple infrastructure: roads/trails, water tanks and toilets. The first day, it was reported, 4,800 people crossed over the border and into the Khow-I-Dang camp. By the end of the next month there were 84,000. In the next three months the population expanded to 160,000.

Sister Katryn bounced off the balls of her feet as she walked; as if her sensible shoes were mounted on mini pogo sticks. Her wiry gray hair protruded randomly from under her tidy headscarf. She carried a Swiss passport.

We met on the fringes of the Killing Fields. She took me by the hand and pulled me toward the epicentre of the camp where we sat cross-legged on a mat with a group of Vietnamese. They discussed the situation in French and Swiss/German sprinkled with English adjectives, gliding seamlessly between languages. Sister Katryn used Swiss/German, the Vietnamese knew French. I faked it and tried to get the drift of the conversation. I could fumble through Amharic and Tagalog, and some Spanish. I needed Vietnamese, French and German. After a few introductions, she took me on a tour of the huge 2.3 square kilometre site.

The entire encampment moved about in slow motion, like a scene from a black and white film clip. Slow, dark, silent and fragile; there was no colour, no laughter, no energy, little life. The Khmer Rouge wore black, wide-leg pants, cut too high above the ankle; their bare legs and feet extended through the pant-legs like broom sticks on a scarecrow. Black Mandarin shirts, with straight wide sleeves, exposed bone-thin arms. They wore red scarves tied around their heads like sweatbands controlling their shoulder-length black hair; like unkempt hippies from the Beat Generation. They milled about listless, reminiscent of emaciated representatives of Goth. The silence weighed down on the encampment like a dense cloud. No shoes. No laughing. No singing. No running. Death, illness, weakness permeated the oppressive, humid camp site.

The chirpy nun, still springing off the balls of her feet, ushered me through the maze. Off to the side, still in full view of the campsite, she pointed out the area where they stacked cadavers. Behind a stick fence, bodies slumped respectfully on top of each other, a mound of distorted faces enfolded in black pyjamas; just from the day. I looked away. Intense heat and humidity of Thailand demanded immediate disposal of the bodies. Large black crows circled ominously adding to the gloom.

As we completed the orientation tour, I asked,

"How can I help? What do you want me to do?"

Sister Katryn looked at me with great hesitation and compassion. She saw right through me; saw my youth and naiveté. I felt over dressed in my jeans with my fitted t-shirt and little gold chain. Her kind eyes peered into my soul. She tentatively suggested,

"If you would, walk through the tent every 15-20 moment and roll everyone over on their opposite side," she paused. She pronounced all 'W's like 'V's and didn't bother with 'TH.' It came out like,

"If you vood: valk srough ze tent every 15-20 moment..."

Then she added,

"Ve need to be sure zere is circulation in zere bodies unt and ve need to determine if any half died." I sucked in my breath.

I hesitated; my hands shook. I had no medical training; well I had Red Cross life-saving certificates and several CPR courses. I had never been exposed to death. I took a deep breath; Sister Katryn forced me to stretch. Inside the dark tent my eyes adjusted as I walked down narrow aisles between rows of fragile bodies. Comatose refugees rested side by side, shoulder to shoulder, on straw mats against the earth without the luxury of cots. A rotten odour hovered in the tent. I knew it was exhaustion, plus dirt merged with sweat, merged with filth, merged with vomit and urine.

Wretched clothes enmeshed in grime, stuck to frail sweaty bodies. The atmosphere felt like death. They needed cleaning-up. First, they needed to survive. I kneeled down. I gently rolled-over the first body, hesitant, reluctant to touch the person's dusty clothes and thin frame. Was I touching a corpse? Was the body dead or hopefully alive? As I did, I felt a warmth flow from somewhere deep inside, which passed through my arms and hands and fingers to his shoulders and body. From this simple gesture we both felt strength.

Robber Docky

S ister Katryn gave me a large green World Vision t-shirt. She said it would help with identification and security within the camp. Over the days I crisscrossed the camp talking with peasants and children through an interpreter. Their stories broke my heart. Cambodians, forced to flee their simple villages, hiked and marched day after day, week after rainy week. When the grains of rice ran out, families survived on plants, grasses and leaves. Wet, damp children were easy prey to influenza and pneumonia. After months of abuse and malnutrition only the fittest staggered and crawled to the camp, some to die days later.

The Khmer Rouge ruled Kampuchea from 1975-1979 with a unique philosophy of communism. It was their aim, under the leadership of Pol Pot to create an agrarian-based communist society. First, they deported all city dwellers and forced them to the countryside to work in compulsory labour with the local villagers. It was their aim to eliminate, by death, all capitalists or people involved in free enterprise.

Part of the philosophy of the Khmer Rouge was to develop a society that was self sufficient, including producing their own medicine. Many died because common illnesses were not treated, especially malaria. Other villagers were executed and tortured on trumped-up excuses.

When it became clear that the leaders had not planted enough crops, and thousands died of starvation, the villagers began a mass exodus to the Thai border.

One afternoon I noticed a twelve-year-old girl the age of my own healthy, exuberant daughter. She sat up on her sparse cot. Her bone-thin arms hugged her knees. She could have been any gangly teenager, but she wasn't. She was alone. She said her name was Samnang; the translator told me it meant Lucky. Her wide grin belied her personal tragedy as she clung to the hope that I might locate her family. I wondered if she had been separated from her parents because they were 'polluted by capitalism;' if she had been sent with other children to be re-educated in the new ways or if they were separated in the throngs along the way.

I sat on the edge of her cot. We didn't talk about hot music hits, or hair styles, or prom dresses. Still, we connected. She told me about her family, I showed her pictures of my daughter and son. She sparkled. What was my daughter's name? How old was she? Did she go to school? Then, more importantly, could I find her family? Would I tell her parents where she was staying? Would I please see her tomorrow? This young girl was not symbolic of the broken families of refugees. She had attitude. I knew Samnang would make it; I knew she was Lucky.

Most families were wrung-out; families who lived for days and weeks on grass and leaves, gnawing on bark stripped from trees, families who crawled to the border. An old gentleman grinned. Able to sit-up on his cot, he talked and chatted about his family. His name was Piseth, which meant Special. Without his shirt every bone of his torso was exposed. His concave stomach made me cringe, though he was animated and optimistic.

Two young brothers however, Ratanak and Raksmei, sat glassy-eyed and speechless and I was never able to break through their trauma. Ratanak, was said to be ten, the age of my strapping, loquacious son; the younger child was thought to be seven. He looked four. I showed them the photos of my children, especially my ten year old, mango-eating son but they could not respond. They stared through me, eyes glazed over. The interpreter told me their names meant Treasure and Ray of Light. I was not hopeful.

Sister Katryn gave me hands-on training for administering intravenous injections. The weakest required intravenous feeding. She sat on the edge of a cot and instructed. I followed step-by-step, practicing with the refugee on the adjacent cot. Holding the thin arm, with pressure applied, pulling the skin taut, I aimed for the vein. She asked if I felt ok giving

Samnang, age 12

Raksmei age 7, Ratanak age 10

the injections. I had never given anyone a shot.

"Not to vorry, about a fatality.

"If ve don't feed zees people, zey half no chance," she encouraged.

"Vill it botter you if za needle hits za bone?

"Zees people half no meat on zeir bones; is easy to miss-your-aim."

She was matter of fact. I went on to the next cot; there was no time for a full internship, too many to assist. I plunged the long needle nearly through the thin arm. The next person I stabbed at a better angle.

Gotcha!

I proceeded with great gusto dripping the nutrition into the skinny arms of refugee patients. I became moderately adept. That is, I hit my mark more frequently, and realized again, Sister had forced me to stretch.

Within several days professional volunteers arrived from around the world. Doctors from France, Belgium and Sweden, missionaries from Australia and New Zealand, and international religious and health organizations offered assistance. As a group we developed an instant camaraderie. The French doctors, with Medecins Sans Frontieres emitted adventure and enthusiasm, oozing charisma speaking English with sex appeal. Ooh-la-la, le men and weemen are sooo sexy.

At the end of the day, we grew incongruously, outrageously silly, hysterical with laughter; a relief from the oppressive environment. We laughed about politics. Manila had Imelda, the great dramatist, China had the Gang of Four and Ching Chi'ang, the former dramatist, America had Nixon, and everyone had Sesame Street; It's Not Easy Bein' Green, we all sang in French, German and English.

> Robber Docky you're zee von,
> You make zee bat time so mush fon,
> Robber Docky I'm 'fully fund doff yooo,
> Vuu, Vuu Bee Duu.

We laughed about our clothes, dusty and rumpled, we laughed about our mothers: if they could see us now.

In a quiet place, in the local two-star hotel, each night I listened to my battery operated shortwave, turning to the BBC. Two weeks before, Iranian student radicals stormed the US Embassy in Teheran. Seventy employees were captured, some later released. Fifty-two Americans remained.

Where were Marie and Bill? William Sullivan, Marie's husband, was appointed ambassador to Iran after leaving Manila; Marie, my scuba partner; Marie, my open water, Whoo Hoo, certified SCUBA diving partner. I wondered if Marie escaped the students and waited-out the news with the rest of us. Was she hiding or was she captured, held hostage in Teheran? Did she escape to a secure place outside the country to wait for news? I also waited to hear.

One night, after a particularly difficult day of deaths and infant deaths at birth, I confessed to the medics about my first attempt with their needles. The doctors leaned forward on the mats to hear the details. I over dramatized with California Valley-Talk for effect.

"The Sister tells me," I started, "You VILL give shots to zee refugees."

"Moi?" I re-enacted gesturing with ten fingers pointing inward toward my chest.

"Like, fer sure… like, I mean… I, like totally, do not know how to do this."

The French doctors leaned in and listened carefully to get the drift, while they laughed at my dramatization.

"Ve neeeed you, she told me most convincingly."

I continued, impersonating Sister Katryn who sat on a nearby cot not sure where I was going with this story.

"Here's vat you do," I exaggerated.

"Oh-m-god. How could I say 'no'? She made me do it; I had no choice.

"Does anyone say 'no' to Sister?

"I'm sooo glad you reeeal doctors finally arrived," I sounded like my kids.

"She made it look so easy.

"When I took hold of an arm I felt the bones.

"I pulled the skin taut.

"I searched for a suitable place to insert the needle.

"I stabbed like someone throwing darts at the club.

"I missed.

"The problem is your bloody needles don't behave under my tutelage.

"They're way too long; they just go right through the arm; in one side, out the other.

"Oops. That can't be right.

"Geeze, I nearly missed the arm altogether. Once, I even hit the bone.

"I'd never make it in med school.

"'Not to vorry,' Sister says to me.

"'Try again, up here.' Sister was hopeful. She made me do it.

"I was shaking sooo hard with every frail body on each cot.

"They were individuals," I whispered. "Each with a horrific story,"

"And while I hoped I might save them, I actually thought I might, like totally, kill them."

"I tried so hard to be brave, I tried to be brilliant, even confident," I confessed.

"Thank God, you professional doctors arrived.

"I'd still be out there piercing those skinny arms like stabbing shrimp at a cocktail party."

Tears rolled down their cheeks from the incongruity of it all, then from genuine gratitude for my being there before they arrived. Sister Katryn giggled and said, "You vas brilliant." We all laughed again. She sparkled, like a single drop of humidity on the dusty mat.

I continued to listen to my shortwave radio. I listened; the world listened. The world focused on the daily drama unfolding in Tehran. The hostages had not been released, or rescued. Few were aware of the emerging crisis in Thailand, in the refugee camp; too many tragedies playing out at one time. How much could the world absorb?

Charlie's Angels

Each night, news reports from Iran counted-out the number of days of the hostage siege; with no hint of release. It was now 21 days.

In Thailand, the press reported the annihilation of two to four million citizens by the Khmer Rouge, the Cambodian Communists, under the leadership of Pol Pot.

At Khao-I-Dang families carried limp bodies of relatives and gently placed them under the canvas of the hospital tent. On the other side of the tent, volunteers set up a paediatric unit for new mothers who struggled to nurse dependent children from their own emaciated, malnourished bodies. Many babies were born in the camp, some died within days. They whimpered at birth with no energy to wail out their birth announcement.

Women suffered during deliveries often giving natural childbirth with no medications. The screams came at unexpected hours. I did not know about midwifery but women know such things instinctively, to hold a hand, to place a cool towel, to offer comfort.

The screams disturbed me; babies hardly had a chance; mothers suffered pain and loss. But the strongest mums survived and their infants miraculously did have a fighting chance at life. What a gift those newborns represented; symbolic of positive possibilities.

In a huge white tent, the mess hall, nutritionists prepared thick grey bisque to approximate the local porridge, a cross between oatmeal, and miso soup. Many could not tolerate even this bland, glutinous mixture when they first arrived.

Atop gas burners, the steaming grey gruel bubbled-up on the surface of huge black kettles. Unlike the witches from Macbeth, the chef stirred each pot, one by one, with great compassion; with optimism and hope.

When I wasn't stabbing fuel into a pencil-thin arm, three times every day we ladled-out the thick provisions to anyone who could sit up and hold a spoon. Flatbed trucks slowly delivered large drums of soup to each tented area.

The porridge sloshed to the rims of the containers, and like the surf at high tide, sometimes lapped over the sides. Unable to get off their cots, some sat with bowls in hand as I walked down the aisles scooping from a red plastic bucket like the lunch server in the school canteen.

Those able to walk brought their plastic bowl to a distribution centre where we dished-up the nutritious mix. The weakest required intravenous feeding for which I was now infamous.

That night i did not know that Marie and William Sullivan left Iran earlier in the spring and were not part of the hostage group. That night I also did not know that Bill Keough however, was entrapped at the embassy.

Bill was head of the International School, Islamabad, Pakistan. His previous work had been in Iran as head of Tehran American School. As the Iranian Revolution evolved and the Shah was overthrown, the school was forced to close. As a temporary precaution, he stored vital school records and text books at the embassy. On November 04, 1979, he flew back to Iran, from Islamabad, to collect the school records from the US Embassy.

As he unpacked the files from the secure safe-room, radicals stormed the embassy; wrong place, wrong time. I didn't learn of this until later. The following year, when he was released, we met at international education meeting, perhaps in Athens, several months after his liberation. He didn't say much; didn't talk about his ordeal. I read he died four years later.

I followed Sister Katryn across Khao-I-Dang, scuffing up the dirt as we hiked through the camp. Sister bounced along; I ploughed. I vowed to learn that bouncy stride; walking like Charlie's Angels, without the wind-blown flaxen hair. Under the shade of leafy eucalyptus, make-shift language schools accommodated students who sat on the ground. Sister Katryn waved.

Clusters of refugees, young children, older men and women, some families, studied English for the first time, in preparation for relocation.

> They learned how to board a plane.
> How to wear a seat belt.
> How to use the airplane toilet.
> No, you cannot wash your hands in the toilet;
> you must sit on it; you must not stand on it.
> And about airline food service;
> no, you cannot cook rice on the plane.

They learned what to anticipate, as these displaced persons vaulted into an inconceivable new life. As I strolled by, they tried their latest phrases or two-word sentences.

"Goo moh-ning Mad-ham. How ahh yoooh?"

As refugees proceeded with paperwork, passports, and entry visas, they prepared to leave Khow-I-Dang. They left with little more than the few possessions with which they arrived. They hugged loved ones who could not yet leave, and reluctantly, with much reservation, some with rubber slippers, some still barefoot, climbed onto busses which took them to Bangkok and international destinations.

One hour to the border, three hours through the Bangkok traffic.

It was on one of those evenings in the quiet, reflective hours, that Sister Katryn, my tough, Swiss nun confided to me,

> "Soup, soap unt souls.
> "Dat's vat ve belief.
> "First ve feed zem,
> "Zen ve clean zem up,
> "Unt zen, unt only zen,
> "Ve save zem."

Today, television coverage continues to portray the plight of refugees and one sees today's victims of Milosevic, victims of Darfur, victims of Rwanda, the targeted population of Robert Mugabe, victims of Afghanistan, the Marshlands of Iraq, in the same light as the victims of Pol Pot.

Refugees traverse borders throughout Africa, and Afghanis push their way into Pakistan. I know these refugees: I have seen them in Peshawar, in Islamabad, in San Diego, Miami, in Mumbai and Delhi, in Saudi, in Beograd. They come in different costumes, with different languages, with different causes and different reasons to flee. I wonder: where is Sister Katryn? Wherever she is, at a campsite, a refugee centre, I know she is serving up soup, soap unt souls.

Reflection

Bill and Marie Sullivan transferred from Manila to Tehran where he again served as US Ambassador. I was surprised to learn that he moved out of the Asia region where he had developed his area of expertise. In Iran he served as the liaison between the Shah of Iran and US President Jimmy Carter. I have read that there was conflict from the beginning of his assignment. Sullivan wrote his own book on the subject regarding the relationship of the US and the Shah.

The gap between Sullivan and Carter grew; escalated to a level of mistrust. Sullivan left his position in the spring of 1979 and Charge'd'Affaires Bruce Laingen took over months before the storming of the embassy by revolutionaries.

I came to the border compelled by the plight of the homeless. I came not as a nurse, though I did nursing, not as a nun, though I did counseling, not as a teacher, though I did teach. Did I make a difference? Can any individual make a difference? Perhaps not. Compelled to offer assistance, I left my family to fend for themselves while I went to save the world. I gained sensitivity to suffering, to death, to hunger, to determination and drive, to survival and strength. I gained an appreciation of the enormous number of professionals willing to give their careers to service, if on a temporary basis. Most of all, I learned the difference between need and want. I know now that I have no needs; only the need to be needed.

The Gift

I knew he bought me a gift. My husband brought me a gift from the Bangkok open market. I loved the market but had not been there on this trip. I was glad he could go.

The Sunday market bristled. A cacophony of merchants, vendors and tropical animals screeched and barked at a rapid cadence. While attending professional meetings in Thailand, Daryle spent his only free day at the Chatuchak, Jat-u-Jak, Market in Bangkok, famous for its mixture of odors, colours and sounds. The market vibrated. Everybody loves a bargain, and the open bazaar teemed with great deals.

Unusual items often showed up on a small table or on a shelf. Exotic animals and pets perched on vendor's shoulders, or more commonly, crouched in cramped cages. The conditions were often offensive; inexcusable.

One found iguanas the size of baby alligators, snakes from boas to mambas, from squeezing constrictors to eye-aiming spitters, to fanged ankle-biters. And monkeys; the only monkeys I recognized were henna-orange orangutans and gibbons, though there were others. There were wild cats, diseased cats, yapping dogs, chickens, roosters, red birds, blue birds, yellow birds, big billed, hook billed and always squawking birds. As in China, many people bought these animals for lunch.

Sculptures of stone and wood, paintings, carpets and baskets delighted the senses. When I went to the market I touched everything; I couldn't keep my hands off the woven baskets. I liked to touch the weave, to caress the round or angular shape. I offered them up to my nostrils to take in the scent of plaited, twisted grass. The colours emulated subtle earth tones in contrast to vivid colours of African baskets. I wanted each one. I called them functional art.

Other aisles offered used books with stained, brittle paper. I'm tactile; I leafed through the dusty, parched pages. I never touched the animals. Vendors sold funky clothes, fabrics, plants, antiques, shoes, silver and house wares, Thai silk and jewelry and always, tacky plastic flowers set against elegant silk flowers.

Daryle met me at the hotel with a gift. Was it ethnic jewelry? Gold? Something to wear? A basket? "I know," I thought. "A wall hanging!"

At the hotel I savored a long, hot shower, fresh clothes and cool drinks poured over crushed ice. The room dripped with orchids and I reveled in their beauty, the sweet aroma, the soothing colours.

What was the gift? It must be a tapestry, easier to pack back to Manila.

Ah, no.

The man came back with a gibbon.

He brought
a baby *monkey*
to the beautiful
Dusi
Thani
Hotel.

It was a gift for me. What was I supposed to do with a golden gibbon? He found the baby gibbon irresistible: it did have bright, black, alert eyes. It was smaller than a fat paperback book, a tiny, furry, tailless, golden gibbon.

He could not know how emotionally drained I had become working at the Kampuchean border. He had no way of knowing that raising a baby monkey was low on my list of priorities, that I would be repulsed by its long, furry arms and legs, thinking only: why should this remnant of our past be allowed to live when thousands of human-kind suffer miserably.

As he moved about the hotel room retrieving lettuce and milk from the minibar I concealed my thoughts. I wanted to see Jessica and Ian. I wanted news of their events, their activities. How was swim practice, how was the meet on the weekend? What happened with the science projects? Did they manage the sleep-overs? Did they remember to go to the dentist? I tried to absorb what this creature was going to mean to me and my family and our future.

The short weeks I spent in Thailand felt like years. I was ready to return to Manila, to my family. Although physically and emotionally exhausted, I felt a small sense of fulfillment at being in the refugee camps before and until the professionals arrived and I gladly turned the work over to them. I realized a great sense of appreciation and sensitivity to those I met, refugees and specialists.

It was time to talk with my children to catch up on what I missed in their lives. With my husband, it was as if I never left; we quickly picked up where we left off. With the children, every day was a milestone, measured in small disasters and small successes: a spelling test, a new boy in school, a lost tennis shoe, the latest Speedos. I missed them in my life.

The Airport

As cute as the monkey apparently was at the market, caring for the gibbon, getting it out of one country and safely into another became, parenthetically, my responsibility. The next day we headed back to Manila. Suspecting there might be a lengthy quarantine time, we decided to make the departure and arrival of Baby as inconspicuous as possible. This meant concealing the gibbon inside the backpack as carry-on luggage; his, not mine.

We arrived at the Bangkok airport as late as we dared for an international flight with Baby, newly christened Mai-Thai, snuggled comfortably at the bottom of the hand carry. From the unzipped, ventilated backpack came an occasional "yip" immediately followed by diversionary coughs from my husband and me. Our plan was to allow only twenty minutes ground-time before boarding.

Within moments of settling-in at the departure lounge, airport officials announced,

"Attention.

"Attention please.

"Departure of Philippine Air Lines flight 0234 to Manila has been delayed.

"Estimated departure is now 1250."

Delayed? What on earth was I supposed to do with this creature? The monkey, that is. How could my husband have done this to me? Cute though it was at the market. The man was mad.

We should have, but we did not, anticipate the impending departure delay. The Philippine word-on-the-street in Manila was that PAL was an acronym for Plane's Always Late. I announced that I would not carry the backpack with the animal. If my husband encountered any problems with any officials, I did not know him. He agreed. Neither of us, planned on a departure delay. He rounded up a four ounce baby bottle, a wash rag, a dozen Pampers, and a banana to get us through the short flight, and home to organize the gibbon in a more settled way.

What could I do? My second language is body. I snatched the backpack, stomped away, slinging it on my front side and paced the duty free lounge. I stalled while waiting for a new departure time. I sampled perfumes, spraying myself all over. Who uses those little white tester strips? I fondled the scarves, each the size of a tablecloth, the type Imelda loved to wear. I wandered to the eyewear boutique and tried on designer sunglasses, the bigger the better.

As a diversion, still trying to comfort a restless child, I made my way to the ladies room, so indicated by the black silhouette of the lady in the too short flared skirt. I went quickly inside a stall. I shut the door, pulled out the bottle of now warm milk and fed Mai-Thai, who gulped with appreciation. When she finished, I removed the bottle and she started to screech.

I reached for the chain above my head to flush, in order to conceal the shrieking. The noisier the environment, the more she screeched. She seemed to become intoxicated by the racket and responded with delighted squeals to more noise. I shoved the bottle back in her mouth and the hysterics subsided. We stayed in the cubicle a long time hoping anyone in the WC during the screeching and flushing would have washed, lipsticked and left. We emerged: the infant and the surrogate. The backpack and its precarious contents dangled 'round my neck.

Within the hour, the milk flowed right through the gibbon. My husband's backpack reeked and I endured another trip to the ladies room. Not that I cared what happened to his backpack, but it was attached to me. And I did care about that. Removing the aromatic and full diaper, I cleaned the baby with warm water, no simple task moving between sink and toilet stall with a backpack on my chest, and re-diapered her with quartered, infant size Pampers.

Then, a new worry: I traversed the security station several times. Officials peered into a large x-ray machine for all hand-carry items. Attempting to ascertain the power as well as the sensitivity of the x-rays, I asked the security technician,

"Does, ah, this machine accept, aaah, film?"

"Aye, yes, Madam! No Froblem. We take feelum"

Oh-m-god. There it was again. 'No Froblem,' he says. A sure sign of a pending problem. I worried. I envisioned a radiation-saturated monkey, a totally bald primate, with fingernails falling out, and re-tardation due to radiation-induced brain damage. What was I doing with this animal? I watched the x-ray screen as bags glided by. The entire contents of lipstick, brushes, coins, film, books appeared on the screen. I visualized a miniature skeleton gliding along the con-veyor belt materializing boldly for gray and white animated viewing, arms gesticulating wildly inside the backpack.

We queued for security check-in. The madman was now in pos-session of his own backpack which he slung over his shoulder. I stood three passengers behind. Remember, the agreement was that if there was a problem, I didn't know him. My eyes fixed on the backpack. As I watched, to my horror, a thin, furry arm made its way through the zipper opening, groping about in the air. I pushed forward and gently placed the furry arm back into the pack then returned to my place in the queue unnoticed.

As we inched our way toward the monitor, Daryle placed his bag on the conveyer belt. My attempt at remaining aloof failed as I el-bowed, shoving past two unsuspecting passengers. Although I saw it but a split second, the tiny ribcage appeared superimposed over the baby bottle, a few coins, house keys and Pampers.

I snatched the backpack, and raced down the concourse to-ward the plane. Not sure what happened, and shocked at my aggressiveness, Daryle grabbed my bag and followed. On the concourse we exchanged hand-carries so that he was again in possession of the gibbon.

The Flight

I wished the film would start immediately upon takeoff. It did not. All lights on, the attendants went through the dismal drill of on-board safety.

None of this made sense to me. What's the big deal, according to Daryle's line of thinking? We already had a big golden lab, a little, neurotic frou-frou dog that looked like a floor-mop, tropical birds, tanks of aerated saltwater clown fish, angelfish, various nudibranch from our diving trips, and an overly prolific young cat and her litters. Always room for one more. Arg. It was like running the Ark for singles, except for the cat. Might as well add a golden gibbon.

Cabin attendants sauntered up and down the aisles hovering over passengers before serving drinks, then dinner, then turning-off the lights for the film. Mai-Thai must have been hungry too, although with all of the milk, she could have just been restless. In the dark, I fed her part of the banana. She started-in again. "Yip, yip, yip."

This time I popped her inside my shirt and lunged down the aisle to the toilets at the tail of the aircraft. I threw the latch; the light over the door flashed "occupied." I lowered the lid on the toilet, placed the plug in the sink and permitted the baby to frolic and play. Like a kid, she needed to run. She yanked the tissues from the container one by one; she leaped atop the cabinet, and placed the air-sick bags on her head, looking like a mini hotel-chef, and then discovered the roll of toilet paper. She delighted in pulling the paper off the roll. She strung it, draped it, and looped it all over the cubical. Fortunately, passengers were distracted by the film. No one checked on us, thank god. I was "occupied."

We were almost home. If we could get through the flight and then through immigration and customs in Manila we would be home-free. As Mai-Thai, My Thai Baby, bounced off the walls of the toilet cubicle, I realized that this was going to be a wondrous and challenging gift. I was still not sure what I was supposed to do with it, but the imposed hours spent in mandatory monkey care, began a bonding process; a process which joined us together like white glue collecting glitter.

During those eight hours from leaving the hotel to arriving in Manila, I probably spent four hours in toilets. When we reached the

Manila airport, we disembarked and the lark began one more time. All went well as we gathered luggage and queued for various inspections of passport, customs, and immigration. We passed through all but the last without incident.

As we approached the final counter with our luggage, as if on cue, Mai-Thai let out several yips in succession. Our coughing routine was perfected, yet the customs official queried, "Brought 'yur gat?" "Mmm," I replied. No further comment. It was over. The airplane excursion was the prelude to a well orchestrated symphony with the gibbon in first chair.

Ask Your Father

J essica and Ian met us at the door, already brushing their teeth, jumping up and down. Everyone started to talk at once, still hugging and laughing and clinging as we brought in our bags.

"You brought a what?" from Ian.

"Ask your father."

"What's that? What is it?" from Jessica.

"Ask your father."

"Mom! Where did you get it?"

"Ask your father."

"She's so cute." Mai Thai clung to me, not sure of the noises and excitement.

"How was your trip? What was it like?"

"Where's her tail?"

"Ask your father."

"Where will we put her?"

"Definitely ask your father."

In Manila, the primate adjusted quickly. The kids were thrilled. I should have known. She instantly adopted me as her surrogate mother. In the hierarchy of her small world, Daryle, who rescued her from certain death in the Sunday Market, took second place as the other adult figure in her life. Our children got in her way as older siblings and with them she was alternatively hostile, jealous, boisterous, gregarious, playful, and a big tease.

The bathroom bonding was instant and from the moment we arrived in Manila, she never left my side. Lucky me. If other people were in the house, she scampered across the floor and grabbed onto my leg. I wondered how she knew me from others. If Daryle offered to take her, she shrieked like a spoiled baby. Lucky me. When she played with the kids, she came to me if she perceived some infraction, some injustice. She sometimes pulled Jessica's long, swimming pool-green hair, or tugged at Ian's shirt. I watched carefully to see if she would bite. Most toddlers do. She never did.

The Menagerie

Mai-Tai loved Pepe, the golden lab and Pepe tolerated this crazy monkey-baby. I worried when they first met, concerned about the relationship between the lab and the primate. Not to 'vorry,' as Sister Katryn would say.

That thought took me back to the refugee camp. It took me to children sitting on cots, alone, hopeful; to dying men and women lying side by side on mats, and corpses heaped in piles.

Pepe, ever gentle, ever forgiving, ever tolerant, even enjoyed Mai-Thai's antics. To the golden lab, she was a constant companion. Lucky dog. She rode on his back; she swung from Pepe's long golden tail or pulled at it. She chased the kittens everywhere, up the stairs and down.

She leaped on the bird cage and I feared the birds would croak-over dead from heart attacks. Not to vorry. I even saw her swipe at the angelfish; such trauma in a fish tank.

Muffy, the frou-frou dog, the floor-mop, was the dumbest dog I ever met. She was a small, low to the ground dog. Her hair hung in her eyes and over her ears. The pelt on her back reached the floor because her legs were so short. When she ran, she took four strides to one of Pepe's. Mai-Thai pulled her stringy pelt. Muffy ran around and around chasing her own tail. Muffy was cute, but Muffy was dumb. She was also inherited and we soon bequeathed her to some other unsuspecting caring family who didn't yet have a menagerie.

Mai-Tai sat in Raggedy Ann's high chair for her meals and progressed from pabulum and milk to fruits and vegetables. There she sat. She was just the right size for the doll's high chair. I popped her on a pillow on the chair and fed her with a small caviar spoon. Soon she grabbed her banana with total control. I tried to remember this was an 'animal' not a baby with a spoon.

Even now when I remember those days, I don't believe a monkey sat on my outdoor, orchid-drenched deck for lunch. In the early days I fed Mai-Thai three times a day at formal, sit-in-your-chair, meals. Probably it should have been feeding on demand, but that didn't work with my life style. I didn't feed anyone snacks or on-demand. We ate regular meals at regular times. The healthy way: for Homo sapiens. What did I know about primates? Ah, no. The primate never sat at our table. I wasn't that nutzo.

We could never bring ourselves to cage her. She swung from lampshade to lampshade, curtain to curtain, bedpost to bedpost. When Alice made bread Mai-Thai antagonized in the kitchen. She didn't seem to like Alice. Thinking back, Alice didn't have much affection for the monkey either. Who would want a monkey in their kitchen?

Mai-Thai bounced along the counter tops helping herself to unbaked cinnamon rolls. When fresh warm *pandasal* came from the oven, Mai-Tai snitched one, took a bite and threw it on the floor. Then she snitched another, took one bite and threw it on the floor. Alice was not amused. She was furious. I suspect she took a few swipes at Mai-Thai, which enhanced the game.

Alice never said anything. Out loud. I knew this was difficult for the house staff. They did not understand why we had all these animals. While some Filipinos did have dogs, it should be noted that they sometimes ate dogs as well. Black dogs were especially prized. Not sure why this was so, but we often saw flatbed trucks with wire cages full of black dogs heading toward the market in Bagio, the mountain province.

Domestic workers were not comfortable with pet dogs. Cats they tolerated, but it was extra work for them to prepare food and to care for the madam's animals. If the kids had hamsters, while it was their responsibility to care for their pets, the household helpers ended up with the final responsibility, sweeping up the seeds or nuts that fell on the floor. I fed the birds and the fish but often asked them to clean the tanks and the bird cages. It was Alice and Perla who dutifully cooked up vats of dog food as there was no commercial dog food available.

When the bunnies from the school carnival grew up, don't look now but there was one male and one female. They reproduced immediately and new bunnies ran around the garden every 32 days. The next year the kids came back from the fair with pastel chicks; several pink, lavender, and yellow. I tried to prepare them for the fact that for many reasons the chicks would not have a long life expectancy. Not only did they live, the dye on their feathers faded, they grew little red combs and look again, they were all roosters and all started exercising their newly developed vocal chords. At three in the morning they cocked their doodle-doo. That was enough. The end of that chapter was that we ate the chickens; we wrung their necks. We skinned and ate the rabbits too. Couldn't even give away the rabbits due to the local stigma that they were related to rats.

Alice never said anything except, "Aye, Madaam, Mai-Thai is eating

da cinnamon rolls." She had a habit of saying loudly under her breath what sounded like, "*Sus papaya.*" For years I thought it was some slang phrase related to wonderful Philippine tropical fruit. She was actually saying something like, "Oh my God, Holy Father of mine, my Pope, our Papa"

Ian and Mai-Thai

Inside, Outside,
All Around the House

Outside, Mai-Thai sat on the engine of the car and swung 'round the antennae when Daryle was fixing parts under the hood. Inside, she learned to skid on the terrazzo floors. She scampered on her two legs as fast as she could, sometimes using her long left arm for added traction. Just before coming to an obstacle, she dropped on her backside to slide the last meter, like a baseball pro.

She swung on the bottom branches of the Christmas tree and batted all the ornaments. She rode Ian's Tonka trucks and played with Jessica's dolls; she loved the teddy bear and was thrilled with a ride in the red wagon. Mai-Thai leaped into the wagon clutching each side with her furry little fingers, jumping up and down, squealing. For once someone manipulated Ian into pulling the little red wagon. He towed her up and down the drive and around the deck.

As we watched her development we wondered, rhetorically, if she was human or if we were primate. From research I learned that gibbons grow to be four feet tall, and have no adolescence. Their childhood of six years moves directly into adulthood. The gibbon, highly advanced of the primates, has no tail, and walks upright making it closely related to Homo sapiens.

The tiny creature, brought by locals to the vendors at Sunday Market, our Mai-Thai, survived the trauma of the Bangkok airport and grew up with thick fur, fingernails and highly advanced brain cells.

Her contributions of laughter, and noise, chaos, astute awareness, tenderness and sensitivity were immense. In a short time, Mai-Thai made an enormous impact on our family. During the summer break, she disappeared. I suspect Alice let her escape or sold her whispering 'Sus Papaya.' The house staff offered lame excuses; we never got to the bottom of it. I like to think she was taken to the Philippine rain forest. We missed her, and we talk about her still.

Ethics

Today, for ethical and environmental reasons, there are movements to halt trade in exotic animals. We were naïve. We learned from our primate baby. We gained beautiful insights. Was it fair to Mai-Thai? Was she doomed in the Sunday market? We thought so at the time. We thought we were doing the right thing, though my mind-set was not in place at the start.

Working with Vietnamese and Cambodian immigrants who escaped the *Killing Fields*, I came into Bangkok from the refugee camps sober and somber and exhausted from hours of non-stop assistance to equally exhausted refugees. I was thinking of my own children whom I had not seen for several weeks, of my husband and his work, of which I had not thought for several weeks, curious to learn about the fifty-two hostages who were captured at the American Embassy in Iran while I volunteered at the border of Kampuchea; thinking of getting back into the routine of life in Manila. A baby gibbon was the last thing on my mind.

The abrupt adoption of Mai-Thai into my life, under the juxtaposition of the Killing Fields helped me reflect. I rejected this gift in the beginning. I was not ready for her. In time, however, in a very short time, the gibbon gave me a perspective on death and life. Mai-Thai won me over. Through her antics we all realized this was a magnificent gift.

Island in a Lake On an Island In a Lake On an Island

Ming Ramos, wife of General Fidel Ramos, worked with Daryle at the school as registrar. This future First Lady of the Philippines entertained the office staff with pleasantries and no-nonsense daily work: steady, consistent, unflappable and unpretentious. She graciously on occasion included us in official functions with General Ramos, whom we all called Eddie.

Fidel Ramos, a graduate of West Point, also received a Masters Degree in Civil Engineering at the University of Illinois. At the US Army Infantry School at Fort Benning he completed the Special Forces Operations Airborne course.

His outlook, his point of view, reflected Western thought. I wondered at his ability to govern in the Philippines. He was considered one of the good guys not prone to bribes or the typical Asian style of management. Good guys frequently come in last.

Eddie was a survivor through it all; through the politics of corruption and assassinations and was elected president of the Philippines to serve from 1992 to 1998. Ming and Eddie Ramos gave us a special farewell *despedida* at their weekend home on Tagaytay Ridge. Their residence overlooked Taal volcano which remained periodically active.

In fact, Taal volcano erupted in 1977. Without a thought, we piled into the car with sandwiches and drinks and drove to Taal Lake, 50 km outside Manila. Taal boasted to be a volcano within a volcano. The island is located in the centre of Taal Lake. They like to say, "It's the largest island in a lake on an island in a lake on an island." I guess because the volcano and lake are on Luzon Island.

Ash and dust spewed for two days so we were excited to observe our first active volcano. As the kids have often reminded us, every trip was a field trip and this was no exception. We weren't sure how close we could get so we drove down the ridge to the lake, now choppy with sharp whitecaps.

The plume of smoke was steady with occasional bursts. The wind blew the fine ash away from us. Along the shoreline cattle nibbled at the dusted grass between village huts and small roadside industry. The pace of life seemed unchanged. If there was tension, it did not show. Fishers repaired nets, boys watched over cattle and venders sold fresh bananas, papayas and mangoes along the winding narrow road. The landscape resembled the pallid appearance of an early, unlikely, dusting of snow.

We parked the car at the shore of the lake and watched the explosions burst open from deep inside the crater. Detonations, friction and lightening scared the beejabbers out of us. At the same time the unnatural forces commanded respect as we stood gawking at this unique volcano in the middle of the lake.

"You like take ride?" The *bangkero* balanced his bare feet on the outrigger and gestured toward his newly painted bangka christened in cursive letters, Baby.

"You mean around the volcano?" Daryle asked. "It's kind of rough."

"Aye, no froblem, Sir."

"How close can we get to the volcano?"

"Aye, no froblem. You can climb der."

"You mean we can go on the volcano?" Our bizarre logic reasoned that these people lived there, they knew the lake, they would not do anything to harm their *bangkas* or themselves.

We climbed aboard Baby as the *bangkero* fired up the little engine by pulling a string the length of a shoestring, and we bounced across the choppy whitecaps. The explosions grew louder. The lightening crackled closer. Boulders, launched from deep inside the cavern of the mountain, catapulted high in the sky before crashing down the side of the volcano. Lava dribbled-down red and gold fire in narrow rivulets to the base of the slope near the shoreline where we docked the *bangka*.

"Don't get too close," I ventured as the giant rocks dropped around us.

"Watch out."

The reality of our logic now sank in. While the *bangkero* and others did live on the lake, they were uneducated. They were self-taught about fishing, about rural village survival, agricultural proficiency with skills we did not possess. We failed to take into account their lack of understanding, their lack of scientific base. Nor were volcanic eruptions a common occurrence, even there.

"This is close enough." We were all thinking the same thing, so

I just said it out loud.

"If you want to take a piece of volcanic rock for school, grab a small piece and let's go.

"Yikes! It's hot!"

"I can't touch it."

"Well, what did you expect?"

"Get in the boat."

"Now!" I was suddenly uncomfortable.

Peelings

Five years later, we stood in Ming's garden overlooking the volcano. Ming and Eddie were gracious hosts, informal, intelligent and humourous, easy to be around; but I never overlooked the fact that Eddie was a very powerful person in the Philippine government and indeed was to become President Fidel Ramos. Ming, a talented musician often played with a jazz group and, when enticed, entertained at dinner parties. All Filipinos seem to be musical and even Eddie was known to sing out at dinner parties. Of course, Imelda was infamous for singing Dahil Sayo, said to be her favourite. The song we always heard the first lady sing was "Feelings."

In moments of disrespectful giddiness, we gathered 'round to sing our own impersonation of Imelda singing:

"Peelings, no-ting more dan peelings.

"Trying to porget my peelings off loff.

"Tear drops rolling down my pace,

"Trying to porget my peelings off loff."

Daryle and I stayed in Manila sans our kids for the summer while he administered the summer-school program. In July he answered a phone call regarding a possible position in Riyadh. Without details, without a contract, we mapped our course. Another possibility it seemed, as we scribbled on our yellow pads, was to work with the international division of a technology company. I called the packers.

We packed-up our lives and put everything in storage until we had an idea of where we might move. I personally packed all the beautiful shells from hundreds of beach trips. I would never trust anyone, professional or not, to pack the fragile, individually

Mabuhay / Best Wishes
to Daryle & Dannie

President Fidel (Eddie) Romos and Amelita (Ming) Ramos

selected cleaned and researched shells from our home of the past ten years.

I personally packed the Chinese pottery, collected from the shops of small villages. I learned about antique ceramics from Bill Sorsby, Daryle's longtime friend from Oregon. He came on a buying trip and asked me to go around the country looking for Chinese pieces. I didn't know a Ming from a Ch'ing, but immersed myself in the dynasties learning about celadon, spotted ware, egg-shell, and Tang wares. I studied by the same method I used for learning the classification of shell life. In this case I learned the dynasties, then the ceramics and pottery typical of the period. It was a new field for me, and more interesting than talking about problems with the maids all day.

Because there was a possibility of traveling to Saudi Arabia, I labeled the Christmas tree, decorative house plant; the ornaments as decorative toys.

Pilipino Bulletin

I read an article about two fishermen who made a big catch off one of the small islands.

Der was dis pisser-man? Who libbed in a pissing billage? On one of da islands? Ebery morning he got eento hes boat and pissed. Sometimes hes prend went wit heem. Day sat to-geder in da boat and pissed all day. By golly, eet was berry hot. Dey ate a leettle lunch den of course needed to piss more. Dey pissed and pissed all day.

One apter-noon, dey saw some-ting berry big een da water; a bery big piss. Dey rowed der pissing boat closer to see wat was dat? Der in da sea. Dey knew. Eet was da biggest piss dey eber had near der billage. Eef dey got dat piss, dey would be reech. By golly, dey would not haff to piss da rest off da week.

Da two prends prepared der pissing rods wit heby line and hooks and cast out ober and ober again. Eet was berry hot. Dey were berry mga tired.

I tink I got eet! Now, I reely need a big piss!

By golly, you got eet!

Da pissers worked berry hard to reel in da piss, berry close to da pissing boat. Eet was heby. Dey took turns reeling. Pine-ally, neerly as da sun went down, and dropped into da water, dropped into da sea, dey landed der piss eento da boat.

Sus papaya! Wat wass eet? Eet was not a piss. Dis was a buddy. A dead buddy. A dead buddy ploating in da sea at der billage.

By golly, now dey were in trouble. Dey had no big piss, but dey had a dead buddy. Da folice would ask questions. What were dey doing wit a dead buddy? Maybe dey should trowe da buddy bak. Eet was getting late. Pine-ally, da pisser-men decided to take da buddy to da folice. Dey wood tell da trute. The trute wood make dem pree.

Now da folice didn't know what to do. Dey had a dead buddy. Day beleefed da pissers por dey knew dees men prom da billage. What would day do wit da dead buddy. Who waz dis? Dey had no reports off missing feefle. Da buddy waz starting to smelling. Baho naman. Berry stinky. Da pace of da buddy wass rotting away. Maybe dey wood neber know who waz dis.

Den, dey remembered. Der waz dis reward por pine-ding da pig, olt mahn who wandered off. Dis must be dat mahn.

Da pissers were so hoppy. Dey had no piss, but dey had a leetle reward to share. Dey would buy a piss and rice prom der billage. Tomorrow dey wood get into der boat and piss again.

And by golly, dat's da trute. I read it in da Bullytin.

Departure

A decade in the Philippines came metaphorically to an end in the airport departure lounge. Ten years before, we waded through puddles, whipped by gusty outer bands of a devastating typhoon. We made our way through the bombed-out hanger of the Manila International Airport, which would be renamed the "Ninoy Aquino International Airport," after the assassinated Senator Benigno Aquino.

We stood at the departure lounge in a clutch, one last, long hug. Tears welled up, and pooled. I blinked but they still spilled over. One by one the droplets slid down my cheeks until they became parallel rivulets against the sides of my jaw.

The separation, the kids leaving their home, friends, teachers, teammates of ten years, foreshadowed loss of innocence for each of us. Leaving us, they flew on their own, their first international solo flight from Manila to Tokyo, overnight, and on to swim camp in Canada. No cell phones, no computers, no iPods. They were ready; we weren't.

Standing there, we watched them walk through the final security check; ten years flashed back in an instant. They had no idea of our present jobless state. They were 13 and 15. Old enough, but still naive. When I lost it, Jessica started to cry. Daryle was already unable to control the tears. Jessica and Ian had never seen their father cry. The tears, like salty drops of the South China Sea, as if part of our lives over the past 10 years, now dribbled down, making spatter paint of my mascara and splotches on my silk shirt.

"We're cool. We'll be fine," from Jessica.

"Don't worry," from Ian.

"We're not worried. Keep your passport safe and your money and your tickets safe.

"Request a wake-up call at the hotel in Tokyo." I tried to be strong.

"Don't miss your flight to Ontario or you are in deep Kim Chi." They snickered.

International travel could be complicated and they did have to pay attention. I knew they could handle it.

Still.

I dabbed at my soggy cheeks and hugged them one more time, biting my lip. Their dad hugged and turned away until they passed the check point. We watched the backpacks bob-off and mingle with other passengers until they were out of sight. We walked to the car in silence.

After ten years, Daryle decided to leave the district and find another position. The Board assumed he would stay in an advisory position, but he wanted to move on. There were few recruiting fairs; headhunters were limited. We wrote on yellow pads, organizing our lives.

On the one hand, on the other hand;

The positives, the negatives;

The advantages, the disadvantages;

Stay or leave.

We both agreed, since nothing was forthcoming, we could always pick apples in Washington. We could pump gas. We could make our lives work.

Still.

It was the end of exotic house animals, the end of Mai-Thai, of Pepe, and tropical fish; the end of scuba trips on hundreds of archipelago islands, orchid trips to the rain forest, swim meets as we had known them; the end of the business group and women's group in Manila. The end of fam- tours, scuba trips on gifted yachts, the end of rice terraces. The end of typhoons, and security issues as we had known them, bombs in book bags, bombs in supermarkets, bombs in toilets; the end of shell collecting in the South China Sea. It was the end of crazy politics through the Watergate years, the Marcos years, birthday parties in the Aquino years and farewell despedidas during the Ramos years.

The Minimalist

M oving is a way of life in the expatriate community. It's not that easy, it's not so much fun and it's never routine. Appraisers show up at the appointed time, or they don't. With clipboard in hand, they scrutinize the squatters with the vigor and chutzpah of a tenacious customs agent. They traipse through your home, peer through your rooms, probe your closets, peek in your drawers, and invade your privacy, all under the guise of estimating the weight and cost of your household shipment. The appraisers are just the beginning, authenticating the move.

The physical act of moving challenges the most organized planner. The whole family becomes dysfunctional. No matter how often we are thrust into transition, no matter how many times we pick-up and pack-out all of our transportable possessions, the task remains colossal. There is, however, a catharsis that goes along with most moves. The sorting process helps families psychologically prepare for the pending relocation.

We start by culling the closets. Dunes of debris pile up in previously tidy alcoves. Where does all of this stuff come from? At our house, each room seems to accrue several piles. Considering the new posting, whether going back home or to another country, we first select-out the things to be sold. Can't use 110v appliances, wrong voltage; can't use the skis in Saudi or the scuba gear in Pakistan; don't need down jackets in Manila.

The best therapy is simply to throw-it-out like crossing items off a list. It feels liberating, as if in edu-babble, completing action plans en-route to attaining outcomes. Of course it is not easy to toss things out. We become ridiculously attached to trinkets and village souvenirs, a hand-woven basket, a sword from the *suq*, or to lesson plans from five years ago. Throw-it-all-out. Write something new.

Making decisions, however, can be the impetus for splitting the family. Permanently. Great dissension may ensue over what is essential and for whom.

"You're not taking those books to Saudi; they weigh too much."

"Of course I am, you're taking your golf clubs."

"But you've already read them."

"They don't even have grass in Saudi."

I've always admired the minimalist. In fact there was a time right after college, when all of our worldly possessions fit into two cardboard boxes. Whatever happened to those carefree days of poverty and freedom, days sans children, possessions or pets? We grew up. We developed a sense of style supported by our possessions. We needed stuff to do our work better. And once we could afford them, we wanted toys, even when they were the wrong voltage, or there was no power at all.

At the confirmed date, more or less, the packers show up, or they don't, in flatbed trucks, or smoke-belching beaters, and in one country rode up peddling black bicycles, balancing cardboard flats atop their heads, a vision which did not generate confidence. To these men, often toothless, bearded and shoeless, sometimes turbaned, usually smoking and typically pungent, we entrust our treasures.

One time, the moving company sent one man, a meticulous wrapper, who spent more time drinking tea than wrapping teacups. At our next move, the moving company sent in a swat-team that invaded the house like army ants attacking every room at once, leaving us totally incapable of overseeing any or all of the pending devastation. Belongings are swaddled in tissue and newsprint, clothing is layered and forever creased in the bottom of cardboard cartons, the furniture is padded, taped and crated, dishes hand-packed with local-language newspaper, and if you are lucky they may bring a meter or two of bubble wrap for your most fragile toys. These realities remain; the packers come and go.

There is something seductive about minimalist philosophy which rears its head each time we move. We always affirm to never, never accumulate such massive amounts; ever again. There is something therapeutic about giving things away, yet disturbing, to observe locals skirmish for our seemingly worthless belongings, the third world a lingering gripper-snapper at our rubbish bins.

Taking up a new assignment is energizing. The environment, the people, the newness of the job invigorates and stimulates the new arrival. The air freight, meant to arrive as accompanied baggage, inevitably arrives weeks after the sea freight, which is not, after all on the Princess Lines and predictably takes many months longer than the promised 6 weeks. What to do? Buy more stuff. So much for the minimalist. When is market day? We're off to the *suq*.

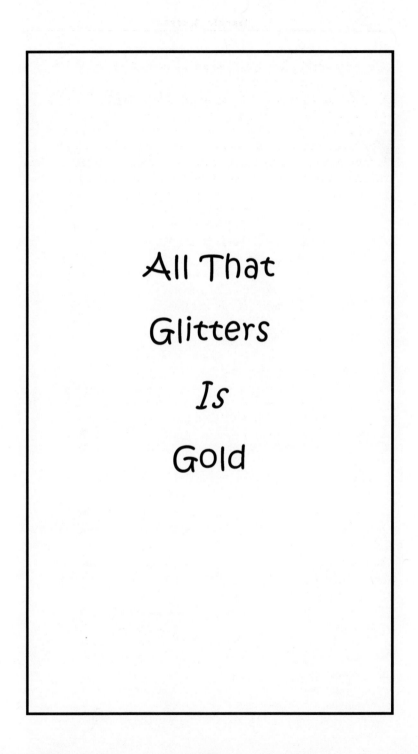

All That

Glitters

Is

Gold

They Never Said it was Easy

Without warning or emotional preparation, we left Jessica to fend for herself in an American boarding school. We waved goodbye and drove off. Or so it seemed. We lingered at the car, lingered at the parking place. It was the most wrenching, agonizing decision about the move to Saudi Arabia: leaving Jessica in America.

Northfield/Mount Herman was every parent's dream of the perfect campus. Small town, rural atmosphere, idyllic, safe environment; farm houses, large land plots, churches, rural streets and middle class values; every parent's dream; every teenager's nightmare. No discos, no pizza dives, no clubs, no nada.

We all cried; for days. Nobody said it was easy. And it was not.

"I hate it here. It's (sniff) raining.

"It rains every (sniff) weekend.

"The food is awful," she sobbed, gulping the air.

"I hate it here." It wrenched my heart.

By February, she announced that she was not returning to her school the following year. We met her in New York while recruiting new teachers. She and her dad sat on the edge of the bed during that weekend.

"I'm not going back." Was this teenage rebellion?

Wait a minute.

This was our call.

But she was right.

The mistake was not regarding the decision to board, but the abruptness of the move and the incorrect choice of schools. The carefully thought-out school choice was a miss-match; not a fit; at all. How she maintained her academic discipline, I'm not sure. She joined all the water sports. She was a human phenomenon on the swim team and a water polo animal as a result of her years in Manila. She also joined the kayaking team. Still, she hated the school. And she faced social issues.

The choice was wrong. She was lost in the crowd, another blondhair, blue-eyed American student. Of course she wasn't American at all. Only her passport was American; she was a foreigner in her own country. She looked like everyone else, used the same words, spoke the same language, but she was different. She knew nothing of American TV, the latest Hollywood stars, she never heard of Bubble Yum. We went to a market. The clerk asked her where she was from. She told her, Manila, Philippines. "Oh, your English is very good." Jessica looked at me then replied, "Thank you."

She did know where Hong Kong was, but this was perceived as arrogance. She learned not to talk about things non-American. Typical of Third Culture Kids, the students she related to in her home country were students from other countries; the foreign students on campus.

Jessica was miserable. When she met with the counselor, he asked her if she wasn't harbouring a lot of hatred toward her parents who forced her to attend boarding school. Didn't she feel they really didn't love her by sending her away? If they loved her, why would they leave her? Perhaps he was trying to help her sort things out. The effect was an abhorrence of the counselor for attempting to pit her against her family. We weren't too happy to hear about this either.

The dean of students wasn't much better. He attempted to meet with the out-of-country students. His idea of assisting with the adjustment to America was to hold an afternoon tea at his residence. This did nothing to facilitate her adjustment.

It was many years before she forgave us for taking her from the Islands of East Asia where she grew up. The following fall she transferred to an American boarding school in Cyprus and things turned around somewhat. She was a year older, a graduating senior and understood more of the dynamics and necessity of her displacement; she was no longer in the U.S. where she clearly did not fit.

Being of a rebellious nature and a wanna-be free spirit, she faced social issues and social choices, not untypical of her age. In Cyprus, at least she was with a group of like-minded equally zany kids living in Nicosia. Reeeally glad I wasn't the dorm mom.

Notwithstanding her rebellion and her defiance of the regulations, she was invited to make one of the graduation speeches. Her commencement remarks acknowledged that leaving home had been difficult. She began,

"I have attended high school graduations since I was six," when she sat squirming in the front row of the sweltering gymnasium to hear President Ferdinand Marcos and of course her father.

It wasn't easy, but in the end, we had, each of us, sacrificed and stretched for common family goals. We attended high school graduations in Cyprus and Bruxelles and college graduations in Washington. I guess we survived boarding schools and so did the kids, but it wasn't easy.

Rome

Boarding school was difficult for Ian also although he had a year to prepare mentally and psychologically before heading off with his classmates. He celebrated two early graduations. In Manila he graduated from eighth grade middle school, then spent his ninth grade in Saudi and graduated again from junior high school. He and his buddies all headed for schools around the world. A bunch went off to Europe and he studied in Rome and Bruxelles the following three years.

"Are you sure you want to go to a boys' school?" Ian was the kid who came home from the pediatric ward looking around for the girl babies. Ian loved life from the moment he burst into it and always seemed to enjoy having friends around. His notion to attend Notre Dame School for boys in Rome shocked me. I assumed he would handle the catholic bits, but I wasn't so sure he would be happy with no girls around.

What I was soon to realize was that the Marymount School for girls was just across town. He had it all figured out. A chunk of students from Riyadh and Jeddah were attending the two schools. Daryle and I visited on several occasions. Why not? Rome was a wonderful place for a parent conference. The first time we went, Ian was keen to show us around town. He gave us a tour of the campus, but he really wanted to take us to some of his favourite restaurants. He was a man of the world it seemed.

He showed us little spots for pizza, thick-crusted and sold by the slice.

"*Buona sera* Ian. What I'm a gonna make for you today?"

"You know these people? By name?"

"Yeah, sure. This is Antonio. He owns this place. Rosa is over there," he gestured.

"Hey Tony! These are my parents. They are visiting from Saudi Arabia."

At dinner he took us to another restaurant in the city.

"*Buona sera*! *Ciao*, Ian. You want a table in the back?"

"You know these people also?"

"Well, yeah; Italians are very friendly, Mom." How worldly was this?

"So, you come here often?" I guess I expected to eat in the dining hall, or walk along the streets and find some interesting looking place.

"Ian, *scusa,* you want the house red or something different tonight? Are theez-a your parents?"

Ian was in the tenth grade. I wasn't quite ready for this. It wasn't the drinking with his parents that I thought about. It was that it seemed perfectly acceptable for Ian to order wine in a public restaurant. Coming out of Saudi, ordering a glass of wine was bliss for us; but we were of age.

The Italians had some informal logic: if you could see over the top of the bar, you were old enough to have a glass of wine. Or something. Well, I hoped this was better than binging on beer his first year of college if it came to that.

"Donatella, per favore, you choose for us tonight." Oh my. The child is fluent in Italian.

"We lova your bambino, Ian. He's a so cute." I thought she might pinch his cheeks.

The following year, Ian requested to transfer to another school.

"Jessica did."

"But why? Why do you want to change schools?" He had many reasons. There were problems with the staff and many of the boys transferred out that year.

"Where do you think you want to go?

"If you do the research, and you have a good alternative, we will consider it.

"You tell us your plan." In our family you have to have a plan. It's the Russell way.

He decided to attend the International School of Bruxelles. He did have one friend there. Amy was a tennis player and good friend from Riyadh. Their system of boarding was to place boarders in homes with Belgian families. We went to interview with several families and the fit was with a family whose teenagers attended the Belgian school across town. The boys, Ian and Pascal, got along famously and by the end of the first semester, Ian knew everyone in both schools.

The International School Bruxelles was large. They offered a broad based American curriculum and presented a large choice of athletic opportunities. He wanted to play American football.

He and his dad sat on the beach in Spain with a yellow pad and a football. They threw passes, played catch for hours on the beach, then discussed the arrows and circles on the yellow pad. That summer, he left early, before the start of classes, for two weeks of football practice. He called us in Saudi the second week.

"Hey Ian, how's it goin' in Bruxelles?" Daryle answered the phone.

"How's your football practice?"

"Man, I had no idea about those plays. I didn't know you had to memorize them.

"I thought it was like soccer.

"I've been working out every day, practicing the plays.

"I don't get it.

"I think I have to quit. Is that really bad?

"I'm not sure I will ever be any good at this game, or figure it out."

"I didn't know you had to memorize the plays," he reiterated.

"Yeah, you have to know the plays, the offensive and defensive strategies.

"Ian, you've never played American football."

"Dad, it's not like soccer."

"Nope. So what's your plan?" There it was again; Ian knew he had to have a plan.

"I'm joining whatever team travels.

"At least I will travel and see the area.

"I'm thinking of volleyball."

Ian grew up with soccer. Instead, he played volleyball and continued with competitive swimming traversing Europe, even Cairo, with the teams, all the while babbling in colloquial Italian and French. He could say, "Kiss me, I love you" in fourteen languages. He and his sister were both more social in Europe than we wanted to know.

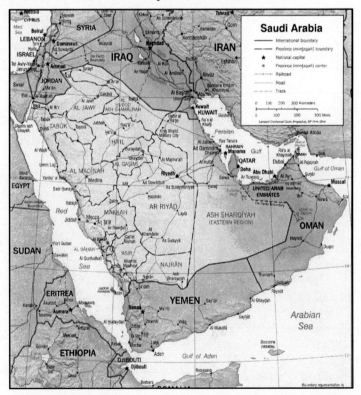

Not Allowed

I read everything I could get my hands on about Riyadh before boarding the plane. The twenty-seven hour flight to Saudi promised to be long and promised to provide much time to ponder our new opportunity. Whatever I read, it wasn't enough. I was not prepared.

In a way, I felt as ill prepared at the Riyadh airport as I felt nineteen years before when I stepped off the plane in Addis Ababa after studying at UCLA, learning the language and reading heaps of books for that assignment. Nothing prepared me for the tension, perhaps self imposed, and for my first impressions on arrival at the Riyadh airport. But why was I tense?

We lived in Africa, pretty different from California, like fer sure. We lived in the Philippines, which was joyous, colourful and predominately Catholic. I never anticipated the sober, somber tone, whatever it was, that I felt when I looked around the Saudi airport. Would I do something wrong? Would I offend? What would they do to me if I did? Would I be arrested for some infraction?

We deplaned at the old airport. Nervously, I entered the customs and immigration area with Jessica and Ian; Daryle went ahead. I'm not sure what I expected, but I guess the uncertainly kept me off guard. I wore a long skirt and scanned the crowded area for other women. There weren't many. Most of the men were workers from Asia, wearing jogging pants and jackets, and there were a few business men, Saudis, Lebanese and other Arabs, and a sprinkling of western types.

A number of Saudi women bundled in black stood at the front of the lines. A few western women wore head scarves and long skirts and very modest dress. No women wore pants. I decided I was okay in my long skirt. I deflected my eyes, just in case.

Everyone knew Riyadh was strict, conservative and restrictive. What I did not know was that while the women were segregated, they were also given preferential treatment. Women and children were ushered to the front of the line accompanied by their spouses, fathers or brothers. This was good. This could work for me.

As we moved through various branches of airport bureaucracy, shoving our passports through windows, to be validated and stamped, two men from the school waved at us from the other side of a barrier, their friendly faces a welcome sight.

The last step was to collect our luggage and move to the last counter.

Where was the green line for customs? Where was the fast track? I had nothing to declare. I submissively heaved some of the bags onto the low table for inspection. The agent yelled at a woman in front of me and removed three videos from her bags.

"Not allowed. Video not allowed."

"These are Disney videos for my children."

"See? Cinderella, Dumbo the Flying Elephant," she pointed to the illustrated covers.

"Not allowed.

"You want? You come back two weeks. Then you get."

What did this mean? They wanted to copy them for their own children? They wanted to verify they were really Disney? Was there pornography on the end of the video?

The next man in front of me received the wrath of all the agents.

"What is this?

"You have alcohol!" he said yelling at the man loud enough for the entire airport to come to a halt. The man carried a miniature bottle of airplane Black Label in his suit pocket.

"Not allowed."

"Why you bring alcohol? Forbidden. Not allowed." Several agents now gathered around shouting at the man all at once.

"You go to jail for this."

"I'm sorry. You take it," the passenger whispered.

"You bribe me? Not allowed." It got worse.

"I guess I forgot. I didn't know I had it in my pocket." Even I wasn't convinced. They wrote in his passport and hauled the passenger off. I never saw him again.

What offending things would they pull from my luggage? With two hands the customs agent rummaged through my bags one by one like tossing a large green salad. Everything on the bottom churned up to the top. He found nothing of ill repute. He tried harder with the next bag as I struggled to re-zip the first. Again he found no grounds for yelling.

Then bonsai. Jessica packed a box of chocolates.

"What is this?" he said shoving the box in her face.

"It's chocolate."

"What is in this chocolate?"

"There is alcohol in this. Not allowed."

"No! It's chocolate," her voice rose in decibels.

He opened the box and fingered several pieces.

"What is inside this?" he asked again as he pinched several pieces open.

"You can see. It's chocolate," she reiterated. I stepped in to give her breathing space.

"You can read the ingredients here, on the box." He continued to pinch each piece of beautiful chocolate. He knew about liqueur filled chocolates. He didn't know enough, but knew enough to harass.

"Fine. You keep it. There is no alcohol in this chocolate." She was furious; I could tell by the way she manipulated her shoulders forward and back, one then the other, accompanied by a hefty exhale.

He threw the chocolate back in her luggage and pushed the bag to the end of the table. When he went through her backpack he had a field day. The inspector took the photos from the pocket and started to rip them up.

"What are you do-ing? Those are my friends."

"Not allowed.

"No boys, girls in same photograph," and he proceeded to tear the photos lengthwise as if to separate the boys from the girls.

"Those are my friends. These are girls. They are all girls." Big tears welled up. Admittedly the girls wore baggy pants and heavy sweaters from Massachusetts. He threw the torn pieces in the bag, leaving scraps of friends littering the customs floor.

It was over; the humiliation, harassment and reasons for anger. The men from the Saudi Arabian International School, Riyadh met us, rescued us and ushered us through a throng of long white *thobes* toward the waiting van.

Change is sometimes traumatic but this move was especially so. We unwittingly entered a slimy can of worms. We arrived in Riyadh, unknown and unaccepted by half of the divided community; we were viewed with suspicion as newcomers. Daryle's predecessor, the former head of school, refused to leave, convinced we wouldn't last. He was almost right. It was a mess.

Ray, chairman of the board, and David another board member, met us at the airport and drove us to the Marriott Hotel. We left the kids to check out the hotel rooms then dashed downstairs to meet the men in the coffee shop. We sat in the family section; I was not allowed in the main dining area of the segregated restaurant. They told us that they came directly from the board meeting to meet us at the airport.

I ordered a strong, Arab coffee, though had it been legal, we both could have used a glass of wine. I listened as Ray told us that the board meeting broke-up in a fist-fight amongst the board members; a real fist fight, not a metaphorical disagreement. It sounded like the Wild West. Who were these members of the school board who conducted discussions with their fists, without apparent verbal mediation? It was by then 3am and I hoped I didn't really hear any of this. Two days later, we were to be introduced at a special parent meeting at the school.

Shamal

Ian pulled aside the heavy beige drapes. It was light out but we couldn't see a thing. Visibility was limited to several meters across the street. A desert *shamal* blew across the road; across the city. Everything was sand-brown: the sky, the road, the cars, the faint outline of buildings. The landscape blended together in one dusty image of the Arabian Desert.

Sand-covered cars and Toyota trucks crept slowly along the sand-paved road; their dim headlights searched the way like parallel flashlights with low batteries. As we looked down on the tops of the white-beige cars from our twelfth floor room, they seemed to ferry a layer of sand making them nearly indistinguishable from the road, from the other vehicles, like a slow moving diorama sprinkled with brown dust. Mounds of sand accumulated along the edge of the curb and against parked cars like beige drifts of snow.

"What is this?" from Ian.

"Look at this.

"Can you believe it out there?" I could not believe it. I had never seen anything like it.

"Man, are we going out in that?"

"Think it will blow away?"

"Look at those people down there."

A few determined souls walked with purpose, their heads tightly wrapped allowing only an open slit across their eyes. Two women in ankle-length black *abaya*s cautiously made their way with haste; with one hand they clutched at their wraps wadded up in one fist, and with the other they clutched their headpieces trying to maintain dignity in distress. I thought they might fly off across the dull, brown sky like witches in black capes.

Men wore long white *thobes* which flapped and whipped at their legs, their faces and heads enfolded in red and white *ghutras*. They hurried, pushed along by the force of the *shamal*.

This: was Saudi Arabia.

Ray picked us up after breakfast and took us briefly around the city. Visibility made it difficult to get a sense of where we were. The roads were torn up and detours diverted all the main roads. He left a car for us and said if we were comfortable, we could drive to the parent meeting in the evening. He told us the street names, sort of, and gave us a hand-drawn map.

It seems incredulous now, looking back. After an early hotel dinner, we left our teenagers in the room as we headed for the introductory meeting. The kids were watching Charlie's Angles dubbed in Arabic. For four hours we drove in the city, looking for the proper turn-offs to locate the school. We went around and around in an endless maze of diversions. All the green 3-M signs looked alike in Arabic. We were four hours late for the meeting where the new superintendent was to be introduced to the parent community; the new superintendent who would never make it; the new superintendent who wouldn't last.

Ray called the hotel asking Jessica and Ian if we had left yet. He phoned the hotel every half hour and by then the kids were concerned. Jessica and Ian fanaticized some Arab kidnap plot on our second night in Saudi Arabia.

"We passed that sign before."

"Let's go back and try again. The turn off should be after that sign."

"There's another flight, so we are still near the airport."

"There's the green 3M sign, or is that a different one."

"I can't tell. The Arabic words all look the same in the dark." We continued to drive hoping for a miracle in the blackness; hoping the parent community would still be there, waiting for us.

At 11.30 pm we finally made our way back. We never found the school for the 7pm meeting. The only way we found our way back to the hotel was that it was near the airport and we used the flight patterns to guide us.

We were sick; sick with frustration, but sick from the knowledge that this first impression would confirm to the cynics that the board made an appalling decision to deny renewal of contract to the former school head. Ray was on the phone when we entered the room. He and the kids were relieved we were not in physical danger. They did not know the depth of our mental anguish.

The Suq

Ray escorted Daryle to the school in the morning and I took the kids to the open market and the gold *suq*. I did not cover my head, but did wear a long skirt and long-sleeve top. The weather outside the hotel approached 40 degrees centigrade. The *shamal* blew away like smoke from the campfire leaving the sky bright, clear and cloudless; leaving the street sweepers to clean up the sand dunes now relocated

along the city streets.

We wandered up and down the hard-pack dirt aisles of the old *suq*. Like any market, each commodity had its quarter. Unlike the bustling markets of Bangkok, the gold *suq* seemed subdued. It was not crowded; it was not noisy. There were no live animals to animate the sounds or activate the sense of smell. The aisles were wide. There was no threat of theft. They chopped off fingers, hands and heads for punishment; an unambiguous deterrent.

Row after row, shop after shop gushed with gold. At first glance, each shop looked alike. How many designs could there be for bangles and necklaces, rings and head pieces? The initial vision of this gold market was of overwhelming glitter; overwhelming opulence; overwhelming gaudiness. Who wore these extravagant pieces? And for what occasions?

Under glass counters, or push-pinned to the walls, hanging on rusty nails and tarnished hooks, kilos of gold dangled for the eager shopper. A man sat on a stool behind a small table in the middle of one lane with an open box of glittering gems; rubies, garnets, emeralds, even pearls. He tapped with small tools to replace missing precious stones and repair gold bangles.

"Wow! They sure have a lot of brass here, Mom," from Ian as we walked around the *suq*.

"That's not brass, Ian."

"What? What is it?"

"Look again. It's gold."

"Hanging like that, out in the open?"

"Yep. Gold dripping from those rusty hooks.

"Gold necklaces hanging there," I gestured with my chin.

"Gold bangles stacked up there and head pieces. Yep. All gold."

"Mom. Are you sure?"

"That's what they tell me."

From my peripheral vision I noticed the patterns of stacked, folded carpets. And in another section we absorbed the aroma of the spices. Huge sacks of colourful seasonings lined the rows. Orange saffron, dark dried limes hard as rocks, red chili, russet cinnamon and black cloves heaped up in a basket like miniature black shooting stars. There was cardamom, curry, thyme and rosemary, but much of it I did not recognize in this format or quantity. And seeds: huge woven sacks of sesame, almonds, walnuts and pistachios; pine nuts purchased by the kilo. I did not yet know about Arabic cooking, but we immersed our senses in the bouquet. The new culture started to sink in. I was hooked. This would be wonderful.

Right away, I noticed many Filipino workers in the shops; men, of course. They did not wear Arab dress but were conservative: not the casual shorts and t-shirts and rubber slipper they might have worn in Manila. There were lots of Filipinas as well, enclosed in black *abaya*s, but no women of any nationality worked in the stalls. I later learned the Filipinas worked as nurses and some were domestic workers in homes. These workers from the Philippines were to become my life-line; my link; my transition between cultures. I could use Tagalog in the supermarkets and shops to communicate.

Coming abruptly from the noisy, colourful, predominately Catholic culture of Manila, what I observed that morning seemed a sharp contrast. Even the Islamic culture of Southern Mindanao was colourful and musical. Muslim ladies in Mindanao danced with candles balanced on their heads exhibiting exquisite poise and beauty; in the Philippines no one wore black.

In Riyadh, dry sand replaced green, verdant grass. No majestic mango trees or palm trees, fragrant frangipanis or strong avocado trees. No orchids or ferns. No trees at all lined the streets and muted colours replaced the glamour of Philippine life-style. Riyadh women were shrouded in black; the men wore long white *thobes*. Everyone covered their head in black drape or checkered cloth. There was nothing sexy about the city, as opposed to Manila which even extolled delicious, sexy cookies at one bakery.

I was unsure and uncomfortable, feeling somewhat out of place that morning in that very foreign *suq*. I watched as a gaggle of corpulent Arab women wrapped in black shuffled up to a glass counter. They looked unkempt and disheveled with henna hands and nails.

I wondered what they wore under their black bags. Though wealthy, I doubted this group was wearing Oochi, Gucci or Couchi. But who would know?

Like any group of women on a shopping spree, they looked at gold bangles and rings pushing the jewels onto their pudgy fingers like sisters of Cinderella squeezing a large foot in a tiny slipper. The women yakked away, barked at each other, gazing at the bracelets and long gold necklaces trying them on, looking for approval in the mirror.

They seemed loud. I didn't understand the intonation or the words and it sounded aggressive as they shouted back and forth. The words came from deep in their throats, like they were coughing up phlegm; a forced guttural sound, it seemed. I tried not to stare, but they were engrossed in their purchases and did not notice. I knew how to bargain in Mexico, in Addis, in the Manila markets, but this seemed very different and I did not yet know the words.

Compound Welcome

"**W**elcome to the compound," from Darlene the music teacher, as she got out of their car. It was very welcoming. Then, from the other side of the parking lot,

"You're staying in my best friend's house. I hope you can handle it," from the library person. She turned a cold shoulder and walked away.

We moved onto the teacher compound with our suitcases.

New members of a community are wined-and-dined and supported by company employees. In Saudi there was no wine. Community members help introduce the new staff, help out with shopping, setting up the house and introducing children to new playmates. At social functions newcomers are often invited 'sight unseen' to get to know the community. The new family is supported by corporate staff and community support groups, even churches. There were no churches.

At this move, there were no invitations. The school community was profoundly divided. Half the board members perpetuated the negativity. The business community, above all the pettiness, ignored the school when it most needed support. We were not included in social events or business meetings. The school had become a non-entity in Riyadh; a negative blight. The attitude in the community seemed to be: 'What is going on? Two heads of school? Who's in charge? The management is a mess.' Of course they were right.

The board of directors, which had done the hiring, was divided.

Those who supported the new director were embarrassed to go public. This compounded our transition. Half of the split board felt the new director would not succeed and the former school head should remain in town.

I had no job assignment, possibly because we were not expected to stay. I was offered the nursery program, a daycare centre for staff children on the housing compound. Daryle advised me to stay away from it because the teachers would eat me up. He was probably right. They would have used any excuse to rip us apart. I was not enthralled with the daycare prospect.

"How's it goin', Dannie?" One afternoon Barb waved as she walked by after school.

"Are you getting along okay?"

She came inside for a few minutes and I walked her around the house to see the set up. For some reason, upstairs I showed her how I arranged the towels to line up a certain way. Even as I spoke, I realized how pedantic I sounded; how concrete sequential. When she left a few minutes later, I collapsed on the bed and sobbed, heaving convulsive sobs. An hour later when Daryle came home, I was still crying uncontrollably. When he asked what was wrong, I didn't know.

I learned that there was an International Women's Group. No one invited me to attend or to go with them. I took the driver because of course I was not allowed to drive. Shugher, was a Bedouin relative of someone at the school or around the school.

Shugher was straight from the desert, fresh from the desert, ripe from the desert. His generous girth filled his white *thobe* and he spoke no English. I quickly learned, *Assalam alaykum*, peace be with you, aka how are you? and *shukran*, thank you. If we were in the car at prayer time, as designated by the news paper and announced by the mosque, Shugerh pulled over to the side of the road.

He popped open the trunk of the car, extracted his prayer rug, placed it on the shoulder of the road or in the sand and began bending and kneeling in dedicated prayer. The first few times he did this, I was aghast at his presumptuous behavior. I was on my way someplace and he stopped driving to perform prayers. Not all cars pulled over, so I was furious that he became so pious when I needed to be somewhere.

Shugher had a Bedouin habit of scratching his crotch. He also dug deep when picking his nose. He was quite crude having learned no social skills to serve him in the city. He coughed up phlegm and spit to the side. He carried sticks in his pocket and picked his teeth with his clean hand.

One day, I ventured out with Shugher to attend a meeting of the International Women's Group. He cleared his throat and spit out the window. It was closed and the thick mucus disseminated across the glass and slid down the window. He thought nothing of it, raised his arm and smeared the mess around with the sleeve of his white *thobe*. Daryle's secretary called him Sugar. That was a reach.

When Shugher drove up to the meeting at Festival Palace, I realized the immensity of the group. Between 800-1200 international women attended IWG each month. It was highly organized to accommodate so many women under one roof.

It was also a threat to the authorities I learned, and was closed down on several occasions because of the enormity of the group. All those women under one roof must be trouble. Muslim men were permitted up to four wives, but very few availed of this opportunity. The extra wives were too expensive and just too much trouble. What mischief could 1200 women drum up! The authorities worried.

The front lobby vibrated with information booths arranged all around the enormous entrance hall advertising a myriad of activities. Ladies tennis, bridge, newcomers, gourmet cooking, stitch-n-bitch, I took it all in. No one was particularly forthcoming. I heard many languages. Friends connected in French including Lebanese, Canadians, Moroccans and Parisians. Ladies conversed in Italian, Chinese, Japanese, Urdu and Tagalog. The morning was overwhelming. I brought home a few brochures, the newsletter of community events and the program for the next meeting. I met no one, but I knew that day I had a fighting chance in this bewildering community.

My new goal: meet one woman each month. It was with that goal that I met a handful of women that year.

Tuna Fish and Fishing

For months we went about our work without the support of the community, and with divided support from school staff and the board. The previous superintendent stayed on the compound until Daryle finessed his departure.

And it was finesse, a strategic strategy, working through a preferred future, to use edu-babble. On the compound, Daryle challenged Tom on several social fronts. He defeated him in tennis; he beat him at chess. In a bizarre competition, the men agreed to a fishing competition; they would have a casting completion across the grass field. At the end of the day, Tom turned over his unsigned contract and left at midnight. It was something like that.

The next month I again attended the meeting of the International Women's Group. Mission accomplished. I met Joan whose husband worked with Westinghouse Corporation. I was thinking washers and dryers. Westinghouse supplied the Kingdom with air conditioners, elevators and escalators. No small business. After the meeting Joan spontaneously invited me for lunch.

Lunch.

She prepared tuna sandwiches. I remember as if it were yesterday. Who remembers a tuna sandwich lunch?

Joan invited me to lunch.

And then we met again. I joined the Newcomers group from IWG and we met together with husbands for dinner. It was a start. Slowly, one month at a time, woman by woman, one by one I started to cultivate contacts and friends.

Spring Break

"**W**here would we be without our kids? ….. Probably Bali."
In fact, we often become acquainted with members of the new community as a direct result of the kids. It seems I'm always somebody's wife or someone's mother.

"Oh, you're Ian's mom."

"Why do you ask?!" I was never sure I should confess, but it did open doors. Our teenagers became the conduit for community friendships.

The boarding school students returned to Saudi for spring break. Stuck in lengthy airport delays they renewed friendships and made the best of their 15 to 36 hour flights back to their parents in Riyadh and Jeddah. That first spring break with kids in tow, we caravanned through the desert, over the red sand dunes and across the stratified escarpment on a camping trip with two other families whose children also just returned from school.

The kids were the perfect and precise definition of teenagers, if there was a definition:

Wonderful kids; crazy kids.

Worldly kids; naïve kids.

Socially sophisticated; not street-smart.

Creative individuals; harmless groupies.

All alike, all different.

Teenage Third Culture Kids.

In the desert they cavorted with complete abandon in the solitude of the dunes. Like a gaggle of geese, they bummed around in baggy jeans, floppy hats, desert boots, and for shock appeal, stuck earrings in their noses and safety pins through the tops of their ears. Collectively, they were from Andover, Exeter, Notre Dame and Northfield. They sang, strummed guitars, made up words and roared at their own breed of humour, gawky arms dangling over each other's shoulders as they made their presence known to the vast wilderness.

When Bill and Marie Sullivan, Marie my diving buddy from Manila, transferred to Tehran, David Newsom came to Manila as ambassador for six months. We never understood why his mission was so short. Six months later Richard Murphy arrived as US ambassador to the Philippines. Their son Reeechard, as he was called by his peers, attended IS Manila with Jessica and Ian; the kids brought us together. We learned Newsom took the position of Under Secretary of State for Political Affairs. He headed a special commission to negotiate the release of the hostages in Iran.

Several years later Richard and Anne Murphy were assigned to Saudi Arabia. In the Middle East we saw them infrequently. Although he was U.S. Ambassador, they were not yet living in the diplomatic quarter in Riyadh but lived at the residence in Jeddah. Anne Murphy: product of the American East and graduate of an eastern university, bright, articulate, east coast formal, intellectual, professional.

In the Philippines our teenagers traversed back and forth between houses. Jessica and Reeechard had the lead roles in *Diary of Anne Frank*. They were great buddies. I respected Anne's professional skills in Manila and especially while we were living in Saudi Arabia.

Camping out with the Murphy's was not a typical camp-out. As U.S. Ambassador, Richard Murphy was required to travel with an entourage of secret service personnel, but on this occasion he was not obliged to take the bullet-proof limo over the dunes. The secret service men were a good bunch and much less formal in the desert, only occasionally talking into their cuff links.

The excursion took us to spectacular new territory. Early spring rains encouraged tiny desert blooms and giant blue irises. The Gaspereti's, bug and insect specialists, identified iguana, dhoubs, other giant and small lizards, red foxes and wolves, and a variety of butterflies and insects.

Michelle Suddarth from France, mother of Mark, wife of the U.S. Deputy Chief of Mission, identified wild herbs collecting samples which made an aromatic potpourri for our tents. Rocky Suddarth prided himself, and made us proud, in speaking deep Arabic with the locals.

The teens headed in one direction dragging guitars and the adults poked around in various other directions. While Michelle gathered herbs, and Gasparetti gathered bugs, Daryle turned over rocks.

What did he expect? He should have anticipated: he was stung by a large spider-thing residing under the rock. Gasperetti's confirmed what we already knew: the spider was a scorpion, a brown species seldom seen in the area. They planned to capture it and send it off to labs in Texas for identification. The hunt was on.

Grown adults scrambled about in the sand like rugby players landing the ball. One of the men apprehended the thing and they stuck it in a glass jar. Daryle's fingers, hand and arm bloated and inflated like a giant balloon from a Macy's Thanksgiving Day parade. His glands were red and swollen. His arm was instantly paralyzed, though he remained conscious. It was Daryle's Stone Fish Moment.

Resting in the sweltering dry heat, hundreds of kilometers from the next village, he ate all the pain-killers from the first-aid kit. Months later, when the specimen was returned from the bug lab, the institute confirmed that the brown scorpion was a deadly species. Had the victim, Daryle, been slight or in a weakened condition, he would be dead. A child or an elderly person would not have survived the dangerous sting.

Daryle didn't miss a beat. Not to be left out, he joined our nightly animated after-dinner conversation, even as he waited-out the poison in his system. We discussed the world-wide problems of education, the problems of the U.S. Congress, the issues of the Saudi monarchy, and the dilemmas of the Middle East. By late evening we solved every one of the world's tribulations as sparks of the fire glittered in the air like confetti tossed on New Year's Eve.

Invited To Tea

Michael Jackson

Several weeks after the camping trip, Anne Murphy hosted an afternoon tea at the Riyadh residence. The guest list merged the names of prominent Saudi women with women of the international community.

The conversation started, not with the rising cost of oil; that fact hardly impacted any of us living in Saudi Arabia. The conversation started with Michael Jackson, of all things, of all people.

> The local *imam* spoke
> from the mosque
> at Friday Prayers
> to the community at large
> through deafening loud speakers
> about the evils
> of Michael Jackson
> his music and videos.

"What do you think? I'm a leetle waried. My kids love Michael Jackson." The princess spoke with a soft accent.

"I like Michael Jackson," from Patti, my new California soul mate.

"Maybe da wards have double meaning?

"Maybe it's hees dancing. Do you think it's suggestive?"

Drivers lined up along the narrow lane as we inched up to the front of the residence. Shugher was long gone after hauling goats around in the back seat of the car. This time we hired a Pilipino driver.

Inside the residence Saudi ladies, with the nonchalance of wealth, flung their black *abayas* into a front closet. I imagined how they tossed furs or Prada handbags in London. How could I cultivate that wealthy abandonment? A great look; so not-teacher.

My contact lenses flashed back and forth across my eyes. Chic designer dresses adorned these beautiful people. They wore smart suits with short skirts which exposed long legs in beautiful designer stockings with provocative dark seams up the back and rhinestones on the ankles like embellished henna. Or long skirts with stitched seams, skillfully lined by Italian, French and Japanese designers. Who knew what stunning apparel hid beneath the conservative black wraps?

Noleen, from New Zealand, married to the head of the Saudi Chamber of Commerce asked,

"What were they saying from the mosque? My Arabic's not good, and I don't have teenagers, so I only half listened last week."

There was some discussion on this amongst the Saudi women. The western women also pondered the aura of Michael Jackson.

"Why he wears the glove? My daughter wants a glove. Why is that? What it means?"

"There are so many influences out there; if it's not Michael Jackson, it's something else."

Nameless princesses from the immense royal family nibbled tea sandwiches. Patti Abu Husain from California married a Saudi entrepreneur. Michelle was French and married to the American DCM. Everyone knew Michael Jackson.

Anne introduced me to Mrs. Zaki Yamani, expecting her third child; the attractive, young wife of then OPEC oil minister. Oil prices recently spiked from fourteen dollars a barrel to thirty-four dollars. The Iranian revolution followed by the Iran-Iraq War caused the inflation, but we hardly noticed since gas for us in the Kingdom, was .25 US cents per gallon. That year the average price in the States was $1.30 per gallon.

"The *imams* suggest he is homosexual," Soad offered.

"Do you think he's homosexual? Does it matter?" I wondered. I couldn't believe we were having this conversation but no one seemed uncomfortable.

"He khan dance, I know that. I like very much his videos."

"Once, at a wedding party, in the ladies tent, we were all dancing the hair dance.

"We swished our hair back and forth to our favourite Lebanese and Saudi music."

In this dance, the women wear long beautiful thobe-like robes, decorated elaborately with stitching and beads at the neck, and down the front. They gently toss their waist-length black hair from one shoulder to the other, sometimes in a circle or figure eight. Their shoeless feet pad quietly right, left, right; left, right, left gently rocking the pelvis.

"Have you seen the dancing?" the princess asked.

"I do like the hair dance. How long would it take me to grow my hair?" Forever, I knew.

"At the party, about three in the morning someone changed the music to Michael Jackson.

"We had so much, how you say?

"We enjoyed ourselves and the new bride danced in the centre of the tent.

"Her sister, Maryam knew how to, how you call it? Moon Dance."

"Moon Walk," several of us corrected. "Really!"

"Well, it wouldn't be acceptable in Islam," Patti asserted, a little too loud.

"Does it matter to you?" I looked around the room not wanting to single anyone out.

"What? If Michael Jackson is homosexual?" Joan jumped in. "I think he's ambiguous."

"I'm not sure," Georgia shifted in her chair and sipped her tea. "I'm not sure if it matters.

"What do I tell my children?" Each woman seemed lost in private thoughts.

"It's all about relationships, don't you think?" I felt brave; I wanted to draw in the Saudis.

"Well, yes. I want my kids to have relationships with the opposite sex. I really do.

"I have some trouble with same-sex affairs.

"But I want my kids to be open-minded," from Georgia again.

"We actually have some families in mind for the proposed marriage of our daughter, but we'll respect her thoughts if she does not want to marry into that family when she is older," Leyla almost boasted. "She's already six."

To me, she sounded like a soccer mum lining up summer camp to assure a place on the girl's little league team; the harried child syndrome, but I knew it was cultural; what they were expected to do to assure an acceptable match for the families; to blend wealth, or properties.

Ranya talked about her pre-adolescent daughter wanting to wear the *abaya* to show by being totally covered, that she was old enough to be noticed. Little girls were not required to cover until teen age. It was a status thing and at puberty young girls went back and forth, one day ready to cover, the next day not.

"Well, isn't that the point?

"Aren't they too young to be going around with boys?" Noleene asked.

"There is no way teenagers can date here," Patti reiterated.

"Do you approve of dating?

"We would never permit our daughter to be with a boy unchaperoned." Soad tossed her head and adjusted her thick dark hair.

"Well, there is no place for them to go anyway."

"Our daughter does go out with her friends to the mall," Sarah spoke for the first time.

"But she is with girls only," Soad validated.

"Yes, and I know they wander about, you say 'hang-out.' And they do flirt with the boys there. I did the same thing, so I know it's going on. I just want them to be very careful. We don't accept that behavior." Sarah seemed conflicted because she knew the thrill of risk.

"You know, I've seen those activities, the flirting, toward my son," I noted, not sure why.

"Your girls get a lot of mileage out of the *abaya*," maybe I was going too far.

"Just a wee bit of henna on the ankle, just a slit to allow the eyes to sparkle, the girls have it figured out. They are cute; quite coy at the malls," I should have stopped.

"And don't think the boys don't notice. I think they are very creative to pass phone numbers in tiny folded notes so they can pretend-date on the phone." There was no comment.

"Patti, what does your husband say about the sermons from the mosque?"

"Well, we do have our differences. What can I say? Hey! I'm from California. But, I am raising the kids in the Islamic tradition. We are very conservative at home. They attend the local schools, as you know. When we are in California and the kids are with their American grandparents, they don't have the restrictions.

"So how do you deal with that?"

"They know the difference.

"However, my kids are not thinking about dating yet. *Al humduli-lah.*" Thanks be to God.

The conversation was what I came to define for myself as different behaviors in different situations. People used to tell me, 'Saudis are hypocritical because they kick up their heels in London and are pious in Riyadh.' I also exercised different behaviors in different situations. I certainly respect the lifestyle and beliefs of my mother-in-law when I am in her home. There is no drinking, no glass of wine with dinner and no cigars after dinner. I didn't see it as hypocritical. It seemed the same for Patti raising her children.

Anne circulated during the discussion while Filipina maids in crisp white uniforms passed silver trays of canapés around the room. I wondered if she brought the maids with her from Manila.

She engaged Ms.Yamani on the other side of the Early American living area. It's my least favourite style of furniture and American embassies tend to flaunt it. I guess it wouldn't send the right message to furnish the residence in Scandinavian IKEA or black lacquered Chinese, French Louis XIV or over-stuffed Saudi Gaudy. Still, Norman Rockwell paintings don't give off the same sophistication as Picasso, Monet or Michael Angelo. Wall hangings in the residencies usually include quilts stitched in traditional patterns. Early-Ugly; they belonged at the state fair.

Topics from the Friday mosque disgorged over loud speakers tended to be wrathful, negative, often about the infidels or the ways of the decadent West. This was more of the same, but there was a morsel of substance for thought: enough to make these women ponder, days after the message. Isn't that what all clerics hope? Was the West decadent? Probably so. Was music and dance the cause of a degenerate generation? Did we in the West have our values askew? There was an argument.

I was struck by the dilemmas our children impose, wherever we are, what ever our culture. I felt invigorated by the discussion; frenzied, over-stimulated like drinking too much coffee in the evening. Who cares about Michael Jackson? Yet, the perspective of his influence on another culture was of interest. Values, morals, social norms, acceptable, unacceptable: raising children was not natural. We all wanted babies; who wanted teenagers?

Anne Murphy's invitation opened the doors to the community and opened my mind to sneak a glance into other-thinking, into a world of other-culture; an introduction into this new land which seemed rigid, all-the-same, controlled, polarized between the sexes, black and white, even in exterior dress. It seemed the issues weren't so black and white.

I Play By The Rules

Riyadh was strictly segregated and segregation strictly enforced. Even restaurants were partitioned in the dining area. Behind a curtain or in a separate room a family-section permitted husbands to join women and children. I never violated the rules. As a guest I accepted the regulations, unlike some of my crazy western colleagues.

I never jumped behind the wheel of the car to drive around the compound in a baseball cap, just to say I did. We heard stories of female Israeli pilots who flew onto a Saudi air base, touched down, jumped out of the cockpit and took off their helmets, long hair flowing. They took photos of themselves and flew off again, just to say they did. It was forbidden on all levels. Israelis are not allowed; women do not drive, let alone fly. I never broke the rules. I wore long skirts when I went into town and at religious holidays, Hajj and Ramadan, I wore a scarf, babushka style, out of respect.

When people later asked, and they always asked, 'What's it like living in Saudi Arabia, as a woman? I usually told anecdotal stories. I still love telling stories about the women's banks. No men allowed; women bankers, women tellers and women managers. The Saudi women have their own money and manage it as they like. I liked the idea that Daryle sat in the car while I went in to make my own monetary transactions. That rocks. I like the idea that women don't have to drive. Who wants to drive around looking for a parking place? Who wants to change a tire? Hire a man for that. The Saudi women have it right.

When our shipment arrived from Manila, months after our arrival, Ian began his adjustment. He and Daryle went to the warehouse when the customs inspectors finally allowed them in. They did not tell me what they saw and I'm glad I did not go with them. When Ian finally told me the circumstances, the details shocked me.

The agents opened all the boxes for inspection. They dumped the contents on the concrete floors then after some scrutiny, shoved the items back into the boxes. Several things in the repacked cartons I did not recognize. Candle holders belonged to someone else. Where did that jacket come from? Not mine. Black tire tracks appeared across our linens and clothing as if some maniac drove a tractor back and forth while learning to drive.

They ripped pages from books. The inspectors impounded a teak sculpture from Nigeria, no graven images allowed. They confiscated our Salvador Dali prints, not allowed, and marked up the art books with black markers. They scribbled Jane Fonda out of her aerobics books, to die for at the time; blacked-out her illustrative photos which showed her in leotards; my yoga books blacked out as well. What an awakening. I knew to write decorative house plant on the Christmas tree box, and ornamental toys for the ornaments on the declaration forms. I did not anticipate this outrageous manipulation.

At home we unpacked. Once Ian regained his personal effects, he morphed into a different person. I missed the clues. As soon as he sorted his clothes, books and treasures, found his guitar, music and soccer ball, he started inviting friends over after school. When I suggested he do so before, he claimed no one wanted to come to the teachers' compound. Well maybe, but after he sifted through his possessions and arranged his room, there were guys hanging around often after school, after sports and on weekends. He had his stuff. He was validated. He was settled.

Everyone knew the basic rules: no alcohol, no pork and no pork products like makeup or lipsticks. Even nutmeg was forbidden. If desperate, as a lark, we drank Listerine over ice. All medicines, including cough syrups, which contained any form of alcohol, were banned. On the other hand, the supermarkets sold Rauch's grape juice, red and white, in corked bottles and sugar by the bag in the same isle. Everyone made an attempt to grow their own wine; all of it bad.

Authorities banned girlie magazines and culled *National Geographic* issues which featured photos of partially dressed natives. They screened *Time* and *Newsweek* for content and censored-out any mention of Israel, oops, the Zionist Occupied Land.

One December just before Christmas, known as Winter Holiday, inspectors showed up at school unannounced. They walked through the congested animated clutter of the elementary hallway. To my chagrin, I watched as they ripped down winter snowflakes, hung by invisible nylon, gently fluttering in the air-conditioned breeze; snowflakes lovingly cut-out with little blunt scissors clutched by tender first grade fingers. They claimed these six-pointed flakes represented the six-pointed star of David; the star of Zionist Occupied Land.

They opened text books and scribbled Israel off the map. They relished ripping out drawings of the human body in the biology books. We learned to scrutinize everything.

I turned my head around early when I learned the translation for daughter. In Arabic, it roughly translates, at least insinuates, 'the protected one'. Once I saw it in those terms, it made sense to me. It was less the suppression of women and more the protection of women. There is something in our own culture about father-daughter, mother-son relationships. I didn't see it that way while living at home. I saw discipline, with the switch off a tree, not protection. Now however, with my nuclear family I see it as support, rather than protection. It's a fine line, perhaps; or perhaps a cultural line.

As western females, we recoiled at this. Women's rights inferred that we women could protect ourselves, thank you very much. We, Americans in particular, fought for years for the privilege to vote, then we fought for equal rights followed by equal pay and now we teach our daughters to be confident and assertive because we can become anything we want to become. To be protected was not a liberating concept. I made it work for me. I told myself I was something between a precious commodity to be protected and a princess to be served. It worked for eleven years. I played by the rules.

Mouna

I sat at a round table for eight in a British diplomat's garden. All tables are round tables at diplomatic affairs; never a head of the table, avoiding the protocol issue of who sits on the right or left of the host.

"And what is your work in Saudi?" I ventured to the man on my left. He gave me a vague work description having to do with helicopters, Mc Donnell Douglas. And the polite response,

"What do you do in Saudi?"

"We are with the International School," I replied.

"Oh." The typical response. He did not need to add, what else do you do. He scooped a mussel from his bouillabaisse.

"You're a teacher," he continued with undisguised disinterest.

"I work with admissions." He drank from his scotch over ice. Diplomatic immunity allowed shipments of alcohol for official events.

He let this sink in; I noticed a slight shift in his attitude.

"Who actually attends your school?" He was American, living in Riyadh; his older children lived elsewhere.

"International students from multinational corporations and the diplomatic community."

"How many Saudis attend your school?" He was more than polite; I sensed an agenda.

"We have no Saudis. The government won't permit them to attend, and we are committed to leaving places for international students," I continued.

"We would like to have some local students because they add a great deal to the dimension of the school, but the ministry won't allow it."

Servers removed the soup bowls, placing Cesar salads in front of guests. I turned to the gentleman on my right who was picking the anchovies from his plate. As the waiters refilled the tall white wine glasses, Mr. Helicopter chatted with the woman on his left.

"Do you have a card?" he asked me later. I sliced the rare Beef Wellington. Bulbous stemmed glasses filled with red wine replaced the white.

"I would like to talk to you about a Saudi family." Before I could put him off, he added, "They are very well connected."

"I would be happy to give you a tour of the school.

"They're all well connected," I said between bites.

"We have gone down this path with the ministry before.

"No exceptions. No Saudis." I tried to be gracious. It was a dinner party and we were both working it. No such thing as a free dinner.

He called the following morning and set an appointment for his sponsor. Mouna Al Rashid swaddled in black and escorted by security, walked into my office punctually at 11am. She started by telling me about her son, diagnosed with leukemia. She lifted the elegant black veil from her expressive face but remained bundled from head to toe in her designer *abaya*.

She spoke quietly in a deep gravelly voice. Fahad her first son was seven years old and ill. She would do anything to save her son; anything to make his last few months tolerable. For a fleeting second I wondered, was this a sympathy ploy? The ministry would not allow Saudis in our school.

Mouna Ayoub studied in Paris where she met Nasser Al Rashid. They married when she was nineteen, twenty years his junior. She was intelligent, beautiful and young. When we met in Riyadh she had two children and was in her late twenties. Nasser Al Rashid, Rashid Engineering, studied at the University of Texas where he

211

received a Bachelor of Science and went on to receive his Doctor of Philosophy in Engineering from the same university.

In a desperate attempt to save his life, young Fahad and his mother spent months at a time at St. Jude Children's Research Hospital in Memphis. She bargained with God. If He would save her son, she would do anything for God. Mouna al Rashid was originally Christian Lebanese. In this instance she was not unlike Imelda Marcos, pleading with God. Also like Imelda, she was beautiful and wealthy.

"Ms. Rashid, I think I can arrange for you to borrow some text books.

"Maybe library books for Fahad's grade level.

"Perhaps some classroom materials."

Although we had a no-fly policy and books were to remain in the Kingdom, I thought there might be an exception for her when she and Fahad traveled to Memphis. Perhaps some arrangement was possible.

The hospital link was logical on several levels. St Jude Children's Hospital was founded by Danny Thomas, famous American actor, born in the US of Lebanese immigrant parents. The hospital committed to research for catastrophic children's diseases, especially childhood cancers. Mouna was Lebanese.

Just when you think you know the answers, they change the rules. There was no question if the Al Rashid child would be admitted to the Saudi Arabian International School-Riyadh. Nasser Al Rashid played a large part in the development of the country and was engineering consultant to King Khalid and later King Fahd. There was no question regarding the enrolment of their son. I didn't meet Nasser until some time later.

At school, Mouna played the role of poor little rich girl. We became friends on a first-name basis; she was everyone's friend; magnetic and personable. Every week she volunteered in the classroom; she pitched-in enjoying the parent volunteer program; just one of the moms. She was at first surprised that no one wore an *abaya* and eventually stuffed hers in her large, elegant bag. Week by week she seemed to expand outward from the Saudi culture. I didn't know her in Paris, but I watched her evolve at school.

One week she was too busy or not sure how to laminate a large scarecrow for the classroom.

"I'll just buy a laminating machine for the house and do it there," and asked her maids to laminate the life-size door decor. Another week she didn't know how to make coffee in the work room.

"I've never made coffee.

"So that's how you do it." The teacher was patient.

One week she spilled hot coffee on her hand as she poured herself a cup.

"I'm so helpless. Someone always brings my coffee to me." The school nurse patiently wrapped her hand in gauze. On Valentine's Day she wore a ruby the size of a strawberry on her finger. It was possibly garnet but the colour was very ruby-like. While she pretended to be just one of us, she lived on another social level. It was condescending, but she was so charismatic about it, we overlooked the charade.

"I love this ruby. I bought it from a jeweler who sells cut stones.

"It's very large for a ruby.

"Nasser had it set for me, by Bvlgari.

"Do you like it?

"Here, try it on."

I attended small luncheons at her residence. Once we each received favours of gold bangles carefully wrapped and placed on each napkin. The discussion across the table centered on haute couture. I only recognized a few of the names as the ladies discussed which shows they planned to attend in Paris, London and Milano. Another time I received exotic perfume carefully wrapped and placed at the top of my plate at the table for 14. She was generous hosting classroom parties as well. Al Rashid constructed a mini playland on their property before Michael Jackson ever thought of Neverland.

One year Jessica was home for spring break. Mouna invited us to come for lunch and a swim. We sat around the pool as she phoned the kitchen for lemonade and sandwiches and salads. The afternoon was interrupted by a phone call from a European designer. Most of the conversation was in French. Then,

"Pierre, don't worry about the visa. I can get you the visa.

"The vest should be waist-length.

"I have a private jet. Don't worry about it.

"You have my measurements. The fabric should be silk; exotic.

Then more French. Jessica and I sipped our lemonade.

"I already talked with Oscar and he never got it right.

"You need to come here next week.

International Day

And then there was Moudhy. Moudhy al Rashid was young when Fahad entered our school. When she turned five, Mouna and Nasser registered her as well. This time there was no question about admission to the school. She entered the kindergarten class as feisty and spirited as her mother. Fahad grew stronger each year.

On International Day, Moudhy, Mouna and Fahad, the only Saudis in our large school, came in national dress. Moudhy wore a colourful long dress adorned with gold necklaces that hung to her waist, her long hair swishing down her five year old back. Fahad, shedding his jeans and polo shirt wore a white *thobe* and white *ghutra*. Mouna was stunning in Saudi dress, highlighted by kilos of gold, her hair also long and flowing, her black eyes flashing, tinted with shadows and mascara.

The Al Rashid's provided tables of Saudi food, as the only Saudi family in school. Mouna arranged for mounds of Saudi Capsa: large chunks of lamb on top of savory rice prepared with onion, garlic, tomato, carrots, the rind of oranges, plus cloves, cardamom, cinnamon, raisins and almonds. Every nationality loved it.

The Lebanese community prepared mezze of hummus, pita, olives, in addition to tabbouleh, baba ghanoush, eggplant and sweet diamonds of baklava; the French, Italian, Swedish families brought in food courtesy of their embassies: cheeses, crepes, pastas, olives, herring, meatballs. No, we did not serve wine at any school function. Ever. The Koreans prepared kim chee, the Japanese sushi, Filipinos prepared pancit, fried rice and chicken adobo. The Africans grouped together to prepare hot stews; the Indians prepared curries.

The Americans never got it right for the international dinner, it seemed to me. In fact, we never got it right in any school. Parents boiled hotdogs and made chocolate chip cookies and brownies. It was popular food, but always gave the appearance of tacky junk-food. More appropriate, I thought, would have been stuffed turkeys that would feed lots of people and showcase our national feast day. The school enrolled nearly three-thousand students with as many parents who loved the occasion to wear their national dress.

The Japanese wore silk kimonos with meter-wide obi sashes, the Dutch wore wooden shoes, the Germans wore lederhosen. Silk saris, colourful African turbans and wraps sauntered by tables of mushroom crepes, Swedish meatballs and Turkish stuffed grape leaves. The Americans invariably showed up in jeans and T-shirts.

After some time Mouna outgrew her role as parent volunteer and ran for a position on the school board. By then she had three children enrolled in school. She was bright, intelligent and added sparkle to the group. Daryle asked Mouna to preside over the Arabic weekend program. Arab parents complained about the quality of the classes and qualifications of the instructors. Mouna took it over, hired excellent teachers and made sure they were there on time. She always read her board packet and contributed to the discussions.

She matured in her education outlook; learned along the way and over time, developed a vision.

It was through that experience with western education augmented by her own experience in catholic schools that she planned to open her own school on Mallorca, fostered by the knowledge that she needed a place for Fahad to attend after he graduated from grade nine in Riyadh.

Fahad gained strength and his visits to Memphis became less frequent. He graduated from the Riyadh school a respected student leader and budding philanthropist.

Newcomers

One night the Meade's hosted a dinner party and as always invited a gaggle of interesting guests. Those in the garden represented various embassies and businesses including several Saudi tycoons. I looked forward to meeting the new Russian ambassador and his wife. I wanted to ask about the Soviet invasion of Afghanistan. It was rumoured the US supplied Kalashnikovs to the Afghans. Well, maybe I couldn't ask that.

I wanted to ask about *perestroika* and the restructuring of the Soviet economy and bureaucracy. I wondered if one could ask such questions at a dinner party. I wanted to ask about the implications of *glasnost*. How did transparency affect their work in the diplomatic arena? Did they find it difficult to be transparent in Saudi Arabia with the royals, with the monarchy? I wanted to hear about it. What really happened at Chernobyl? How did officials respond, react to the immediate problem in the area, and the global problem of international concern?

I conjured up a zillion questions that I wanted to ask of a captive audience; captive interviewee. Although maybe a first meeting, a dinner party would not be the appropriate venue. But I wanted to ask. Maybe someone else would ask and I could listen in.

We were perhaps the only guests who made our own terrible wine. The embassies were granted a diplomatic allotment and the business men seemed to have contacts. The Meades served real wine with labels, and duty-free liquor from the embassy. I thought to myself, 'Oh my god, they serve real wine: cabernet, chardonnay, pinot noir,' but in this crowd it went unnoticed; it was expected.

Inside the Kingdom of Saudi Arabia people served alcohol with

discretion. We all knew when we invited Saudis to our home not to offer or serve them alcohol. Hosts typically set up a bar with soft drinks
and juices and if you had access, alcohol. If Muslim guests wanted
wine or scotch or vodka they themselves asked the bar tender.

Fran and Dick Meade, long term residents in Saudi Arabia, hosted
lovely dinner parties; some casual, some more formal. Dick, a diverse
businessman, later purchased and brought in the Saudi franchise for
San Francisco Cheese Cake. It was so popular that for a while every
dinner party ended with some flavour of cheesecake. At first they
stocked the standard favourites: lemon, blueberry, mango, coffee,
caramel, rocky road, and my favourite, Reese's peanut butter cheesecake encrusted with chunks of Reese's pieces. In October he flew in
pumpkin cheesecakes. Over the months owing to the huge success of
the venture, they brought in apple-cinnamon, strawberry, raspberry,
white chocolate and pecan. In December he tempted us with eggnog
cheesecake. There were, however, no amaretto cheesecakes, no Bailey's
Cream or Kahlua flavours.

Fran at one time headed the Riyadh International Community
School. In the early history of the school RICS held classes in villas at
various sites in the city. There were 35 children on the first day of classes. Today 20 years later there were over 3,000 expatriate kids: pre-K
through grade nine. There were no high schools for western students
in the Kingdom; we sent our teenagers to boarding schools. She later
worked as protocol assistant to four US Ambassadors and contributed
as educational director of a Saudi women's organization for continuing
education. Fran served California wines.

I located my place-card and after cocktails, joined the table. The
conversation was light as waiters served giant prawns that dangled
on the side of ice-packed goblets. The newcomer from Moscow
talked about her adjustment to Riyadh. Table guests added anecdotes about their own arrival to the Saudi capital because everyone
had a story.

We laughed about restrictions and segregated restaurants, about
covering up and told and retold the latest horror stories of stonings
and beheadings at chop-chop square. It helped to know that others had
similar stories of adjustment. The beheadings were the most disturbing. We didn't laugh about the primitive punishment, but it helped to
talk about it. I stabbed a prawn and dredged it through cocktail sauce.
Most of us lived several places before landing in Saudi. It seemed we
rotated cities like a game of musical chairs. The list of countries read
like the table of contents to National Geographic.

Waiters surreptitiously removed the goblets and just as covertly
substituted shallow bowls of pale carrot-ginger soup. The elegant meal

juxtaposed a double image, an optical illusion of life inside the compound and life outside the gate like a hidden image in a Salvador Dali painting. We sipped our soup in defiance as if unaware of the surreal nature of our circumstances.

"I vant to bring-in cultural groups for the diplomatic community," Marina, announced.

"In two months. In May I am wanting to bring in a small group of belly dancers."

Every person at the table sat up straight at this notion, soup spoons suspended mid air.

I looked around and exchanged looks with the man on my left, then at the woman across the table. Belly dancers in Saudi Arabia? What on earth was this new woman think-ing? Surely she would have sensitivity about what was allowed and what was prohibited.

"Really!" someone said.

"Yes. I think the diplomatic community vould enjoy cultural experience." She spoke with a faint accent.

Waiters again circulated, removing the soup while we sat stunned contemplating this notion. I made small talk to the man on my right as a server in white poured more wine. Belly dancers as cultural experience; in my few years in Saudi, I had never heard anything so outrageous and so potentially dangerous in the eyes of the *mutawwa'* in the religious police. I looked around the table again.

"Oui, I'm sure zey vould!" from the French Ambassador. Marina continued, determined.

"I vould like to set up several verk-shops if there are residents who vould enjoy;

"while the group is in the coun-try."

"Oh, I'm sure there will be lots of interest in that," the men were shocked at the thought; bizarrely delighted too.

"Think my wife could join the classes?"

"Si, si, my wife also," from the Italian Ambassador.

"Where will you host these performances?" I asked, knowing the strict gender apartheid and difficulties in staging-logistics. I hoped to see a glimmer of understanding.

"Vell, the verk-shops can be held at our resi-dance." Marina sliced at the medium-rare beef fillet.

"I have a large open room vit new hard-vood floors." She waved the beef, stuck on the end of her fork, in a circle to indicate the space of the hardwood floors.

"Vee are still looking for a venue for the program.

"If ees in Diplomatic Quarter, vee can permit men and women to enjoy together."

No one rolled their eyes, but I was so tempted. These guests were diplomatic, after all. I looked at the woman across the table again. She quickly lifted one eyebrow. As we individually processed this ambitious proposal from the newly arrived public servant, Marina added, piercing a small parsley potato,

"Vee have many famous Russian belly dancers."

"Maybe you know Rudolf Nureyev; he is famous belly dancer."

"Ooohhh. Ballet dancer," everyone said at once.

Marina never slowed down and continued projecting her thoughts, oblivious, punching the air with her fork.

"I have never seen him, myself," she said while chewing.

"He is always performing in a coun-try where vee are not posted." She looked around at each of us. I pushed the peas around my plate.

"Ven we vere in Paris, he vas dancing in Vienna.

"Ven we vent to Vienna, he was vas dancing in Denmark.

"Of course, I don't expect to bring Neureyev into Saudi," she said to quell our perceived expectations.

"Vee have many Russian bel-lay dancers and traveling bel-lay companies." Now I could hear the slight pronunciation variance.

The soviets were still in Afghanistan and no one brought up the issue during dinner, at least at our table. No one mentioned perestroika, glasnost or Chernobyl. Marina never received permission for the ballet troupe to enter Saudi. We saw the diplomats from the Soviet Union only occasionally at large receptions. They transferred after twenty months.

We were momentarily excited about the belly dancers, even ballet dancers; it was not to be. In Cairo, perhaps; Riyadh was not Cairo. Not yet.

The Candidate

B uilt like a well-oiled body-builder, the candidate, a stocky man, glistened from the roots of his greased pompadour to the toes of his shiny wingtips. He entered the room, briefcase in hand and marched directly to the overstuffed chairs in the crowded, private interview area. He sat on the edge of the cushion and rested his hand on his swinging knee. It jerked as if victimized by a doctor's mallet.

We needed a French teacher, preferably one married to a chemistry instructor. Putting together the pieces of the puzzle, assuring the fit for the number of candidates with the number of matching positions was like working a Sudoku solution. Each year we made the pilgrimage to the recruiting fairs in Canada, England and the US; always in February. Always with the promise of delayed flights, missed flights, and canceled flights. Sometimes we split the recruiting between us in order to interview more candidates.

Much has been written about the recruiting trail, but not so much about the candidates. Aspirants come in all shapes and sizes and are as creative and diverse as the schools and positions we seek to fill.

"I vant to teech French," he blurted by way of impatient introduction; his name ended in 'vich.' He was not married to a chemistry teacher, a primary teacher or a librarian, but he did teach French.

"Tell us about your background," we began.

"Vell, I half vorked vit cheeldren from all over zee vorld, and I like vorking vit American cheeldren," he offered.

Sometimes you suspect the outcome of an interview in the first minutes; this was one of those sessions. Something was not quit right.

"You like teaching French," Daryle continued. "Where did you study?"

"I learnt in Saint Petersburg and von many competitions in my coun-tree.

"I have received especial avards for my pro-noun-ci-A-tion.

"I like to talking vit natives; like you and you," he nodded my way.

"That is vhy I vant best to teech French." He clearly wanted to be around Americans, and wanted to use the school as the venue.

"And what else have you done?" Was there anything redeemable here?

"I can do anna-thin." After some minutes of light exchange which yielded no knowledge of organizational skills, lesson planning, methodology, or text books, we submitted one last unlikelihood. I asked,

"Have you done anything with yearbook?"

He answered too quickly, "I tell you, I can do anna-thin. Vat is yeerbuk?"

Glossing over the yearbook question, he stammered on like a jackhammer,

"I-can-teech-dance." His short, stubby body belied his confidence.

"I teech Rrrrrussian dance," with a trilled rrrr. "I von a competition."

"You teach Russian dance?" as if repetition would make it go away.

"Do you have a US passport?"

"Not exactly, but zat is vhy I vant to vork vit yur school. Zen I vill get a ceetizensheep vit yur coun-tree." Espionage, KGB, security, where did this man come from? He would be viewed in our conservative Saudi community at best with suspicion, at worst as a plant.

"You can do famous Russian dance?" we asked in diverted curiosity. We were amused. With skepticism we questioned,

"Can you jump high off the ground, as high as famous Russian folk-dancers?"

He nodded, then grasped his briefcase and stood up to leave. In the middle of intense interview schedules with other candidates waiting in the hallway, this was a good sign. But then, "You vant to see?"

Dropping the case, he folded his arm across his chest and lifted his elbows shoulder height, parallel to the ground. His dark suit strained across bulging rhomboids as he began squatting, kicking his legs out straight in front, in classic Russian form.

He had our attention.

His leaps from a full squatting position were spectacular. As he ricocheted off the ceiling, the pictures rattled and the floor heaved. If we'd had a full-time, full-credit course for ethnic dance, he might have been our man. We were momentarily hypnotized. However we were, after all, looking for a French teacher and not, as it seemed running a competition. We looked at each other, looked at our watches and shuffled papers. We stood up, locked elbows and performed our own improvisational Pas de Trois all the way to the door. Next?

I Do Taters

B ack in Riyadh I worked the crowd. A large man stood in the open lobby of the embassy, his outsized feet planted firmly to support his bulk. He clutched a tall drink like it might be the only one of the evening; it looked like beer. Others milled about. He held his ground. I surveyed the crowded room. It seemed I had no choice.

"It was warm today," I initiated.

"Yup."

"What's your work in Saudi?" the standard opening.

"I do 'taters."

"Taters?"

"Yup."

"Have you been here long?"

"Friday night."

"Oh! Are you here on a business trip, then?"

"Yup." This was hard work.

"Where do you work?"

"Idaho. We do 'taters in Idaho."

"Oh! Potatoes!"

"Yup."

"Hmm. Most Saudi's eat rice. Do you work with the embassy commissary?

"McDonald's. Yup." I was shocked into reality check. Maybe he meant McDonnell Douglass aircraft.

"McDonald's is opening here???" I queried in disbelief.

"Only if we get the 'tater contract."

"I see." I didn't see at all. "What is the link? Does it work like a franchise? Do you think the Saudi's will be an important market, or is it for the expatriate community? How does it work?"

"The Saudi's are interested. It's McDonald's who is demanding consistent standards."

"What does that mean?" Then I continued, "You want to sell the potatoes."

"Yup. We have the biggest, best 'taters in the world in Idaho. We have a quality standard. Our 'taters are long, perfectly straight, for long, perfect fries. Up to McDonald's standard; to international standard. If I get that there contract, we can do business here."

"Well, sir, I'm sure the Golden Arches will be profitable here in Saudi, at least in Riyadh."

"Yup. We see Jeddah and Dhahran as big markets. Riyadh, they tell me is conservative. Jist might be a better market in those other environments. Know what I mean?"

"I do indeed. I hope your negotiations go well." I noticed he had drained his tall glass.

"Think I'll git myself another Budweiser. Sure am glad to know I can git I drink at the embassy, anyway. Still, I gotta be sharp goin' into the talks tomorrow with the Saudis."

"Good luck with your meetings; save lots of time for drinking tea during your talks." I was already moving toward another group. I was working the crowd. Needed to meet with some parents and couldn't wait to pass on the latest gossip: we might have McDonald's in Riyadh!

The Fast

"It's Lent! What are you giving up?" as a teenager I asked my high school friends.

"My parents are giving up meat; I'm giving up dessert," Julie started.

"I'm giving up boys," Rachael said as she smoothed her twin sweater set.

"That sounds good to me," from Marianne.

"I'm giving up chocolate. The prom is next month," again Julie.

"You afraid you might get a little bitty zit on your nose?" I ragged.

"You're gross. I just want to look good in my dress."

"Yeah, and it's almost beach time.

"If I don't stop eating, I will sink the surf board," I said like 'fer sure I was a surfer. The truth was we were all self conscious and consumed with teenage vanity. And boy-crazy.

It was a status thing to participate in Lent. I was not raised Catholic but all my girl chums fasted during the Easter season. We thought we were very superior. Fasting was in. It was what we did in the spring. It was cool. Even at the time, I viewed the exercise as self-serving. Lent was observed in the spring. It provided a great excuse for getting in shape for the summer season. Some girls gave up chocolate, others gave up dessert or ice cream. Some even went so far as to give up lunch. I never went that far. Sometimes we claimed we gave up boys. That lasted until about third period.

When I was very young, I wanted an ash mark, a grey bindi, a third eye. I had no idea what it symbolized, but it represented the start of the fasting for Lent. On Ash Wednesday kids came to school with a mark on their foreheads and that was the beginning of the season. They looked special; everyone noticed. Once I bent over and scooped up some loose dirt to rub on my face between my eyes. I looked like a dirty kid.

Perhaps the Islamic month of Ramadan can be compared to the Christian Easter season of Lent. However, unlike Lent, Ramadan in Saudi Arabia is not optional. Unlike Lent, Ramadan is not always in the spring. The holy month of fasting is the ninth month of the Islamic lunar year, and only determined by the sighting of the new moon. If the crescent is obscured by clouds, the Fast does not begin. Or end.

My first year in Saudi, catapulting directly from Catholic Manila, I learned that the Ramadan Fast is imposed on all citizens of the country including non-Muslim guests. All restaurants close during daylight hours. All restaurants. Full stop. No exceptions. Non-Muslim hotel guests may, by special request, order room service but may not walk around with a cup of coffee. No snack, no shawarma sandwich, no cigarette, no water, no chewing-gum, no sex. Now there's a thought.

Pushing my shopping cart down the wide supermarket isle, I asked the manager of the impressive Riyadh Safeway,

"Ramadan must be a slow time for you every year. Do you take a break now?"

"Ha! It's our best month, our biggest sales," the American supervisor told me.

"Our revenue is based on our Ramadan sales."

"Really."

"While everyone is fasting, the women cook all day preparing for the end-of-the-day meal, iftar. Muslims eat like crazy all night. And we count on it. It's festive."

It's also nerve-wracking to be on the road at the end of the day during Ramadan. Men drive like madmen trying to get someplace, usually to their neighbourhood mosque, to break fast. The drivers in Cairo are terrible during the month, irritable and angry and the Emiratis are not only crazy behind the wheel, they drive at break-neck speed, throwing caution to the shamal. They go faster because there are not as many cars and they weave in and out of traffic at turbo speed like preprogrammed projectiles heading toward their target. Maybe they are lightheaded at the end of the day due to low blood sugar. Of course I did not drive, but tried to read a book in the back seat; anything for distraction.

"Oh my gosh, what was that?"

Thank god I wasn't driving. I would have driven off the road or plowed into a wandering camel. The Ramadan cannon exploded at the exact moment the sun dropped out of the sky. The Fast for the day was over.

The Commission for the Promotion of Virtue and Prevention of Vice Religious Police

The buildup for Ramadan, in the form of public awareness, starts several weeks before the holy month begins. *Mutawa*, religious police, are visible and numerous. These disheveled men always appear rumpled. Their beards are untrimmed, unruly and wiry. Their *thobes* are too short and sometimes brown. They wear black shoes and black socks, undoubtedly a British influence; seldom sandals. Never mind; they cover their ankles. They wear checkered *ghutras* draped over their heads like Shakespearean crones, not held in place by black cords, certainly not pleated in front, cowboy style.

They patrol the markets and malls reminding everyone that all women must have their heads covered and should not wear makeup; a good reason to favour the veil or beg for a *burqa*. Men must not wear any gold jewelry. *Mutawa* carry sticks, useful for smacking exposed ankles or wrists. And they use them. Men have had their *iqamas*, critical identification cards, taken because their wives, shopping with them, did not have their heads covered. Women have been scolded and sent home. You have to know the rules, you have to play by the rules and even then they sometimes change the rules especially during significant religious times including Fridays.

The religious police act separately and apart from Saudi police. They are members of the Commission for the Promotion of Virtue and Prevention of Vice who roam about instilling fear. These slovenly men are scary.

I knew a woman, a large western woman, who was shopping at an outdoor market. She wore a long, rather full dress which covered her arms and legs. As she bent over to examine tomatoes one of these old-fashioned terrorists came up to her and smacked her on the ankles with his stick. With automatic, uncontrolled reflex she whirled around and slugged him with her bag. They were both stunned. She was promptly hauled off infuriated, was interrogated and released.

Recently, there has been a trend toward changing attitudes in Saudi. The public is slowly standing up to the abuses of these stick-wielding conservative men. The stated role of the *Mutawa* is 'to ensure strict adherence to established codes of conduct. They may detain people.'

Until recently, they detained people on the spot, taking them to a district office. The law now requires that any arrests be made only in the presence of an accompanying policeman. It was not always that way.

The Mosque

Significant events across North Africa and the Middle East often evolve after Friday prayers. The topic may be about the moral influence of Michael Jackson or the burning of the Holy Qur'an. It may be the toppling of a dictator, or inciting demonstrations over wages or increasing food prices. Fridays are traditionally days of statement; days of finality; get-out-the-vote days; Final Friday; Freedom Friday. Revolutions often come to fruition after Friday noon prayers.

Mosques act as gathering places, like the squares of ancient Greece where citizens gathered to listen to orators. Isocrates, Plato, Aristotle met in the Agora and open markets of Athens to discuss and debate. Today, Arab men gather to talk about political issues, to verify and pass-on news and share stories. They argue and deliberate. As in ancient Greece, effective orators not only inform; they persuade, generate emotion and influence opinion.

In the mosque, unlike the ambience of churches wherein protocol suggests stillness for inner reflection, mosques are often venues for animated discussion as well as communal prayers. During Ramadan men share their common sacrifice and break fast together. Special prayers are said and one-thirtieth of the Qur'an is recited each night.

In front of the mosque, rows of plastic, rubber and leather sandals line up like multicoloured centurions. During Ramadan, at the sound of the cannon and the call of the *muezzin* men praise Allah. Inside the mosque, dehydrated devotees sit on patterned carpets, in ample white *thobes*, cross-legged and barefooted. They drink water from paper cups filling and refilling from oversized red Igloo containers, quenching their parched throats from a day of denial.

Young and old, educated and illiterate, labourers and executives, as equals, consume traditional fresh dates. As the fruit is passed, men reach with their right hand for nourishment to cut the edge off the hunger. For now, the men are quiet. *Alluh Akhbar*. God is great.

I decided early that I wanted to experience what my Saudi neighbours felt during this important month. I had no plan to wear an *abaya* or convert to Islam or go native. I wanted to acquire a more genuine empathy; to learn how this annual ritual enhanced ones spiritual life.

The first year that I tried to fast, I skipped breakfast and lunch and pushed dinner up an hour. I cheated just a wee bit. When I felt hungry, I sneaked a cup of coffee behind a closed door. Around ten in the morning my stomach growled so loud, people heard it. By three in the afternoon I experienced cramps. Sometimes I squeezed my stomach to relieve the stabs. Everyone else went through it. I would survive.

As the month progressed, I learned to think outside myself; to get on with my work; to stop being so self centred and to stop obsessing over my uncomfortable sensations. If my stomach growled, what was it like to always feel hunger? The Fast forced me to wonder: what would it be like to be without food; to fixate over where I might scrape together provisions for my family. I was privileged. Eventually I gave up water and all meals during daylight hours. However, in the manifestation of full disclosure, it is only fair that I mention that I have been known to break my fast not with water and dates but with a glass of wine and a chunk of cheese. I am reflective, not pure.

The Fast helps me understand the significance of going without. It helps me identify with colleagues who celebrate a minor accomplishment at the end of each day; a feeling of control, of discipline. In the winter it is easy. The days are short. During spring and summer fasting is more difficult. The sun in the Middle East bears down without mercy, the days are long.

The kids lined up, noses pressed to the kitchen window waiting for the sun to set.

"Mom, this is so unfair," from Jessica.

"Why do we have to fast?" Ian demanded.

"You are so mean."

"No one else has to fast."

"We're on spring break. We're supposed to be on holiday."

"Yeah, Mom. You're forcing us."

"It's not fair."

I decided the kids should experience what the Muslims experienced. Ramadan that year came during spring and the kids were home for holidays. I only did it once and they only participated for a couple of days. Of course I never heard the end of it. They were not as reflective as I had hoped.

Travel Exemption

The International Women's Group invited a speaker one year to discuss the topic of Ramadan. He explained that students, children, pregnant women, the elderly and the ill, as well as travelers, are exempt from the fast. If you miss a day you can make it up.

"One year I was traveling to San Francisco from Riyadh," he started.

"Although it was during Ramadan, I didn't see any reason to give up my Fast.

"Who would give up fasting for airline food?" We laughed at this notion.

"If I'm going to break my fast, it's sure not going to be for airplane chicken and green peas, right?" Everyone laughed again. I never believed for one minute that he sat in coach. However, he made his point.

"I have made the trip before," he continued. Everyone in the hall had made the trip and identified with the 26-34 hour endurance flight.

"My strategy," he said, "was to sleep most of the way." He continued, "The drinks-cart rumbled down the aisle. I slept.

"Sometime later the meal-cart bumped along, nudging me. I went back to sleep.

"The lights lowered in the cabin and I slept three more hours.

"When we arrived in New York, it was still daylight.

"The sun never set." The audience moaned.

"I was exhausted. Not from lack of sleep. Physically, I was fine.

"Emotionally, I felt drained. I wanted to do the right thing.

"I didn't calculate correctly.

"Psychologically, all my senses seemed to scream: 'starving, starving.'

"Discouraged, I claimed and rechecked my luggage and boarded the flight to San Francisco.

"As the plane landed, the sun dropped into the Pacific Ocean.

"The minute we got off the jet, I grabbed a loaf of sourdough bread.

"No Arabic pita ever tasted as satisfying as that chunk of San Francisco sourdough.

"I gave thanks to Allah.

"Now I understand it.

"The scholars are right. I appreciate the reason for the travel exemption."

The Commerce of Christmas

S tudents are also exempt from the Fast. However, no surprise, the older students like to fast, want to fast; it's that status thing. It's cool. The Fast singles them out. The American and International schools comply with special hours determined by the Ministry of Education or the Ministry of Tourism or Culture or the ever important Vice and Virtue Squad.

We set aside a separate room for Muslim students where they sit or pray or study during lunch break. Such status.

But that get's old. Who wants to sit around doing homework during lunch break? The first few days the boys line up in prayers, but that get's old too. They want to be back in the action, hanging with their non-fasting peers. Students are exempt from the fast but they covet the recognition, the attention of participating. Unlike my high school chums these students don't give up ice cream or chocolate. They give up all food, all liquid, all day.

"Aye, I'm so tired," from Nada resting her head on the desk.

"I was with my family for iftar and had no time for homework."

"Ms, I'm so thirsty. I can't think, sorry, Ms," whispered Farida.

"I have headache, Ms," Mohammed whined holding his head with both hands. Mohammed always had a headache. Mohammed gave me a headache.

I look forward to Ramadan; but many westerners do not. It's a challenge, a chance to reflect, and a feeling of unity with colleagues who sacrifice for the month. It's not convenient. There is a slow-down in hours and efficiency. Business colleagues find the adjustment annoying. For those working in international business, the frustrations mount. Four days are already potentially lost because the Saudi weekend is Thursday-Friday and Europe, the US and much of Asia maintain a Saturday-Sunday weekend. It's always somebody's day off.

We in the west are a bottom-line culture and shortened work hours don't fit in our go-go-go lifestyle. We are aggressive, assertive, a money-driven culture and sitting around drinking tea or going home early are not concepts we embrace. The rest we measure as wasting time, as letting the competition get ahead. If we do get it, do understand the system, most likely the big boss in the home office won't get it and will require a more enhanced explanation for the slowdown than, "Everyone here is fasting."

According to the Qur'an, one may eat and drink at anytime during the night "...*until the white thread of light becomes distinguishable from the dark thread of night at dawn. Then, you shall fast until sunset.*" Sura II.187.

The challenge and conflict for expatriates is working a western schedule and a Ramadan schedule simultaneously. Accustomed to an 8am-5pm work day, or more likely 10am-8pm allowing for a generous lunch break, during Ramadan the entire country, the entire Muslim world, is in tilt. The days are topsy-turvy and for many, it's a scenario of up all night, sleep all day.

One year I was having therapy for a frozen shoulder. When Ramadan started, all of my appointments were scheduled for 10pm. I should have been in bed. I was scheduled for alternating women's nights. I sat in the reception area, the only woman not shrouded in black, the only woman with my face showing, though my head was covered with a scarf.

When called in, the doctor and nurse strapped me into various contraptions to pull and stretch and rotate my arm and shoulder. At the end of each session, I was relieved to be out of the torture chamber and painfully left the office into the throngs of pedestrians. Like everyone else, I battled late night traffic jams and got home around midnight. In a few hours I would face students equally exhausted.

Muslims break fast when the sun goes down, pray, prance around the malls, eat and shop all night, take a mini nap, get up before dawn, take suhoor then go back to bed. Some have a light meal for suhoor, but many eat a huge capsa of lamb and seasoned rice. Everyone gains weight.

For me, it's easy to fast in Muslim countries. In the west it's more difficult because there is no support. I don't talk about it. Unlike my teenage years, I don't want the attention, the questions about what I'm doing or why. It is very personal. I have been at luncheons where I pushed the food around, a trick I learned from my kids, then asked the waiter to box it up. You can only do that in America; take your food home in a box. I admit I've done that. It's tacky.

The sacrifice is easy. The discipline is not. For the faithful, the reward is a humbling focus on surrender, appreciation, and dependence upon God; a reflection about poverty and hunger; a time for self discipline, self control and patience. So why is the driving so crazy before iftar when patience and control are so important?

The three days of *Eid* are festive celebrations at the end of Ramadan. Twenty-nine, even thirty days of denial and discipline deserve celebration and jubilation. I love the thought that I did it. I made the challenge. I only cheated once or I only cheated twice or I didn't cheat at all; that the entire country fasted together; made it through the challenge like the entire city reading the same book at the same time; to agonize, celebrate, relate together.

Two years in a row I purchased eccentric furniture during the Ramadan Sales at the malls. I called the pieces Saudi Gaudy; silver chairs with original burgundy padded seats, coils protruding under the surface nearly poking through the thin velvet like chicks trying to hatch. Another year during *Eid* I found a garish silver hexagon table to place between the chairs. Really gaudy. I later realized the work is from India. I like it, outlandish as it is.

Reflection

In recent discussion there is concern for the growing commercialism of Ramadan. It's-beginning-to-look-a-lot-like-Christmas; like the commerce of Christmas. In Lebanon, I've read, Ramadan has become self-serving and known for extravagant entertainment, great shopping and lavish meals; Lebanon, the fashion centre of the Middle East. Retailers now charge higher prices during Ramadan. Rather than focusing on the poor, they focus on the wealthy. Copious *iftar* banquets and buffets offered by five-star hotels for the wealthy, do nothing to highlight the plight of the poor.

The common Saudi breaks fast along the Cornish or in the parks or with family and enjoys traditional simple foods. He doesn't have money to spend on opulent dining and entertainment. In Lebanon, I have read that the season is so festive, other cultures and religions fly in to take advantage of extravagant festivities. It's a time for special clothes; a dress-up occasion with fine jewelry and elegant attire, for those who can afford.

Television advertising promotes entertainment and elegant iftar meals, and malls that twinkle with luxurious lighting. The emphasis is no longer on equalizing the population, but on polarizing the wealthy from the poor in a commercial frenzy.

The intent of the fast is to emphasize sharing, giving up, making small sacrifices; to experience hunger. Excessive celebrating, excessive eating, excessive shopping is not appropriate at this time some argue. It is better to spend the time in prayer. In Lebanon, the fast is not imposed as it is in Saudi Arabia. In Egypt, Indonesia, Pakistan and other Muslim countries, the fast is optional, though shops often close during the day.

In countries outside of Saudi Arabia, the number of those who fast is dwindling, as numbers of worshiping Christians decline. Some question if prayer is being lost. In mixed cultures, where diversity thrives, Dubai, Jakarta and Beirut, everyone enjoys the culture of Ramadan; some question if Ramadan has become self-serving. Maybe it is like my teenage experience with Lent after all, becoming more about self, less about others, less about serving the poor, less about identifying with poverty.

It Takes

Less Time

To

Boil an Egg

Aerobics

Pink plastic petals bobbed up and down on the rubber swim cap as the woman plopped around the pool.

"It's weird over there where you live; it must be a real problem."

"Well yes, I guess it is; sometimes it is."

I assumed the swimmer wanted to comment on camels or women's rights, the usual Saudi topics. I was cold in the indoor pool and timidly tried to tip-toe into the water. I never got the habit of plunging right in. I preferred the slow-is-better technique. We had four days left of our summer break before returning to Riyadh.

Jessica and Ian, completing undergraduate degrees in Spokane, led the water aerobics class for community women. On my first day when the women worked out with water-jugs as weights, I felt very confident. I could lift my water weights, push them together and pull them through the water as well as the other women who attended all year. I was awesome and proud, and somewhat amazed that I could keep up.

I felt good; firm and fit to start another school year in Saudi. I huffed and puffed to get my heart rate up; kicked my kickboard with all the fury of a camel jockey. I jogged in place trying to get warm. The discussion about Saudi Arabia never materialized.

232

At home, at lunch, bragging on myself and my brilliant ever-so-fit state, Ian told me, "Mom, your water-jugs were only half full."

Later in the day, I understood what my pool-pal was talking about. In the early pre-dawn hours of August 02, 1990, Iraq invaded Kuwait. The world sat on edge. "It's weird over there." 'Weird' might not have been my descriptor, but there was now an element of uncertainty and immediacy, an urgency to our remaining holiday time in the US, our last four days.

The invasion started on August 02, 1990. Two days later most of the Kuwaiti Armed Forces were overrun by the Iraqi Republican Guard, many escaped over the border into Saudi Arabia.

As the news of the invasion broke, our phone lines jammed between Spokane and Saudi. The skeleton staff already in Riyadh sent updates and hourly communication using phones and faxes. Kuwait, a weensy country, was easily overrun by Iraq. What were the implications for Saudi Arabia?

We decided to stay in the US for another week to contact board members and all new staff. Would they come? Should they come? Why should they come? Daryle wanted to be practical, sensible and sensitive to feelings and emotions.

We spoke with returning teachers. We talked with their parents. This contact was essential for determining our procedures and strategy for the opening or closing of school for the fall season. Kuwait was a small country; if Iraq steam-rolled across Kuwait, would Saudi be next?

We reentered Saudi a week late, with restrained confidence. Television news pumped everything up. We needed to deal with reality; needed to be on the ground, on site. We needed to reassure families and staff that life was a 'go,' that school was a 'go.' At the airport there were no tanks. In the streets there were no tanks.

We talked with Ellis and Kay Melton, Riyadh teachers from Arkansas who called the compound several times, way too many times, before heading back to Riyadh.

"Hey Bob, what is the lay-of-the-land? How's the climate? Are you staying?" Bob Tinney was Personnel Director.

"Should we come back to Riyadh or wait to see how things develop?"

"It's fine Ellis. Come on back. It really is fine. There is no activity and the streets are quiet."

The Meltons booked a flight as far as Paris. They waited three more days then called the compound again.

"Hey Ted, Ellis here. How's the environment? I've been watching CNN." Ted Burgon worked as Manager of Building and Grounds, now self appointed as Security assistant.

"Should we come, or wait it out in Paris?"

"Ellis! Come on in. Someone will meet you at the airport. It's fine. Really. We've been at the pool all afternoon. It is safe."

"Ted, are people evacuating? If you're going to evacuate, there is no point in us flying to Riyadh just to evacuate out."

"Ellis, no one is evacuating. People, just like you, are coming back. Lots of families are already back. It's fine; it's safe."

They boarded the plane in Paris, arrived in the early hours of the morning, when all overseas flights arrive, and slept immediately in their compound villa. A few hours later the Meltons, in the dead zone, the deep sleep one finally achieves after the adrenalin relaxes and intense sleep takes hold, faintly heard a pounding at the door. It was not the prayer call; it would not stop. Ellis finally staggered downstairs toward the unrelenting pounding. Bob knocked at the door. Outside stood Maxine, Nancy, Ted, and eight to ten others, all with suitcases, hand luggage, and the school van loaded with bags.

"Sorry Ellis. During the night, sometime after you arrived, the situation changed. We all have our paperwork and are evacuating out right now. You have no documentation and Al Matar will try to get you an exit-reentry visa in the next week or so. We couldn't do anything without your passport. I hope you get out all right.

"There is a stack of papers on my desk, all in Arabic. I'm sure you can find someone to translate them and help you get out of the country. It has all been very fast. There is no time; I wish we could have helped you escape."

They waved goodbye, hurried for the van and skidded out the compound gate. Ellis stood devastated and in shock. He slowly shuffled back upstairs. Kay, now fully awake begged for an explanation. Ellis looked at Kay, shaking his head, dumbfounded.

"Kay, something happened and they are leaving. We can't get paperwork for an exit visa."

"What? What's happening? What are we going to do? Why didn't they tell us?

"You called from Arkansas, you called from Paris. Why didn't they tell you?"

"Don't yell at me."

"I'm not yelling. I just don't understand why they told us to come into the country, and now they are leaving? Why didn't they tell us the truth?"

"Turn on CNN."

As Kay moved toward the remote control someone knocked at the door. Ellis peered out the upstairs window. Who was it? Who was coming to get them? He grabbed his jeans and threw a shirt over his pajama top. He saw no tanks; he saw no one. He slowly made his way down the stairs; Kay hunkered down and peeked over the banister toward the front door. Ellis pulled the drapes slightly aside to look out before answering the persistent knocking. There stood Bob and the others, waving and laughing.

Ellis did not recognize the waving, just the familiar faces. He threw open the door still in shock and wonderment. They came back for them after all.

"Kay, they have come back for us." Kay stood up tall and grabbed her jeans to pull on with her night shirt. She bounded down the stairs to join Ellis and those at the door who had come for them.

Waiting for instructions they stood side by side while Bob and Maxine, Nancy and Ted and the others clutched their sides with laughter. Ellis looked at Kay. Still groggy and disoriented, their reactions delayed. What were these merry-makers saying? Should they grab their unpacked bags?

The gang waved and laughed, amused by their black humour and elated by their theatrical success. Maxine gave Kay a bear hug. Then, for Ellis, the great aha! There was no evacuation, no crisis.

As we assessed the situation in Riyadh, we talked with colleagues in Jeddah and Dhahran. We decided to postpone the opening of school by one week hoping our school population would return from their summer holidays as the situation in Kuwait mellowed. It did not and they did not. Not all families. Not right away. Parents were reticent to return to Riyadh with their children.

Companies which lost everything in Iran during the revolution were not willing to take another financial bath; they did not initially send their employees back to Saudi Arabia. Several major corporations refused to send in spouses and families including Boeing which represented a large student population. This decision also impacted several of our teachers. The spin-off was that it lowered the enrollment figures hence tuition revenue.

On opening day, we mustered-up sixty-two percent of our students. However, we lost thirty-eight percent. In the good ol' American way, we immediately set in motion try-outs for cheerleaders, sports teams, music groups and pep squads. We posted the schedule for student council elections and meetings for honour society. Everyone wanted a diversion from the news.

The appreciative and relieved students concentrated on reports, projects, term papers and violin practice. But the constant news barrage had a draining effect on all of us, the students being no exception.

It was widely acknowledged that the recently created 24 hour CNN was a good thing, but it also generated an overpowering presence and dependence. It was not news until CNN gave us a visual; if CNN told us it was true, then it was true. It was parenthetically acknowledged that a hardship post was one without CNN.

Mohammed

I sat cross-legged on a stack of folded silk carpets in the corner of our small villa. I clutched a dog-eared copy of *To Kill a Mockingbird*. I read hoping to be ahead of the eighth grade language arts students. I used skimming-and-scanning and then performed a deep-reread of each chapter, dredging up middle school reading skills. The teacher was unable to come in: uncomfortable, afraid, parents were afraid, company refused? I took the class.

When school opened one week late, there were three guys named Mohammed in the grade eight class. My favourite Mohammed was a tall, lanky kid from Kuwait.

He looked out his window in the early hours of the dawn on August second. He stood at the upstairs window in his pajamas and watched tanks drive through the streets. It was not the usual scene, but he did not recognize that an invasion was in process. Never had he seen a line of tanks driving past his window, 'round the round-a-bout and down the street: big tanks; army tanks; not the usual colour of the local Kuwaiti tanks.

On August second, while I splashed about with my water aerobics group in Spokane, Mohammed reflected on the approaching head-lights in the street; the uniquely distinguished sound of oversize tanks rolling in convoy past his home.

Now in Riyadh Mo, as he preferred to be called, slumped at his desk. His legs were too long; they stretched under his small table, across the floor, sometimes crossed at the ankles. He sat like a Picasso version of Don Quixote.

Everyone liked Mo. He was new; he was quiet. He seemed reticent to converse in class, simply introducing himself, "My name is Mohammed." I wanted to draw him out.

"So Mohammed, do you have family in Kuwait? What have you heard from them?"

"Everyone came with us."

"What do you mean, came with you?"

"We all drove across the dessert to the Saudi border."

"Do you mean you were actually in Kuwait when Iraq invaded?"

It was as if Mo never thought about this; as if he never had time. It was as if he never processed the idea of war, displacement, relocation. Of course: he was a teenager. How could he be expected to comprehend any of it?

He slowly told us what happened. We enrolled a few other Kuwaiti students, but most evacuees chose Arabic schools. Mohammed was fluent in English. His choice in Riyadh was the Saudi Arabian International School, American Section. As the story unfolded, I prodded, giving him gentle prompts to get his narrative out. He began to speak rapidly telling bits of the story as it occurred to him.

"I knew it was strange, ya know? Those tanks going through the streets.

"And they didn't look like the regular tanks we saw sometimes on the bases.

"I got my parents up. I don't know why I was up at that hour. Something woke me."

He rousted his parents who stumbled to the windows and stared. They turned on the television. No news. A blackout. They turned on the radio. No news. Marching music. Through phone calls to friends and relatives, they pieced the story together. Iraq invaded Kuwait.

He and his family shoved as much as possible into their cars. Nothing was meticulous about the move. His mother grabbed armfuls of beautiful long dresses and thrust them into a box. She threw elegant shoes into a bag with rice and sugar. Mo grabbed the family computer while his father forced bags and boxes into the trunk of the car. No time to go to the bank, they gathered the family gold and jewelry and cash and stuffed it under the floorboard of the back seat.

Mohammed, his sister and several cousins squished into the back straddling containers of petrol and drinking water. Suitcases bundled in bedding were lashed to the roof of the car. With nine people in his car, and as many in the other family cars, their convoy headed toward the border joining other convoys forming a small procession across the sand to the Saudi border. Two weeks later, he was in my class at the International school in Riyadh.

I asked Mohammed to write about what happened in Kuwait. He obliged, and the story became more focused in his mind. He was anxious, but not traumatized as his parents might have been. His experience was about going through the transition of the move.

In the beginning, he didn't seem to realize he escaped. He missed his friends, the familiar surrounding of home, like most kids who shift from school to school, from country to country. The act of relocating and attending a new school was abrupt. He had no friends in Saudi and little communication with his former friends in Kuwait. The move was sudden and unexpected. He had no time to prepare; no time to process the move.

He prepared assignments conscientiously and never missed on the homework. Once he got his story out he was talkative in class though relatively focused. Sometimes I thought he would never stop talking. But he was under control and always participatory in class discussion, nearly to distraction, but never over the bounds of appropriateness.

Shannon, a student from America, viewed life from a different perspective. She was a serious learner. Not as gregarious as Mo, but very studious. She too prepared her homework thoughtfully, ready to discuss the novel in class. Shannon's deep dimples slashed down the centre of her pale cheeks and when she smiled, her cheeks bisected. Somehow, her cavernous dimples made her appear very American, the way freckles indicate wholesome. Shannon later told me that her parents engaged in lengthy discussions regarding whether or not to stay. "Ultimately my mom wouldn't leave my dad and my dad couldn't just leave (his) work, so we all ended up staying."

Rania embellished the class as a bright and sensitive adolescent. Her dad was a good friend, often around school and her mom was equally supportive. Her younger brother gave her grief, but they were all good friends. Rania's skin was as coffee-brown as Shannon's was snow-white.

Others in the class added a mixture of dynamics. Each student represented a different nationality, presented dissimilar backgrounds, perspective and voice. When I read their essays I was often surprised at the accurate, if cultural, perception they brought to any given assignment. None of the students took ESL as a class, but they demonstrated various abilities related to their linguistic background. As we made our way through To Kill a Mockingbird chapter by chapter, we talked about the story, the themes, in class.

Rania began a journey of self awareness as the discussions evolved, becoming aware of her blackness, aware of her sexuality. I think she never noticed her skin colour, or knew she was black or that the colour of her skin might influence how people thought of her. She was Sudanese.

Along with the others in the class, Rania had little understanding of rape, or seduction and I rather skimmed over it; there were other themes in Mockingbird to discuss. Rania took it all in and expressed her thoughts and some of her anxieties in her papers. In class discussion she listened, then processed ideas. It was difficult for her to comprehend that black people could be singled-out rather than included-in, as she had always been in her international life style. Rania was thirteen. She questioned how 'those' adults thought. Did Americans really feel that way?

"Is that what you think, Ms Russell?

"You are different I know Ms Russell, but Ms Russell, do most Americans discriminate against black people?

"Why do they do that?

"What will happen to me if I go to your country?

"Will they know I'm from Sudan?"

"Rania, does it matter where you are from?"Mo stated rather than asked.

"Well Yes, I'm Sudanese."

"Rania, it doesn't matter where you are from; it's called racism and it's bad.

"Right, Ms Russell?" Mo hopefully affirmed.

Mohammed, who watched his country's assault, viewed Mockingbird from a perspective of invasion. There was something on a subconscious level of threat, killing the mockingbird and intimidation which resonated with him as he read this story of a small southern town in America. How did these things happen? Why were people, races, countries persecuted? He and his family fled Kuwait in fear for their lives and under threat, just as the fictitious Tom Robinson, the convicted, innocent black man, fled the jail but was murdered. Mohammed was more fortunate.

Mo's anxiety in the early hours in Kuwait soon became our anxiety as we waited-out the various phases of what was to become the Gulf War. It was no longer a story of the Mocking Bird. Or was it? You could shoot the blue jays but they said it was a sin to kill a mockingbird. To kill a mockingbird is to kill that which is innocent and harmless, like the characters in the story, like the civilians in Kuwait, in Iraq.

Though Kuwait was threatened and warned, the invasion was unexpected. Kuwait was unprepared. Denial? Perhaps. The Kuwaitis refused to forgive the $14 billion loan to Iraq during the Iraq/Iran war. Kuwait was warned. They ignored the threats. On August 02 the intimidation ended and Iraq entered by force while Mo stood in pajamas at the window naive and vulnerable, and I bobbed around in the pool equally naive.

It Takes Less Time
To Boil An Egg

The rhetoric heated over the days and weeks. Talk turned to gas and chemical warheads. Pat Freeman, then wife of the U.S. Ambassador Charles 'Chas' Freeman, was mater-of-fact. She might have said, 'bring it on' about the pending Gulf war, thought the quote was never attributed to her. One afternoon we stood around her spacious open kitchen talking what-if scenarios. What if SCUD missiles were employed by Iraq? Would the SCUDs hit us in Riyadh; would Iraq focus on Dhahran; if they did aim for Riyadh, how long would it take for one to reach us; what kind of damage would it impose; how effective were the ever-so-expensive Stingers. The press reported that a rocket launched from Kuwait would take four minutes to reach Riyadh.

"It takes less time to boil an egg," from Pat. One could boil a three-minute-egg and serve it before a rocket launched from Kuwait would arrive in Riyadh.

Well.

That put the issue into perspective. "There is plenty of time when you hear the sirens to get under the stairs." Everyone talked of safe rooms, gas masks, and evacuation. An editorial in the Saudi Gazette urged people to look to the trees. If the birds fell out of the trees, it would indicate there was gas in the air: chemical war heads. People were encouraged to stuff wet towels under the doors to prevent the chemicals from entering the house. Many people duck-taped Xs across their windows to prevent shattering glass.

As tension mounted, everyone devised a plan. Maxine and Bob designed their own strategic escape. They placed their scuba tanks by the front door. At the first sign of danger, they planned to zip into their wet suits, masks, weights, fins and tanks and sit on the bottom of the pool till the external air was uncontaminated, buddy-breathing if either ran out of oxygen. The Mc Arthur's and others, including Jeanie and Vern Cassin and the lawyer-group planned to camp in the desert in the event of missile attacks. Bill Fisher, the dentist who lived near the airport also planned to camp in the desert.

While trying to maintain normalcy, Steve Wentworth and I hosted a week-end leadership day. Eighty-seven kids attended the all day conference, a training session for student council and upcoming student body elections. The campaign lasted all week, with speeches on

Monday, and computer voting on Wednesday; another diversion.

For a nearly-normal United Nations Day, students waved all kinds of flags and pretended that all nations were united. The choirs went to the British school for a program and sang Rock-Around-The-Clock and Stars-And-Stripes-Forever, with lots of red, white and blue. Patriotism was contagious. The same week, students from Jeddah came for a massive volley-ball tournament and a pep-rally. My ESL students wanted to know, "Ms. Lasso, wassa pep-lolly?"

By October, the buildup of US troops in the area was formidable. Two months into the school term I made contacts after chasing numerous numbers, names, phone calls and conversations, to carry-out the Great Cookie Lift. I planned for student council to choreograph this effort and take the cookies to the troops. Shattered, I discovered that some staff believed that an anti-American element among the students or their families would sabotage the effort. I never heard that or sensed it in any way. When I pursued this line of thought, I was shocked to learn that some said students would bring cookies with ground glass or poison to incapacitate the soldiers.

I did not believe there was support for this feeling. My 'inspiration' of having the new student council officers push this project as a trick-or-treat Halloween gesture for the troops was crushed. Surely there was no support for this line of thought. But the school principal supported this fear, so there was no sanctioned SAISR support for the forces.

I admit I took it as a personal affront. We were so positive, and determined to work at calming fears and feelings and individuals, while others seemed to work at flaming the gossip fires, stirring things up, spreading rumors. Well, they won this time. Determined, I pulled my self together. We all had to work here, and we had to work at calming students. I just became more determined to continue the calming strategy. Perhaps we needed it more than I realized. If this element was inciting or reacting to students or rumors, the more I needed to stay visible and calm and continue in a quasi counseling role, if you like. That's how I saw it at the time.

Helen Fields, a military wife, told me she had been out to see some of the soldiers; they were easy to find in the desert. The new recruits whom she had seen were eating MREs and they concurred that Meals Ready to Eat were pretty bad.

"Dannie, our soldiers are so grateful to see anyone who speaks English," Helen was proud of the recruits.

"They love homemade cookies even more than they love junk food." What would she think of our teachers and staff if I told her they feared the students would sabotage the soldiers?

The ongoing embassy functions fostered the illusion of

Author making notes in Desert Storm

parties-as-usual and one week in October we sent regrets to the Austrian Embassy, the Turkish Embassy and the British Council. Everyone determined to stay busy. In fact, the socialization helped us all keep our sanity and sense of humour. We 'regretted' because there seemed to be as many compound or staff meetings as there were dinners and receptions. Daryle always met with anyone at any time to hear-out their concerns or to field rumours.

It came as a surprise to us that our young teachers harboured the most fear. Where was the life-on-the-edge group? Where was the sense of adventure most conspicuously identified with the young? Contrary to our expectations, the older staff members seemed to take circumstances in their stride; the more mature staff reflected, whereas the younger teachers panicked with no scaffolding on which to build.

The Lunch Bunch gatherings were animated. Patti Abu Hussain, Pat Freeman, Helen Fields, Jeannie Cassin, Noleen, Joan, Fran Meade and others sipped sherry (someone always had access), and attempted to analyze the events of the month while trying to project into the future.

These professional women, unemployed in the Kingdom, thrived on the luncheons which gave us time to blow off steam and enjoy the conversation of our jobless colleagues. I was the exception with work at the school. That month, the conversation centred on politics including the governments of Saudi, New Zealand, and the U.S. We also discussed women in politics, which we determined would never happen in the Kingdom of Saudi Arabia. One should never say never. Still, it seemed unfathomable.

The ladies had various concerns of getting out of the country with their families in an emergency, what to take besides water, passports and gold, and where to go to wait-it-out. I voted for Paris with makeup and earrings, but Cyprus, Rhodes and Athens were more realistic. Pat wanted to have an American women's group called American Women Of Riyadh aka AWOR or American Women of War aka AWOW. She was feisty, wanted the world to know: Don't mess with American Women. I already knew it took less time to boil an egg.

The Great Cookie Lift

Johnny, my Pilipino cook, baked 1200 cookies and Daryle and I headed to the desert toward the Kuwaiti border and the U.S. military troops. If I couldn't include the student council or school support for the Great Cookie Lift, 'I would do it myself; and I did,' like The Little Red Hen from the children's book. I bought nuts and chips, popcorn and candy bars to supplement books, board games and junk food.

The wife of a military friend gave me information and instructions. As we drove we would see the troops, but we should not drive directly up to the tanks because they would see us long before we would see them and they would have guns on us. We should stop, let them approach us, and check our car, to be sure we were who we said we were, then they would be keen to talk and visit. They were particularly concerned about terrorist acts at that time.

We headed for Nasariya, to the north of Riyadh, near the Kuwait, Iraq, Saudi border, not sure how far we would get. At Joudah we drove off-road toward a rocky area, took a trail, and rounded a bend smack into the centre of an army brigade. On top of the nearest rock was a strange stone formation covered with cloth flapping in the breeze like camel blankets out to dry; a lookout bunker. Large green netting covered other rock-like formations. On closer scrutiny we made-out tanks, trucks, more tanks. We stopped for a minute, thinking that all the guns were probably pointed directly at us, then, as no one approached our land rover, we made a u-turn then abruptly left, for the first time, uncomfortable.

In two hours the sun would drop behind the dunes. We headed further along the escarpment, into another group of tanks and trucks, as unfriendly as the first troops. We headed toward a Bedouin encampment, feeling more comfortable with the Bedu, camels and sheep than with the tanks and guns. With less than an hour 'till sunset, we set up our campsite before dark.

The wind blew at a terrific force whipping us about like a vengeful *mutawwa* thrashing his stick. We found a secluded spot between the dunes and although fairly close to the highway and nearby town and very near the Bedouin, we stopped for the night. The power of the wind required all my strength to hold down the dome tent while Daryle tried to insert the rods to stake it to the soft sand. We tip-toed around wondering if someone would come and tell us we couldn't stay, then finally sat down to read by a hot fire.

A young camel herder with his wife and son drove up in their white Toyota pickup to check us out. Satisfied that we were not in danger, they left us and continued the camel roundup.

As I sat by the fire I thought about the party last night held in my honour. The compound threw a surprise 'Glitter and Glitz' bash for my fiftieth birthday. I was surprised. I staggered home from school late, tired from preparing for the Boarding School Fair. The teachers practiced total OPSEC (operation security). I never thought about my birthday with my swirl of commitments at school. I never gave one thought to the idea that I would be fifty. It was enormously fun, we drank really bad home-made wine and the party was not totally unbearable; a Bruce McMillan production. The 'gifts' were complete bling; very glitzy and the party theme emulated the Golden Girls, apparently based on a TV series; yet another diversion from the tension of the war build-up. What would it mean to be fifty? Maybe this would be the year I would go off-the-bottle and become a natural gray. Maybe not. Barbara Bush was not the look I was going for with her white hair and pearl chokers.

The Bedu, who earlier came to check us out, continued to round up his camels. They ran every direction but into the pen. The sun set and soon it would be dark. Thirty minutes before, the camels followed the Toyota back to the tent but then it seemed they each had their own scheme of self-determination. In a futile attempt he blasted the horn and bellowed at them, *"Yellah! Yellah!"*

He turned on the Toyota headlights, squirreled around in the sand and tried to round them up like a Texas cowboy. They disbursed all over the desert in the region of his large black tent. Although only about twenty in number, the camels refused to be corralled. The young herder drove off with the camels still scattered. I thought, I hope they don't bed down here. Camels are noisy when they sleep; they snort and bark-cough and blow through their flutter lips sounding like un-tuned bass gadgets in the music room. And they smell; like never-washed filthy wool carpets.

As we sat in the cusp of the evening, I heard a staccato, broken-wing cadence; an irregular shape silhouetted against the sand dune, its shadow clear and black against the red sand illuminated by a full white overhead moon; it was Halloween. Even in the desert, it seemed the bats came out for full moon. The evening seemed surreal so far from Halloween or western customs, sandwiched between a makeshift military camp and a Bedouin encampment.

This thought barely complete, as I reflected enjoying coffee and the fire, I saw it peripherally before I heard it. It was noiseless until it was just at our side. A low-flying aircraft, wings swept back, an F16? a drone? came flying so low over the horizon it seemed to brush the dunes. It was followed minutes later by another on the other side of our tent as our campfire flickered.

Bernie

They showed us their Stinger missiles, weapons designed to deal with low-flying aircraft and helicopters. Bernie said he was 17 as he placed the Stinger on my shoulder. I wasn't sure he had a mustache yet.

"Whoa. This missile is heavy."

"Not really, Ma'am. It weighs 25 pounds, Ma'am."

"That's one-fourth my body weight."

"We add the launcher which weighs another 10 pounds.

"This-here launcher is reusable, but 'course once we fire the Stinger, it's gone fer good.

"Yes, Ma'am. Ninety thousand dollars each.

"Costs a lot 'cuz it's so lightweight, it's portable.

"But me 'n my buddy usually work it together; at least in training.

"Haven't had a chance to use 'em yet out here. Sure wish we'd get some action.

"We are ready, yes Ma'am."

Bernie and his buddy explained how the computerized chips were programmed. He was articulate and although a high school dropout, this young man found his niche through army training and learned the technology.

"So how does it work? You just aim and fire?" I knew nothing about guns.

"Yes Ma'am, something like that." Bernie was patient with me, but I knew he was proud to share his knowledge of this highly specialized, costly weapon. He was elated to have this tremendous responsibility.

He was confident and, I was sure, competent.

"This-here rocket is fire-and-ferget. So when we see a low flying aircraft, we aim the missile at the target. The infra-red, here on the tip of the rocket, this-here locks on to the heat of the enemy airplane's engine. When we hear that 'click,' we pull the trigger.

"This-here rocket is so smart it can correct itself and readjust in a tenth of a second."

Bernie leaned against the side of the Humvee and started to twist and pull the Stinger apart. Each piece of the weapon had a name. They took it all apart, cleaned each section and put it back together with all the pieces in the correct order and none left over.

"How did you learn all of this?"

"Yes Ma'am. I hated school. Every day I just put in time. Didn't learn nothin'. One day I looked at the clock in my math class. Two hours till school was out. I jist stood up, left my algebra book on the desk and walked out. I finally quit. My ol' lady was pissed. 'Xcuse me Ma'am."

"Did you need some math to understand these Stinger missiles?"

"When I told my ma I wasn't goin' back to school, she yelled, then cried, then told me I had to get a job or join the army. I couldn't sit around the house.

"I went to see the army recruiter the next day and signed up. I sorta lucked-out. First I thought the workouts were gonna kill me. Man, ferget about combat, they were trying to kill me just runnin' me 'round boot-camp. I couldn't do 5 pushups. Man, now I can pop-off a hundred at time, but I thought it would kill me every day when I started. Funny. I never thought about quittin'.

"When I saw the signup for the Stinger program I just thought it was like rifle practice or sumthin'. I thought we would go for target practice, learn how to shoot and care for guns. First thing we did was sit in a classroom and I thought I was back in math class.

"But it was real different, Ma'am. The commander respected us. He told us this was important technology and we would be expected to learn it properly. The way he told us was way different from the math teacher who made us feel stupid. The commander diagrammed on the board. He showed us the Stinger, right there in the class.

"He took it apart and I knew right then, I made the right decision.

"I never expected to be in Saudi Arabia. Everybody wants action, but I thought I would go to Europe. That sounded cool. Who ever heard of Kuwait? I didn't do so good at geography neither.

"On August 2nd our platoon was ready. We knew how to use the Stingers and received orders to come to Saudi. It's not like Germany or nothing'. No Ma'am, it shore aint Europe."

"Were you scared when you received orders to travel to a war zone?

"What did your mom say?"

"I wasn't scared, but my ol' lady, she was real upset. I try to write her three times a week. She's real proud of me now, but she always worries 'bout me."

"Mom's are like that."

"You got any more of them cookies?"

Humvees, Stingers, Cookies and Kids

Victory Main

The parachutes drifted closer. Wide-eyed, I watched the jumpers make their drop right at our tent, their chutes translucent in the moonlight. They came closer, dangling over the dunes, dropping in front of our tent. I was not afraid, but astonished. I don't remember hearing the helicopters, but perhaps that is what woke me. The dream was strangely exhilarating. I went back to sleep to continue the vision, learn the outcome, and watch more airborne troops touch down in slow motion, their toes teasing the tops of the dunes.

I slept in fits drifting in and out of sleep. My sleeping bag wound around my neck and twisted at my legs. The night was reminiscent of our first few nights in Vietnam just before the Tet offensive. I slept with one eye open and both ears fully exposed to rocket and gun fire. When I woke, my fists were clenched and my jaw tight, my teeth grinding.

We set out in the morning, still headed toward Kuwait and pulled-in for petrol where a number of army personnel also filled their tanks. The men, in the Kingdom just two weeks, started to get mail. They missed their families and planned to be home in June; were guaranteed eight month rotation unless, the pause, something happened. We offered to phone their families in the US, "You could do that? Could you really call for us?" as they handed us phone numbers of their mums and wives.

Along the highway every vehicle, the colour of camouflage-ar-my-beige, blended into the desert sand. Our lone burgundy Toyota stood-out with a few civilian Toyota trucks used for ferrying goats and herding camels. Tanks loomed at every rock formation; armored personnel carriers inched along the highway. Wide flat-beds crawled along, laden with enormous undulating bloated bags which stretched across the width of the vehicle. They heaved from the weight of the liquid: propane, gas, chemicals, water? Thousands of brown vehicles merged into the landscape.

We drove another hour and a half that morning north toward Kuwait. At the turn-off at Victory Main the scene overwhelmed us. The vision emulated a scene from *Apocalypse Now* choreographed by Francis Ford Coppola. We estimated five thousand tents; hundreds of Quonset huts aligned the sand in orderly layout in a grid across the desert.

Hundreds of helicopters swirled overhead in a deafening roar. It altered the wilderness. Low-flying choppers flew in tight formation to our right. Their blades whirred so close it seemed their rotors would touch. I expected at any moment to hear *The Ride of the Valkyries* from the third act of Wagner's second opera in *The Ring*.

A helicopter sat atop a knoll. Behind and on top of every escarpment we observed rows of tents perch. Planes circled overhead and there were hundreds and hundreds of 4x4s and Humvees. We gawked at the enormous desert buildup; the military presence surrounded us from every direction; we found ourselves in the centre of a mammoth military encampment, without doubt disturbing to the Bedouin, their lands occupied by this massive influx of outsiders. This was Operation Desert Shield.

Inside the camp, we wandered about talking with military personnel and left batches of cookies inside the tents. The first impression I formed was how very young these men and women were. The second impression was how well trained they were. As they dove into the cookies, "Man, these cookies are just like my mom's," "Brownies? Man, awesome!" they told their stories.

"What are you doing here? Sir! How did you get out here in the desert? Sir!"

"Sir, are you with the military?"

"Excuse me Ma'am, are you visiting from some US senate committee?"

"You live here? Sir! Why? Sir! "

"What do you do here? Sir!"

"You run a school for international kids? You mean Saudi kids? Sir!"

"American kids??!!" He forgot the 'Sir.'

Then it was our turn to ask questions. "Where do you call home?" Most of this group seemed to be from military bases in the American south.

"Where are your families?"

"Yeah, like my girlfriend, she's like waitin' fer me?

"I try to write her a lot, 'cuz it kinda fills the time while we wait for some action."

"Yeah, sittin' around is real, like, boring. Thanx for bringing them games n' stuff."

"Naw, I don't read nothin', but my buddy, here, he reads all them paperbacks."

"So, how do you spend your days?" I asked.

"Mostly like tellin' bad jokes.

"That girl over there, man, she tells the same jokes we've already heard.

"Lame. Otherwise, she's cool." The 'girl' was very cool. She grinned and said nothing.

"Yeah, like waitin' fer the mail, then readin' our letters over and over."

"We spend a lot of time makin' sure our equipment is ready. This-here sand gets into everything. Gotta clean our guns all the time. It's a constant battle, Ha! Battle! Keeping the blowin' sand outa' yer guns and tanks."

"Yes Ma'am. It gets in our tents and on our cots too. It's real bad 'cuz it sticks to ya in this-here heat."

And then, out of nowhere, "Hey, Sir! You ever seen a Stinger?"

"Ma'am, you wanna' see our weapons?"

"Ma'am, you wanna' ride in my Humvee?"

Who could resist? They whisked us off to their Humvees. We climbed in and drove over the dunes. What a great machine. We went right over the tops of the dunes, regardless of the slope, to demonstrate the flexibility and mobility of the Humvee. One of the guys explained about the High Mobility Multipurpose Wheeled Vehicle, HMMWV, about the portal axles and something about tire inflation. It was lost on me. Daryle leaped at the chance for a turn behind the wheel. He wanted one, his own Humvee.

The Hummers serve in various capacities as cargo and troop car-
riers, ambulances, missile carriers, and weapon platforms which
we saw. They are known for fording deep water, but none of these
soldiers had seen anything approaching water even in the wadis.
The HMMWVs were probably gas guzzlers, but that was a non-
issue in Saudi Arabia.

I was impressed at how well they knew their vehicle; how to
maintain it, keeping the sand out constantly and understanding
how the vehicle worked over the terrain. I wanted one. These young
men knew their vehicle as well as park rangers at Fothergill Island,
Zimbabwe. Impeccable knowledge for both the rangers and the soldiers was a tool for survival.

Aysha

In Riyadh we salvaged the wadded-up papers with scratched-down
phone numbers and called the wives and mums of the men we met.
The relatives could not envision that we lived in Saudi Arabia and
were not connected to the military. Americans knew little about the
desert Kingdom.

"You saw my husband? Is he hurt, is he injured? Is he having
trouble?"

"How did he look?"

"What did he say?"

"Where did you see him?"

"You mean you live there?"

"You just drove to the border of Kuwait to talk to our troops?"

Another mom could not wrap her head around the idea that non-
military personnel lived in Saudi and would drive five hours just to
spend time with the troops and that we spent our weekends in the
desert because we liked it.

"You like it? Down there in Saudi 'RAbia? You like it?"

"So, what's it like?" They all asked the same question in various ways.

"The men are frustrated with the sand and the heat; and they want
some action.

"Your son looks great, but I think he's not used to the desert heat."

"Your husband said he doesn't care if he ever sees sand again." His
wife laughed, "That sounds like him alright. He doesn't even like to go
to the beach."

"He has plenty of water for showers, but it's a constant effort to keep the blowing sand out of their guns, tanks, tents and cots. "

"The sand sticks to everything and they spend most of their days cleaning their weapons.

"Yes, your son looks great in his uniform. I'm so glad I got to talk to him," to a worried mum.

"You don't know what it means to us that you have done this for our men and women, and that you have taken the time to phone us from way over there where y'all live.

'Y'all take care over there. And God bless y' hear?"

The buildup continued in Saudi. Reporters arrived on a daily basis representing all of the major news networks, international newspapers and periodicals. CNN was one of the first. Christiane Amanpour held her own with the others; became the face of CNN; the face of the Iraq-Kuwait War. Tom Brokaw became a household name along with Sam Donaldson, fondly known as Mr Toupee. Reporters from the BBC as well as ABC, NBC, CBS and a string of Asian and Middle East agencies lined up equipment to monitor the news. The barrage of news pressed down on us like a heavy blanket, warm and secure but weighty and stifling. We headed to the desert to lessen the stress.

October 15, 1990

Hi Jessica…. Great to hear about your student teaching; middle school is a squirrelly age. … Next week-end we are going out with a Saudi conservationist group to look for ibex and build some retainer walls to aid in water drainage, as I understand the project. It sounds like an African safari but searching for illusive ibex rather than rhino. We will camp Wednesday and Thursday night, bring our own food Wednesday and they will provide a goat-grab Thursday. The weather is beautiful now. Once we get to the sand, we can forget the tension and relax. We are always on alert, just-in-case, but we have to get out of the city to relieve the stress.

The Wildlife Commission set up several base camps along the way. They hope to introduce gazelle into the Quarter. We later talked with Peter Jenkins, game warden in Kenya and Siana's father, about the conservation going on in the Kingdom. There are two breeding centres, one for ibex and one for gazelle. The centre outside Riyadh, Thimama, is at the King's farm.

As we sat on the patterned red carpet, our Saudi hosts offered us Arab *qhawah* and dates, then *chai* and just when I thought my knees would give out from sitting cross-legged, one of the men brought out large platters of sliced melon then passed the traditional incense, wafting in the air, signaling our exit. Exhausted, we set up camp in the dark, heated the chicken stew and fell onto cots.

At double-oh-dark in the morning we indulged in steaming Arabian *qawah* with great hopes of finding the ibex and at sunrise drove through a series of dry wadis. The valleys so deep, the escarpment so high, I wondered that anything could ambulate in the environment. The conservation site is located toward Wadi Diwaser, past Kharj, just a few *wadis* over from Baloom.

In the car Yusef discussed his background in botany. He worked fulltime with the Wildlife Commission and worked out of Riyadh. He told us about a recent trip and survey of the Rub al Kahli. They were 45 days in the Empty Quarter.

"How did you manage 45 days in the Empty Quarter?" I interrupted.

"We had a lot of support including a petrol truck and several water trucks.

"We ate a lot of rice and were pretty glad to get back to Riyadh at the end.

"The Saudi military was a big part of the project in that they paroled and checked on us. They brought food, so we did have fresh food once a week. One week we killed a goat and roasted it over our campfire.

"Water is always an issue in the EQ so we appreciated the water trucks supplied by the army. Don't try this on your own; it can be very dangerous." I was already thinking how fabulous it would be to make that trip.

"We won't see gazelle today, but I hope we can find the ibex," Yusef continued.

"There are several large herds and always the possibility of seeing some singles.

"Help me scout." We trained the binoculars on the sides of the escarpment.

Traveling in Le Blank's car, which Ted Burgon borrowed for the weekend, we beat-the-stink out of the body and wheels over rough terrain. Ted drove up seemingly endless *wadis* searching for ibex. We drove to the end of the dry riverbed, got out and walked to places where no car or truck could maneuver. I noticed a young girl hiking by my side as we trekked into a narrow rocky gorge.

We walked under pristine, blue skies, along dramatic escarpments and rocky foot paths intersected by smooth, narrow camel trails leading to the bend in another wadi of palms, verdant cat tails and clear water, probably laden with schistosomiasis.

She, a child of the desert, had seen it all before. The girl tagged along by my side picking up colourful stones like I used to collect magic rocks and wishing pebbles as a child. Ostensibly, we searched for ibex.

"*Assalaam alaykum*," 'Hello! Peace be with you, how are you?' she chirped in Arabic. Aysha was now my new *asdiqaa'*, my new ten year old best friend and daughter of the Chadian environmentalist. Her huge round eyes twinkled like faceted brown topaz as she giggled skipping along at my side. I felt like the Pied Piper of Hamelin as all the little girls followed me down the wadi and across the escarpment.

"Ma'da'am, *Umm*. This for you, *Umm*." Aysha extended her arms toward me offering a 30 cm desert *dhab*. Startled, I jumped back and laughing, she clutched her side with her free arm. My response to the prehistoric lizard was just what she was hoping.

Primordial looking with their spiked tails, these lizards, *dhabs*, are vegetarian, and not thought to be harmful, though their mating ritual is known to be aggressive and violent. They can grow to 60cm, 2 feet in length.

The girls carried the *dhab* around like a favourite pet. They rigged up a leash of plastic string, loosely tied around the reptile's neck. We sometimes saw *dhabs* on the side of the road or at a distance in the sand. I had a flashback to my own fascination with chameleons from the California State Fair, that I proudly wore pinned to my dress in first grade. My chameleons always died in the shoebox but I knew Aysha's *dhab* had a fighting chance because her father was a conservationist. The *dhab* walked alongside like a spoiled Chihuahua.

The ranger located a large herd of ibex near the base of the cliffs. There were 17-19 in the herd. Two large rams, with great horns curving backward over their heads toward their necks, led the group of juveniles. They shortly spooked and made their way up the sheer escarpment wall. Slowly, they ate their way up the cliff- side like Billy Goats Gruff.

As official camera people set up their equipment, the ibex climbed higher and higher up the side of the escarpment. Invisible to the untrained eye, they were difficult to spot even with binoculars. Coloured the same shade as the desert sand and jagged rock they merged into the environment like individual grains of sand.

"*Ma ismak minfudlak, Umm*?" what's you name, Mother? from Aysha and her *dhab*.

"*Ana* Ms.... Well, *Umm*." I started to say, 'I'm Ms. Russell.' Then I decided, "*Ana Umm*." I am Mother. The girls already called me *Umm*, so they could stay with that. There was no way they could wrap their tongues around 'Russell.'

The weekend project was to build simple stone structures to capture water, if any, which would redistribute silt to encourage plant growth. In the heat of the day, we began gathering rocks and stones to build miniature dams. The temperature climbed above 40 degrees Celsius as we wandered off looking for rocks and stones. We carried as many as we could physically load onto our outstretched arms and trudged toward the designated spot.

I became painfully aware of Pakistani and Yemeni workers who do this manual labour on a daily basis in Saudi, not for any philanthropic effort, but for wages to send home to their families; workers who strain and sweat in the blazing sun day after day, year after year. The structures were easy to construct after a professional stone-layer from Mecca instructed us.

"Aysha, *asadiqaa*, for you," I said handing her an exploded geode for her collection of stones.

"Ayee!" she exclaimed running to her friend and mentor to explain what it was. He explained in Arabic the crystalline elements found within the stone. She was delighted; we were forever bonded, though after the weekend I never saw her again.

We assembled rocks and stones of various sizes, carried, loaded them into wheel barrows and Toyota trucks and arranged and fit the pieces together to cobble miniature dams. The stone-mason from Chad demonstrated how the stones should be placed. We made four such water holds, two before prayers and two after.

The Saudi conservationists enthused with the whole effort broke into song with the loading and unloading of stones. They fetched and carried, stacked and assembled with us, with me, a mere female.

"Misses! You drive pick-up! Ha!"

"No problem, *mafi mushkala*. Really! We're just Saudi conservationists."

"We will say nothing. *Aiwa*, yes, you drive."

"*Mafi mushkala*." No problem.

"Well, *shukran*, thank you," I said. There was no way I would drive in the desert as a female with these Saudi men. I said thinking on my feet,

"I don't drive pick-ups.

"I only drive automatics." Then I added,

"Or Lamborghinis." The men looked at me, then at each other. Then simultaneously exploded in laughter.

When we stopped, they paused for prayer, kneeling and bending in the afternoon sun and sand. It was a reflective time and renewing to observe their faith.

Back at work after prayers we completed two more dams with Brits, Dutchies, Americans and Saudis and by sunset we traversed the top of the escarpment mesa back down the steep approach.

Everyone enjoyed the promised *Capsa*. On the shoeless carpet, with our right hands, we dipped into the savory almond-raisin rice topped with succulent roast lamb. I tried in vain to imagine how they prepared the meal in the barren, sparse desert, but there it was on steaming platters and most welcome. I knew the Bedouin prepared meals in the same manner. We greedily consumed everything on the trays. I knew to eat with only my right hand, and only the fingers of my right hand. It was considered rude and uncultured to place more than the first knuckle of your fingers into the food.

Meal completed, guests and hosts stood up to wash their right hands at the spouted water truck before we enjoyed fresh melon slices with spiced ginger *chai* and cardamom *qhawah*.

In the morning we dissembled our tent. I waved and blew kisses to Aysha. "Be good to your *dhab*," I hollered out the window. As the desert disappeared, thoughts of Kuwait and Iraq merged and the tension slowly crept back.

Eid

At the start of *Eid*, a three day holiday celebrating the end of Ramadan, the month of fasting, we forgot about Desert Shield and again headed to the desert for a couple of days. Everyone seemed to be out on the road, walking out of the city to visit family and friends.

Eid Mubarak!! Ramadan was finally over after extending one more day of fasting because no one could sight the moon. It made me grouchy. Although fasting becomes easier as the days and weeks pass, by the end of the month everyone is ready to celebrate; ready to eat at normal hours and get back to some semblance of order in their lives. It makes me irritated that scholars know the exact date of the new moon, but the clergy insist on a visual sighting. Last night it was cloudy. No moon. The fasting continued.

What a spectacle to see people out on the streets in the morning as we headed out of Riyadh. Everyone felt the same. It's over. The Fast is over. We did it. Let's celebrate together. Neighbour ladies bundled up in black *abayas*, eyes shining through slits in their veils, crammed into cars en route to visit friends and family.

The country was in a celebratory mood: little girls in ruffled polyester pinks, yellows, whites and white bonnets; little boys in clean, pressed *thobes,* shiny black shoes, one hand thrust in a pocket, the other clutching a flapping *ghutra*; men walking in the streets, smoking again in broad daylight.

Young boys clustered in front of doorways. Today the barefoot, *thobe*-skirted legs were not kicking soccer balls but supported the shifting weight of 9 and 10 year olds in dress-up *thobes*. Little girls scampered about with the energy and adrenalin of knowing it's *Eid* today.

Older students stood demurely in groups. Draped in black *abayas* the girls presented in style; they made a striking presence; more mature and poised than their little sisters. One, then another moved, ever so slightly to adjust a veil, eyes cast downward, with some small secret amongst girls.

A sense of pride and accomplishment accompany the completion of the Fast. With the conclusion of abstinence comes a renewal, a spiritual cleansing. The strict discipline committed by peers and colleagues brings a feeling of acceptance, forgiveness and genuine kindness which is the result of new commitments, devotion and dedication to God.

There comes with this discipline, the discipline of the Fast, a new dependence on God and on giving; a renewed awareness of those who suffer from hunger. There comes with this discipline a thankfulness which transcends but which integrates into daily life with ones friends, associates and neighbours.

The city is alive again in the morning sun. *Eid Mubarak!* Happy Festival. Congratulations!

Right But Wrong

"You did what?! No way." I heard her, but I didn't get it. It sounded like cocktail conversation: all the things one is going to do to save the world, after one glass of wine.

They had it right, but it was all wrong. International media including television, news outlets and experienced freelance reporters came to Saudi Arabia to cover the invasion of Kuwait. CNN, ABC, NBC, CBS, BBC and a host of non-English language countries covered the Gulf War.

Sarah giggled as much from nerves as from boasting. Jane Lewis confirmed; she was there as well with her camera and equipment, but Jane wasn't laughing. Jane got in on many special Saudi events in order to document them with her exceptional photographic skills. Women called on her for weddings, children's parties and ladies events. They could not hire a male photographer for any segregated events, and all events were segregated.

We sat in the women's section of the restaurant drinking cappuccino, picking at Danish pastries. All restaurants were divided for gender apartheid.

"Sarah, tell me this again," I beseeched.

"Donnie," her Arab pronunciation was soft and flowing. "Donnie, we met in the parking lot and drove to the Ministry of the Interior, dhown King Fahd Rhoad."

"Who?"

"We where eleven cars," she whispered loudly.

"Eleven cars? Why? Why did you all go to the Ministry?" I repeated, still not getting it.

"No, not like that," she said lifting her cup. It seemed to take forever to get the story out.

"Jane, what is she talking about?" Maybe my American friend would speed up the story.

"Yep. That's about it. We met in the parking lot with our drivers and drove to the Ministry."

"So what's the point? Why did you go to the Ministry?"

"Dannie! We were driving!" Jane blurted it out; the critical point I missed; disbelieved.

"Okay. Slow down. Who was *driving*?" still wanting to confirm this incredulous story.

"Mouna, Sarah, Leila, Salwa, Aliyah, Fadia; do you know Salwa?"

"They were all driving? Behind the wheel? Mouna was there?"

"There were lots more. We all met at the parking lot in front of the Mall." Now Sarah became animated. "We were standing around trying to decide how to do it, exactly. The reporters were all there. I do not know who called the press-es."

"I don't know either, but I recognized some of the western guys," from Jane.

"I ask-ed my driver to get out of the car. Everyone did the same."

"We all jump-ed into the eleven cars, stuff-ed in the back and front like grape leaves stuff-ed with rice. I think we were eleven in my car." I knew she had a Mercedes.

"Dannie, you should have seen it; a collective adrenalin rush. Everyone buzzed-down their windows, hooting and shouting, in English and Arabic, 'Saudi-Wo-men-Want-To-Drive, Saudi-Wo-men-Want-To-Drive,' and 'Let-Us-Drive. Let-Us-Drive,' honking to the cadence." Jane got into the description.

"We drove dhown the high-a-way, to the Ministry, then around the median and back dhown the high-a-way the other direction; tree times. Oh my God, Donnie, we were so excited, we forgot the time. When we finally stop-ed at the Interior Ministry, it was clos-ed for prayers."

"Oh no. What did you do?" I looked around. "Shh." I motioned to the Filipina server.

"Can you bring more cappuccino, *midfudluk* please? *Pakidala mo* ang *cappuccino*? Many Filipinos lived and worked in Saudi, helping in the service industry in supermarkets, running shops at the *suq*. They were well educated and fluent in English. I loved that they helped with my own transition from Manila to Riyadh and I enjoyed using some Tagalog when I could. It seemed to establish a bond: I know about your country. I know something of your heritage. I see you as a person, not a worker.

"Whatever did you hope to do?" I continued as the Filipina removed our empty cups.

"We expected to speak to the Minister of Interior and discuss our demand-es to be allowed to drife. We plan-ed to discuss that we can make a contribution to the country by doing our own drifing; that we do haf jobs in Saudi and that sometimes we need to drife for our families. We expected to point out that no other Islamic country forbids women from drifing and finally, Donnie, we were prepar-ed to show that the *Quran* does not ban women from drifing."

I leaned in. "This is amazing. So what happened? Did you meet the Minister?"

"Fadia wrote everything dhown to present to the Minister for a *Majlis*, petition.

"We got out of our cars and decided to wait for the Ministry to open after prayers. We were a big group and a leettle bit noisy and very excited to have the Minister hear our demands."

"Dannie," injected Jane, "they were cackling like a noisy gaggle of geese. I took pictures of everyone driving then waddling around the Ministry lot, more like penguins in black *abayas* than geese. Everyone was properly covered in black, including the lady drivers. It was a great scene."

"Jane, I can't wait to see your photos."

She cupped her hot cappuccino, then stirred it slightly with a demitasse spoon. Both women were silent. I looked from Sarah to Jane, to Sarah.

"They confiscated my camera and all my equipment and put us all in jail; locked up until our husbands came to get us out." Sarah and Jane looked at the marble table top. Sarah pinched a piece from her Danish then whispered, "It was mortifying and degrading. We were made to feel shameful."

Saudi Arabia denied women the right to drive. It was not a decree from the *Quran*, but a Saudi custom to protect the dignity of women. When the American forces arrived in the conservative Saudi desert, American army women drove all over Dhahran as part of their military assignments. They drove trucks and tanks. They also walked around town in body clinging, sleeveless camouflage tank tops, oblivious and insensitive to Arab custom.

Now it seemed the Saudi women overstepped their bounds. There were some jokes. The husbands laughed and said they should have left them all in jail. But, in fact, the government made it very difficult for the men who could not control their wives.

The backlash was not pleasant. *Mutawa* religious police broke into Jane's home confiscated all of her photography equipment and smashed it. They were all harassed on the phone by authorities. Most were forced to change their private numbers. Authorities confiscated passports and *iqamas*, personal identity cards.

Immigration refused to allow Salwa to fly to London the following week to present a paper at a medical conference. Mouna's husband was furious, though he was superficially kind. Her rebellion, defiance of the laws, proved a problem for him and his work with King Fahad. Educated at the Sorbonne, she epitomized intelligence and wealth and wanted to make a statement. Saudi Arabia clipped her wings.

As a result of the incident, the few women television anchors, though swaddled from head to toe, were removed from the news shows; war coverage was not dignified for women. The *mutawa* harassed everyone after that, especially Saudi women.

Because of tight censorship control, my liberated Saudi friends did not get the press coverage they coveted. They had it all right, but wrong. Inflamed religious police and ministry officials on every level lashed out. Saudi Arabia would not succumb to decadent ways of the west.

Twenty years later, the driving issue continues to reverberate. Today, Saudi women are 20 years more what: courageous? More edgy? More likely to be thrown back in jail. However, and read this slowly, a new *fatwa*, religious ruling, declares that Saudi women can breastfeed their foreign drivers. What?

Every household requires a driver. Saudi men drive their own cars; fast and expensive, often Lamborghinis. Therefore unrelated Egyptian, Sudanese, Yemeni, Pilipino and Pakistani men are hired to drive women and children to school, to market, to activities. This inadvertently violates gender apartheid laws.

Pondering the perceived rampant violation of illicit mixing of the sexes, the renowned *Quranic* scholar, Shaikh Abdul Mohsin Bin Nasser Al Obaikan, member of Saudi Council of Senior Scholars and advisor to the new King, announced that Saudi women can breastfeed their foreign drivers enabling the men to become their sons, consequently brothers to their daughters.

Outraged, the country bustled with unbridled, impassioned argument over the controversy. According to Islam, breast milk kinship is as good as blood kinship. A wet nurse, for example, becomes connected to the family because of this relationship. In order to change the status of unrelated males, the women are encouraged to breastfeed their mature, adult, male drivers.

This ludicrous ruling, this farcical notion had women bustling like frenzied shoppers during Ramadan sales. They buzzed like Drones on a mission. They bristled like hedgehogs under *abayas*. They aimed to turn this absurd *fatwa* to their advantage. A group of women organized an ultimatum: "Allow us to Drive or We Breastfeed Foreign Men."

Some say the driving problem for women is trivial. That would be men. It has for many years been a divisive, explosive clash. Of course, if women are veiled, it is difficult to drive with accurate peripheral vision; difficult to maneuver the car; difficult to get a license with photo identification of a veiled image. There are issues. Yet it has long been acknowledged that by permitting women to drive, work productivity will improve. Women require transportation to their place of segregated employment, to fetch and carry children, to shop for food supplies. Without transport they are housebound, incarcerated and symbolically imprisoned.

The women jumped all over this. They decided to push it to the edge. In discussions all over town, they pressed various scenarios.

"What if I'm breastfeeding my foreign driver and my husband comes home unexpectedly.

"Who will protect me?"

"I'm allowed to breastfeed a foreign man, but I'm not allowed to drive. What is this?"

"In reverse," one woman sarcastically questioned the Shaikh, "can my husband and the men of the household breastfeed from the maids, so everyone is related?"

This is not a paragraph about *fatwa*s, though there is fodder for this one which is off-the-bubble. It is not a commentary about Islam. This is a post script about long standing local customs and passion for social reform.

My predictions? The Saudi king cannot give-in to the demands of women. The religious council, however, does have the power to overturn the *fatwa*. At a later date, when the timing is favourable, the king has the power, in the semblance of modernization, to permit qualified women to obtain a license to drive. It will be choreographed and orchestrated and it will be a win for everyone.

Twenty years ago, the women removed male drivers from their cars. Twenty years ago, I would not have made a prediction. Today, I predict it is closer to a reality; in maybe twenty more years. Perhaps the 2011 Arab Spring of revolution will influence Saudi leadership. Perhaps.

"Allow us to Drive or We Breastfeed Foreign Men." This is edgy. You go girls!

Gasmasks and Stress

G asmasks symbolized stress which morphed into fear. Some companies bought masks for employees and families, others did not. Some embassies recommended gasmasks, others did not. Shops offered masks for sale at inflated prices, others offered discounts. I saw a marketing sign in a window promoting their gasmasks, "Satisfaction Guaranteed." Think about it.

Instructions came out on television demonstrating how to wear a mask and how to determine the right size. One size did not fit all. Everyone talked about getting a mask or not getting one.

But not all masks are created equal. The popular Israeli masks arrived with expiry dates 20 years earlier. The filters were bad and valves and seals questionable. American masks arrived with no filters or expired filters.

The masks coming into Saudi were often of obsolete design. The filters were rotten and valves and seals questionable. The quality of the masks became an issue. Nobody wanted a mask Made-In-China with a reputation of cheap price and tacky quality. Many American masks retained filters from the 1950's with expiry dates making them useless. On the other hand, what lay person knew how to determine a quality product? Who knew? Who had experience in selecting proper protection from gas or chemicals? No one wanted to skimp on life-saving gear.

If you are going diving, your equipment better be in perfect condition. Your tanks better not be empty. If the boat is sinking, your vest better not have a hole in it. Several countries offered army surplus masks.

Kids started toting gasmasks to school. Those without felt they were at a disadvantage. Adults fell victim to the same psychological warfare. The US Embassy issued mixed signals neither recommending nor condemning the use of masks for American citizens.

By the end of November, the UN Security Council authorized the use of force if Iraq did not withdraw from Kuwait by midnight EST, January 15, 1991. The ultimatum was set.

In December embassies began to evacuate staff and send families home. The US Embassy received no such authorization from Washington. Was DC in denial? Did they think it, the war, would go away? That by January 15th Iraq would back down and leave Kuwait, claiming they made a mistake and really didn't want to annex the small country?

Teachers reeled from the stress. Did we not care about their safety? Did we not love children? What did we plan to do about gasmasks? Stress morphed into fear.

Danny Sales had a deal for us. He supplied gasmasks for the Royal Family, or some of them; there were hundreds of princes. He could obtain enough protective masks for our teachers and their children. His wife Louise worked as a teacher in the elementary section.

Danny and Louise were sweethearts from grade school. They hung out together for so long they looked alike. Danny and Louise both sported bleached-yellow hair from the same bottle. Louise sported a pageboy cut; Danny wore Dutch-boy bangs like Captain Kangaroo from the long-ago children's TV series; he even sported a navy blue captain's blazer like the Captain Kangaroo. They had no children of their own, but every child who came through Louise's classroom was her child.

She ran the resource room for several years and one year came back from a Kenya conference dragging a life-size giraffe for her students. She strapped it into the seat next to her on the aircraft in coach class. The wood carving measured nine feet, three meters. Danny had a special deal; he could get enough masks for us. How many did we want?

No one knew what kind of gas to expect, or if they did know they were not at liberty to disclose the information to the public. The masks should be NBC proof: should resist Nuclear, Biological or Chemical agents. People remembered the awful mustard gas reportedly used on the Kurds in northern Iraq and before that used by Iraq on Iran.

People discussed visions of blistered skin as a result of 4 hours of exposure; of itching, burning blisters; of swollen and sore eyelids, of conjunctivitis and blindness, of internal blistering and bleeding. I hated those discussions. Thinking adults allowed themselves the privilege of panic and fear.

Danny agreed to get masks for everyone on the staff including dependent children. When others offered surplus masks, with no filters, for twenty-five dollars, Danny offered us 'reliable' masks from Israel for quadruple the price. I guess he forgot we were not working for the Royal Family. With the loss of tuition revenue, the administration and the school board hesitated to dole out the thousands of dollars necessary to obtain the masks. At 400 dollars per family, the board seemed unconvinced. The embassy refused to support the need, so the administration and the board made the decision not to purchase Danny's gas masks.

The verdict did not go down well with staff. Stress turned to fear; fear turned to anger and staff lashed out: Administration did not appreciate teachers enough to purchase masks. We did not love children. The ultimate insult: We, administration, did not love children.

Within the administrative staff the tension barometer varied too. Don and Tim building principals, Ted, self appointed security guru, Duane, head of procurement and Bob, in charge of personnel, registered up and down the Richter scale from 2 to 9 at any given hour, depending on the seismic events of the moment. The men thrashed out the hourly rumours, discussed critical issues constantly and attempted to maintain calm. The gasmask decision sounded calculated and callus based solely on monetary reserves; it sounded like money over people. Not everyone was rational.

By the time teachers realized that masks would not be provided as a hand-out, supplies on the open market or from personal contacts were limited. Some days you could feel the air taut with tension. A few teachers purchased their own masks. Not all, of course, but those who were most concerned attempted to make intelligent decisions on the purchase of a personal gasmask. Several admin also bought masks. Others started to think about evacuation.

Shannon and other kids hauled their masks to school every day. Rania had no mask but she showed no outward evidence of anxiety; a very together girl. We conducted air raid drills at school. When the bells went off all students filed into the large middle school library carrying only their gasmasks and water bottles. They lined up against the walls and sat on the floor. By this time, all windows were duck-taped throughout the campus and many western nationals, those who had a place to go, departed.

One European ambassador swung by school one afternoon. He had open seats on a charter and teachers were welcome to fly out, first-come, first-served and leaving in two hours. I think a couple of people were tempted, but didn't have time to process the implications.

Of all of the free advice, all of the recommendations on how to save the school from disaster, one of the more ludicrous plans and suggestions generated from fear and offered in good will, came from Louis, the Argentine ambassador, who offered the school his Bubble Scheme,

a plan for constructing a large inflatable bubble;
like a bouncy-castle;
on the school athletic field;
on the Astro Turf
soccer
field.

This was his plan: At the sound of the first siren, designated staff would dash to the field to pump-up the deflated bubble. All students would quickly evacuate classrooms and rush to the field, lunge into the partially inflated bubble, to be zipped-up until the danger passed. Enrollment was down by half, but we still had over 600 students. The young scholars should cram inside the rubber blimp and staff would zip the sides tight to prevent any gas from entering. *Voila! Bene!* Everyone, students and staff, safe.

It takes less time to boil an egg. We did not order the Bubble.

Desert Christmas

"Last night? What'd we do?
"Oh yeah. Christmas.
"We had a real nice meal with everyone together.
"We all gathered to play guitars and sing songs. Yes Ma'am."
"Yes Ma'am, we're gonna have more guitars and banjos for New Year's Eve."
"Are you on full alert? Red alert?"
"Well, ah…," they exchanged glances.
"Yes Ma'am, sort of.
"Cuz of the holidays, Ma'am."
"We heard Saddam Hussein has gathered all his top advisors."
"Yes, Ma'am. We heard that from the British news.
"We get British news here, Ma'am, from England.
"D'you hear that news, Ma'am?
"And they're gonna attack Israel.
"All depends on what happens January 15."
Everyone tensed at the mention of the January 15th deadline. Christmas day for the army was very low-key in deference to Saudi conservatism. The US military held no services outside in an open amphitheatre or arena. I read that US chaplains and rabbis were asked to remove crosses and stars-of-David from their uniforms. They were to be called morale officers.

The chaplains went around to the tents. They brought the message of the season inside living quarters as soldiers gathered in clusters squished on cots, sitting on the ground, leaning against each other reading familiar Biblical Christmas passages.

No entertainment in Saudi Arabia. However, as usual, Bob Hope showed up to be with the troops. As unusual, there was no publicity; no cameras, no girls. It was announced only after he left. We knew Hope was in the country because he was with the men in Karj, a somewhat accessible area, and later went into the desert, into the remote army camps we visited on the border of Kuwait.

Jessica and Ian completed their student teaching and came to Riyadh for the holidays as real people with diplomas and certification. On Boxing Day we made our annual desert safari. Occasional palm trees dotted the sand near infrequent black Bedouin tents. This year we drove north to camp, again toward Kuwait, and for the first time observed the ever important tap-line stretching across the sand like a rigid black snake suspended above ground bisecting the dunes in some blatant, out-there naïve, nonchalant display of oil.

The pipeline, tap-line, at least this section, pathetic and unimpressive at 6-7 inch diameter, seems so vulnerable. Oil, Black Gold, the wealth of the nation, necessity of the world, stretched across the arid region through a puny pipe, through a skinny black tube. The desalinization pure-water pipes, on the other hand, are suspended above ground also, and are approximately 20 inches in diameter; this puts things in perspective, water versus oil.

A convoy of trucks headed toward the highway from deep inside the desert. Tight security of armed escorts surrounded the front of the procession. The highway intersection came to a halt in all four directions as the convoy wound its way along the sides of the dunes; headlights beamed in broad daylight as it made its way toward the wide blacktop road. One by one enormous vehicles rolled across the sand and pavement.

The sight was one of power and strength. I was overwhelmed with emotion. At trucks? Why was I consumed with sentimental passion, this stirring of patriotism? I don't like war. Nobody likes war. Why this personal reaction of pride? That's what it was: pride. Was this Arrogance of Power? Had I become the Ugly American? Whatever happened on January 15th I knew we were ready.

Many vehicles ferried soldiers: Syrian, Egyptian, Saudi soldiers. Not just the American trucks displayed Free Kuwait bumper stickers. My heart pounded. This sight of the international force, the coalition, stirred and exhilarated. I wanted to shout, "YES!" The coalition, as much as anything, was reassuring. We were not in this alone, this effort. I would later look back on that sense of pride and wonder that we were once so proud. It was a foreshadowing of a terrible downward spiraling of events which led our country and the world into economic recession eighteen years later.

Convoys with tanks and rockets were everywhere. I have never seen so much armament in one place. This is what reporters called a "massive buildup of strength, power and might." It brought new meaning to the word massive.

One can't escape the incongruity of it all. We drove along the new eight lane highway in our dusty, burgundy four-wheel drive, as out of place as a camel in a shopping mall. The highway scene was surreal, Daliesque. Army brown vehicles, Bedouin white trucks all blended into the landscape.

A carload of young Saudi men emptied-out alongside the road to kneel in orderly lines for afternoon prayers. Across the road a single man spread his small carpet and knelt in prayer beside his car, facing Mecca, head bowed, red and white *ghutra* blowing against his dark grey, woolen winter *thobe*. What were their prayers? I could only imagine their distress and conflict. Was he praying about January 15th?

The surreal scene surrounded us. Behind us scores of army-bile busses transported young American men and women wearing sand and earth fatigues. I waved enthusiastically, giving the thumbs-up. I felt giddy, like a groupie teenager driving by busloads of movie stars.

In the slow lane, a non-air-conditioned van with all the windows down, hauled Yemeni workers to a worksite somewhere in the scorching heat.

In front of us, khaki army jeeps full of troops occupied several lanes. I waved again.

"Yes! You Go Soldiers!" I shouted to no one and everyone.

"Moth-er, puleeze. Control yourself." Jessica and Ian slithered low in the back seat. It occurred to me many times that they could have been in an army tent with any of those young soldiers. They were the same age.

In the lane next to us a Bedouin shepherd drove a white pickup filled with large, dirty, black and white dread-locked sheep. Crowded into the back of the densely populated Toyota, the long-haired livestock heaved from side to side on wobbly legs. I maintained decorum. White, beige, burgundy: everything the colour of sand but our four-wheel claret coach.

Across the highway the scorching hot-orange flames of the oil fields burned. The fire charred the earth and polluted the air. With this scene, the convoy, the highway diversity, the burning oilfields, bordered by the pipeline, that night I wrote:

surreal highway scene is daliesque
bland desert cubism splashed with orange.
busses of yemenis; busses of americans,
truckloads of rastafari sheep; jeeploads of soldiers.
and the pipeline
the reason for the build-up.
along with freeing kuwait
of course.

The pipeline bordering it all was the real reason for the build-up, along with freeing Kuwait, of course.

A New Year

No one knew it was New Year's Day; at least we didn't remember until we punched our shortwave radio after dinner. We depended on international broadcasting, a flashback to Ethiopia nearly thirty years before, where we learned the relevance of international news wherever we were.

We got to the wadi early, set up camp, scouted the narrow channel, then hiked to the top of the knoll and found several fossils. We walked with eyes glued to the ground, with scotomas toward anything but a narrow tunnel vision searching for whatever treasure the wadi offered. We seldom found arrowheads in the rocky valleys but often found fossilized shells and echinoids.

We found terebra, sturdy bivalves and other forms of fossilized sea life. The spiny murex seemed too fragile to survive 'one-hundred-thousand years of inspired design.' It always astounded me that the dunes and escarpments were once covered by the sea. Searching for fossils replaced our hobby of diving for shells in the Philippines. I knew most of the names after years of serious study and classifying, and to see the ancient fossils of the same species we found live or recently dead ten years before, humbled me.

As we poked along the top of the escarpment turning over stones, nudging rocks with a toe, we were joined by three Saudi men who decided to fossil-hunt with us. Oh great. They were nice men, polite, Arabic speaking, not too intrusive, but Jessica and I had to find a way down the escarpment without the men, on a ladies-only trail as we would not be allow to gender-blend.

The sun lowered. Daryle, Ian and the Saudis came down from the table top of the escarpment; Jessica and I retreated from sitting on the red-patterned prayer carpet into the tent as proper Saudi women, grumbling beneath our breath once inside. The men took our spots on the carpet, sat cross legged and talked about the fossil shells. In broken English they invited Daryle and Ian for *qhuaw* and *chai*. We should have offered them refreshment but I was afraid they might find our bad homemade wine concealed in the salad dressing bottle. The Russell men declined the offer but were invited for the following morning. Again they made an excuse. The illegal liquid was almost vinegar; the choice of salad dressing bottle wasn't much of a reach.

We sat 'round our fire, sipping covertly from our liquid stash; the shortwave news focused on the invasion of Kuwait. Reporters told us the French gained support for the Gulf Cooperation Council meeting to be held on Friday, January 04 in Bruxelles. It was New Year's Day but the news and editorials focused on the January 15 deadline. Potentially this conference could split the allies. The GCC included Bahrain, Kuwait, Oman, Qatar, Saudi Arabia UAE, but not Yemen.

It sounded like the GCC wanted to postpone the UN date for withdrawal on January 15, stalling, to hold talks with King Hussein bin Talal. Hussein of Jordan wanted to meet with England and Europe as well as the GCC, to plan an "Arab" solution.

Everyone wanted to be the peace maker.

Ego nourished the chaos. Saddam Hussein first, then Mitterrand, Hussein bin Talal and Hosni Mubarak have all been participatory. King Fahd attempted to be silent, as an unwilling observer. His Saudi kingdom could be next. I bet George Bush was packing his bags for Bruxelles to be there for the Friday meetings, to be part of the Peace Making, one of the decision makers.

Dan Quail came to Riyadh. Daryle was invited to a December 30th dinner reception with Quail hosted by Crown Prince Abdullah; men only. He decided to go camping. Surely, Quail couldn't possibly be the one to sit in as US representative at peace talks. The poor Vice President gets a bad rap and would probably spell it 'piece' talks. He must be with the troops now, somewhere in Saudi. How do bad politicians keep getting good jobs?

At the time, all of the negotiating for the perfect peace deal, led by the flavour of the day, fed by ego and desire for international leadership recognition made me angry. Everyone had conditions. The French seemed arrogant and egocentric. That would later be what nations thought of America and its policies to go-it-alone, as isolationists. But for now, America was in a leadership role, its international reputation undamaged.

We spent the night at Balum. Not the Palace. Instead we drank bad wine in the desert. We slept under a chalk white full moon camping at Balum after stumbling onto an ancient site at Hole-in-the-Rock. Primitive stones outlined houses and boundaries. Some rocks stood upward at a diagonal, but not typical burial stones. We've not seen anything written on this prehistoric place. There are wells; even some undeciphered graffiti.

We jostled home over washboard roads, over dunes, skirting the round, green pivots, driving between fences, through a herd of baby camels till we arrived at the highway, our bodies beat-up from the travel, our skin covered in soft, fine dust; the silt powdered our pours. Tonight we generate New Year's celebrations including hot showers and affirmations for the year.

The world waits for January 15.

International Jobs

found this letter written on my Mac 128k. It was the world's first Macintosh Computer introduced with much fanfare in February, 1984. With a 9 inch monitor and a funny mouse thing, it operated with floppy disks. I bought one that February while on a recruiting trip in the US. No one in Saudi yet owned a Mac. The men from Jaycor Engineering were jealous and begged me for demos. Although their facilities were state of the art, they did not yet possess the miracle Mac. I found this letter saved on a floppy. Ian's fiancé used her second name Janice at that time.

riyadh, jan 3, 91

dear janice;

i have just put jessica and ian on the flight to dhahran. they were so lucky to get jobs. i guess much of life is a matter of timing. of course the circumstances are bizarre and difficult during a war, but everyone has to start somewhere.

yesterday was quite unbelievable. jessica completed most of her packing to return to spokane, via zurich and we had two parties to attend in the evening. ian was as usual, kicked-back. at three in the afternoon the phone rang and they were both offered jobs in dhahran. they needed time to think through their lives, but dhahran academy needed an answer in the afternoon and they should plan to be on the flight for dhahran in the morning to get their house and some orientation before classes started on the following day! it was a difficult decision for jessica because she wasn't really prepared to leave spokane. ian, on the other hand, took about 10 minutes to make his decision after hanging up the phone. they expect opening day to be hectic and chaotic tomorrow. they have no idea what they are getting into or what to anticipate but it should be a wonderful learning experience; 'a chance to grow,' as they say at whitworth. for our part, we also wait with anticipation to see who will actually return from holiday break. there seems to be some sort of magic in the january 15th date, as if everything will be normal on the 16th or there will be instant war with rockets and gas and germ warfare.... hmm. i guess we'll just wait. the community fluctuates between panic and calm.keep me posted on your wedding plans. we're excited.

that's all i have.
love you, Dannie

With all the war uncertainty and nonsense, teachers in Dhahran left and Jessica and Ian ended-up with jobs at Dhahran Academy teaching a variety of subjects as we all scheduled and re-scheduled according to enrollment fluctuation.

War is Not the Good Way for the People Everywhere

As the January 15 deadline became a global countdown, tension on campus, on the compound and in the community intensified. Nerves frayed. What would happen? How would Saudi be affected? What would be the physical ramifications for Riyadh? What would happen in Dhahran? Most people sent their children out of the country. We brought ours in. Emotions festered like blisters from mustard gas. We all read of collateral damage. Would anyone knowingly target a school? Was the operative word 'knowingly?' It was a fine line between flipping out on the what-if scenarios or being ignorant; being careless and naive versus wise and prudent.

On January 7, with one week to the deadline, the local television station presented a discussion on how to prepare for chemical attack or air raid. The conversation opened with four doctors sitting on bar stools, what would be called bar stools in any other country, except there are no bars in Saudi Arabia. They sat in a semi-circle, as in an open forum. The program was presented in English by the medical doctors of King Faisal Hospital.

"Seal the room with curtain and you can wet it down," doctor one.

"If it is an air raid you shouldn't be on the top floors of a high rise," doctor two.

"Watch the birds. If birds drop from trees, it indicates gas in the airs," doctor one again.

"When the attack comes stay in your room which is already prepared," doctor three.

"Do not panic," doctor one.

"Use towels to stuff the door," doctor three

"Follow instructions on radio," again doctor one.

"Put your mask on. Your mask should be in your room," this from doctor four.

"Always use a wet towel," doctor one, the assertive one.

"Stay home. You might endanger yourself and the others," doctor four.

"Here is the mask demonstration." Doctor three reaches for a mask on a low table.

"The mask is a sealant," he continues. It looks, to me, like a diving mask.

"The trick with the filter is that you can't use it for long time." Doctor two now lifts a mask to his face.

"When you feel dense in your brain you have to change the filter," doctor four.

"Or if your eyes are burning," he concludes.

"The trick about having a mask: don't just have it lying around." Hmm.

"Try it on, and try it on your children. Rehearse the use of the mask," doctor one tutors.

"Be sure there is filter.

"Release the strap to the maximum.

"Then put on chin, then head, and tighten straps and seal the filter."

"Then you can't talk even for the demo." Doctor one is adamant on this point.

"Then you are short of breath and can't keep your eyes open."

"Then you have to change the filter." Doctors two and three, in masks, face each other.

"No leak."

"Hold your breath and change the filter." Masked men mumble something.

"You should have the new filter available immediately."

"When any problem in the attacked area, first:

"Do not try to help in transporting people.

"Secondly, don't drive.

"If you have to drive," the doctors conclude, "go sideways; don't block the main road."

The next day, January 08, John Major, England, arrived in Riyadh while James Baker, Secretary of State, met in Germany attempting to drum-up solid support and a united position of the allies. There must be no backing down of the UN resolution. Everything should be peaceful and sanctions should work. It seems there would be no military assistance from the Germans. They had there own problems. Baker met in Paris earlier assuring a full understanding that Iraq must accept the UN resolutions.

There must be total agreement in this: Iraq must pull out before January 15th. There must be no cracks between France and the US. There must be total consensus. The goals must be unified; no room for grandstanding or special interests. They must be UN goals and resolutions. They said.

It was a wishful flurry of diplomatic shuttles all in passive voice: would, should, could and must scenarios, where the theme, the receiver of the action, is more important than the agent.

"War is not the good way for the people everywhere." Tariq Aziz has new ideas to take to the meetings tomorrow, January 09. Aziz says if there is war it will be long. Iraq wants something new from the meetings. Saddam Hussein met with Yasser Arafat. Baghdad protests at several embassies. Now, a Middle East conference would be held. President Bush insists on mandatory rules or guidelines for the discussion: no negotiation and no linkage to the Palestinian issue. John Major says partial withdrawal is not acceptable. This sounds like a foreshadowing of Afghanistan. Tomorrow's meeting will tell all.

On January 09 James Baker, Secretary of State and Tariq Aziz, Foreign Minister for Iraq, met in Geneva. The meeting lasted 6 hours, but there was no progress and there were no results. The meetings ended in an impasse. The talks failed.

I now suspect that Baker would not give an inch; would not budge on any items. Bush was determined that none of Iraq's demands be met or negotiated. I now suspect that these were the same reasons that Jordan switched sides, deciding to support Iraq.

Three days later, January 12, three days before the withdrawal deadline, the House of Representatives voted 250-183 and the U.S. Senate voted 52-47 to authorize President Bush to use military force. War is not the good way.

Desert Discussions. Water colour. Ian Russell

A Line In The Sand

C hris Johnson, corporate lawyer, hosted a gracious, cordial and most welcome dinner. With some hesitation, we drove to his residence for a seven course meal with Vern and Jeannie Cassin and several other couples. We sat at the long table as each course whet our appetite for the next.

The roads were empty. It was a dicey time and no one knew what to expect. We left full instructions with Alvin, the security guard at school, regarding where we were going and how to reach us should there be any incident. Anything at all, he was to phone us at dinner. We thought it might be an anxious night, worrisome for us, but saw no point in sitting home, just-in-case, playing out what-if scenarios, watching endless analysis on CNN. It was January 16 and all was quiet; eerily quiet. January 15th came and went.

During drinks and horsd'oeuvres we tittered nervously about occupational issues, labour laws, interpretations of the Koran, news items, anything but the elephant in the room that was on everyone's mind. I sipped at the soup leaving most. Was it because I was a bundle of nerves or because I knew there were six more courses? I nibbled at the pate then devoured the illegal pork tenderloin, disremembering where I was. We lingered over the courses as the plates came and went. Following dessert, we retired to the sitting area for thimbles of Arab coffee, fruit and cheese.

When the phone rang everyone stiffened. Chris handed the phone to Daryle.

"Dad, it's coming," from Ian in Dhahran.

"What's happening over there?" Everyone inched to the edge of their chairs.

"The whole air force is flying out.

"They are roaring over the house.

"The sirens are blaring. We were having dinner with Dan Tighe.

"We all ran home, leaving our plates at the table.

"Dan wanted to bring the brownies into the safe room under the stairs, but everyone flew out the door, barely hearing his offer.

"Dad, we didn't even say goodbye."

"How is your sister?" Daryle asked.

"She's fine; she ran faster than I did; she still had her fork."

"Okay. Thanks for the call.

"Keep your head down. We will call you as things develop here."

"Dad, they're on their way."

"It's okay Ian. We are heading home now.

"And thank you for the call.

"You're better than CNN.

"No, there are no sirens here in Riyadh, nothing yet."

We dialed Alvin, the gate guard, and told him to expect some action, that we just heard from Dhahran and would be returning immediately. We ended our coffee as abruptly as Jessica and Ian ended their meal in the eastern province. The Russell Juniors accepted their first overseas teaching jobs in Dhahran. We often told recent graduates that if they wanted to work internationally, they should be prepared to start in the trenches, thinking of some of the war-torn schools in Latin America. We did not expect it for our own two children who had recently completed student teaching. But there they were, in the trenches of Dhahran, phoning us in Riyadh to prepare us for what would be coming our way, and theirs.

Over the months, throughout the buildup to the withdrawal date, we received tremendous support from our international colleagues and concerned US friends including the Roenschs from Manila. This week we have been more down and a little depressed at the end of the day. The phone calls from around the world helped a lot. Scott Chambers called from Norway last night, David Daly called from Boston, Dick Krajczar called from Kuala Lumpur, Roger Hove called from Dubai plus calls from friends in Pakistan, India and Greece; school people have called me from TASIS Leysin and Bahrain; plus faxes from the US.

My father never did connect with the international part of our lives. I got the feeling my father thought I was foolish; still thought I was throwing my life away. Why didn't I stay home and help people in America? I called him one evening as the SCUDS started coming in. I just wanted to let him know we were okay and watching events carefully.

"What events?"

"Well, you know, the Gulf War."

"Oh, I know you guys are fine."

"I hear your TV; what are you watching, Dad?"

"I like the weather channel."

I recently read through remarks, made by Peter Arnett, formerly of CNN, who commented on the lack of information they were given access to while reporting in Iraq. He remarked that apparently President Bush didn't want the Americans at home to know everything as seen from inside Iraq. Perhaps my family and others were not aware of the enormity of the buildup of tanks, troops, weaponry and the destruction perpetrated on Bagdad and to some extent Kuwait and Saudi Arabia.

We sped through the empty streets as sirens started to wail in Riyadh. We were never so glad to roar through the compound gates, Alvin standing ever ready and eager to hear what we knew.

We did not sleep, waiting for the unknown. We cracked the sliding glass window to hear any air-raid sirens and slept with the shortwave radio under the pillow. I punched it every hour to hear the headlines then tried to drift off again.

Marlin Fitzwater announced, via the shortwave," The liberation of Kuwait has begun…" The air war started at 02:38 Middle East Bagdad time with an air attack on Baghdad and other military targets in Iraq and Kuwait.

President Bush addressed the nation and the world, but we missed it. We did, however, catch the incredible filming and reporting from CNN which recorded events live, in real-time, as they unfolded in Baghdad. Newsmen John Holliman, Peter Arnett and Bernard Shaw reported via audio reports inside the Al Rashid Hotel while other networks provided live visuals of incoming missiles and explosions. Although there were tight restrictions on reporting, there were incredible stories. The success, popularity, of CNN was due to the spontaneous coverage. At any time of the day or night we turned on the television to find out what was happening; we no longer waited for the six o'clock news.

The following night Iraq launched the first SCUD missiles at Saudi Arabia.

Sam Donaldson, Jessica Russell, Ian Russell, Dhahran

SCUDs and SSATs

B ill Fisher, an American dentist, lived near the airport. The runway was an obvious target. SCUD attacks continued sometimes night-ly, sometimes sporadically. Every night he sweat rockets; he sometimes slept in the desert, then sent his driver in the morning to find twist-ed bits of shrapnel out of which he figured art objects and jewelry. Shannon lived near the airport also. The Patriot missile launchers were located there and each time the SCUDs launched, the Patriots fired back both in Riyadh and in Dhahran.

Shannon, my clever American student, later told me, "… when-ever SCUDs were fired and Patriots retaliated, our windows shook. We taped the windows with duck tape. When the sirens went off, we (sic) went into my parents' room and (sic) put on our gas masks—scary." I thought about Bernie, the young man in the army, and his training with Stingers and Patriots.

Not unlike anticipating the GRE, with fear and trembling, the Secondary School Admission Test, given twice each year internation-ally, is feared, dreaded and anticipated by students. Young academics believe, at least their parents believe, their entire futures are dependent upon taking the SSAT and scoring well in order to be placed in private schools around the world.

The international date for this year's SSAT, January 18, established a year ago in Princeton, was already going to be a problem for us. With the buildup of troops, mail delivery slowed; mail was nearly nonexis-tent and no packages were permitted.

After the December holiday break, enrollment dropped to an all-time low of 329 students from an enrollment of over 2000. Many fam-ilies elected not to return, but to wait-it-out until after the January 15th deadline. Families were hopeful, but cautious. Some left for two weeks returning to their home cities including Cairo, Seoul, Istanbul and Omaha, while others were able to request to sit for the exam in Jeddah, Amman, Delhi, and St. Louis. Still others had nowhere to go. Those students remained in Saudi and attended classes when school reopened after the winter break.

As the January 15th deadline inched closer and closer and hope prevailed, crested then sharply deteriorated, the tremendous let down and depression gave way to anxiety and tension which increased hourly. Students who registered for the test left the city, others left the Kingdom. Some remained because they felt obligated to take the SSAT.

Normal test-tension coupled with the possibility of SCUD attacks intensified the anxiety and brought new meaning to 'anticipatory set.' Again I offered the SSAT mini-course to focus on practice exams and test-taking strategies, but we rewrote the book on fear. Routine, a basic combatant to stress, preempted other strategies.

With bulky gas masks slung over their shoulders, jostled against overloaded book bags, students faithfully reported after school, wanting to concentrate on the material from the mini-course, but needing to discuss all the what-ifs.

What if there is an attack?

What if the sirens go off?

What if we don't take the test?

What if we don't get into a good school?

What if something happens while we're taking the test?

What if the tests don't even arrive?

Coping: Making Yourself Calm, the last two hand-outs for the mini-course, were prophetic. Reassured that Riyadh is a long way from Baghdad and from Dhahran as well, I sent home that scenario to help avoid piggybacking stress. Parents, students, staff, the entire community was edgy. Even those who handled the stress were still uneasy. The idea of a good night's sleep was a fantasy from calmer times. Students anticipated midnight strikes and intermittent sirens. No one slept. Three days before the exam, the tests arrived.

Sirens began wailing early the morning of January 18th, the scheduled date of the Riyadh exam. At three AM we knew there would be no SSAT at eight in the morning. At six AM we began calling all students. Although confident that there would be no attacks during the day, everyone's nerves were shattered.

We talked it through daily. The students were okay and the parents were relieved that the exam would be postponed, not cancelled. Amidst nightly attacks, intermittent wailing of sirens and midnight lunges into safe rooms, students reported for the rescheduled exam two weeks later.

No scuds, no attacks, no sirens, and no disruptions; students remained focused and determined throughout. SCUDs or no SCUDs they were jubilant. Upon completion of the final bubbling-in, test takers released tension by ravenously devouring hand-carried brown-bag snacks. All that energy, intelligence and tension bottled inside, they were now free, liberated at last! The exhilaration and relief mirrored exceptional emotions for an exceptional time.

The admission of gas masks into the security-tight ETS test centre was the only deviation from the norm. No calculators or slide rules, a figment of the way past; no books or notes, no food in the room.

Students were instructed to bring two #2 pencils only; gasmasks optional, the one exception to the tight security rule. This time security meant physical security, not test security.

Spud Attack

O nce the SCUD attacks started, they were fairly regular. That's not to suggest we became used to them. Schedules went well enough during the daylight hours, but hanging over everyone's head: what will happen tonight? I felt guilty, but I hoped the missiles were headed to another country. In a warped sense of ambulance chasers, we sometimes went outside to watch the rockets stream across the sky. The men thought this was particularly macho and delighted in taking videos which they narrated with breathless adrenalin gasps. We were all scared.

We remained on high-level stress. Sirens went off intermittently and no one knew where the SCUDs were headed or where they would land. As the SCUDs approached Saudi, especially Riyadh, the Patriot missiles went after them, usually cutting them down, sometimes missing. Some nights there were no strikes at Riyadh, but we never knew and never slept, in anticipation.

As tension built during nightly SCUD attacks, we felt we needed a stress-breaker for our staff; I choreographed a SPUD ATTACK, a baked potato bar with heaps of condiments and terrible homemade wine which we scooped from the basura bin with big pitchers.

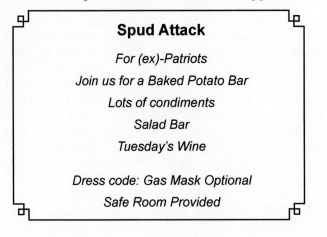

Spud Attack

For (ex)-Patriots

Join us for a Baked Potato Bar

Lots of condiments

Salad Bar

Tuesday's Wine

Dress code: Gas Mask Optional

Safe Room Provided

The invitation provided the levity for the evening that I hoped; the bad brew helped too. But some still asked, "Where's the Safe Room?" Though sensitive to growing staff stress, I underestimated the extent of the tension. Some brought their personally purchased gas masks. I indicated the small space under the stairs for a safe room. Bob and Maxine brought their masks, Margie and Justin brought masks. Barb laughed her contagious whooping-cough-laugh through her nervousness, her gasmask slung over her shoulder the whole evening like a Gucci bag from Bangkok.

We baked the potatoes in foil. In addition to the usual butter, sour cream and chives, I served as condiments chili, jalapenos, guacamole, cheese, caviar, diced boiled eggs and black olives. The salad bar included oriental slaw, green lettuce, artichoke hearts, marinated baby asparagus, chicken chunks, red tomato wedges, purple sliced onion rings, more cheeses, salted nuts and dressings. In addition, Johnny the cook prepared a three bean salad, a pasta salad and a huge fruit salad.

I kept a shortwave radio, a flashlight and paperback book in the crawl space and quickly offered the undersized enclosure to anyone who felt nervous during the evening, or in case we had an air raid warning of a SCUD attack during our SPUD Attack. Barb checked it out and whooped-up a good laugh. In reality, had the sirens gone off, had there been a warning, most could have dashed home to their villas on the compound. It takes less time to boil an egg.

Two days later a SCUD hit an apartment building a kilometer from the house. We were home at the time. The way the house seemed to buckle, I thought the missile landed in my garden. My knees shook like uncooked liver, as I wandered about the house in the dark.

In the morning we drove over to see the building, what was left of it. Is that what they call collateral damage? Some of the cement frame still stood, but the windows were blown out and the occupants, if living, were gone. No one could have survived the direct hit on the upper floors. The implosion and blinding light at our villa was the final straw for some; but by that time there were no flights out and they fled across the desert by car to Jeddah.

Recruiting For A War Zone
February 1991

Recruiting teachers for Saudi Arabia presented a huge challenge. It was all about marketing to convince a person that living in the oil-rich Kingdom was not only possible, but enjoyable. That's why I started recruiting with Daryle. Teachers wanted to know, 'What's it like for women living in Saudi Arabia?'

"Oh it's great there. My wife loves it."

Right. What kind of weirdo is his wife?

So I started attending conferences and participating in the interviews. I found I could answer concerns about children, housing, dress-codes and culture as well as questions about student activities and later curriculum questions. Tim Hanson and Don Shoemaker, school principals, provided information about text books and specific curriculum concerns.

This year, people knew all about Saudi Arabia due to extended media coverage. They knew too much. Who of sound mind would sign a contract to work in a war zone? We started the conference in Boston, after a twenty-nine hour flight, and did persuade a few couples to come upstairs to interview with us and with Bob Tinney.

When we registered at the front desk in Boston, we received messages from recruiters and colleagues, including a fax from Gail Barilka, Daryle's secretary in Riyadh.

"Don't worry, it wasn't our school."

As we sat on the edge of the bed, the first teaching couple sat in the chairs as we started getting to know each other. From nowhere, in the middle of the conversation, came a deafening bang. Bob and I dropped to the floor and Daryle grabbed the side of the desk. We looked around and realized the noise came from the construction site across from the hotel.

The confused couple stared at us. Bob and I got off the floor and started to snicker, then laugh from embarrassment and nerves; that gasping forbidden laughter when you know you shouldn't laugh, but can't stop; when you know the timing is terrible, like in a worship service or funeral. Daryle tried to gain composure stating that things were really fine in Riyadh, but we were all a bit jumpy. That made it worse and we guffawed out of control. The couple left the interview without signing.

From Boston we split up. We had several days midweek between conferences. I stopped in Spokane to see Jessica and Ian who were also between job-fairs looking for first-time, full-time teaching positions. Daryle traveled to freezing, snowy Iowa to interview candidates and Bob and I headed toward sunny California. In those few days, Jessica met with her former junior high class to talk about her first-hand experience with the war, and Ian got married.

February 19, 1991. Up early with few hours of sleep, Jessica and I went to her student-teaching school at Shaw Junior High where she was scheduled all day for classes which had signed up in the school library. Everyone was eager to see her again. The junior high is located in a depressed area of Spokane; the housing dumpy and small and run down. The students ratty looking, tacky, tough, worse than public school, lots of ear rings, nose rings, rat tails, torn jeans, but well behaved in the large group sessions. She handled them professionally, walking around to vary attention and calling names if any wandered or attempted whisper sessions on the side.

"Hi everyone. It's great to be back at Shaw Junior High." She sort-of lied.

"I went to Saudi Arabia for the holidays to visit my family. Jeremy, sit down please.

"Remember, I told you that before I left?

"Yes, they live there. Yes, now. My parents.

"Yes, they still do, now in Saudi.

"Well, this is my mother. She's here now, but she is going back next week.

"Lots of teachers in Saudi Arabia left the country.

"Yep. Guess what! They offered me a job and I teach 4th grade now.

"What do you mean, Freddy, 'Why did they leave?'

"Ha! Maybe they are the smart ones, you're right!

"I brought my gasmask. Would you like to see how it works?"

The students and the teachers inched to the edge of their library chairs as she placed the prehistoric looking apparatus over her head and face. Walking around the room she let the students get a good look then offered several of the boys a chance to put it on.

"Awesome, man."

"That is totally way out, man."

"Where'd you get that?"

"Could you get me one?"

"How'd you know when to wear it?"

"You sleep in it?" they all talked at once.

"If you will sit down again, I will show you a video that my brother made last week."

She showed parts of Ian's courageous home-made video, showing the compound at Dhahran, their school, her students in Saudi, and the best part, the SCUD missiles gliding across the sky, all caught live on video.

"Cindy?"

"Ms Russell, did you ever have to use your safe room?" she leaned forward in her chair.

"Well, this is what happened. My brother and I are sharing a house in Saudi Arabia.

"The night of the first air raid, the first night of the war, we ran home from a friend's house.

"We were so scared we didn't want to hide in the safe room."

"Ms Russell, why? Wasn't it safe?" she asked as she pushed her hair behind her ear.

"We slept in the living room in our sleeping bags. You know why?"

"It's safer than your safe room?" from one of the boys.

"No, it's not." Jessica paused briefly. The students waited.

"We wanted to watch CNN." They laughed, thinking she just wanted to watch TV.

"The only way we knew what was really going on was by watching CNN news. We knew most of the reporters were waiting for action, and when it came, they were the only ones to inform us of what was really happening."

"Ms Russell, were you really scared?"

"Jonathon, I was so scared. I'm still nervous thinking about it."

"Why are you going back there?" Jessica paused, then said,

"I'm a teacher."

What she really meant was that she had a real job with a real salary. And what she also did not tell them or her former teaching colleagues was that she and her brother received hardship raises twice in the first month of the war. Not bad for a beginning teacher.

Call Your Mother

"Janice, you need to call your mother."

That afternoon we sat around a kitchen table in Spokane. Janice Klesch and Ian planned to marry in the summer. Janice would need a passport wherever they intended to work in the fall. As always, there was a backlog in the U.S. passport office. It would take weeks to obtain the document, her first, then more time to obtain the proper visas.

Janice called city hall. A formal name change could not be handled by the post office, or even the county courthouse. They would need a marriage certificate. Before I caught the implications, and certainly before it sunk into their heads, they were talking marriage; wedding; legal documents. How would they get married? Should they get married? Could they get married? What should they do? They called for wedding information in Spokane: a three week waiting period for blood tests and for processing other tests. They did not have three weeks.

"Janice, you need to call your mother," was my neutral advice. She ran downstairs.

"What did she say? What does she think?"

"She's not home. I left a message on her answering machine."

"About getting married?? You left a message?

"What about Idaho?" I remembered.

Jessica and Ian were returning to Saudi in two days; they had a day and a half left. I suggested they phone Idaho. I had some recollection that they might be able to get a quick wedding across the state line. Ian phoned the Idaho courthouse. Marriage was possible without witnesses or blood. The Hitching Post would be open until 5pm. No regulations, no waiting, just seventy-five dollars.

"Should we?" We all looked at the kitchen clock. It was 3:15pm.

"Do you think we can make it?"

"Janice, I think you should call your mother. What will your parents say?" I didn't want to harbour the full responsibility for this life altering decision.

"Oh, she'll be okay. She'll understand. Probably would be okay."

"Call your mother," I pushed.

"Should we?"

"No, probably not."

"This is ridiculous."

"Probably should, for logistics, then we can get going on the passport."

"Janice, do you want to change your name," trying to think of details.

"Definitely. I'm only doing this once," meaning the marriage thing.

Tomorrow was out. More looks around the table and at the clock.

"Well, maybe we should."

"Then get going!" My age showed, already showing signs of being the mother-in-law.

"You have an hour and a half to get there," I encouraged.

"What shall I wear?" Janice vanished and emerged from her room cute and smart.

"What did your mother say?" still hoping.

"She's just not there."

Ian shaved, we gave Janice the fresh tulips from the kitchen table, and off they went to Idaho. It only occurs to me now, that maybe she never did phone her mom, and just did what she felt she had to do without reinventing the whole conversation over the phone.

"We need to make this festive," I said to Jessica.

"If they really pull this off, and actually get married…

"Cellll-e-braaaa-tion," we broke into song. "Come on!"

"Let's go. I'll get big, thick, red steaks."

"I'll stuff mushrooms,' from Corey, a house mate.

"You have any rice?"

"Rice?"

"It's traditional, right?" I still cringed at throwing rice away, but it was tradition and it was symbolic. We were reaching to make this special, since it was so spontaneous.

"Maybe a bottle of champagne."

"And a card."

It was Tuesday night. They had a standing date at Big Foot, the local bar, for trivia night.

"Hey! Wassup?"

"Hey!"

"Hey!" No one says hello anymore.

"Ian. Jen. Hey Ms Russell. Glad you could come."

"Kim, Paul, wassup?" We found places round the bar jawing back and forth. Everyone ordered a beer, except me; I was out of college. I asked for a glass of wine.

"What'd you guys do today? They addressed Ian. He looked at Jen, then at me.

"We got married."

"Right."

"No Way."

"What??"

"Yeah."

"What'd your mother say?" They looked at me, then at Ian.

"She said it was one more thing we could cross off our list." I was there. I could not deny the comment, though I don't remember making that statement.

Thursday, February 21. When Jessica and Ian left for Saudi, I had one more day before heading to Carmel, California for the final recruiting conference of the season. I took out my files and in the silence of the empty Spokane house I sat on the edge of the bed and phoned all the private boarding schools where my Riyadh students had applied.

"How are you doing in Riyadh?" from the admissions officer at Exeter.

"Did you receive the SSAT scores?"

"We did. Is it still pretty tense in Saudi?"

"It is. It's very tense, but the kids are holding up well."

"We aren't ready to announce any decisions at this time, as you know."

"I understand. I'm just following up to be sure you received the application forms.

"Mail is a bit erratic.

"We had 6 applications this year for Exeter.

"All the boys took the SSAT and their files were mailed last month."

"I have them all. I'm glad to hear everyone is alright.

"By the way, can you add any more information on Matthew?

"We were assessing his file yesterday."

I reviewed all the student files, discussed the SSATs, and I was pleased to learn many schools were willing to waive the exam results this year for our students. I called Princeton to determine that the test scores had been received and spent extra time explaining that the test was given under SCUD attack, but that the kids were disciplined and cooperative and focused. Colleagues in America were interested in our circumstances and in our story. I was the personal face to the TV news.

When the War's Over, You Want to be in Riyadh

Friday, February 22, 1991. In Carmel, beautiful Carmel, California, I met Bob Tinney at noon to look at candidate paperwork. Bob Infelise and Lou Fuccillo seemed casual and unstructured at their Carmel Conference. They seemed to wing-it; at least that's how it appeared to most of us. The structure for the weekend was intended to be stress-free.

"Eh! Daniela!" It was Lou. Gregarious, happy, rose-nose, rosy-cheek Boston-Italian.

"Daniela," as if I didn't hear him across the lobby.

"Ya takin' ova fa Dahryle!

"Ya just get in?

"Ya know your way 'round, so any thing I can do fa ya, ya let me know. All right?"

"Thanx Lou. Always feels like I'm coming home when I'm in Carmel."

The Carmel teacher hiring conference was abstract, relaxed and California-casual. Bob and I asked when the files and paperwork would be available. Nothing. Not set up for early review of the files. The system at Carmel was an evening introduction presented by some-one from each of the schools followed by signups for interviews. Bob and I, both borderline type-A personalities, wanted to review the files. We asked Bob and Lou who finally agreed that the secretary kept the candidate files. We were the only ones to have access to the candidate papers. No one else knew they were available.

Adele the secretary-coordinator, by contrast was very organized. She inquired about the Middle East and about Riyadh in particular. She asked if we saw the interview with Riyadh teachers the day be-fore. She told us she taped an interview with some Riyadh teachers whom she had seen on the satellite feed. The men drove to Dhahran and were interviewed there. Thinking we would be interested she taped it for us. Of course Bob and I were very interested to know who it was and what they said about their circumstances, especially with the school.

We carried boxes of files to a grungy open room and separated the folders of candidates selecting out non-Jewish, married couples; regu-lations from the Ministry of Whatever. After several hours we knew the names of several promising candidate couples to look for and in-vite for interviews.

We returned the boxes to Adele and she offered to show us the teacher video. When we saw it, we watched Jim and Jack of all people. The irony was in their aggressive compound anger directed toward Daryle; that they ran-out during the chaos, escaped to Jeddah, and now had become thrill-seekers driving to the frontlines of the Kuwait border. As a result of their genuine fear factor, Jack lashed out at Daryle in his office and in compound meetings meant to squelch rumours and calm nerves. Now they wore their macho manners and were off hot rodding in the dunes of Desert Storm. The interview did not set well with SAISR staff.

"President Bush issues an ultimatum of February 23rd for Iraqi troops to withdraw from Kuwait."

That would be tomorrow. I watched the news as I prepared for the evening reception.

I felt rotten; depressed from the war scenario. Lou introduced the recruiters. I had to be upbeat; positive. I had great clothes; I should feel great. And I loved the energy from Carmel. I was not a weirdo who lived in Saudi Arabia. But I felt down. I had to be up. When I was introduced I said simply, with as much enthusiasm as I could muster, "When the war's over, you want to be in Riyadh." It broke the ice. We made contacts and talked to couples we had seen on paper and introduced ourselves to others whom we did not know. Bob worked one side of the room while I worked the other.

Saturday, February 23, 1991. No one wanted to come to the Middle East. In the morning, sign-ups proceeded slowly. We worked the day hard. Bob was frustrated by the pace. There were so few couples to talk to. We gave several courtesy interviews. It was cold, the rooms were unheated and the classrooms in horrible condition. We were in a terrible classroom yesterday, and today we were in a computer room that was dreadful: dirty and chairs falling apart, old tables, ugly walls and no windows.

California candidates showed interest in Latin American schools and European schools; the safe ones with great weather. The sign-ups were disorganized with no interview times listed and no times indicated to show school videos. We decided on 30 minute blocks of time. But others had different time frames. We blocked a time to show the SAIS-R video and most couples came.

"Wow. Is that where you live?" The SAIS-R video showed the villas and the compound.

"Your school is modern."

"Your teachers are American."

"You have Pizza Hut and Kentucky Fried?" That was Bruce McMillen's bit for the video.

"A couple can save one salary?"

"I never knew Saudi Arabia was modern like this." A picture is worth a thousand words, but apparently, money isn't everything. We offered no contracts.

When To Pull Out

Sunday, February 24, 1991. I slept fitfully in my California hotel room. The Iraqi troops did not pull out of Kuwait.

"Last night the ground war started with Marines, Army, and Arab forces moving into Iraq and Kuwait." It must be true. I heard it on TV.

Two more SCUD attacks showered and destroyed a boys' school on the outskirts of Riyadh. I was sure it was the school next to us. The devastation was massive. No children were there, schools have not re-opened, and the attacks were during the night hours, but the impact was major. The community will be jittery again. I knew no one in Riyadh slept. The night raids continued. Because we were the only school open, I guessed there would be much discussion again, about the wisdom of remaining open. I assume we are the only school open. The French school closed, the British school closed and the Saudi schools never reopened after January 15th.

In the morning I turned to the news; I was addicted to the stupid news. I didn't want to watch it, but I did not want to miss anything. A marketing tool no doubt: get the latest news; be the first to know. I fell for it. I nibbled at breakfast then walked into the fresh air and sun. The day was bright, clear, sweater-weather, and I needed a diversion. I felt miserable and didn't understand the emotion. I knew what it was, but didn't understand why I was so affected.

I strolled across the street behind the hotel thinking about troop movement over the Kuwaiti border and the continued SCUD attacks. The Barnyard, an elegant, smart-casual California mini strip of shops was a pleasant diversion displaying beautiful cards and thoughtful art work in several small galleries and everywhere yellow ribbons and American flags fluttered; war reminders ever present. It was my first time to see the Chinese symbol for crisis. Black brush strokes emblazoned a simple white card. The combination of strokes suggested crisis (or) opportunity. The back of the card explained that the characters depicted danger and opportunity, which defined the word crisis, wei ji.

Of course. It was my aha moment. Crisis creates Opportunity. Crisis permits the occasion to be bold with solutions; to think the unthinkable, enables outside of the box thinking. The bold strokes of the Chinese characters jumped out at me. I purchased several cards.

Easter must be soon. Fluffy bunnies, books, cards, baskets, pastels and flowers conveyed a spring message in all the shops. Also

CRISIS AS OPPORTUNITY
(wéi jī)

bright green sparkles and shamrocks reminded the consumer of Saint Patrick's Day. Aggressive marketing. It was February.

Absorbed in an exquisite book shop I read, selected then eliminated all but the most essential books. I purchased a few gift items for compound kids and when I could carry no more, made my way back to the hotel room to regroup, though it was much too beautiful to stay inside. The people and stunning art displays cleansed my head. Never hurts to purchase a few good books; I started to feel better.

I headed out again, this time across the highway to another shopping centre of unique boutiques and restaurants. Carmel was decked-out in Sunday dress; casual chic, looking very smart, as my Kampala friends would later say. Carmelites brunched and shopped in an outdoor market for strawberries the size of tennis-balls. I walked and walked and while invigorated, I also felt a blanket of emotion and concern. I wandered around like a hippo stuck in mud; heavy, ponderous, without focus. Was this a form of depression?

Absentmindedly I bought peanuts to eat in the room and looked at war buttons and patriotic stickers. I walked aimlessly, pausing for long stretches in front of windows, all displaying flags and yellow ribbons, looking at everything, looking at nothing. For no reason, I wandered into a Christmas shop. An enormous evergreen wreath, with American cocktail flags embedded between the pines, decorated the front entrance.

At the front of the store, a couple stood talking to the owner about the ground war. The shop radio was tuned to a war-coverage station, a radio talk-show. The owner of the shop, an older gentleman, wore 'I Support Our Troops' buttons on his shirt. The couple talked about the ground war, about the military hitting the sand; getting on with it, supportive and positive, but wanting their boys home. These were Americans; real Americans. I'm a native, but I'm a global American. I think differently. I want to think like an American. I saw those kids on the front lines; met with the soldiers who might be hitting the ground. I thought of Bernie and the others. I thought of Jessica and Ian the same age; they could have been soldiers.

The tears welled up. I walked to the back of the store to gain composure and the drops slowly trickled down my face onto my sweater. I bought all the tiny flags he had left and headed out into the sunshine. Not sure why I have become so overwhelmed. And so patriotic. Maybe all the weeks of putting on a positive front never left time to release a pent up anxiety and apprehension.

In the next shop I bought window flags as giveaways in Riyadh and party decorations of red, white and blue. Was the spending a binge to cover my emotions? As I headed out, I saw the last T-shirt. I bought it:

it featured a head-shot of Saddam Hussein, a forbidden slash through the circle which read 'So Damn Insane.' In my right mind, I would never buy anything like that. I don't even wear T-shirts.

It was by then 4:00pm. I had been wandering around since 10:30 in the morning. I headed back, the sun still clear, though the cloud bank began to roll in from the ocean front. I was still moping about. I packed out, cramming things into my bags, now bulging. Daryle will strangle me. I wish I could connect with him. I wanted to hear the results from the Iowa recruiting. I tried to call Janice to learn what she heard from Ian, but their phones were dysfunctional every time I called, turned on to fax mode which screeched in my ears.

Later in the evening Daryle called from Iowa. He called Riyadh. It had been a very difficult day. Ted was scared. He wanted to close the school and inadvertently stirred up controversy. He was convinced it was not safe. Tim tried to keep the lid on and called board members.

Vern Cassin and Dick Jones both urged that the Board keep the school open. The SCUDs, along with the tension of the beginning of the ground offensive, made for a very difficult day. It was hard for Daryle to be away. The following morning we returned. Jeannie Cassin handed me a bag of condoms of all things, a fundraising project of her sorority sisters at Radcliff. Each packet featured a photo of Saddam Hussein. Printed under his photo: For the Man who Doesn't Know When to Pull Out.

And Then It Was Over

The news indicated another school was hit and destroyed outside Riyadh. We later learned it was the Nejd School. The night raids continued. The following evening, February 25th, an Iraqi SCUD missile hit a US barracks located in al Khobar, just outside Dhahran, killing 27, mostly American military personnel. Over 100 US troops including an Army Reserve unit and several female soldiers resided in the converted warehouse. We watched the coverage of dazed survivors wandering around in shock wearing shorts and sweat suits milling about with rescuers.

Accounts of the disaster varied. Some witnesses claimed they saw a Patriot intercept the SCUD; others noted a large explosion before the missile hit the ground. American command suggested that the SCUD broke up in flight. Iraqis hailed the attack. Whatever the exact cause, the barracks disintegrated within an hour, leaving only a skeleton of the building. I felt personally devastated. It was too close; too tragic and only kilometers from Jessica and Ian.

The next morning, resistance leaders in Kuwait declared they were in control of Kuwait City. There was a lot of happy-fire aimed into the sky, lots of honking in the streets and flag waving in Kuwait. The day after that, President Bush ordered a cease fire effective at midnight Kuwait time, February 27, 1991. And then it was over. Five days later Iraqi leaders accepted the cease fire.

A cease fire, a prisoner exchange, and it was over. The troops went home and we resumed our lives. It was something like that. It was over. As quickly as it started, it stopped. Teachers returned and families came back boosting the diminished enrolment.

The unexpected turn of events, which we failed to anticipate, was the lingering problem with the attitudes of some teachers who returned. There seemed to be an overriding feeling of survivor's guilt, departure guilt; quitter's guilt. Returning staff voiced the opinion that they knew they would not be accepted back, socially, because they left to escape the war.

I never heard this opinion voiced by any of the staff who stayed in Riyadh. Everyone had their own mechanism for dealing with the war. Some expressed anxiety for their children. Some felt pressure from their parents. This came from the young staff. We were surprised that some of the macho, young, fearless, adventurous teachers and families were the first to bolt, to flee to Jeddah, to fly to Cyprus, or to enroll their children back home, where ever that was.

Early in the build-up to the war, Daryle drew up several plans to make it comfortable for teachers to leave on a temporary basis, or on a permanent status if they chose. There was never any condemnation of teachers who made those choices. It was anticipated and helped with the problem of attrition.

To learn that they felt guilty, for anything, came as a shock and an interesting revelation. It was clearly self-imposed. It never crossed anyone's mind that people were deserting, jumping ship. Apparently, this feeling surfaced and festered while the families or teachers were away. It bubbled to the surface when they returned.

It was not until the following August when we came back to peaceful Riyadh that we realized the emotional strain we had been through the previous year. The nightly SCUD attacks on Riyadh, and on Dhahran, where Jessica and Ian were living, sleeping with the windows open in order to hear the screaming air raid sirens, the psychological threat of chemicals, safe rooms, sealed windows, gas masks, the ever-charged emotions of teachers, staff, children and parents, security and contingency plans, evacuation plans, and the tremendous responsibility of trying to keep everybody up, including ourselves, was in the end, enormously draining.

While other people sent their children out of Saudi during the conflict, we brought ours in. Jessica and Ian stayed during the war to teach at Dhahran Academy.

The Gulf Crisis which so drained us was now back page news.

Empty Quarter

Rub al Khali

Addicted

It was not an easy camp-out; not a Thursday overnight in the *wadi*. The chances of becoming lost in the Rub al Khali were great. The dunes in the Empty Quarter measured over 300 meters, 1000 feet; taller than the Eiffel Tower, as the books like to describe. Severe conditions make it uninhabitable with summer temperatures reaching 55 degrees Celsius, 130 Fahrenheit, but not in December. We left Riyadh late. We planned to leave at 8am on Boxing Day but finally pulled-out at three in the afternoon.

Our mission was to locate the *field of dreams* as we called it: a dry lakebed thought to be littered with ancient artifacts of carved stone tools and weapons from the Paleolithic and Neolithic periods. Our point of reference: numbers on a GPS.

Thinking about the trip made me tense. Camping in the dunes, especially those dunes, required meticulous planning. The stature of the formidable sand mountains and the austerity of the region required accomplished driving skills and full attention at all times.

We used Global Positioning Systems, and carried radio phones plugged into the cigarette lighters of our cars. However, we were not Bedouin; our skills in the sand were limited to weekend driving. The GPS guided our direction, but did not guide us over each dune; the reading of the satellites told us where to go, but not how to go.

I worried about navigating: no roads, no trails, no land marks, only soft sand. Each dune looked like the last; each dune looked like the next. The giant dunes shift with the wind and the season. Nothing remains exactly the same.

I lost my breath just thinking about traversing colossal mountains of sand. Food, weather, water: no problem. But the ruggedness of the dunes sobered the psyche. The late departure forced us to drive at night. We left Riyadh at three in the afternoon with only two hours of daylight left. How would we navigate in the dark?

We took three cars. Ian drove Vern's Nissan Patrol, Daryle drove our Toyota Land Cruiser and Vern drove an Italian La Forza. We often went to the desert with Vern and Jeanne, both lawyers. This trip Ian and Jen joined us from Dhahran on our last big trip to the dunes, the big dunes.

"Why's Vern driving that Italian car?"

"Who knows? It's supposed to be a big deal; very expensive."

"So why's he taking it to the Empty Quarter? Must be a macho thing."

"He said he was testing it. Maybe they will import them."

"Who?"

"Some Saudi entrepreneur; probably a prince. Vern has lots of contacts."

We drove for three hours and at 6pm stopped for petrol and hot *shwarmas* at a small town near Wadi ad D'wasir. The moon, a mere crescent, dangled from the edge of a white cloud like a silver earring.

The rural town sparkled for three blocks with little white lights. Strands of lights framed the doors and outlined the tops of each small shop along the desert strip. Neon tubing jumped like disco pulse and glittered in self-important circles around otherwise dull signs.

Lighted yellow and purple Arabic shop names vied for attention on the short strip of the main street like a tacky strip mall anywhere. In the centre of the roundabout stood an arresting gray concrete sculpture of a four-sided, angular 6 meter high incense burner; vintage fifties, a spinoff of Russian modern art; ugly, dreary, but symbolic.

The *shwarmas*, swathed in warm pita and wrapped in paper towels, filled the car with an aroma of garlic and spices. We were hungrier than we thought and devoured the cumin-garlic-cardamom- nutmeg spiced lamb wraps. The *shwarmas* were Lebanese style and stuffed with fries. I looked out the open window of the Land Cruiser, as I dabbed at the yogurt-tahini sauce dripping down my chin. Ian, Daryle and Vern stood outside stretching their legs and leaning against the cars clutching their own *shwarmas*. Jeannie and her kids and Jen and I sat inside the cars to eat. The restaurants were segregated.

A *thobe* shop stood next to a small photography shop, next to Al Ankar Textiles, next to Salajed *'Office of General Services From Government Offices and Man Power Supply,'* the sign said in small English cursive letters. On the corner of this small strip of stores, a dry cleaning shop displayed several rows of six-foot long *thobes* hanging in crisp formation, not one touching the ground; Each *thobe* looked like the next; each *thobe* looked like the last; clones, all white, all starched, all exactly alike to the untrained eye.

Three hooded, masked, fully covered ladies ambled down the street like black carrion crows. Their stiff masks folded down the centre, covered their noses like black beaks. Across the street a lady clutched the top of her head-covering with one hand and slightly lifted the hem of her full length *abaya* with the other as she ascended steep concrete steps to the bakery.

Men from Cairo and Lebanon wandered the street in leather jackets, while those from India and Pakistan walked in groups wearing polyester pants and thin crew sweaters. We pressed on toward the formidable Rub' al Khali.

At eleven-thirty we stopped again for petrol in case there was nothing else open. In the car we listened to four tapes of Alvin Toffler. It helped us stay awake and pass the time as we drove on and on. Toffler, the great futurist, talked about a power shift, based on violence, wealth, and knowledge. It seemed profound in the expansive desert. I remember his thoughts on the illiterates of the future. He said illiteracy of the twenty-first century would not be about reading and writing, but about unlearning and relearning. I think we're there.

At one in the morning we pulled off the road, let air out of the tires and prepared to enter the sand.

Vern led in the La Forza. Jeannie took the wheel from Ian like Jeanne d'Arc leading the troops. In the middle of the night, in the desolate Empty Quarter, no one noticed the illegal female driver behind the wheel. No one saw anything. With the moon but a sliver, the sky black, the night dark, the forbidden female driver slipped through the desert darkness unnoticed. Daryle followed in the Land Cruiser. We drove fast in the soft sand not wanting to separate or get lost, or get stuck although the radios were there for backup.

Vern flew up and over the top of a red dune and the La Forza was out of sight. Jeannie soared to the top of the 100 meter dune with the Nissan Patrol, but failed to have enough momentum, and slid back down.

"What should I be doing?" she asked over her radio. "Is third gear ok?"

"Take it again, girl," Vern answered as we listened-in.

"The RPMs need not be too high. Second gear will be fine."

Already in four wheel drive, we let more air out of the tires. With a running start, she tried once more, got to the crest of the dune, but still couldn't get over the top. She slid back down and tried again. Vern encouraged her over the radio and waited on the other side.

I felt her anxiety as she made a third attempt. I sensed the tightness of her muscles as she tensed her thigh to force the gas pedal to the floorboard, giving it all her strength to get over the top of the soft sand. This time she made it over the first mound and again over the second dune before dropping out of sight.

Then it was our turn. My palms were wet as I clutched the wimp-bar with both hands. We floored-it top speed over the first dune but made a hesitation at the second sandbank and lost it. Roaring back down in reverse, we tried again with a running start, gunned-it, made it up the first mound and without shifting, sped up to the second sand dune and soared over the top. The sand deteriorated under our wheels as we attempted to maintain control down the back side of the steep dune. The other cars waited at the bottom.

It was nearly two AM and dark. As we pulled up we saw Vern in the parallel beams of our Land Cruiser squatting on his haunches on the hard-pack of the lake-bed.

"What do you think? Shall we stay here?" He crouched over a perfectly formed, perfectly carved, one inch flint arrow head.

It was two in the morning. We dumped the rolled-up tents on the lakebed. Then set about bent over, pencil flashlights held between our teeth, scooping up stunning arrowheads, scrapers, small blades, even cores. The *field of dreams* did not disappoint. We made it with GPS, deflated tires, in the middle of the night, in the dark, over enormous dunes. Although exhausted, we surged on fresh adrenalin. There was no way anyone could sleep.

"You are addicted," Jen kept saying.

"You're all addicted.

"This is narcotic. You have to stop. This is really stupid."

We all agreed. It was stupid. We were addicted. It was nearly three in the morning. Then Jen found a scraper, then an arrowhead and she was among the last to hit the cots. At three a.m. we scrambled to set up the 'stupid' tents. We reluctantly crashed but everyone was up 3 hrs later by seven, some at six searching for Paleolithic and Neolithic artifacts.

It was insane.

We were addicted.

Global Position Systems

We toppled off our cots, stumbled out of our tents and before even a mug of hot coffee, began to genuflect on the hard-pack desert surface; on our knees scanning the landscape for more artifacts. In the daylight the smooth flint reflected in the sand like pebbles in a shallow brook and we picked up a few more pieces. These dry flatbeds, once lush lakes rimmed with reeds, teemed with fish, water birds and turtles. Now they were cracked and dry or dusty with no hint of water.

We drove on toward our next planned stop, searching for lakebeds or dunes that might be potential sites for flint. Andrew and Ionis were to meet us in the evening. Like hunter-gatherers we pursued our mission. We hunted and found flawless scrapers, knives, blades and a diverse variety of shapes and sizes of arrowheads.

Jen found a chiseled three inch blade and a unique blunt scraper with a shaft which looked as if the carver changed his mind midstream; a unique piece. Each stop revealed a few treasures for the novice anthropologist. We pushed on over formidable red dunes to the final lake bed of the day, after several attempts at the site-reading. The GPS gave us the readings, but often the dunes got in the way; a classic case of you can't get there from here.

Nearly comatose as we set up dragging tents, chairs, cots and food, Andrew drove up, entirely on navigational finder. This in itself seemed miraculous as we drove from opposite directions in the immense Rub al Khali. The Thompsons, Andrew, Ionis and kids, thrilled to have found us by navigation only, remarked again and again at the wonder of us all connecting in the vast desert by means of a few numbers and a satellite.

After last night with three hours sleep, we were not social. Daryle poured the red homemade wine, decanted in salad dressing bottles. I brought out caviar and crackers, heated meatballs and simmered tagliatelle 'till al dente. We ate, cleaned the plates, hit the cots and never moved. It was remarkable that we all connected through GPS. We crashed without acknowledging this brilliant phenomenon.

Shamal

Refreshed, I boiled up steaming coffee; we ate a quick breakfast, loaded the car, then hunted for scrapers and arrowheads in the dunes and flats another hour before heading out for the next spot. We were addicted. This was, after all, the purpose of the trip, the subplot to the expedition to the Great Rub al Khali. For several days we headed overland deeper into the Empty Quarter tackling the dunes one by one.

We surged over the crest of a great red dune one morning but Vern, in the lead, crash-landed nose first down the steep slope. The La Forza, engineering wonder of the Italians, was embedded in the base of the dune, wedged into the soft sand like a wafer in a dish of sorbet. He revved the engine through each gear including reverse. The wheels dug in deeper.

We grabbed sand ladders and shovels to dig him out. Hiking back up the dune, with sand filling our shoes, the men dug around each wheel. Daryle placed our two ladders under the front wheels, heading forward, down the slope and placed Vern's two ladders under the back wheels. Again Vern revved the engine. *L' macchina* lurched forward, then sank again with the wheels spitting sand in a radius around each of us.

With our short-handled shovels we repeated the procedure to dig out the ladders, buried from the attempted acceleration. This time, putting our body weight behind the Italian marvel it lifted out of the sand enough to make it to the base of the dune, to the lakebed pan.

Pressing on, Andrew got stuck; we dug him out, Vern got stuck again; we dug him out. We forged on searching for a campsite.

"Watch it! Soft sand at the bottom!" came the urgent warning.

"We're stuck!" Andrew barked over the radios.

"Don't let up your speed as you come over the top. Take it fast.

"Keep up your speed.

"It's soft."

Andrew charged down a steep dune and was stuck this time in fine, soft sand at the base. He tried to warn us. He was not in our line of vision, but we heard the message just in time to speed over the crest of the dune accelerating all the way down through and over the soft sand.

Once again, we walked back with sand ladders and shovels to dig him out. It took a long time to free him from the supple sand and we still had not located a campsite for the night. After all the digging, we were ready to stop; ready to eat. I pre-cooked curry which sounded pretty good about that time.

We diddled along, up and over the length of the breathtaking dunes, picking at artifacts along the way. With one hour of sunlight remaining, the wind picked up and we watched a dark, swiftly approaching *shamal* moving in our direction.

We monitored the brown wall, quickly found a level spot and set up tents. We attempted to park the cars to block the blustery weather. The wind was unrelenting. As the *shamal* came up, my contacts scratched across my eyes.

While digging Andrew out, I wrapped a red and white *ghutra* around my head, but the wind was strong and laced with grit. By dinner, everyone's eyes burned.

There was no way to control a fire for cooking in the dirty wall of sand and wind. Dinner would be cold. The thought of cold curry sounded disgusting. We decided to eat tomorrow's lunch: pre-fried chicken, hard boiled eggs and pre-baked potatoes.

According to my meal schedule I planned to heat up a big pot of chicken curry for the evening meal. In Riyadh, I planned and thought through the meals for each day. I prepared a spicy curry and froze it solid to last as many days as possible and to act as insulation for other perishables. We were camping. Cold fried chicken would be fine.

We started with a little homemade red, emptying another salad dressing bottle and munched dried salted peas for hors d'oeuvres. We ended with Kahlua cake, a holiday gift from the kitchen of Janet Rehman, our colleague. The Kahlua was a big deal in Saudi Arabia. Though it was only flavouring with not a drop of rum, it was still illegal. The fried chicken worked. Although we visualized a hot meal at the end of the day, the cold, crusty chicken and hard-boiled eggs satisfied. The homemade red helped. It was all good and better than cold curry.

The wind lashed and whipped the sides of the tents with violent force. We carefully lit a small lantern inside the tent and were fairly protected, but the weather gusted and blew all night, nearly flattening one side of the tent in the gusts.

We stayed inside as much to anchor the tent as for our own protection. Since four in the afternoon the *shamal* blew dark sand in our face, stinging our arms and legs. By nine-thirty it was still howling and black outside. We gave up, put out the light and burrowed into our sleeping bags like moles searching for earthworms.

The Find

In the morning, everything was wet. It was cold but the wind was down. The intense thick fog hung suspended in the air, a miasma draped over the tents and trucks like a heavy wet shroud. Visibility was limited to one car length. We ate breakfast in the tent, put away the dishes then Jen and I packed the lunch while the guys took down the wet tent. We covered the duffels with rain tarps as we packed in the thick drizzle.

Since we ate our pre-cooked fried chicken lunch last night, we tried to find something interesting in our ice chest for today's lunch. What did we have left? It was a balancing act to eat the perishables first, leaving the frozen items to the last, hoping they would not defrost too early. Lunch must be quick and readymade; no time to drag out the burners to heat food or water. The prospect of cold curry was for a second time not appealing.

Peanut butter and celery worked. Ian's summer sausage and crackers and hot bullion would be good on this misty wet day. Jen boiled-up the water and filled the thermos. We could easily pop a cube in a cup. In the cold wet air my fingers felt brittle like a pencil starfish. I thought they might snap off as we loaded the trucks. Everyone wore all their clothes, layered like immigrants crossing a border. Attired in

Qatari with Galactica and plastic bullets and Ian

leg warmers, mittens, hooded sweatshirts and jackets, we looked more like we were set for a Nepalese trek than a desert drive. We loaded the trucks and drove off to make our way back to the site we visited the previous night that was so interesting in the early stages of the stinging *shamal*. There it was, the A-word: addicted.

Vern encountered trouble with the La Forza. We headed across the sand traversing two sets of dunes looking for new, first-time virgin fields. He was not stuck, but there was some malfunction with the starter or engine or pistons. We stopped to wait for him.

Some of the sand was hard pack, partly because it was wet from last night's wind and rain, partly because it was winter and cold. In the summer the sand expands and becomes soft. Part of the driving challenge is the problem of sameness. There is no depth perception on the rolling dunes. There is no contrast of shadow or colour. You can drive along a seemingly level area which suddenly drops off and you find yourself air-borne.

Another challenge is propelling to the top of a dune, 500, 600 feet high, climbing steadily, hoping the back side will be navigable. Sometimes it is possible to get out of the car and have a look over the other side before making the decision to descend or, if not, whether to try another spot to attempt the descent. The going down is always nerve-wracking. I think it's the nose-first perpendicular to the ground angle which produces the adrenalin rush like sitting in the front seat of a rollercoaster.

We needed water. To get to the next site we needed air for the tires and moya for the throats. We drove out of the sand back to the highway with deflated tires to a service station for water. We rolled along going 75 klicks as opposed to 120-130k when the tires were full.

At the petrol station green over-sized 100 gallon garbage bins blighted the place. In Riyadh we used large 20 gallon rubbish bins stashed in the extra bathroom tub to ferment our fine red wine. These barrels at the petrol station stored 100 gallons and bulged, overflowing with garbage. I wondered when or how or if they disposed of the rubbish. Pop cans, plastic containers and cardboard spilled over the top as we added our litter to the repulsive heap.

A Qatari drove into the station from the other direction. He wore a curved *jambiya* knife on a belt slung low across his hips like an exquisite silver accessory over his white *thobe*. He wore a long suit coat, white sandals and white sox; his checkered *gutra* held in place by his tightly coiled black *igal*.

"You must go *Shura*." Was this a place? A council meeting?

"You go left to Doha." That would be Qatar.

"Then go Abu Dhabi." This was a route. It was possible to get back to Dubai through Qatar. But why? I think we missed something in the translation.

"Yes, that would be a good expedition. Maybe next time."

We took his photo. He also proudly carried his gun and spare magazine for his Galactica, he called it. No metal, he declared, only plastic so they can go through the metal detectors; bullets can be made of anything he correctly pointed out. He posed confidently with the automatic, then posed with Ian. Probably wanted someone to mail a print to Qatar. I didn't offer. The man was charismatic and friendly and he carried it all off in English.

The men squatted beside the tires and filled them enabling us drive along the highway. We tested the pressure with our individual hand-held gages. Vern decided to leave the La Forza for service and maintenance. He, Jeannie, the kids and all their gear bunched-up in the other cars and we headed for another site.

With air in our tires we drove along the highway toward Najaran and stopped off-road in the desert for lunch. The weather changed. By eleven in the morning, the clouds lifted. Sweatshirts came off, leg warmers off, mittens stuffed in the backpack, we peeled back layers of shirts and jackets; the inner stratum, the final layer, the lonely T-shirt once again the fashion statement of the morning.

We no longer looked up at the beautiful horizon or across the sandscape. We disembarked from our trucks and walked with heads down, scanning the ground as if looking for a lost contact lens; but the flint was not as difficult to find. Flint lies on the surface and has a glaze; it's easy to spot if one is focused.

Reluctantly we brought out the lunch coolers and spread out camel blankets on the sand. Jen and I plopped down cups and napkins then meandered into the sand scouring the area for treasures. Everyone went a different direction from the trucks. Vern, Jeanne and the kids dispersed from their trucks, Andrew, Ionis and their kids spread out. Ian and Daryle, Jennifer-Janice and I meandered in the warm sand. No one attacked the lunch boxes.

I wandered, kicking the sand, turning over obstructions with the toe of my tenni' in the fine grains. Standing, bent over in my wind-blown T- shirt, I scoured the sand. Then looked again. I hunched over further, stretching out my arm and fingers. Like scooping a beautiful shell from the sandy bottom of the sea, I reached forward with both hands to touch then lift up an incredible piece lying on top of the sand. On my knees, I pushed forward one hand, then the other to clutch something flint-like glimmering on the surface of the sand. As I placed both hands together to frame then touch what I thought I saw,

I brought my fingers together to grasp the most magnificent, spectacular piece of sand-coloured flint. Gently, I reached for the piece, placing my fingers almost tenderly under the sand to excavate what I thought I saw.

As my fingers laced beneath the flint, I brought up a blade; a remarkable blade that measured 9 inches in length. It was not a deception. It was a worked, carved Clovis-like blade. I turned it over and over again and again. When the reality sunk in, I screamed to the universe, and performed my own end-zone dance in the sand, "I won! I won! I won!" and waited for others to gather around to confirm this magnificent Paleolithic carved stone piece.

The hunting stopped as if the jackpot emptied; there was nothing left. The Blade was the centre of all discussion. All hunting stopped. We joined together for lunch. A feeling of exhilaration mixed with some resignation, some feeling of 'it's over' permeated the picnic. Then with renewed vigor, after a cup of soup, some crackers and a chunk of celery we leaped off the blankets and began an energized hunt for yet another blade. If there was one, perhaps there were others. There were not.

Curry

"You take the lead," over the radio.

"No thanks, I'll follow."

"NO! You lead."

"Need to be heading west, probably should traverse two sets of dunes."

"Okay, okay."

Radios in hand, we set off, an enormous area to search: another set of dunes. We climbed to the top using whatever gear worked.

"Whoa. Watch this one." We were air-borne. "Whoa."

"Thanks a lot, Daryle."

"Vern, watch the small dune."

"Where?"

"Where we stopped."

"Where was that?"

"How are we supposed to know?"

"Daryle, you are giving me a great compliment of Bedouin tracking skills."

We negotiated the slope easily onto the black flatbed of the next wadi but lost communication with the third car until they finally called out and asked for a reading.

"46.56.0...North," or something.

"Roger. Stay where you are. We are probably too ridges away."

While waiting, we looked in the sand on top of the dunes and found arrowheads lying on the ridge. In 15 minutes Vern radioed that he was with Andrew. We joined them. This was an outstanding site; lots of tiny arrow heads for small birds and game. Vern tossed back imperfections, carvings with chips or damage. Vern's rejects looked good to me.

Unlike raping the sea for shells, I didn't have a problem taking whatever I found in this desert that once was the sea. My thinking was that these beautiful artifacts could be exploited in a collection. I was not destroying the environment; not taking valuable antiques or personal property like wooden doors or carved windows. And my most convincing self-talk was that the Saudi museums were not interested in preserving the stone tools of early man. The Saudis are interested in the future, in being modern. They express no interest in Stone Age man, lest it draw attention to the fact that they are not progressive; no interest in early man or modern woman.

The wind and sand came up again. In the morning, we picked up the La Forza at the station and drove to the Najaran turnoff. Hissing and fizzing was the sound of air escaping from 16 spitting tires before we headed back into the soft sand. Vern decided the car would be okay so we traveled with *l'macchina* along the highway then across the sand. We drove parallel to each other in order to locate more sites. We found nothing and stopped for the day.

We pulled in behind huge dunes in a small hollow as the wind picked up. The sand blew off the top of the dune. It formed new shapes and carved new sculptures as we watched. In the raging wind we set up the tent and the rain fly, still soaked from the day before.

The sand won the battle and overpowered us. With no choice we ate inside the tent again. After some discussion, we cautiously lit a small burner inside the nylon tent to heat the curry. We needed the hot meal and the curry beckoned.

My oh my. The curry tasted like fire. The spices burned all the way down.

"Wow!" Jen said waving her hand up and down across her mouth to put out the flames.

"What?" from Ian, seeming nonchalant.

"This curry's hot," stating the obvious.

"This is the way we always eat curry. It's supposed to be hot.

"Curry means hot in Urdu."

The curry warmed our souls; the chutney soothed the flames; peanuts and coconut added the texture to this already rich environment. We sat cross-legged on the ground cloth inside the now dry tent. Jeanne came to invite us to the campfire which somehow blazed in the wind. The discussion began with: The Blade.

Author with The Blade

L'Macchina

I slept with the chiseled knife under my backpack pillow. In the morning Daryle lathered-up in the side view mirror of the truck in an attempt to shave with the Blade.

"What are you do-ing?

"Give me that.

"Give back my Blade!"

"Hey. You want me to look like a Bedouin? I'm only thinking of you."

"Use your 21st century plastic Bic blade. Not my prehistoric Paleolithic blade."

I fondled the polished, worked stone as we made our way through the dunes, cross-country to the highway. We traveled several hours on the blacktop until we reached a petrol station at the edge of Najaran.

The place was filthy; the weather harsh, the environment unforgiving. Heaps of aluminum cans and non-degradable pink and blue and yellow paper-thin plastic bags littered everything. Plastic will be our demise. Plastic water bottles flattened by trucks, dead milk containers, Marlboro packs, corrugated cardboard boxes crushed lying where the wind dictated, blue plastic marked bags and the ever-indestructible, non-biodegradable green plastic feed sacks; it amounted to a junk yard dump.

Propped up, a greasy, oily pump rested beneath an aluminum roof. An older Bedouin filled a gas barrel in the back of his army green pickup; his *thobe* belted by a Yemeni sword, his *ghutra* loosely hung, *Igal*-less, his un-manicured toes spread wide in his sandals.

The service station, if lacking in service, did miraculously have cold drinks. No *naan* bread, but cans of sugary pop. We took it; even the non-alcoholic Moussy beer was welcome. The beer was cold, the weather unseasonably hot. True we were south, but it was December. We were not prepared for the heat. *Ma fii moya;* no water. We needed water.

The men worked on Vernon's car. Something was very wrong with the La Forza. Something was always wrong with the La Forza.

Another bearded, brown-*thobed* Bedouin strolled over to inquire where we were from and if we saw rain. Rain, Vernon tells him, in Wadi ad Dawasir. They had rain here two weeks ago. It was an important question on the edge of the Empty Quarter. The Bedouin offered to take us into Yemen.

"You go Yemen. Good place. You like Yemen."

"Yes?"

"*Aiwa*. Fifteen minutes." Did he say 50 or 15? It sounded the same to the untrained. I didn't question.

"You get paper here." He means official stamp or government permission to enter.

"Well, that sounds interesting."

"I guide you across sand." This is tempting. Then I remember all the kidnappings for ransom in Yemen. I further remember the US doesn't pay ransom. Still, sometime I want to visit Yemen.

I looked at Vern. He stood on a small mound of greasy oil cans smashed and flattened, aiming a hand-held, remote control device at the La Forza like a kid with a remote control toy in a parking lot. The doors locked and unlocked and the burglar alarm wailed on and off.

The Sudanese attendants leaned on the side of the car, not having the slightest idea what to do or how to help. They postulated some theory. They wondered about this, they questioned that. Perhaps when the car bolted to a stop in the dune, the sand caught on the low pan under the car frame, it shut off, causing the smoke to billow out in black oil. The question now was how to get the system turned off and the oil and gas flowing back into the engine, or something.

The button for such was located in the door panel and was controlled by the automatic remote control. After numerous tries under the hood, and into the door panel, they gave up, unpacked *l' macchina* and merged their family and gear with the other cars. Ian and Jen jumped in our truck with several bags of equipment and dusty tents for the drive back to Riyadh. Not a particularly glamourous ending to a spectacular week in the Empty Quarter.

Matching driving skills with GPS, matching gathering/hunting skills with bumbling along, matching frozen pre-cooked meals with wing-it snacks, it was a marvelous week. We saved the best for last. Of all our camping trips, this was by far the most challenging, most beautiful, most profound of all. We knew, though we did not voice it, we would miss Saudi Arabia.

The End

I t was a difficult weekend, the run-up to several culminating weekends; eleven years in Saudi Arabia coming to a close. We celebrated Day with the Arts at school all day Thursday. Daryle traveled to Oman and Jessica and friends from Aramco, Arab American Oil Company, came to do Riyadh. The guest villa was not available so everyone stayed with us. Jessica's husband could not get time off work to come which proved to be most unfortunate.

The three arrived Wednesday evening. Joe and Marlene, an articulate energetic couple from Hawaii and Vietnam, had not been off the Aramco compound much except for occasional trips into Dhahran. Marlene and Jessica worked together; Joe was an engineer for the oil company.

"Marlene, just take these skirts. You have to wear long skirts in Riyadh," Jessica offered.

"Come on, no way."

"Really. It's not like Dhahran, and it's nothing like your Aramco compound."

At dinner we talked about the culture of Saudi. They had just read *Princess, An appalling indictment of the treatment of women in Saudi Arabia,* by Jean P. Sasson. The book was banned, but there were a few dog-eared copies making the underground circuit. The paperback was the allegedly true story of a princess, a member of the Saudi Royal Family, told anonymously through journals, diaries and notes given to Sasson.

We discussed different elements of the narrative. Joe and Marlene didn't believe it; they arrived in Saudi 9 months earlier and were not exposed to much outside the Aramco compound. The manuscript seemed to sensationalize Saudi culture. We believed it; over the years we heard the stories. My own thinking was that Sasson compiled several stories of stonings, beheadings, arranged marriages and slavery to portray one princess. In Riyadh, whenever there was a stoning or beheading, the news circulated faster than a desert *shamal.* The anecdotes were not made up.

Jessica was up at six, her dad already gone. Joe and Marlene ate a leisurely breakfast and the three of them followed the *suq* bus then planned to go off to find the furniture store. They intended to come back at noon prayers when everything shut down, have lunch then maybe attend Day with the Arts.

I saw them briefly about 3:00 in the afternoon. They stopped by school, walked through a few displays and decided to do something and perhaps come back for the finale at 4:30pm. There was no sign of them. I went back to the house at 6:pm. They were not there. Their note on stairs read, 'We are off to the *suqs*, we'll be back after sunset prayers.'

At 7:30 they were not back. By 8:15 they were not back. It was important that I stop by Ted and Barb Barlag's to congratulate them on organizing a brilliant Day with the Arts. The staff would be there as well as the art department staff from Dhahran and Jeddah. Daryle was in Oman on NESA business. Where was Jessica? Again, I left a note, and walked to Barlag's, at least for an abbreviated visit. We were on the same compound and as I walked across the parking area I met Jessica, Joe and Marlene.

"Where have you guys been? I was worried," I hoped I didn't sound angry.

"We had some trouble," Jessica bit her lip as we walked back to the house.

"What happened?"

"We were arrested by a *mutawwa* at the *suq*." Joe and Marlene didn't say anything.

We went into the house to get the details. Visibly upset Jessica cried and tried to explain what happened through intermittent sobs and gulps for air. I poured them each a glass of bad red wine to help calm them and help them relax from their ordeal.

Before sunset they purchased a few pieces of antique jewelry. As they went to the dusty parking lot a *mutawwa* confronted them at their car.

"Mister. You, *wa* you," he said pointing his stick at Jessica and Marlene.

"Must wear *abaya*.

"You must come to police station." This notion was ludicrous. I never wore an *abaya*. For eleven years I dressed conservatively with long skirts and long sleeve shirts and no *abaya*.

The *mutawwa* rounded up a policeman who accompanied them to the Batha station. Jessica and Marlene waited in the car while Joe nervously walked inside. The stories about Riyadh now resonated. This was turning into a nightmare. Joe admitted his fear; it felt like a bad dream of a Turkish prison.

Inside, he produced their papers. Jessica carried a photocopy of her husband's *iqama*, work permit identification and a separate letter stating that she had his permission to travel to Riyadh with another family in order to visit her parents. She begged Joe not to show the letter unless necessary; she didn't want to lose it.

In the small room there was a lot of discussion in Arabic. They took all his papers and Jessica's and went into another room. Then it was prayer time. Joe waited. An hour later, he was told that the women must write an apology for not wearing an *abaya* and for not covering their heads. The police dictated what the letter must say.

"I _____ visiting Riyadh from Dhahran, wish to apologize for my wife not wearing an *abaya*. I was told that she did not have to wear one by my company Aramco. I promise that in future she will wear an *abaya* and cover her head. Her ankle was showing."

They told Joe that Jessica must write a confession and an apology and promise that she would always wear an *abaya* and cover her head. He said he did not know if she would agree to such a statement. I can't imagine Joe would argue, even question at that point but he did.

Jessica did write the statement tongue in cheek. I wish i could remember how it went. She said that she had not intended to *offend* (they wanted to know what that meant), and that she would wear an *abaya* as they liked and that a little ankle was *apparently* (what was this word) showing. And further, that the Muslims were *ostensibly* (they wanted to know what that meant) good people and always led by example. I wonder how Joe explained this sarcastic apology.

It was such a negative experience for her. She has always loved it in Saudi. She treasured roaming the old *suqs*. To be harassed in a place that she respected so much, disappointed her and hurt her deeply. She felt she ruined Riyadh for her friends, I'm not sure how. It was frustrating to be so extremely sensitive to Saudi taste and culture, wearing a long sleeve blouse buttoned to the neck and long skirt, even providing one for Marlene, and still be spit upon.

It was enough to turn one around. It was hard for me not to be very bitter; not to want to scream Three-More-Weeks! Ninety-one more prayer calls! Get me out of here: to start the count-down to be caught-up in the pessimistic short-termer's attitude. I wanted to remember all the positive years, to not allow the negatives to creep into the last impressions; to not allow the conservatives, the jerks, the misfits to spoil my positive experiences of the past eleven years. That was difficult.

It was not easy knowing Jessica and Jen would still live in Saudi with all its eccentric idiosyncrasies and have to live with the issues, carefully tip-toeing through the quagmire of unusual regulations and customs and I would not be there to walk them through it, to talk them to the positive side of the negative situations.

Had it really come down to this? It occurred to me that we were getting out just in time, something like our timing in Manila leaving just before the coup which finally toppled Ferdinand Marcos by the People Power revolution led by Cory Aquino after her husband's assassination. But if this was so, it disturbed me that my family was not getting out. Ian could get a job in another international school now that he had a start in international education. I wondered if Jessica's husband might have difficulty lining up something international, outside of Saudi Arabia, which turned out to be a non-issue. But I wondered.

Joe and Marlene did not want to go to Barlag's to socialize with anyone. They ate food from the refrigerator then went out for Japanese food at Jade Garden. They encouraged Jessica to come with me for a while. I thought it might be good. At least she could sip someone else's bad wine. She was a mess, but the change of environment did help her mentally regroup. We did not mention the experience, her trauma with the *mutawwa* and police. Everyone was busy patting themselves on the back. They didn't focus on us, which was as it should be.

Duane Root went on about a retirement community for international teachers. I could think of nothing worse. Now, I can see some merits in the idea. There was a fifth grade staff party at Le Blank's and a sixth grade party at Di Silvestro's. The joint was jumpin': the benefits of compound living. We listened to Ted Barlag's story about the Masai woman who spit in his mouth, a gross excuse for why he was so sick while climbing Mt. Kilimanjaro.

Jessica, Joe and Marlene left for Dhahran the following day. I wonder how they relayed their story of life in Riyadh. Jessica knew not to sensationalize, but I had no idea how the Aramcons would relate their story. I never heard back from them.

May 1993

Hi Ted,

What a show! What a day! For all of the work, the late hours, the sorting, mounting, framing and planning.... thank you. Your Day with the Arts is my day of catharsis; my Day of Healing, of Renewal, of Regeneration. I feel as if I have spent a day in the Metropolitan Museum, the Cairo Museum, the Dali Museum in Spain. Invigorated, I think I shall get through the year. Thank You!!

Not to be slighted, the music department, drama and French clubs were an integral part of the Day. Elizabeth's chamber groups were stirring and emotionally moving. Can these be children? With string-ed instruments? Everyone's contributions were wonderful in Elementary and Junior High. Our students are brilliant and talented and it takes gifted and intuitive adults to bring forth their aptitude. Your philosophy that everyone can draw, everyone's an artist (thought some of us work harder at it) permeates the curriculum with astonishing results.

Thank You for making it happen! I am going to miss you both. I have said it before. I guess I'm trying to cope.

Dannie

Thank You Remarks

When Gail called in March she said, "Dannie we want to get together for dinner." Good idea, I thought. We have been trying for two years to have dinner together.

I finally met Gail through a mutual friend who kept saying, "You must know Gail Farha, she is so talented. She's an artist. You must know her...." When we finally met, we worked together on several projects in a row including a Bazaar, an international dinner, an Embassy affair or two, and we kept meeting from one Gala to the next. Gail moved her son from the British School to the Big School and we saw each other rather frequently in the hallways.

As our schedules became more diverse, my children graduated from college, got married and got jobs in Saudi, Gail & Adib made another beautiful baby, and the men continued to meet in meetings all over town.

Literally, two years ago we agreed to get together for dinner. It was postponed, then canceled, the rescheduled all year. Adib was traveling, then it was Christmas, then February recruiting, then Spring break, then Adib was traveling, then summer. The next year it was the same story.

When Gail called in March, I think I said something like, "Great. Shall I put it in pencil or pen?" She said, "We want to have a farewell dinner for you and Daryle." Farewell? In March? She said, "April 01." Farewell was the last thing in my head. Yet here we all are.

All of you are special to us. You are our colleagues and friends. The Farha's are like long-distance relatives. We love to see them, but although we are in the same city, our times together are calculated and rare and very special.

We are not here to say good-bye or farewell. Perhaps, we are trying to bring some closure to our Riyadh phase. It used to be that no one came back to Saudi, but I have taken heart in a postcard I purchased at my favorite shop: Hallmark-In-The-Malls. Don't you love Hallmark? They always know exactly what I'm thinking; what I want to say. Hallmark knows what I want to say before I do. I always want two of everything. Jessica says she and I are the only people who need a shopping cart in a Hallmark store. The postcard says:

AVENGE YOURSELF
Live Long Enough To Be A Problem To Your Children.

That's my new thinking. What I have in mind is becoming their dependents so that we can come back to Saudi.

This country has been good to us. We have lived the cities and the *suqs* and loved the deserts. And you, those of you in this room this evening, have made Riyadh the positive,

wonderful experience that it has been these past eleven years. We don't say Farewell. We say Thank You. We'll see you on the next go-round: Brignoli's in Cairo, Petri's in Florida, Khattak's in Pakistan, Hansen's in Manila, Chlouk, Rashid and Shammas in Lebanon, Moreau's and Anthony's in Canada, Rashid's in Paris-Mallorca-Beverly Hills-Lebanon- Memphis and the rest of you in the US and Riyadh.

Ma,as salama and Thank You.

June 12, 1993

H.R.H. Fahad bin Khaled
H.R.H. Maha bint Fahad

Your Royal Highnesses;

We want to thank you for having us into your home for dinner last week. We enjoyed talking about your esteemed father and of your dreams for your children and for yourselves.

Thank you for listening to our dreams. We both hope now to give back something of all that we have taken in the past years, at least in some small capacity.

We wish you success with your children. They are fortunate to have parents who care so deeply about their education, progress and development. Whatever decisions you reach regarding their future, I know it will not be without considerable thought and planning. We look forward to hearing, one day through the world press, of their accomplishments.

We leave Saudi Arabia fulfilled, enriched, and deeply committed to Arab causes. We shall forever treasure the dunes of sand, the peaceful, elegant architecture which can only be termed 'Islamic,' the cacophony of the morning prayer calls, and our many friends from casual Bedouin acquaintances who shared their qahwah, to the business community and university professors who shared their lives and stories, to members of the Royal Family who have shared their home. We will miss Saudi Arabia. We are forever changed.

Sincerely,

Dr. and Mrs. Daryle Russell

Barrels For Bosnia

!! How You Can Help !!

National Junior Honour Society is sponsoring a Humanitarian Drive for the children and refugees in Bosnia.

You can assist in the following way:

- Cash Donations
- Soap, Detergent
- Tooth brushes
- Clothing for All Ages
- Blankets & Sheets
- Diapers, Shampoo
- tooth-paste
- Shoes

- Cash will be used to purchase:

mattresses	stoves
tables	dishes
fuel	food

National Junior Honour Society will pack the items and arrange the shipment through the donation of SWISS AIR and other sources.

Please Be Generous. Bring all items to the Barrels on the JH patio or to the Placement Centre. (No JUNK)

April 12 first shipment— Thank you

Thank you for helping with—

Burgers for Bosnia
Lunch Fund Raiser!!

Your assignment is to report to the lunch area at 11:10am, SUNDAY, APRIL 04. Please be prepared to assist with set-up and clean-up.

There will be several people helping, so we will rotate the jobs and everyone will work about 25 minute shifts!

If you can not come at 11:10 am, please come at 11:25 am, as soon as the bell rings.

Thank you again for helping. This is a very worthwhile cause, and an excellent service project.

Sincerely, Ms. Russell

Remarks

All staff

Intercontinental Hotel • May 17, 1993

The years we have spent in Saudi Arabia have been memorable and very important to us. The gift you have given to us has been one of support, kindness, professionalism and most especially, friendship.

SAISR is a truly remarkable corporation.

Where else can you attend a Gala affair once a month in a Kindergarten class?

Where else will you find volunteer attendance at faculty meetings?

Where else can you celebrate department and grade level meetings with catered lunches?

Where else in the world can you invite a Prince-Astronaut to present an assembly and visit the classrooms?

Where else in the world are the women free from parking lot duty?

Where else in the world will you get your building principal to cook breakfast for you once a year?

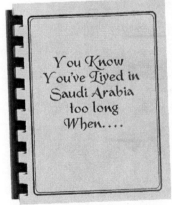

You Know You've Lived in Saudi Arabia too long When....

Where else in the world does everyone teach with their minds and doors open?

Our time here has been remarkable. You have enriched our lives and we will take with us all of your lessons. And now we know it's time to leave.......

You know you've been in Saudi Arabia too long when....

You think black is appropriate daytime attire.

You know you've been in Saudi Arabia too long when....

You enjoy camping in sand.

You know you've been in Saudi Arabia too long when....

You think an evening out is attending the Junior High Strings concert.

You know you've been in Saudi Arabia too long when....

You resign your position a year in advance (and they hire a replacement)

Thank you to all. We wish you a Bon Voyage and *Ma' as-salaama*.

Memories

Things to Remember
a rose sky that accompanies the shamal
the stillness which precedes the thick, fine sand
sculpted dunes that rise and fall in the shadows formed at sunset
quiet fires on cool clear winter evenings
the serenity of the sand
the clarity of the sky, the brilliance of desert stars
the peaceful architecture of arches and marble.

The Ambassador of the United States of America
and Mrs. Chas. W. Freeman, Jr.

cordially invite you at a reception

In honor of the Commander in Chief
General H. Norman Schwarzkopf
and the Officers of The United States Central Command

on Wednesday, the twentieth of March
from eight-thirty to ten-thirty o'clock

R.S.V.P.
488-3800 Ext 323/318

Quincy House
(Informal / Duty Uniform)

Pakistan

Unretired

Teresa

Our retirement from Saudi was intended to be a switch of professions, not a move to rocking chairs; perhaps taking our background to international business or international service. Interviews with American Peace Corps proved futile. We left Florida while our home was being completed and headed to New Zealand for three months of camping and fishing. People asked, "How could you leave the construction of your home?" It was easy.

Building a home was never a retirement dream. I endured pedantic conversations with interior decorators and builders. I never felt we worked together.

"What colour would you like the walls, Ms Russell?" Teresa twisted her hair around her finger.

"White, I have to have white."

"What shade of white would you like?" She opened a paint chart.

"What?"

"Ivory, chalk, snow, vanilla, bone?"

"White. Just white." What kind of question was that?

"What about your bathroom fixtures. What would you like?" Teresa pressed on.

"Separate faucets or a single spout?"

"What?" This was nonsense to me.

"Is there hot and cold water piped into the house?" As I said this, I realized I sounded like the third world Bedouin that I was.

"Excuse me?" Now it was her turn to be astounded.

The conversation went on to tiles and flooring. I wanted black slate in the entry way.

"We don't do black in Florida." She asked about furnishings.

"My centerpiece table is dark rattan," I said thinking of my Philippine dining table.

"Oh, it has to be white. We do natural rattan or white bamboo.

"Black or dark won't work here."

"And why would that be?" I sat up straight; my blood pressure began to rise.

"Interior design does not accept dark colours in Florida."

I fired Teresa. Her public school hair style, shoulder length with wings, showcased her public school education, her public school mentality. We flew to New Zealand for three months. The mundane questions, middle class, compromised, stylized, flippant answers to interior design pushed me out the door to the international dimension of our life.

Fishing is great therapy. Fresh air gave us perspective and space to think through the frustrations and self doubt we encountered while staying in Florida.

The transition to America wasn't easy. We weren't prepared. I suspect it's more poignant for men: pride, ego, big issues. We talked for hours around evening fires in New Zealand hashing out the concept that we would have no work, no employment. We needed health insurance. We would not qualify for social security or Medicare for five more years.

We needed transportation, not a designer car, but something reliable. The house was paid for; the kids were salaried; our parents were secure; we had no bills. What lingered was the reality that we had no contacts. Daryle quickly interpreted this as nobody wants us. He started thinking, I'm useless. I'm perceived as over the hill.

Most of all, it was the blow that we did not come up with anything. Service organizations and volunteer organizations were not hiring or Daryle was so-called overqualified. While I could volunteer

Daryle with Jane Goodall

comfortably with Habitat for Humanity or any organization, he needed to make a leadership contribution. However, he didn't have the political contacts to move into a Peace Corps assignment as country director. All jobs are political, as we eventually learned. We were slow learners; naive in the job market arena. After two days of mindless interviews up and down the floors of the government offices of Peace Corps, he was herded along a horizontal hallway to nowhere. Their loss; we would have been good.

We talked with Jane Goodall several times about joining her organization working in international schools promoting Roots & Shoots. She was interested in the concept, but more interested in our financial contribution to the organization than our need for a wee salary. We were not in a position to fund her.

In New Zealand Daryle fished with intensity, with focused tunnel vision, a scotoma toward everything else. He never sat back in a chair balancing a pole against a paperback book. He read the water; studied the flies and hatch. He worked up the stream, then back down stopping occasionally to stuff his pipe.

In the evening we talked endlessly and regrouped. We bought a local smoker and prepared fresh smoked trout every few days. Graham Bassett, Daryle's New Zealand colleague in graduate school, recommended the smoker which was sold everywhere; we bought ours in a petrol station.

When Daryle fished he released most of the fish back to the cold,

Benazir Bhutto, Unidentified , Dannie, Daryle

clear waters but kept one or two for dinner and a couple to smoke which we enjoyed for breakfast and with sundowners. The instructions for smoking seafood were simple and fool-proof. We bought wood chips, also available at the petrol station, rubbed the fish in salt then brown sugar and covered it until the mixture liquefied. We drained the liquid then smoked the fish, scale side down, over the chips for 15-20 minutes. The blend of smoky flavour, the scent of the wood chips with the fresh trout made for a melt-in-your-mouth succulent sensation.

Away from the banal discussions about details of the house, we centred thoughts on our preferred future. It was easy to converse in the ambience of evening fires at the edge of the stream. Around twilight embers, we focused with no interruptions; no distractions, while we picked at smoked trout and neat scotch.

Our interest in taking on a new responsibility with business or charity gently faded as we realized our contacts, our links, our own brand of political networking, were all with international education. Thanks to unswerving support and the confidence of friend and colleague John Magagna, we unretired and moved to Pakistan for three years.

Cold as it Gets
Markets

Pakistan promised to be an effortless cultural adjustment. I knew something of Islam from our eleven years in Saudi Arabia. Now we would be in Islam-abad, home of Islam. In contrast to the feeling of Saudi severity, guttural harshness and total control, Islamabad felt soft. Muted colours of the feminine *shalwar kameez,* the sultry drape of a *dupatta,* head scarf, the lilt of Urdu, felt gentle in comparison. The sheer translucence of the *dupatta* adjusting in the breeze signaled a shift in cultures.

Everything about the adjustment was seamless except the weather. At the base of the Himalayas I felt the cold move in like an uninvited guest. Standing barefoot on the terrazzo floors of the big house it felt like standing on a Nordic glacier. A board member, obsessed with overspending the school budget enacted a *fatwa* on all staff and faculty. No one was permitted to use their heating systems or, god forbid, their air conditioners in summer. Daryle slept with a ski cap and although the house sported four fireplaces, none of them drew the smoke. We tried various methods, but never avoided a house full of black smoke billowing from the fire places.

Rose Puffer, colleague from Saudi, then a middle school teacher in Islamabad, suggested I pick up some thermal underwear.

"Dannie, I don't know how it works, but I promise, by October 15th it will be as cold as it is going to get." Rose made the transition from Riyadh a few years before.

"Thermals are a great idea. Where can I find some?"

"The covered market behind your house has them. Only for men, do you care?"

The covered market behind the house was grim. Women took me there on a quick city tour when we flew in for interviews the previous year. They liked the place; it represented a functional market where you could find a lot if you knew where to look. It may have been the ugliest, darkest, most depressing market I have seen. Because it was covered, it was dingy. I didn't see them, but I knew there were rats. The meat bits hung like slabs in the Ethiopian markets, but this place seemed dirty. Vendors also sold T-shirts, black socks and towels. In this dark conundrum there was a photo booth for black and white ID pictures. It worked when there was power.

A butcher sat on the ledge, an open counter, of his shop. Between his toes he manipulated a long, wide bolo knife. While holding a slab of meat with his hands, he managed to whack the carcass with the cleaver held between his big toe, while the other toes seemed to grip the handle. He amputated away parts of cows and goats, all while sitting cross-legged on the ledge. I had seen many open markets, many covered markets but this was my first time to see a guy with his feet and hands on the meat while he dissected the parts with a huge knife between his toes.

"I know how cold you are, but I promise, this is as cold as it gets." It was October 15th and Rose was right. I wore the thermal leggings and top, under long skirts and sweaters. "Dannie, there's no such thing as bad weather; there're only bad clothes." She was right again.

As a kid growing up in California, every few years somebody thought it was a great idea to drive to the mountains and play in the snow. I never had the right clothes. Who has snow boots in LA or in the Valley? My sneakers were wet in five minutes and I was miserable the rest of the day. I never thought it was fun.

Islamabad was all about Friday Market. By contrast to the dark, dingy functional market, every week, like an overnight miracle, an open field blossomed into a bustling bazaar. Oversized carpets of burgundy, crimson and deep blue, woven in silks and wools, swayed from make-shift clotheslines strung between trees.

Set up on collapsible card tables or perched on inverted boxes colourful fruits arranged in immaculate, topple-free pyramids never once tumbled. Asparagus and cucumbers lined up in orderly rows like soldiers in precision. Afghani caps, red and tightly woven with hints of interspersed golden thread projected ethnic art and beauty stacked in careful rows lining improvised walkways. The Friday Market was Art in Life; the Friday Market was functional art.

Most of the items that drew me in each Friday, I later realized were not Pakistani. The carpets, glass, porcelain, jewelry and colourful dresses came from Afghanistan, China and the northern 'stans brought in by emigrants and immigrants merging into Islamabad.

Pop the Locks

Tariq's wife annoyed me; it wasn't her fault, but the fact that she came with us. During winter break we hired the school van to take an overnight trip to Peshawar, in the North West Frontier Province and then visited Darra. Jen and Ian flew in from Saudi for the holiday. Tariq drove, and without warning, brought along his wife. The couple decided to make a shopping trip of it in the smuggler's market near the Khyber Pass. Since he was the driver and we hired the van, he decided there was enough space for his wife. Oh great.

Tariq navigated the treacherous blacktop road to Peshawar. Two lanes became three, the centre lane for head-on passing. The closer we got to Peshawar and the Afghan border the more frequent the *burkas*. In this region of Pakistan, many families came across the border. The frontier was, as they liked to say, porous with people gliding back and forth seamlessly between Pakistan and Afghanistan.

The blue full-body covering for women replaced the black *abayas* in Saudi Arabia. As we drove through the village on the outskirts of Peshawar, all the women wore *burkas*, some with head pieces stitched in place, others wearing a simple head cover. The wraps, bordered with lace akin to tablecloth trim, caught the wind. As a slight breeze billowed-up a puff of fabric, the women floated along like bulbous, blue parachutes hovering along the irregular road.

In Saudi, I marveled when I watched a child at the airport gravitate right to their mum when all the black *abayas* looked the same to me. Somehow, children knew which black bundle was their own mum. Even without a word or call to the child, boys and girls identified their mothers.

Although covered from head to toe, one does learn to discriminate, ascertain beauty, desirability. Over the years I observed the flirting and non-dating that went on in the Saudi malls. Passing discreet notes with names and phone numbers was part of the socializing. Whether the sandal flip-flopped too casually, if the skin of the heels was cracked, if the feet were flat and pudgy, if the toes were enclosed in a shoe with a heel exposing just a thin, graceful ankle, one learns to socially discriminate.

The outer edges of Peshawar were ugly, crowded and dirty. The rain left it muddy, adding to the grimy look. Along the road I read, "Knowledge is Power." I liked it. Closer to the city, "Enter to Learn." Then a sign stated, "Asylum = Protection." I wondered what that was about. Next I read, "Revenge," and further on, "Hospitality." We were in Pashtun country. These were reminders of *Pashtunwali*, the Pashtun tribal code of honour which I learned more about later.

Along the road a procession of women carried large aluminium pots balanced gracefully on their heads,
   full to the brim,
      spilling not a drop,
         making their way from the stream bed
            to their village across the road.
               I marveled at their grace in flowing blue *burkas*.

"Have you ever tried to walk with anything on your head?" I asked Jen as we drove by.

"Not really," she stared out the window.

"In middle school we had a unit on posture; in our PE class," I thought back to my life in the Val'.

"We practiced walking around the perimeter of the gym with our social studies books on our heads.

"When we managed that, we put our math books on top of the social studies books.

"I was pretty good when I practiced.

"My mom told me that all beautiful models walked very straight, and of course I wanted to look like a model." It was all about posture. For these women it was about survival.

Further on, graveyards like Saudi desert graves suggested simple dignity: one tall, uncarved stone plunged into the earth at the head of each grave. With no markings or words the mounds clustered together by villages, where others lived on.

In the centre of Peshawar we found a cheap hotel. It was not a city where we planned to lounge around the hotel bar, so we opted for minimalist rooms. Tariq's wife was not happy. The shared bathroom was down the hall. We left our backpacks but retained our valuables and headed out for lunch.

We sat at uneven tables at the Kabul Restaurant on University Road in Peshawar. Afghani food consisted of various kebobs roasted over hot coals outside the local restaurant. Who could resist the exotic pungent spices of grilled meat on a stick? Even the reputation of the Iowa state fair where all the food is on a stick, including deep-fried Twinkies and whole barbecued turkey drumsticks never competed with Afghani kebobs. The chunks of lamb still skewered to thin wooden spears, balanced crisscrossed on individual plates of *naan* flat bread.

"Man, I love this stuff." Ian loved most foods. Exposed to many types of food growing up, he was as a child, cautious with the unfamiliar, like most kids. By the time he was out of college he loved everything, especially smothered in Tabasco.

"You gotta love it," he repeated.

All at once the tables began sliding back and forth across the linoleum floor. Warm tea sloshed around in the cups. It was a good jolt. I looked around. My California training came into play as I looked for the nearest doorframe. I was ready to duck under the table. I looked to see what others were doing. Conversation at the other tables never stopped. In the Hindu Kush, the mountains grew every day. No one noticed. We continued our meal.

Police officers fierce, yelling in English, barged into the restaurant.

"Who you think you are? Where you think you are?" Even his eyes growled.

"This not America; not England." The second officer's belly lopped over his belt in the front and on the sides like handles on a sugar bowl.

"Why you leave car? Why you aren't sitting in car watching?"

No mistake, the remarks were directed at us. The police scared me much more than the earthquake. Tariq pushed back his chair and walked outside.

"Three cars stolen in two days. Yesterday in this area," the officer barked.

"Just pop the locks and drive away," he yelled.

Now everyone in the room looked at us. The van displayed US embassy plates, too high profile. Of course the police came in. Of course we were vulnerable; stupid and naive. After some discussion, Tariq paid money and a boy watched the van, while we finished our rice and post-lunch tea. Did he really say "pop the locks?"

Darra

Everyone writes about Darra: the illicit ammunition bazaar outside of Peshawar. Darra is reportedly dangerous, restricted and illegal. Foreign reporters are still banned from the area. We went to check it out. We drove to a small office shack, while Tariq took care of some business. He came back to the van with two skinny men armed with big guns. Each wore a bandolier of bullets slung over his shoulder like a Boy Scout sash of badges. This private militia of two was mandated to protect us in the bazaar.

We squeezed together in the already full van, to make space for the extra men, the security men. Mentally annoyed, I took it out on Tariq's wife with icy body language as I over exaggerated my move across the seat; anything at all, what-ever (!), to make room for the Kalashnikovs and their curriers.

It wasn't her fault, Tariq's wife, but we were crowded and I didn't see the point. Tariq explained that the security men were an obligatory requirement of the authorities to accompany all foreigners into Darra. So. Darra Adam Khel was still the cowboy capitol of the west; the wild west of Pakistan.

Ammunition shops lined both sides of the alleys which ran parallel to the narrow main dirt road. Every doorway represented a small specialized factory. Some produced bullets, others AK-47s. Children, only boys, ran in and out between goats and donkeys; the lads were also part of the industry. They sat cross-legged next to older brothers and cousins polishing copper bullet casings.

Men crouched in doorways eager to show visitors their specialty. Across the cobblestone road workers sat on the dirt floor assembling Kalashnikovs with as much nonchalance as employees assembling a Big Mac. Each home was a mini factory. In another house, men drilled barrel shafts. They drilled copper tubing then sliced it to fill with powder. Some made gun barrels, others copied all the Kalashnikovs.

Shop workers leaped up to fire a round or two in the air to check out the finished product nearly scaring the beejeebers out of us; caught us off guard every time. Although it was not the dunes of Saudi, it was pretty exciting.

There were no women on the street, no girls. They were not part of the craft. They were, no doubt, inside preparing meals, cleaning rooms, washing clothes: women's work. Every door on the alley opened to a workshop and sales room.

Tariq pointed out the different weapons. I knew the difference between a rifle and a pistol. The rifle was the long one. The names and styles were lost on me although I did appreciate the enormous variety on display. The range went from long thin rifles, the old ones requiring a musket, to stubby automatic weapons, to a clever single shot fountain-pen gun; something one might see in a double agent spy movie. One shop made Italian guns the next, German guns. If you wanted a Smith Wesson they could copy it.

Kalashnikov knock-offs. These were the Ouchi, Gucci, Cuchi knock-offs of the gun world. It was like walking through an outlet mall but the fakes were bullets and guns; like walking through the night market in Bangkok but instead of faux Rolex watches, men ordered faux AK-47s; genuine, copied, Russian weapons; get yours now.

One year I went to an American gun show held in a convention centre where vendors stood behind tables and talked about their guns. There seemed to be a gun culture, a like-mindedness of those attending, walking around the various tables of guns on display.

Everyone at the gun show expressed enthusiasm for weapons, whether they wanted a gun for protection, their right to bear arms, or they were sport enthusiasts, their right to hunt for food or their right to hunt for sport pleasure.

Those concerned about the events claimed that American gun shows were a primary source of illegally trafficked firearms, both within the United States and abroad. Those supporting gun shows pointed out American freedoms and rights. Darra was nothing like that.

Although it was tempting to grab a pen gun to display in one's shirt pocket, a macho thing, the illegal market was aimed at militant groups, drug gangs, criminals, and now, most probably, Taliban; and of course anyone wanting protection from those groups.

Darra is located in the tribal area bordering Afghanistan. Neither the Afghan nor the Pakistan governments have any authority in the tribal region as the area is governed by the clan. Pashtun hospitality reigns and shoppers or visitors are offered tea as if haggling over a silk carpet rather than a crate of guns.

"Try this one, Lady." Jen lifted the huge gun to her shoulder. Simultaneously, a man from the shop walked up to the front door and fired a round of ammunition out into the street. We jumped nearly to the Khyber Gate.

"Was he aiming at anything or anyone?"

"He's just testing the bullets."

"Here? In the middle of the street?"

We wandered from shop to shop, sometimes going underground to additional workshops illuminated by a single bulb on a chord. The only other business in Darra seemed to be a tea shop, a small restaurant and a fruit vendor who pushed a wooden cart.

Tariq nudged me with his elbow, his hands in his leather jacket pocket. I looked up at him. He leaned toward me and whispered, "We have to leave now." I was just getting into it, feeling more comfortable with all the guns and shooting into the air.

"Why?"

"It's getting late. We have to leave before dark."

"Really?"

"Let's go, they are rushing us to get out now."

"Is there trouble?" He locked elbows with me and I tried to keep up with his long stride. I looked back and Daryle, Jen and Ian were following close behind.

"There's not really any trouble, but we don't want any."

Maybe it was like the American gun show as some argued; a primary source of illegally trafficked firearms.

Author and Jen Russell

Tariq's Wife

Finally, Tariq took us to Loktil Landi Kotal, the smugglers market at the top of the pass, the reason he brought his wife. It's a bizarre bazaar. Goods for Afghanistan, as I understood it, were imported from China, Japan, Russia and the US through Pakistan, then smuggled through the pass, which the Pashtun control; this to avoid paying duty.

The fascinating mixture of tribal people of the Khyber Pass, Afghanis who cross into Peshawar and Chinese who intermingle, produces a rich fusion for the local markets of smuggled electronic items as well as tribal carpets, fabric, jewelry, lapis and artifacts.

We sloshed our way to the smuggled appliances. While I tiptoed around squishy puddles trying to keep my shoes dry, barefoot kids and men, oblivious to the muck, beckoned us to their shops.

Tariq quickly separated himself from us as he and his wife began haggling for a blender and a mixer. When we saw them again they were comparing toasters. Jen and I looked around the rather tired and dirty shops and tried to find something of interest. Daryle and Ian did the same. Jen found a bottle of US shampoo probably lifted from the embassy commissary.

The rain started to drizzle again. We were ready to go back to the van in fifteen minutes. Tariq's wife was just getting started. Not even the piles of folded clothes attracted us. Tariq and his wife made their way from shop to shop, negotiating best prices. Jen and I walked past a shop and in the back we saw the happy couple going for a microwave and a big-screen television.

Laughing, Tariq juggled boxes of goods back to the van. Jen and Ian wanted Pakistani or Afghani carpets; Tariq wanted American appliances. Jen and I looked for ethnic pieces; Tariq looked for smuggled GE products and Sony electronics. Even Tariq's wife found the humour as we all laughed out loud at our acquisitions.

In fact, the black market items put us in jeopardy. Illegal goods are illegal. Police at road blocks searched vehicles. They had no authority at the bazaar, but on the road, they exercised authority. The goods could be confiscated. The van could be confiscated, and theoretically, we could all be arrested; better to be deported than banished to a Pakistani prison. The school name would be flashed across the publicity arena. The van flaunted embassy plates which

Tariq wrongly assumed made us, him, immune from prosecution or arrest. Our own car in Islamabad used local plates but we were too many to fit in the Corolla.

We all crashed in the roach motel with the bathroom down the hall. I only saw one cockroach, something remarkable in Pakistan. Not sure how Tariq's wife slept. She had her treasures; she was in heaven and the return trip to Islamabad turned out to be uneventful.

Shopping with Carolyn

On a small space on the small table in the small parking area, a merchant carefully laid-out pieces of tribal jewelry; pieces of silver, lapis, amber and turquoise, tempting us to add to our already avaricious stockpile of ethnic jewelry. For many years I lived in the land of beautiful Bedouin, and my collection of wearable folk art was substantial. Carolyn wanted to catch up. These pieces were guaranteed to be knock-outs in New York at the theatre or at the office

Carolyn Brunner exploded with energy. International colleagues sometimes confused us because of her small frame and punky short hair.

That was before she went from light brown to henna red and from henna red to carrot orange. That was before I went completely off the bottle to flat gray.

She was as dynamic off stage as she was on. She built a traveling career presenting Learning Styles workshops for educational conferences and for international schools. We invited her to present in Islamabad to enrich our staff development program.

Months after she committed to the trip from New York to Pakistan, her family calendar intensified. Her son was to play in a weekend championship game and a few days later, would solo in the school band performance.

Carolyn never flinched. She left the game at the fourth quarter and jumped a plane. In a whirlwind trip, she returned to Buffalo nearly overnight. As the workshop leader, she belted us with academic stimuli on differentiated learning styles integrated with differentiated teaching styles to meet the needs of our diverse classrooms; she crammed-in a city tour and squeezed-in the inevitable, mandatory shopping trip.

Yes, shopping. If operating within a limited travel time, we learn to prioritize. Some people do museums. Serious travelers delight in and understand the value of appreciating a culture through shopping. The experienced traveler knows to combine the museum with the museum gift shop. But if time is severely limited, the shopping trip wins the day.

Between workshops, I grabbed Carolyn for a power-shop; I needed some meat and drug her along. Midweek, between Friday Markets, a few Afghanis set up a small bazaar in the parking area near the frozen-meat shop, a one room meat-boutique of frozen animal parts.

Freezers lined the perimeter of the closet-size shop. Two freezers sat back to back in the centre of the small room. My blue fingers lifted chunks of shrink-wrapped, at least plastic-bagged, meat.

On smudged yellowed papers taped to the wall above each freezer, letters encrypted in Urdu and English the contents of each freezer. I trusted the wall signs and left the rest up to my imagination. I seldom recognized the cut. The choices included chicken, beef, mutton, lamb. No pork.

Carolyn patiently tapped her toe, taking it all in as I selected the mystery meat of the day. This was not a supermarket in Buffalo. She feigned interest in the meats, but kept looking over her shoulder at the merchants in the parking lot. I made my selection, several kilos of ground meat of some kind, a beef bit, not sure what it was or how I would choreograph it. I skipped the chicken as Tanvir, the house helper, could find live chickens in the market. We drifted, as if by magnetic pull, to the shopping tables in the lot.

The driver tossed the frozen boulders of meat into the car while Carolyn and I perused the Afghani merchandise. We scrutinized the portable card tables like professional buyers from New York. By this time in our lives, we were professional buyers. We knew how to power-shop; with great results.

Each folding table displayed an eclectic array of goods. Two turbaned merchants stood behind the wobbly tables in eager anticipation. The vendors mixed their wares, whatever they had available for the day. This day, items included a few pieces of blown glass from Herat, including vases and stemware in characteristic blown glass colours: aqua, amber, sea foam, and beer-bottle brown.

One table displayed a few Chinese decorative implements, hand painted rice bowls and a carved figurine, and colourful Afghani prayer caps stitched in reds and greens. Carolyn and I zoomed-in on the jewelry. We fondled long necklace pieces and caressed earrings set with lapis and amber. The vendor, soon to be my personal *suqi*, talked to us in broken English about each piece. Carolyn didn't understand most of it and kept looking at me asking, "What'd he say?"

His story, they all had a story, involved his family, they always have a family. It seems he and his brothers were making their way from Herat, Afghanistan, across the rugged Khyber Pass to Peshawar, Pakistan, finally to Islamabad. I knew this story. Afghans packed up their wares and stuffed them in matching saddle baskets which precariously straddled donkey backs. Packing up the jewelry seemed safe enough, but I always found it incredible that the glass pieces survived the journey in any form other than shards. His story continued.

"My brother lead donkey. I follow with more donkey. Careful pack glasses wares."

"What'd he say?" Carolyn whispered at me.

"You were coming from Jalalabad?"

"We pack donkey with glasses wares from Herat. Wrap good with many papers."

"What'd he say?" She cocked her head, looking at me for more interpretation.

This trip took days. From Herat, in the far west of Afghanistan, they proceeded across the country to Kabul, the capitol, on to Jalalabad and through the Khyber Pass to Peshawar and Islamabad.

"We come to mountains. Donkey all tired, go slow." He looked down at the small table.

"Bad men come at us. Take brother."

"Did they steal your things?"

"Take brother."

"What's he saying?"

"What happened to your brother?" I repeated this several times to be sure I understood.

"They keel brother. With big knife.

"Bad men. They sell brother."

"They killed your brother? Why did they do that?" Although I had heard of this, no one ever told me their personal story.

As they approached the mountainous region, near the Pakistani border, mountain men ambushed the donkey caravan and abducted his brother. They murdered him on the spot, to hear the *suqi* tell the story, and carved out his body parts to sell as transplant organs. The storyteller became so distraught, tears welled-up around his dark eyes.

"What? That's terrible," from Carolyn, catching about half of the story.

"What'd he really say?" I repeated what I heard, back to the Afghan merchant.

"You mean they kidnapped your brother while you were walking to Peshawar?"

"Yes. They keel my brother. They sell his ice, they sell his key-knee and his leever."

"They get money selling the eyes, the kidney, and the liver?"

"Yes. They make much money from my brother body."

Carolyn clearly understood my translation. The brother had been murdered for his body parts, to sell as organ transplants. It was big money in the medical arena in Pakistan. She looked from me to the leathery face of the raconteur and back to me. What did one say after such a tale?

"I must support my family and now my brother family also."

I saw in Carolyn a glimmer of guilty greed, wanting to get a lock on the beautiful pieces, especially the jewelry, as if it were her last chance for happiness. At the same time the counterpoint tugged at the conflict to get out of there to ask me if this narrative could possibly be true. Was this just a sob story, a sales pitch? I knew Carolyn wanted confirmation. She also wanted his merchandise. We both wanted to be savvy shoppers, not conned tourists. In my own mind, I decided what I was willing to pay.

I picked up a necklace similar to a piece I purchased in Nepal. The pieces, especially jewelry, travel with the Bedouin and it is difficult to know the exact origin, though one can determine the general region. An Afghani gentleman at a Friday-Market once leaned across his table.

He told me, in hushed tones, he had something better than beautiful amber beads. Did I know how to tell real amber?

"I haff some-ting better than ahmbur," he whispered. I leaned in to hear the secret.

"You know how to tell reel ahmbur?"

Not wanting to appear as a novice, I nodded twisting my palms upward. I presumed it was something like how one knows real pearls from faux. That unsanitary method involves scraping ones teeth against the pearl. He took out a match box, struck a match on the edge and held the flame under the amber.

"See, eet does not burn." Now I'm thinking the test is like knowing the hardness of diamonds that cut glass.

"I haff some-ting better than ahmbur," he repeated. He leaned in close, like a master of the pause, milking the suspense.

"I haff," he paused again.

"Plastic." Before I could catch my breath he repeated one final time, "It eez better than ahmbur."

The bereaved merchant wrapped our purchases and we rushed back to the house. Carolyn and I each bought necklaces and blown glass, feeling guilty as we negotiated a better price. We did our best to support the Afghan families of the refugee camps. We dashed home; she packed her bags, while I packed my freezer with frozen animal parts. She wore her new jewelry on the plane and wrapped the blown glass as if it were traveling via donkey through the Khyber Pass. Carolyn made it home to enjoy her son's concert and the Herat glass survived with nary a chard.

Taliban
Tanks
and the
CIA

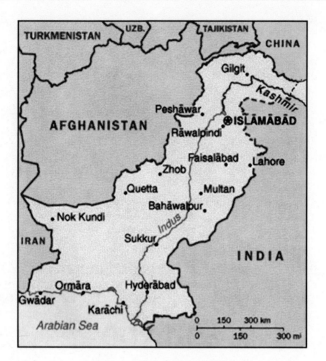

On the Road

Mirwaz drove. He wore a traditional dust-coloured *shalwar khamis,* loose-fitting pajama pants and a knee-length pajama shirt. He westernized the look with a dark suit-jacket. Without socks, his worn loafers seemed preppy. He seldom wore a turban, though the others of this gaggle of characters did. All were present at the dinner in Islamabad, the interview, but it never occurred to me we would be travel companions bouncing along in a Pajero.

Next to Mirwaz sat a thin, turbaned man with a wiry, untrimmed, black beard. It hung five inches past his chin; or rather it stuck out five inches, undisciplined and wild. He was the self proclaimed *Mujaheddin,* an armed struggler, a holy warrior, who fought the soviets and then resisted the pro-soviet government in the 1980's. He saw himself as a freedom fighter and as the religious leader of the group.

The narrow, two-lane road from Islamabad to Peshawar was badly rutted. Years of government corruption and skimming resulted in cheap blacktop road construction. Heavy, overloaded, slow-moving trucks further congested and weighted-down the inferior highway, deepening the ruts. The narrow, restrictive road was the only access between the two cities.

While the men strained their necks looking out the windows, watching for chances to pass, I relished the opportunity to observe the garish trucks and study the naive paintings and caricatures. I loved the lorries. I wasn't driving. Each truck represented a piece of folk art: a painted mural, a visual, functional work of art rolling along the road; a testimony; a personal mosaic. Plodding along, the red, blue, green and yellow lorries projected an art form of ironic energy; overloaded, they listed from the weight of the cargo. One might see anything painted as ornamentation, from Madonna, the singer of pop, to Madonna, the mother of Jesus, often on the same truck.

Mirwaz

The Interview

I wanted to go to Afghanistan and none of my friends would go, even when I used the "S" word. Shopping promised to be unique; beautiful pieces of blown glass, tapestries, carpets, even funky embroidered boots, none to be found in the *suqs* of Pakistan or Saudi, certainly not in the sterile malls of America. What was wrong with these women? It was a brilliant opportunity to Shop. I wanted to see the schools as well. Daryle had no interest in going to Afghanistan, especially to shop.

"I'd like to go, but we're State Department; I can't go with a diplomatic passport."

"You think it's *safe?*"

"My husband would never let me go there."

"Are you kidding?"

"Let's go to Hong Kong; the shopping's great."

I was invited with mutual friends to have dinner with Mirwaz, my Afghan contact, in his Islamabad home. Daryle agreed to join for the dinner. I wasn't sure what to expect but I anticipated that the evening would be something of an interview, not unlike the invitation to Tea at the Chinese Embassy the years before Foreign Friends were issued invitations in 1974.

In this case, there was no engraved invitation; there was no butler to open the door of the Residence. Instead of black lacquered chairs swathed in silk cushions, we sat on straight-back unvarnished wooden chairs lined up against the walls of his small home. Instead of blue and white ginger jars and celadon platters there was a map of Afghanistan scotch-taped to the wall.

In Manila, I was nervous meeting the Chinese Ambassador and his wife in their residence. Twenty-two years later, I was apprehensive because I didn't know this Afghani man and I didn't know if I was being set up. Was I making the right decision? Maybe this wasn't such a good idea.

The more I considered the reality of the trip, the less sure I was about traveling alone, although my new contact was eager to escort me across the border. None of my friends were willing to enter the country, to take a risk, as they perceived it to be. I could not generate interest in Afghanistan.

The night I met Mirwaz, Daryle and I were also introduced to other men who were already at the house. Though fiercely aware of being scrutinized, I tried to be at ease and natural. I told myself it was just a dinner party. No, that's not right. It was a dinner evening. I knew better. I picked at a hangnail while observing the men. I chewed the inside of my cheek. The Afghans sat on one side of the simple, unpretentious living room squeezed onto a sagging sofa. A single *kilim* of dull red geometric design loitered over the terrazzo floor. The men seemed to represent different factions of Afghan politics. We talked about the Taliban who were having some success that week against the government of Burhanuddin Rabbani.

What did they think of the Taliban? I wanted to know; I wanted to know what the Afghanis thought of the new political movement that was having moderate success in their country. Were the talibs a political group? Were they a student group? However, I did not want to be denied an entry visa because of my own political view. I didn't want to be denied the promise of shopping, of enjoying the arts of Afghanistan. I didn't know much about the new student movement of *talibs* but I was curious. During the evening, amongst themselves these men voiced disagreement over the success and/or usefulness of the Taliban group. The conversation lapsed into animated Pashto, then guffaws of laughter, followed by a lengthy translation for our benefit. We laughed in English.

I was further put at ease when Mirwaz' daughter skipped into the living room to be introduced. She proceeded, after gentle prodding by her father, to climb up the sides of the door-frame by spreading her legs and arms to their widest stretch, barely reaching each side as she inched her way, spider-like, from the floor to the top of the frame where she hung swinging until her father plucked her down. His wife, however, did not appear from the kitchen.

Several of the men worked for the Office of the Interior in Pakistan, or was it the ISI, the Inter-Services Intelligence? They might or might not assist with facilitating my visa into their country, depending on how the evening went: the interview. They explained about my passport, saying one of the men would personally take care of my visa. I felt my back go rigid. A tentative date suggested that we travel during a school break. *Who were these men and where was I going?*

Over orange juice we talked about the beauty of Afghanistan and the diversity of the land. The men stood around the dog-eared map on the wall talking about various rivers and streams. This got Daryle's attention. They bragged, like all fishers, about the trout here and the bream there, gesturing with their hands to indicate the enormous size of the fish. Even in Pashto, I got the drift. Fishers are all alike.

And that was it. Daryle agreed to accompany me. With boyish enthusiasm, the men told hunting stories and fishing tales. I suspected their notion of fishing and Daryle's concept of the sport, were chasms apart. I suspected they were of the school of dynamite; the big bang theory of blow 'em up and scoop 'em up downstream.

Black Box

N ow, on the road, I sat with my sub-notebook in the centre seat of the Pajero next to Daryle. In the back seat, a lively man who spent a year in California chatted on and on. "You eat avocado? Everyone eat avocado in California." I was not sure if he was ever legal in America. He inferred that he stayed on after his visitor-visa expired and would now have trouble returning. His buddy, Samerdin, also sat in the back. Contraire to Muji, the *Mujaheddin,* Samerdin's beard was well-trimmed, unlike the scruffy, religious beard. They were good-humored. They laughed a lot; in Pashto. Everyone's face was covered. All were bearded. Only Daryle had a fresh shave. I did not veil.

I never thought about companions on this trip over the Khyber Pass, through the tribal areas of the North West Frontier Province, this wild and rough cowboy territory. Law and order was based on tribal ritual and tradition, and *Pashtunwali,* the Pashtun code of honour. I also knew about revenge.

The *Mujaheddin* was animated. He wanted all of the conversation translated into English enabling us to participate. These jovial men have been friends for many years. I was not sure why each was along on this trip wound-up like kids off to camp. Excited to be going into Afghanistan? They didn't seem hyper at having foreigners along; just having a great time, enjoying each other and the adventure. *Why would it seem like an adventure to these men? They go back and forth frequently.*

Mirwaz pulled off the road at a swarming bus-stop. People milled about leaping on and off busses. Under their arms they clutched filled bags and bulging baskets. Children clung to hands and grabbed at adult legs.

From wooden pushcarts and crowded stalls, vendors hawked fruits and vegetables. They sold deep-fried, greasy spinach and potato pakora and live chickens squatting in woven straw pens. Mothers and maids carted off cackling hens carried by the scaly ankles and claws, dangling upside down, flapping their wings to no avail.

Armed with a bag of oranges, we continued on as our Pajero-mates gaily tossed missiles of orange peel from the windows with naive abandon.

Another hour down road, we halted at a rest stop for tea. *This could take forever.* The outdoor truck-stop was owned by Muji's brother. Travelers rested at outdoor tables and benches, under palm-branch kiosks. I looked around then asked if it was alright for me, the only woman, to join this truck stop. 'Oh yes, no problem.' After joining heads, someone indicated I should follow him. *There must be a separate section for women.* We walked past the crowded tables. I was aware of being the only female but it didn't seem to be an issue. No one stared, they hardly noticed. As I brushed between tables, black clouds of flies lifted, en mass, from the cups of sweet tea and honey-covered *naan.* 'This way, Madam,' through the fly-ridden tables, past the kitchen, down a mud path, to three stalls. Ah. How thoughtful. I think! I tentatively pushed open the first corrugated door. A man stepped out pinching his crotch. There was a drain on the floor. The other two doors were shut. I entered where the man exited.

Back in the Pajero, the bantering continued.

"What kind of beard is that?" mocked 'Khalif,' so dubbed, from his year in California.

"I like it. It's still black, not like yours."

"Mine is much better," chimed in Muji, stroking his chin.

"Yours goes all over the place."

"While you were gone, the Missus," he said twisting around toward me, "put all our names in the computer." They laughed.

"If anything goes wrong, we're already in the black box." Gales of laughter.

Afghani escorts

Lenox

The evening before we crossed into Afghanistan, the owner of the Panasonic distribution centre in Peshawar, hosted us for dinner. Although a wealthy man, he lived in a simple home with a garden of wild flowers. The blossoms bent with the wind, uncultivated, scattered, and effectively un-choreographed. We sat inside on the floor. The only piece of furniture in the living room was a Panasonic television with an oversized screen. Several satellite dishes hid among the foliage and teetered on the roof providing programming from Russia and Europe as well as the US, the Middle East and Asia.

I sat cross-legged on the carpet, grateful for the fullness of my long skirt; and for my yoga classes. We sat around a large cloth placed atop the carpet. Someone from the kitchen came around with a bowl and pitcher of water and a towel for each guest to rinse their hands before the meal.

Large eggshell Lenox platters arrived heaped with lamb. A young boy placed silver trays of chicken, enormous bowls of rice and hot, fresh-baked *naan*, down the centre of the cloth; each placed strategically, in easy proximity to the guests.

I sat next to the host. He began by reaching into the platter of lamb. Using the fingertips of his right hand he deftly scooped up a chunk of meat and placed it on my own Lenox; the man on my left placed a warm piece of *naan* on my plate. Before I had a chance to serve myself, more chicken was placed on the bread. "Eat. Please eat." They sounded like nurturing Jewish mothers.

The lamb, seasoned with herbs, cilantro, garlic, onion and cardamom fell apart in my mouth. With a piece of *naan* I scooped up the fluffy baked rice. Preparing the rice was usually a two part process. It was first parboiled then baked with stock of the meats and flavoured with raisins and pistachios. This process made the rice a bit tricky to eat because it was not sticky, but I had some experience from Saudi. There were other stew-like dishes which blended with the meal. The important thing to remember was to use only my right hand. I wanted to use both hands, the better to scoop, but that would be a crude insult.

The guests included an electronic distributor from Dubai, and the president of the local bank whose son also joined the dinner. He was a bright boy about eleven years old studying in one of the better Pakistani schools, and was confident in English. He planned to attend university in England. The others in the room were of the elite Afghani leadership.

I had many questions: were these men part of the parliament, leaders of the *Loya Jurga*? Were they war lords, tribal chiefs? Did the son attend a *madrassa*? I knew it was a boy's-only school. Was his school private? I was the only female at dinner. I did not question, but listened. I noticed that Khalif and Muji were not at this dinner. The meal was organized because Mirwaz is a well respected friend or colleague. It was not prepared in our honour, but might not have happened without us.

The banker reached across the carpet placing more chicken on my plate. I attempted to decline.

"You cannot refuse. You are sitting between two Pathan tribesmen." We laughed.

"You know about *Pashtunwali?*

"You can never refuse Pashtun hospitality."

I was aware of the importance of hosting guests and I knew of Pashtun hospitality. I was keenly aware of their fierce reputation in the tribal areas. If there was any dispute, I wanted these men on my side. This was the first of many meals on the floor or on the ground and the last meal to enjoy without guns and weapons at the side of each man.

Dinner with right hands only

Border Patrol

Pajamas and Turbans.

The following morning we made our way through the steep and twisting Khyber Pass, through the harsh and fiercely guarded northern territories between Pakistan and Afghanistan. We stopped often; each time we loaded our back packs on and off a succession of trucks and vans. In Peshawar we left the Pajero and jumped into a minivan. We stopped again and got into a truck. *They seemed to have difficulty getting the right car, renting a van or borrowing a truck.*

Rugged mountains define the border. Along the road, through the pass, armed uniformed men guard the territories. It's a rough land: cowboys in pajamas and turbans, guns and military boots. Afghani music blared from the cassette of the rented vehicle. The

345

transport might not have heat or air-conditioning, but there was usually a dusty tape deck.

We arrived at the so-called border crossing for Afghanistan. Usually we crossed borders through airports, clearing customs with official forms. It's different when driving. Over the years, we traversed Europe and Africa by car. Crossings in Africa can be crowded and bureaucratic; the offices are sometimes small shacks. At one crowded African border they handed out condoms with a warning: Don't bring AIDS to our country. I grabbed a handful for the lark of it.

This crossing was different, not like the small African stations, except for the dust. I didn't know what to expect; I never gave it a thought. We were thrust into a small dusty crowd of pushing and shoving residents and merchants waving crumpled papers above their heads shouting in Pashto, Urdu and probably Farsi which I didn't understand.

Our precious passports, surrendered to Mirwaz, disappeared through a small window of a wooden hut. I glanced over my shoulder sobered by the reality of our environment, as someone shoved me along. *I remembered the first and only time I left my college dorm without signing out. There was an accident and no one knew where I was.* My palms were wet. *No one knew where we were.*

Pushed and shoved, we squeezed through the bent chain-link fence. I looked around but went with the crowd like a teenage fan at a rock concert, pushed and shoved across the frontier through a narrow wedge of aluminum fence. *No one knew where we were;* no five-star hotels, no Hilton, Hyatt, Sheraton to list as a contact address. No cell phone connections. All I knew was that we were in Afghanistan, shoved through the commonly called porous border.

Once across the frontier, unable to take the Pakistani vehicle into Afghanistan, we hired another small van. As we drove through a crowded outdoor market, I looked on both sides of the road for *shopping possibilities,* carpets or tapestries; lots of potential here with big crowds and a large variety of merchandise: pots and pans, red, blue and green plastic bowls, buckets, containers and plastic spoons, plates, cups, fruits, sugar and rice.

I zeroed-in on a carpet stall. The *kilims* looked typical but as we drove by, I noticed the geometric shapes were in the form of war tanks. The rectangular shapes made manifestations of Kalashnikovs; the octagonal shapes became hand grenades. I had seen a few war carpets in the Afghani *suq* in Riyadh. Today I noticed one prayer rug with army tanks in the typical pattern, lined up to indicate each prayer spot. Whoa. Stop. Why doesn't he stop?

My nose pressed against the window of the vehicle as we drove on.

The centre lane bisected the village. Moving on I watched the unthinkable as a child ran toward the van. Villagers, as well as each of us on the van, shouted in anticipation. The driver hit his breaks and swerved. Confused, the young boy turned away from the traffic but then back into the van. He fell away with an audible thump to his head. The child seemed alright, though stunned.

Everyone praised the driver for reacting so well. Inching the vehicle through the crowd, he stopped the van and pulled out a wad of *afghani* notes for someone to give to the family of the boy. The father refused, indicating it was not necessary. Finally the driver got out and a discussion followed in the middle of the road. In the end he paid the money. We left quickly. *No shopping here.*

Just beyond the market we changed transportation. This time my jolly bearded companions negotiated a car to take us into the village. They called it a police car. Doubtful. *As I jumped in, I wondered again about the boy at the market. Was the family negotiating for more money? Were they paid more than usual? Would he be alright? Was this the reason we changed cars? If we foreigners had not been in the van, the accident would not have happened, so the thinking goes.* We left quickly. We had no choice.

The police car was a big, fifties era gas-guzzler, when gas was twenty-five cents a gallon; an old, black, American Chevy. A

taped-up, shattered bullet hole penetrated the front windshield on the passenger side. *I could only imagine.* The cracks radiated outward from the hole like a first grader's happy sun in the corner of a finger-painting tableau. The dashboard was rusted, perhaps burned out. Loose wires dangled under the steering wheel and the dash. *Was the car hot-wired? I didn't notice.*

Three of us squeezed together in the front seat. Daryle postured himself in the centre, so I avoided any accidental groping for the stick-shift. On the passenger side, staring at the bullet hole, I clutched the door, partially concerned that it would fly open at any bump. Muji, Kalif and Samerdin tossed their backpacks into the trunk and jumped in the back seat cradling Kalashnikovs, *where did they come from?* aimed inadvertently at our necks. Mirwaz and several other men took a second car.

Networking

We drove through bombed-out villages and towns; Mirwaz networked. He worked the crowd like a politician on a campaign stump. Sometimes he saw someone on the road. We stopped and he was greeted like a best friend, the return of a brother. Men clutched in fond embrace, chests pressed together, heart to heart.

Other times we stopped at a house and Mirwaz disappeared inside for lengthy visits, at times for over an hour. It was clear that occasionally we were not included. Too difficult to translate the dialogue? Not interesting for us? Private discussion? There were a few times we were left with others in the group. Maybe he needed space? During these stops they entertained us with more tea or a walking tour or broken conversation about Pashtun poetry, or the ongoing question of young Taliban who were hopeful of changing the country, or more conversation about the Russian invasion.

"When the Russians came we fought against them." Muji, was eager to tell his stories though they were difficult to follow with the rough translation.

"Why would the Russians invade Afghanistan?" I asked, sort-of egging him on.

"The King was overthrown by his cousin who made himself King, or something, as leader of the New Republic." He became president of the Republic. This in 1973.

"But then, five years later, there was a military thing and the Russians didn't like him."

"You mean a coup? Didn't like who?" I pressed with the terrible translation.

"Taraki, the communist leader, was assassinated by Amin.

"Amin was (then) assassinated by Soviet soldiers." In 1979

"Then we had Karmal then Nagibullah." Who were these people? I couldn't keep up. Mohammad Najibullah, President of the Republic at the time was forced to resign as the *Mujaheddin* overtook Kabul. He was captured and executed by the Taliban in 1996.

"They drove big tanks. We fought from the hills.

"The Russians know nothing. Those tanks ha! Big. Huge. We ran 'round them.

"They left. But there was much damage." The withdrawal was from 1988-89.

"The *Mujaheddin* won with help. I am *Mujaheddin*," he said patting his chest.

"America big help with Saudi and Pakistan." He slowly stroked his Kalashnikov.

"America give Kalashnikov, rocket launcher and big money." America wanted to defeat the Soviets.

This networking, important to Mirwaz, seemed genuine. Part of his sincerity was validated by cultural customs and part of the authenticity was Mirwaz himself. Everything he did was predicated on Islam. He said something from the *Hadith*, a book of sayings of the Prophet Mohammed, Peace Be Upon Him. "One who serves, leads." Mirwaz lived this philosophy. He knew everyone. *They joked about it, his knowing everyone.*

"Ha! Kalif, you don't know anyone."

"Mirwaz knows everyone. Samerdin, you don't know anyone because of your beard."

"And Muji, you only know your *Mujaheddin* brothers."

"Just see, Missus," he said to me, "if there is anyone on the street or in the village who doesn't know Mirwaz."

Often when we stopped on the road we were encouraged to take photographs. They, our bearded companions, took lots of pictures.

We drove through peaceful, clean communities cultivated green; the valleys hosted tranquil villages at the foot of the purple and blue Hindu Kush. In stark contrast, unsightly bile Soviet tanks lay strewn about the landscape like oversized Tonka toys in an empty play yard. Houses and buildings were destroyed. As we drove along the dusty road, the fighters began to tell us their memories, still as vivid and fresh as our own visions of SCUD attacks in Saudi Arabia. Not only Muji fought. They each voiced some involvement and expressed their loss.

"Here a 'copter downed eleven people in this house."

"They all died."

"They were all at home."

"There was no reason."

"Over there we were sending fire," From someone else, "On the top of that knoll."

"They all died."

"Even the children."

"The entire family." They all knew the family, and all were visibly shaken again by the deaths and from the souvenir of the destroyed home.

We drove around another corner. "Here, between those hills, we came across the mountains with Dan Rather. They fired on us and we fired back." Mirwaz, who ten years before took the American news team into the rebel camps to cover the start of the Russian invasion, spoke.

The Russians destroyed the village. For what? They needed the area as a strong-hold between Peshawar, the trade centre of northern Pakistan and Kabul, the trade centre of Afghanistan. Primarily, they wanted the commerce including precious and semi-precious stones, according to the unshaven scholars. Eventually, everyone wanted control of the trade route for the Central Asian republics; it was also about gas and oil.

The former business area was reduced to remnants of mud-brick rubble. No shopping here. No shopping for the locals either. *Perhaps this trip would not be about shopping.* Farming came back as the residents slowly, cautiously returned to work their land or to hire it out, but the business area would take a long time to return. Neighbours carried water from the wells. The governors held regular Friday *majalis* court but there was no plan for electrification; there was no money.

Cemeteries scattered the roadsides. In the countryside flat stone like flagstone stood upright as grave markers in the desert landscape. In the tradition of Islam, the body of the deceased must be buried before sundown the day of the death if possible, the body aligned perpendicular to Mecca, the head facing the Qaaba. In cemeteries, gravestone painted white stood out like exclamation points in the green wild grasses of the fields.

"There, you see that large, new, freshly painted grave?" Kalif gestured out his window. I leaned forward looking in the direction he pointed.

"A university student was shot dead in Queens, New York." The irony did not go unnoticed.

"His body was returned last month.

"He survived the Russians but was murdered in the United States."

This was humble land to overtake. In vivid contrast to rugged mountains and jade wheat, the crude mud-and-straw huts and walls contained compounds of family life. Before.

"All of these cows walking here and in that field belong to one woman.

"She defied the Russians and stayed here in her home, on her land with her cattle.

"She did not ever leave Niseer, even though others left as refugees."

The Russians destroyed the village. *I hope no one can ever accuse the Americans of leaving this kind of destruction, I thought. Sadly, it sickens me, now.* It seems abusively wretched to occupy such impoverished land.

Fishing

The first time we went fishing, we drove out toward the university. We were interested in seeing the campus. We stopped several times along the highway to take photos of the valley below. Mirwaz and Samerdin used a telephoto lens and encouraged us to take pictures. They pointed out the university in the far, far distance; a nice area, but not postcard material.

Mirwaz talked a lot. He enjoyed dialogue. Having a conversation with Mirwaz seemed to energize the moment. Every day something new came up. Daryle asked about the current leadership of Afghanistan. What was going on with the Taliban? They asked the same questions amongst themselves.

Mirwaz, an intelligent man with deep-set dark, twinkling eyes, was at ease discussing philosophy, religion, politics, children and family, education, or any of the above as applied to the United States. What did Daryle think of the current leadership of the US? What were his views on education in the States and in the international arena? Mirwaz discussed with candor and with a broad sense of humour, laughing contagiously. Would he consider standing for a political position in Afghanistan? Daryle asked.

He reminded me of an Afghan superstar of some game show category; able to discuss the Russian invasion with a slant toward Afghan politics. We continued to discover his charisma and later hope for and fear for his life.

We did not stop at the university, but went on toward the river beyond the dam. It was late afternoon and crowds, primarily students, milled about the huge falls of the dam and the adjacent park. I knew we were in trouble if this was their idea of fishing-water. They drove a little further and parked the truck. It was big water.

At the top of the embankment several men threw out nets. Daryle dutifully, and perhaps hopefully, grabbed his bag of gear and headed up the river, the bearded hoard following close behind. I waited in the jeep with my computer and a book. I've been fishing before.

When I could stand it no longer, I closed-up the truck and headed toward the bend in the river. Allahgul, a young sixteen year old, came along. He joined the men on the trip assigned to watch the car. Apparently designated to stay back with me, Allahgul was pleased to be heading toward the others. They were not difficult to spot.

A group of students hovered on the bank while Daryle assembled his rod and flies then paced up the river working his line, trying to avoid snags. He talked to no one. A group of kids floated by on tires hooting all the way down-river. He continued to snag on nets. The water churned with river rafters crashing along on their tubes. I agonized for my fisher and after some time he climbed the banks and disassembled his rod. Our eyes locked for a second and communicated his frustration, aggravation and irritation.

The young college academicians turned to me for their questions.

Who was I?

Who was that man?

Was he important?

What was my work?

Why was I there?

I listened to their typical questions. I was vague. I gave generic responses. I noticed Mirwaz and Kalif watching with unusual intensity. They exchanged glances with Samerdin. Perhaps they thought I was uncomfortable. This was not an ideal setting for fishing, but I did not feel harassed. Daryle wanted to try another beat but curiously, they whisked us into the truck and whizzed past the university.

I hoped to visit the university. Instead, we flew by the school back up the road and were again offered the chance to take photos from way up the highway, looking down on the distant campus. Mirwaz pointed out the large villa in the foreground. This was the home of a former drug czar; others used the villa now. Mirwaz and Muji took photos again.

"Stand here, Missus. You can get a perfect photo."

"That's okay. Thank you, I'm good," meaning, I really don't want to take a photo of this.

"You can see the university from here." Didn't we want to take pictures, the university in the distant background?

Mirwaz pulled out a new GPS, acquired along the way in one of the villages, to take a reading. I watched from the car, then got out and walked along the rim overlooking the valley. The brisk air whistled as we looked down on the huge villa. My skirt whipped around my calves smacking in the rhythm of the wind. Mirwaz fumbled around with the settings then asked for help with the satellite positions.

"Have you used these before?" he approached Daryle who was leaning against the car.

"We used them all the time in Saudi. GPS is the only way to navigate the dunes."

"How long does it take?"

"Sometimes it takes time. It depends on the satellites."

"They have to line up. Here, it's lining up now." He handed the palm size instrument back to Mirwaz.

"What does this mean?"

"When the system comes together, you will have your reading for longitude and latitude."

"This is good. I'll take a reading now, then we'll stop up the road to take another reading.

"Just to verify and practice using this thing."

He wanted to get a satellite impression, saying this was a good place, since we were stopped, then we would corroborate the reading further up the road. *Where did this Global Positioning System come from? There were no electronic stores in the villages.*

Hunting

The cold eggs congealed like coagulated lumps of lard. With flat, warm chapatis we scooped up ghee-saturated scrambled eggs. It reminded me of eating early morning cold fried eggs with jelly, served to us, or left on a tin plate for us in the provinces of the Philippines; lucky if there were no cockroaches. Breakfast was the most difficult meal. We washed it down with tepid sweet tea before heading out, guns in tow. I kind-of got into the rhythm of the men and their guns. This morning they wanted to hunt.

Along the road we picked up a distinguished looking man as we headed toward another village. He looked educated. He was well groomed, his beard trimmed short and even, his beige *shalwar khamis* clean and pressed.

In another culture he might have carried a briefcase and worn a three-piece suit and dark pointed shoes. Today he carried a gun, wore pajamas and open leather sandals. This man I later learned was leader and commander of over 200 troops and controlled two thousand Kalashnikov weapons. He seemed respected and a likely candidate for new political leadership.

Without warning he leaped out of the front seat of the truck, lunged across the road and crouched low to the ground while aiming. He missed, as the pheasant soared back across the road. He embraced his gun like a familiar lover. Clutching it close to his body, he ran back across the road to an adjacent field. Crouching again he took aim but the insolent foul was gone.

We drove through red, orange, yellow, multicoloured poppy fields, brilliant in contrast against the severe blue-black mountains. Again, Mirwaz stopped to greet friends. He knew the village elders and leaders and greeted each with a strong double-handed grasp. He spent much time visiting with his father's friend. Mirwaz seemed to be an honoured and respected son when he returned to each village and met with locals.

While he visited and conversed we met an older, mature gentleman who told us about his time with the Russians while they occupied Afghanistan. The man wrote poetry, spoke Russian and had great respect for the time the Russians were in the country.

I felt my back stiffen. I wondered why this annoyed me. The Russians were supposed to have three heads or at the very least two horns. My background showed as a child of Sputnik; a child who practiced DROP drills, hovering under my desk at the command of the classroom teacher, in case of a nuclear bomb attack by the Russians. Such propaganda. I fell for it; it is what I was taught and now it reared its silly head.

This gentleman, thick white hair under his wool Chitrali, rolled *pakol* hat, attended university in Moscow on a scholarship sponsored by the Russians. He studied Russian literature and poetry. I shouldn't have been surprised; Pashtun poetry is important in Afghanistan. But I was. In his genteel manner, we discussed literature. He talked, I listened. Was I really having this conversation in the heart of Afghanistan with a group of freedom fighters?

We stopped in the poppy fields for tea with more friends; right in the middle of the poppy fields. Even in California, where the poppy is the state flower, I would have been uncomfortable in this colourful garden. Muji propped his gun against the tree; Kalif rested his Kalashnikov across his knees. We sat on the ground, made a little fire out of twigs and heated water. I didn't want to know where the water

Afghan Poet

Dinner with the poet, Muji and others.

came from, but it did boil for a minute or so.

The river flowed beyond the poppies and with it another invitation to fish. I had a painful attack of stomach cramps, but no place to escape. We hiked through red and purple and white poppies lingering for photos, walking and talking, making our way toward the river. Just walking through the poppies made my palms sweat. Although they presented a rainbow of colour, and a photo would be memorable, I wondered, was I being framed? The little old lady from Pasadena with opium. They insisted we take photos. If I was taking the picture, I would have faked it, but Khalif snached the camera and clicked away. He wanted me in the photos. The camera was not digital; I could not delete.

Poppy Fields

We walked passed villagers in the fields. I held my cramping side hoping to forestall the inevitable result of the barely boiled tea. A man stuffed grass into the centre of a large inner tube. I assumed it was for the cattle. However, when he joined us at the river he threw the tube into the water, jumped aboard and floated to the centre of the wide, fast-flowing waterway to cast his nets.

We all sat on the bank, presumably to watch him fish. Daryle took one look at the flow of the water, the width of the river, the steep bank and did not rig-up his line. I, alone, headed back toward the poppy fields and high grass fields to find relief. Things were not good, but for the time, the stomach seizures stopped.

The farmer dangled off the grass-filled inner tube.

Without warning Mirwaz looked to the sky, aimed and fired. The tree took flight as a wing-ed cloud rose and dispersed after the explosion. Then the shooting began in earnest at invented targets across the river. Everyone fired several guns at protruding river rocks. Everyone else. Muji offered me a Kalashnikov.

The last time I was offered a rifle was during afterschool activities in Shanghai. There, the cadet leader found it incredulous that we didn't teach shooting at my school, that I didn't know how to use a rifle. As a kid, my dad encouraged me to shoot his rifle at tin cans in the desert. The kick from the gun nearly threw me to the ground.

"No problem, you can shoot here. You like?"

The clouds moved in and we walked back through the tall grass fields, past the white poppies, past the yellow poppies, past the purple and red poppies now blowing and bending in the rain-motivated wind. The poppies rolled out like an Afghani carpet which stretched for hectors from the dusty road to the craggy mountains.

We walked through the destroyed village to a small mud structure and entered through a carved wooden gate which was wedged between the door-frame and supported by rough lumber 2x4s. In Saudi, the ruins in old, abandoned villages look similar. These ruins in Afghanistan were bombed out, not weathered. There was no roof, so we were not protected from the rain, but further inside, a shelter of beams and straw did help to keep out the drizzle. Inside,

Afghan barbeque

men found several *charpoys*, bed frames with ropes lashed across the frame, which provided the semblance of a fiber mattress. Someone produced hot, sweet tea and it warmed us as they sprawled on the *charpoys*. I sat making notes on my computer, though they encouraged me to lounge resting on one elbow.

We ate all of our meals on the ground. Sometimes the food was placed on a carpet, other times on a piece of plastic. If we were in a room, there might be cushions to lean back against. If we were outside, on the ground, we sat around the plastic. This required some agility, but was pleasant. Everyone ate from common plates. It was better not to think about it, but to be as prudent as possible. On several occasions the men slaughtered a goat and cooked it while we traipsed around the country. It seemed natural and they performed the ritual with ease and familiarity.

When I was twelve and my brother five, we lived, like fer sure, in the infamous San Fernando Valley. One day our dad slaughtered the family pig. Its name was Disposal. Every day it was my job to trot the garbage to the back of the half-acre plot to the pig pen. My father hired a butcher. They captured the terrified pig, tied him up and hung him upside down from the tree at the side of the driveway. The pig squealed at the top of his lungs before, during and while they strung him up. When the knife sliced through his neck, he shrieked and squealed as blood gushed down the driveway. I can hear the horrible screams which seemed to go on for hours. When Disposal was finally dead, they hosed the red river of blood from the driveway and chopped him up into recognizable meat parts. The next day I helped cook pork chops for dinner. When we sat down to eat, I threw up the first bite.

After some time, Muji produced a large, flat pan of sheep parts. He placed it on the ground and the men gathered 'round to inspect and sort and carve the carcass into appropriate sizes. *Please tell me that we will not be offered this meat raw; not with my already vulnerable stomach.*

All of the men participated in the preparation of this meal. Well, they got that part right: men doing the cooking. Someone brought an armload of wood to be chopped for the fire. This could take hours.

I enjoyed goat-grabs in Saudi, pig roasts in the Philippines, luaus in Hawaii. Roasting an animal required most of the day, unless it was a chicken. Khalif and Samerdin gathered up bundles of sticks and with Daryle, began to whittle them to fine points for kebabs; a very good sign. This was hopeful. Long, slender chunks of kebab would cook

Dissecting the goat

Muji, Mirwaz prepare kebabs

much faster. How sensible.

Mirwaz separated the dark, purple organs, the favoured parts, from the carcass. Kalif skewered the cubes of liver onto thick branches. Samerdin speared meat squares onto additional tree-branch skewers. Other sticks pierced chunks of fat. As the fatty strips cooked over the fire, the flavoured oil dripped on the flame and was used to baste the liver and the meat. The liver was carefully wrapped in the stomach

Mirwaz, Black Box

lining which served as delicate filigree around the meat.

The liver, heart, and organs, the smooth red meat, provided gourmet eating: lamb giblets on a stick; the perfect picnic appetizer. Allahgul passed around a plastic bag of coarse rock salt and the bearded chefs, squatting in the dirt, pinched crunchy fingerfuls to sprinkle over the tender meat. Next, they placed skewers of sheep parts on the carefully fanned fire roasting the meat to perfection. The scent of grilled meat drifted through the hut. The chefs snatched hot, broiled chunks off the sticks, tossed them around the *charpoys*, and sometimes sprinkled them with the coarse salt before popping them into their mouths with their right hand.

It later occurred to me that they slaughtered the sheep for us, on our behalf, while we sat drinking tea. There were no markets that day. They killed the animal for us. We should have made speeches to express our gratitude. I expect we were remiss, culturally insensitive to this fact. Following the meal, everyone stood, hands lifted, elbows bent, palms facing the body. Muji led prayers after the meal, as was the custom.

Carriage and Culture

One afternoon we stopped for the day and walked through irrigated rice fields. We hiked single file down narrow mud ridges along the irrigation canals. Mirwaz led. We marched like children following the piper, I with my arms outstretched for balance. The men stepped nimbly over the rice paddies.

Across the fields, Mirwaz visited with family and extended-family. We met another longtime friend of his father. The man showed us his gun. The old rifle was embellished with a carved silver handle. This piece of art almost made me a lover of guns. He caressed the rifle butt and with two hands, presented it for a closer look.

It was antique, perhaps handed down from the man's father before and exemplified a rich tooled artistry in silver. I wanted the old, worked rifle, the first piece of art we had seen. I already gave up on the idea of shopping.

How could I take the gun from this family, this village, this handsome old gentleman? I would never get the firearm across the frontier; maybe I could get it into Pakistan, but eventually the antique weapon would be headed for another border. I felt privileged to touch the cutout work, the silver filigree, the old wood peeking through the silver lacework.

Children ran in and out gawking at the foreigners. I didn't feel that I looked so different; my skin was about the same colour as the Afghanis, not like the blatant contrast with blue-black or brown African villagers. I wore long and fluid skirts intending to blend in. It was not about looks.

It was about carriage and culture.

I grew up making decisions, allowed to make choices; allowed to make mistakes, bad choices. I learned from those bad choices. I wasn't afraid to ask. I learned it was okay to not know the answer; to look it up with an adult. I worked with books, not goats. But were we so different? I carried myself with confidence. I didn't recognize it. We are confident. We do walk with a self-assured carriage. It's cultural.

The village ladies gathered around me, the curious visitor, in a natural grouping of genders, pulled together like little metal bits clinging to a magnet; like the inevitable after-dinner apartheid in western settings. I noticed they wore loose, shapeless garments with simple dusty shawls draped elegantly over their heads. As we talked I fondled the old firearm before handing it back.

The women and girls mingled freely with family members and with Mirwazar. They were not embarrassed or uncomfortable, but shy with me and when I asked their names and the names of the children it produced gales of nervous giggles and they quickly covered their mouths with their shawls.

I brought out photos of Jessica and Ian, then in their early thirties. There were lots of oohs and aahs. This was always a good ice-breaker. Then, together, we girls all traipsed across the dirt road. They wanted me to see their school. Where did all of these women come from? There were just a few, then there were many.

They showed me the simple building where the girls attended school separately from the boys. The building was non-remarkable, a bit larger than the houses and contained narrow tables and benches with no backs. Someone introduced me to the female teacher. When she greeted me in English the women giggled again and the girls clapped.

We returned across the irrigated rice fields to sit outside on *charpoys*. For entertainment before the sun set the men blasted their guns at targets across the field. Between blasts the conversation continued about the Taliban.

"Some say these Taliban are just what we need here: Law and Order.

"Some say they want to bring integrity back to Afghanistan," whatever that meant. Kalif let forth a long barrage of rat-a-tat-tat.

"It sounds like they are dangerous, aggressive fighters; warriors," I wondered out loud.

"They are violent?" I asked between blasts. I was out of my element, but interested to hear this discussion in English. What was the feeling in the country? What was the thinking as we traversed the countryside? Did villagers accept this form of governance where Kalashnikov was king?

"Most of the *Talibs* are Afghan refugees.

"Returning 'home' from Pakistan," Mirwaz pointed out.

"They never lived here. They grew up, even were born in the camps in Pakistan."

He reloaded his Kalashnikov. During the Soviet occupation of Afghanistan, three million families crossed the frontier into Pakistan to avoid the conflict. Refugee centres became Afghan communities. The schools along the border were *madrassas* for boys only.

"These young fighters don't really know anything about Afghanistan." He lifted his gun and blasted another volley of ammunition at his unidentified target.

"They never lived here. They have no sense of history or of tribal history." Mirwaz expressed some empathy with the students. He continued.

"From a young age they attended *madrassas* to study the Qur'an.

"You, Missus, would scare them to death," he teased, eyes twinkling.

"Me? Why?" I repeated, "Moi?"

"Madrassas accept boys only. Many were orphans.

"They grew up with no mother or sisters around.

"Even the teachers at *madrassas* are *mullahs*, always men."

"So…?" I didn't get the link; I didn't see myself as scary; naïve, not scary.

"I think they don't know what to do with women.

"I think they want women to stay home.

"I think they can't figure it out yet." He struggled to define his own thinking.

Mirwaz suggested that as these little Afghani boys grew up in Pakistan, they shuffled about in an Afghan community not in Afghanistan. They went to school together, grew up together and went home to their dusty refugee camp with whatever men were around. The occasional female, he seemed to suggest, had little or no influence on the boys or men in the family, or in the camps. I filled in the gaps reflecting to myself that the women prepared meals and washed clothes as an expectation and no one really noticed. It was assumed and expected. Obviously, they made babies. Many children were born in the camps.

The real issue it seemed was not the influence of women or lack of influence of women, but the gap between Afghani Afghans and the

Afghans who grew up in Pakistani refugee camps with no knowledge of their native Afghanistan. I didn't put this together right away. I didn't put it together until much later as I continued to read background reports and articles accessible on Google.

The village scenes I witnessed with Mirwaz showed compassion within the tribe, the village and the family. The new *Talibs* didn't have this experience. The new *Talibs* came in bands, in groups, from Pakistan and attempted to integrate into their former tribal lands. There was a gap; a disconnect.

Gang Rape

"When I was a *mujaheddin* we fought for our tribe." Muji fired off a round, then sat next to Mirwaz on the string *charpoy*.

Growing up in refugee camps, the young students knew nothing of their tribes. Perhaps they even developed a camp-mentality. Whatever that was, it was not tribal, as in ethnic Afghani tribal.

"In Pakistan, in the camps, we *mujaheddin* taught the students how to use weapons but they don't know about their tribes." Muji stood up and shot again at a distant tree stump. The idea of no tribal background or understanding came up often.

"I shoot good.

"I shoot many Russians.

"I teach you to shoot. You like?" What was it? *Déjà vu*? This need for me to shoot a gun?

Mirwaz suggested that the reason the Taliban were successful was because the religious students found a purpose. The *madrassas* offered little science or math. With no training in farming, business or fundamental arithmetic, being part of a fighting, aggressive family appealed to them. Being part of any family appealed to them like Crips and Bloods from Los Angeles, they needed a symbol of kinship, something to bond them together.

Khalif was sick. I didn't recognize it at the time as he ran off into the fields to relieve himself. Later in the evening we ate communally on the floor, rimming a ground-cloth covered with recently slaughtered goat, rice and veggies; all eaten by hand. We sat around the food cloth with Kalashnikovs in-between, next to each of our mates. I was now a member of the gang and filled my own plate with my right hand, dipping in only up to the first knuckle. Now, only occasionally did they plop food on my plate.

Samerdin chimed in. "One of the first things the Taliban did, two years ago, was rescue two girls who had been captured by a general for the pleasure of the soldiers." He meant Gang Rape. It seemed everyone knew the story as they presented the account during the evening meal. I helped myself to a small portion of goat. Gang rape; that's how it started, so the repeated narrative went, with only slight variations. Mullah Omar headed into Afghanistan with the aim of re-establishing law and order. If the *mujaheddin* were out of control or misguided, Mullah Omar planned to enter Afghanistan with a small group of young talibs from his *madrassas* on the Pakistan-Afghanistan border.

After the Soviets left, there was no function for the *mujaheddin*. Putting the pieces together, it seemed the *mujaheddin* of the soviet war had no jobs, no mission and no government salaries. The soldiers were not paid and the regime deteriorated. Consequently, the *mujaheddin* devised an operable means of financial support.

There were stories of extortion. Attempting to attain financial reimbursement, former soldiers stopped travelers and truckers to extort a travel tax and whatever loot they could pilfer. This morphed into stories of abducting children for rape; boys and girls.

The pivotal story to many was the story of two young girls abducted for the purpose of gang rape. Not accepted in any community, in any country. Apparently a warlord/commander abducted the young girls, shaved their heads and offered them for gang rape at a military base near Kandahar. I found it difficult to eat as I listened to the details.

The story goes that neighbours went to Mullah Omar to report the offense. The Mullah sent 30 *talibs* with 16 rifles. They stormed the compound, freed the girls and hung the commander 'from the barrel of a tank.'

I didn't know if this was fact or fiction, but the story of gang rape and the rescue of the adolescent girls endeared the young *jihadists* to the Pashtun *talibs*. In the beginning there were many stories of injustices. When neighbours and villagers took their complaints and grievances to Mullah Omar he sent the *talibs* to bring about justice and order. The reputation of the Taliban spread like honey over ice cream.

As the tales of Mullah Omar's efforts against community atrocities increased, villagers grew to respect him as one who pursued justice. The students, the *Talibs*, the Taliban, as they became known, gained admiration for defending communities. News of the group of young student-fighters spread like Hollywood gossip. Many Afghans wanted this support, protection and return to law and order.

Every night the men, our freedom fighters, discussed the latest conquests of the religious students; which cities and which warlords they overturned.

"In Peshawar we learned the Taliban took Kandahar. Then they lost it to Massoud," Ahmed Shah Massoud, the Tajik leader of the Northern Alliance.

"As of last week, they had 20% of the towns. But Hekmatyer changed sides, right?"

"Lots of action in the south, but Massoud has aligned with Rabbani (the President)." They discussed and assessed the situation every night and included us with some English.

"I just can't decide if these young *talibs* will make it."

"You think they should make it? Think they are good for us?"

"I can't decide if they are any better, any different from the *Mujaheddin.*"

"I can't decide if they are any different than the warlords."

That evening we slept outdoors, on woven *charpoys* under a palmed roof. I did not undress but slept in my long skirt and bulky sweater in my sleeping bag. I did have a thin foam mat atop the rope-woven bed.

Before I crashed for the evening, Mirwaz asked me if I had any medicine. I really didn't: water tablets, which we never used, lomotil and aspirin. He took the lomotil and they joked that poor Khalif really had a bad problem mimicking him, clutching their sides, as he ran off to the bushes.

This was reassuring. It was not a foreign predicament. They too got Montezuma's Revenge, Delhi Belly, Afghani Affliction, the local equivalent: Taliban Tummy? Kabul Karma? Jalalabad Jinx?

The Goddess and the Serpent

E very night, wherever we were, we all slept in the same room or outside under thatched cover. I never felt nervous around these wild-eyed Kalashnikov-clutching freedom fighters; I appreciated their *Pashtunwali* code of hospitality and sharing, especially with foreigners, especially with me as a guest, especially with me as a foreign guest. Dare I say, especially with me a foreign female guest? I knew they would never cross me. I knew they would always protect me at all costs; it was mandated by the code. I wanted them on my side.

At sunrise I woke up, slid out of my bag, pushed my hair around and started to roll up my sleeping bag. In the crisp air I saw my breath, but the temperature was not uncomfortable, just fresh and bracing. I sensed others watching me. I folded-over my bag intending to head to the bushes. I slept in my clothes, like my Taliban/ Freedom Fighter companions. I tried to be nonchalant, but I did look up.

Kalif and Samerdin stood at the end of my *charpoy* staring at the bed and at me. A bad-hair day? I rearranged my matted mop with my fingers and looked up. Several of the men stared at my cot and then looked at me in disbelief, or some other emotion that I didn't recognize. I didn't get it. I couldn't quite understand what was happening. Again, I looked down at my cot still warm.

There rested a tightly-coiled brown patterned, yellowish snake;
On my bed;
Where I just removed my bag.

I knew my Pashtun partners tried to set me up. I sized-up the situation and decided they were trying to trick me or were playing some sort of bizarre Pashtu, Urdu, Afghani joke with a long, rubber snake. I laughed, I smiled, I continued rolling my bag and looked at them again. They looked at me and back at the snake. They were not

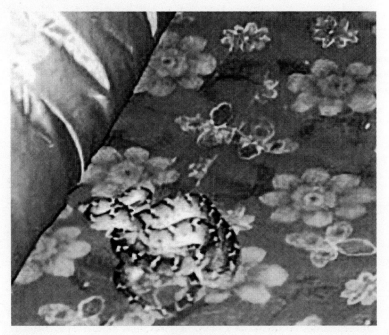

Bed partner

366

laughing. And when I looked at them yet again, the emotion which I hadn't understood, I realized as fear.

In the short time since I met these men, I grew to respect their courage and raw Pashtun pride. I never expected to see them afraid. Fear, not an emotion I anticipated from Muji, or especially Mirwaz; the twinkle in his eye replaced by a grimace and a set jaw. Samerdin's face contorted and twisted began to twitch just slightly. I almost laughed, but that would have been rude and insensitive. These tough, fierce men, fighters of Russian occupiers, who slept with, were wedded to their AK-47s, were afraid of a skinny little snake.

It was indeed a long coiled up yellow and brown reptile which I either slept on all night, or which slithered up during the night to snuggle and stay warm.

I remained nonchalant. I looked again. Their faces reflected panic, horror, terror, and probably a nervous concern for me. I still didn't respond. I grew up in California where rattlers were a way of life. Well not under my blanket, but I was certainly not afraid.

They started shouting and looking for sticks. Whoever found the longest stick flicked the creature, the live snake, across the *charpoy* onto the floor where it slinked across the ground. Someone else grabbed a gun, of course, while others began beating the creature to death.

Daryle grabbed the camera. They reluctantly paused while he snapped a photo. Now it was their turn to ponder why we wanted pictures. For us, the snake was more mesmerizing than the poppy fields and not illegal. As panic kicked-in, everyone caught the electricity of the emotion. Within seconds, they collectively batted the snake off the cot and onto the ground. As the reptile slithered across the dirt, the men lunged, whacked and lurched to annihilate the creature, finally blasting its head off.

When the warriors confidently declared the enemy dead, they grudgingly held out the snake to measure its full length: a meter plus. I wanted another photo and Daryle wanted to look it up when we got back to Pakistan. They did not leave it around but as soon as we had ogled over its length and patterned skin they flung it far out in the bushes to be permanently banned from our quarters.

When the commotion calmed and the battle concluded, the men hovered around me, like Greeks worshiping a goddess. Moi? What did that mean? I didn't do anything; I only slept on a snake. Was I special? Did I represent good luck? A good omen? The snake was poisonous.

It seemed they were now forever mesmerized, captivated by the idea of the Goddess and the Serpent. Was this a problem, that I did not fear snakes? Was it an issue that I was, god forbid, a person who had no fear? I was not uninformed. I knew about mambas. I knew about spitting snakes and squeezing snakes as in cobras and pythons. This snake was dormant, perhaps from the cool morning air. Gender was not a concern at any point during my time in Afghanistan. Why would it be an issue now? I decided it was not about gender. What was it about?

Like a charmer, it seemed as though I surmounted sure death. In fact, if the snake had slept inside my bag, yes, it might have been cozy with a fang in my ankle. It was not inside my bag. The fang was not in my ankle.

It seemed as though I overcame certain death from this most deadly species and I was forever to bring them luck and good fortune; the truth, in their eyes, was that I was spared by Allah PBUH. Who could argue with that? From that day forward, the tale of the Goddess and the Serpent preceded us in every village along our route. I decided to live with it.

Escape

Getting out of Afghanistan proved to be as thorny as getting in. One last time, we climbed out of a borrowed car, another old beater. Two of the men grabbed the bags and Kalif grabbed me by the arm pulling me through the crowded frontier area. Another border scrum: shoving and pushing as the fragile link fence slammed shut. Someone grabbed my other arm and pulled me through. I looked around and realized I was out of breath and panting. The gate closed with shaky finality. The others didn't make it and were forced to climb over the top of the wobbly boundary marker.

Several men in the crowd shoved and hoisted Daryle by the seat of his pants and the collar of his shirt as he tried to get a footing in the chain-link. He made it over the top and fell in the dust. We had no passports. Mirwaz disappeared in the crowd of disheveled Pakistanis and Pashtuns, Afghanis and other hopefuls.

No one knew where we were.

I was yanked through a chain-link fence.

My husband climbed over the barrier like a common criminal.

We were on the Pakistani side and if necessary, we would apply for new passports. Maybe my women friends were right. They were shopping in Hong Kong.

Reflections: Ramzi Yousef

One of the first things we did on our return to Pakistan was research the snake that caused all the commotion. Fittingly, it turns out that the reptile was most probably the Russell's Viper. The markings, length and habitat concur with those of my bed partner. The venom is said to be potent causing pain, swelling, bleeding, decreased blood pressure, decreased heart rate and... death. It grows to a length of 1.7 meters or 5.5 feet. One source claimed the Russell's Viper will coil, hiss and strike with such speed that its victim has little chance of escaping. According to Jan Sevcik of Wild Facts, "the Russell's Viper will transfer a large amount of venom into a single bite... death may occur over two weeks after the bite." This from Wikipedia.

I continued reflecting on the trip several weeks after our return to Islamabad. I found the Afghan culture rich in art. What I saw in Saudi and in Pakistan encouraged me to learn more. Carpets, blown glassware from Herat, tapestries, articles of embroidered clothing, caps, boots and dresses captured my imagination.

The day after we returned, our neighbours came over to inquire about the trip; our neighbour worked on the third floor of the US Embassy. They heard about the snake.

"Mirwaz told us you had a bed partner one night. Uninvited." Tom sniggered.

"Oh yeah? They told you that?"

"What did you do?"

"Nothing, really. I thought it was plastic." I took a sip of wine which they thoughtfully brought.

"By the time I recognized it was real, they had practically annihilated it."

"Weren't you scared?" Norma felt squeamish just talking about it.

"Not really."

"They said it was poisonous," she continued.

"That's what they told me at the time."

We babbled on about the excursion with the men, our companions. I knew they wanted more, but I couldn't sort it out so quickly. It took weeks.

I continued to question and reflect. Why were we allowed into Afghanistan? Who were these men? Was this a drug set up? A sting? While there I wondered: would we be abducted? Kidnapped? Why? Who were these men with us? Did each man have a separate function?

Were they visiting family? It seemed they were not Taliban; it seemed they were sorting out if Taliban were legitimate reformers or renegade students: Freedom Fighters or Terrorists?

Why were we encouraged to take so many photos? Why did we need the GPS? No one commented on the transfer of cars and it was only in retrospect that I wondered why we transferred into so many different modes of transport.

The large villa which we observed from the highway, took a GPS reading on and photographed, in the foreground of the university, was said to be used by Ramzi Yousef.

Who was Ramzi Yousef? Not anyone I knew, though the name was familiar, Yousef being a common name in the region but no one at school, not any of my neighbours. At the time, I had never heard of the man.

The news broke of his arrest. His deportation to the US "under tight security" handcuffed to my friend's husband who also worked on the third floor, his conviction, and the list of his involvements shocked me. Ramzi Yousef was responsible for the first World Trade Centre bombing.

In February 1995, Yousef was captured and arrested two blocks from our house. He *was* my neighbour as it turned out. It seemed the villa we photographed in Afghanistan, outside the university, was occasionally used by Yousef, this man responsible for the first World Trade Centre bombing in New York, 1993. While we lived in Islamabad Ramzi Yousef was in and out of the country.

His plan for the World Trade Centre was to destroy the first tower with the intent that it would collapse on the structure of the second tower and they would both disintegrate killing thousands. His colleague drove a van fully loaded with explosives into the basement parking and immediately drove another car out. Yousef headed for the airport as the van exploded. Reports indicated that he was unable to park in the preferred location, and the concrete support did not collapse as planned. Six people were killed and over one thousand injured. The towers did not disintegrate.

Yousef returned to Pakistan immediately after the Trade Centre bombing and attempted to assassinate Benazir Bhutto five months later. There was a glitch; the plan failed. Yousef went into hiding.

Much of this information came later while I was still processing events. I continued to learn. The more I read over time, I tried to reflect on Ramzi Yousef. What caused this venomous anger? It was difficult to comprehend the rage that morphed into hatred. Yousef, a clever, creative engineer; I tried to imagine his talents put to use in a productive way.

The next project of Ramzi Yousef was termed the Bojinka Plot, bojinka, a made up word to mean bang-bang, big bang, lots of bang. The word was possibly of Serbian origin. In the plan he intended to assassinate Pope John Paul II who was traveling to Manila for World Youth Day; this as a diversion. Simultaneously, while attention was centred on the death of the Pope, multiple bombs would be planted in toys and placed on Delta and United flights out of Bangkok heading to America. Khalid Sheikh Mohammed, Yousef's uncle, who helped finance the World Trade Centre bombing, was also an accomplice to the Bojinka Plot.

As I thought of Ramzi Yousef and read articles, the more I reflected on his presence in the neighbourhood. He perhaps didn't live there. I'm not sure he lived anywhere. But he was in and out. I might have passed him in the street or met him in the open market behind the house where the meat vendor sat cross-legged in his blue *shalwar khamis* and chopped hunks of raw meat with a bolo held between his toes. It was clear from the literature, that Yousef hated America. For that reason, and others not so blatant, I always tried to blend in, but my eyes are blue. I'm not Pakistani; not Saudi; not African, Asian or Middle Eastern. My eyes are blue. I'm American.

In 1994, a year after the Trade Centre bombing, Ramzi Yousef needed to test his new bombs for the so-called Bojinka Plot. On a flight to Tokyo from Manila, he implanted a toy car with a bomb, placed it under the passenger seat, pressed into the pocket of a life jacket. According to press reports, the selected seat was located over the fuel tanks of the 747 jet. Yousef deplaned at Cebu. The plane went on to Tokyo, where the bomb detonated four hours later but only killed the passenger in the designated seat. In the new configuration of the jet, the carefully chosen seat was located two rows in front of the fuel tanks and the plane did not disintegrate. The passenger sitting there was blown apart and others were injured, but the plane did not fragment.

I tried to sort this out. It seemed there was a connection between Ramzi Yousef and our trip to Afghanistan, but I didn't yet have the link to whatever it was. Yousef returned to Manila to work on the plan to assassinate the Pope. In an apartment fire where Yousef stayed, police determined he was assembling a bomb; they confiscated his computer with information of the Bojinka plan to detonate time-delayed bombs on 11 flights across the Pacific. Ramzi Yousef again escaped to Pakistan.

However, the following month, February, 1995, he was arrested at a guest house two blocks from our home. He was extradited to the States with chemical burns still on his fingers. The following year he was convicted and sentenced to life in solitary confinement. Without parole.

Reflections:
Khalid Sheikh Mohammed

Following our return to Islamabad, after being wedged through the chain link fence, we received our treasured passports. Mirwaz and cronies frequently stopped by the house, usually for a cold drink, usually a fake beer. Non alcoholic beer was available in the Muslim capital. Unlike our embassy neighbours we did not have commissary privileges. We worked in international education not the US government, contrary to popular fiction that surrounded our overseas work. It was during those visits that I learned in casual conversation from Mirwaz and his buddies, that other people used the Afghan villa besides Ramzi Yousef.

"Drug dealers use that big villa," Mirwaz divulged.

"They bought it with drug money.

"Only drug money could buy a villa, a mansion of that size.

"Lots of people go in and out, use it like a hotel."

"Interesting," I noted. I always said 'interesting' if I didn't know what else to say.

"You know, opium is a big problem in Afghanistan."

"In what way?"

"Many people make money from the sale of opium, but many more become addicted. The government must substitute other crops to the farmers, but nothing brings in as much money as the poppies. Is big problem, is not going away," Mirwaz concluded.

The day we made tea in the poppy fields Mirwaz showed me how to slice the pod of the poppy and drain the milky opium. I didn't hear most of what he told me that day because I was jumpy about even being there.

"You ready to go back to Afghanistan?" he asked as he took another sip of funny-beer. He was serious.

Khalid Sheikh Mohammed, the uncle of Ramzi Yousef, was thought to be a frequent or occasional visitor to the villa in Afghanistan. In the spring of 1996 when we visited and set up the GPS to get a reading and take photos of the villa, aka university in the background, Khalid Sheikh Mohammed made his way, or perhaps fled, to Afghanistan. He was by then enthralled with his nephew's fame and determined to execute his intensions for the New York Trade Centre.

At that time Khalid Sheikh Mohammed formed a relationship with Osama bin Laden, although reports said he was still, apparently, not willing to commit to the al Qaeda organization.

That year 1996, when we were quickly in and out of Afghanistan, Khalid Sheikh Mohammed was in and out of Pakistan and Afghanistan. It was reportedly during that time that he began to outline the strategy to complete the plans of Ramzi Yousef: to coordinate quadruple hijackings to bring down the Trade Centre towers, the Pentagon and the US Capitol building. This, a follow-up of the Bojinka Plan of multiple flights which failed the first time, combined with the plan to demolish both towers of finance and trade in New York, which also failed the first time.

Two years later, in 1998 when the US embassies in Dar es Salam and Nairobi were bombed, Khalid Sheikh Mohammed apparently became convinced of Osama bin Laden's commitment to destroy the United States.

Working with others, Mohammed began to finalize the plans of his nephew to hijack 4 planes, and bring down the towers. Bin Laden gave the final approval to go ahead with the plans. I learned of this much later as I was still processing our time in Afghanistan. We were at that time working in Dubai. I continued to question and reflect. What did this mean? What did any of it mean?

Slowly it started to come together for me. Over the weeks Daryle and I talked about the various segments of the trip. Piece by piece we started to put it together. The night we met Mirwaz and some of the others who would be our companions, we knew we were being scrutinized; it was more than an introduction.

Were the bilingual men from the Afghani Embassy or from the ISI, Inter-Services Intelligence? Months later at a cocktail reception in Islamabad, with a large generic crowd, I saw one of the men in a dark blue business suit. He was gone before I realized we met at dinner the previous year. He was not wearing pajamas but a blue business suit and polished black shoes and he carried a small radio in the palm of his hand.

On the infamous road to Peshawar and from Peshawar through the Khyber Pass, the men, our companions, laughed and joked like kids on a campout. The giddiness surprised me. We were getting to know each other. Everyone seemed on very friendly terms. The spirit would have been contagious, but I felt reserved. They were on familiar ground; it was all new for me.

"Daryle, when they picked us up at the house, to start the trip, did you expect to see the other guys with Mirwaz?" I asked one weekend. We sat on the upstairs deck in Islamabad as we sorted through our thinking.

"I never gave it a thought, but no, I only expected Mirwaz," he said as he lit his pipe.

"I guess I expected the others to be dropped off someplace."

"Did they seem hyper, over excited to you?" I wondered, trying to figure it all out.

"I don't know, but looking back, maybe."

"They were like kids off to camp, animated, laughing. Didn't you notice that?

"Joking about their beards, stopping for snacks, stopping for tea.

"I thought we would never get there.

"Those men laughed for two days; it was like an adventure." I re-lived the days.

"I think they were surprised to see your computer."

"Think it bothered them?"

"I think they may have wondered about it at the start. They called it the black box."

"Did you feel comfortable? I know you engaged Mirwaz in lots of conversation about education in the US, his thoughts on university education, and the possibility of his political interests."

"I really like Mirwaz."

"I felt reserved, cautious," I admitted.

"They were on familiar ground. They've been back and forth many times.

"It was all new for us," Daryle took another puff.

"That's my point. So why do you think they were so hyped-up this time?"

"You probably got 'em all excited."

"Get out."

Reflections: Ahmed Shah Massoud

In 2001 Khalid Sheikh Mohammed pressed forward with Ramzi Yousef's original plan to bring down the twin towers of the World Trade Centre. We were between jobs staying in Florida, having retired for the fourth time. On September 09, Ahmed Shah Massoud was murdered by two assassins posing as reporters, two days before the horrific multiple attacks, the completion of Ramzi Yousef's Trade Centre plans.

I stood at the edge of the pool in the afternoon, looking out on the sixth fairway. The late sun turned the greens to emerald. When I heard the National Public Radio announcement of the assassination I thought, 'This is not good.' Ahmed Shah Massoud: assassinated by suicide bombers in his office in the northern province of Afghanistan. There was no analysis of the murder. It was not reported as particularly relevant; another warlord murdered.

I didn't know why, but I felt this assassination was significant. I knew that Massoud was a respected Tajik, as leader of the Afghan Northern Alliance. He was instrumental in driving the Soviets out of Afghanistan, therefore appreciated by the US military and political figures.

Intuitive? Perhaps it was a gut feeling. I sensed it would be bad for America, just a feeling, as my Afghanistan reflections continued. I sensed that this meant trouble. I did not foresee that the trouble would be massive. Two days later the world focused on New York.

Many asked, "Why do they hate us?" It was not difficult for me to understand, though I placed more emphasis on our monetary system and American devotion to materialism. In fact, al Qaeda, in the voice of Khalid Sheikh Mohammed, later claimed four symbolic reasons for the destruction.

It was reported that the first two flights into the World Trade Centre were aimed at the US economy. The flight into the Pentagon was aimed against the US military. The flight intended for the Capitol was to represent anger for US policy in support of Israel. Kahlid Sheikh Mohammed was later to amplify his hatred for Israel.

At the end of that terrible year, in December 2001, three months after the destruction of the trade centre, Khalid Sheikh Mohammed sent Richard Reid to bring down an American Airlines flight from Paris to Miami on the 22nd of the month. It was to be a Christmas tragedy. The plot failed. Reid was restrained by attendants and passengers before he was able to fully ignite his shoe-bomb. It was initially assumed that Richard Reid was a lone malcontent.

Daniel Pearl, a reporter with *The Wall Street Journal*, had reason to research further. He flew to Pakistan to investigate a story on Richard Reid and his possible connection with a Pakistani militant. Pearl was abducted while en route to an interview. He was held captive for nine days then murdered by his captors. Decapitated

Khalid Sheikh Mohammed ordered the capture of Daniel Pearl and claimed to have personally severed his head, filming the act for distribution and internet video. Once it became known that Pearl was Jewish American, Khalid Sheikh Mohammed vented his rage and ordered Pearl's abduction and decapitation.

Who teaches this hatred? What cultivates this rage? How can we un-teach it? Is teaching arbitration, intervention or conflict-resolution enough? If the education doesn't come from home, where sometimes dysfunctional environments prevail, can formal education provide solutions?

Education is always the answer. 'Our' kind of education, that is. Education where the worth and dignity of the individual and of others is extolled. Our western conflict comes into play when education incites hatred and revenge. Do we still teach an eye for an eye? When does struggling for a cause cross the so-called line?

Who has the better cause? Who can help malleable young minds distinguish if the death of innocent victims is worth the cause for the greater good? And for the young minds, is this loss of innocence part of the education process?

Would I defend my own land, my family? Probably. By nature, I'm non-confrontational. I'm better with defensive body language. My life is still sheltered and protected. I've faced no such personal decisions. Sometimes however, I grapple with the decisions of my government. Grappling, struggling, is acceptable in our culture. No one is hurt.

The Struggle is the essence of Islam. Personal purification, the Struggle, is the *jihad* to become a good Muslim.

It occurred to me that Ahmad Shah Massoud, head of the Northern Alliance, respected by the US for his role in defeating the Soviets in Afghanistan, would have been instrumental in hunting down the probable criminals of the 9/11 attacks, as they came to be known. Instead, he was blown up in his own office two days before the assault.

Photo Op

Much of this reflection came later, long after we left Afghanistan. But I continued to reflect on what it all meant, our visitation through the villages that spring. When Daniel Pearl went missing we were working in Beograd. I felt close to Pearl. I knew Pakistan a bit. Daniel Pearl was one of us. I wasn't Jewish, I wasn't a reporter. Still, Daniel Pearl young American investigative reporter, a fine musician and husband, represented all the things we strive for in international work. It became personal.

January 2002, four months after 9/11 we moved to Beograd. The story of the young reporter broke my heart. Daniel Pearl was murdered because he searched for truth. Taunted because of his religion, they executed with vengeance and calculated rage. Emotion is contagious; all emotion. Khalid Sheikh Mohammed's misplaced leadership no doubt fomented in an infectious fury climaxing in the heartbreaking conclusion. When Mohammed learned that Pearl was Jewish, he personally, according to released videos, wielded the knife that beheaded the young journalist.

From Beograd we moved to Vienna and the violence continued. In reflection, the stream of world wide violence was often and frequent with devastating results. In October 2002, nine months after the murder of Daniel Pearl, Khalid Sheikh Mohammed was reported to have orchestrated the Bali bombings through a scheme of financing in which he arranged a courier system to send money from Thailand to Malaysia to Sumatra, Indonesia to pay for explosives for suicide bombers. Over 200 died in the Bali nightclub district, including many tourists from Australia.

Khalid Sheikh Mohammed was captured in Rawalpindi, Pakistan in March 2003; we worked and lived in Vienna. I focused to process the new information.

In Afghanistan, we changed cars often. We only later thought about this. We discussed the transportation. We accepted their decisions in blind oblivion. I didn't know where they came up with the vehicles, or why we changed so many times. Now, it seemed they didn't want to be tailed or followed. The scene in the market when we hit the child was high visibility. Though we did not get out of the van, Daryle and I were most probably noticed.

In retrospect, it is quite possible the family or the mayor was paid extra to be sure there was no further incident. Partly they were protecting us, the foreigners, the American foreigners. If we needed protection, we would be their guests, they were Pashtun. But if we were abducted, the US Embassy would have a public relations nightmare on their hands. Our colleagues carried guns, but the risk of that kind of publicity would be way too high profile.

What was going on when Mirwaz disappeared for lengthy stops in the villages? It seemed he did know everyone. It seemed he knew someone in every village. Though he had no datebook, no prearranged meeting times, it appears now, that he was not just dropping by to have tea.

Every time Kalif encouraged me to take photos, he also adjusted his camera lens. From the poppy fields to the villa in the valley of the university, they even encouraged us to take photos of the abandon soviet tanks. While giving the impression of pointing out interesting photo-ops for us, they were fine-tuning their own telephoto lenses.

The surprising use of the GPS also began to make some sense. It was important technology, new to Mirwaz, for pinpointing locations.

The villa, not the university, was worthy of note and was of significant interest.

The trip to the fishing river beyond the university was most probably a diversionary tactic which went out of control. When the university men at the fishing site became too curious, we were whisked away before anyone might determine we were on a fact-finding mission. Of course we were naive. We weren't on any mission. It was Mirwaz who was on the mission.

As I watched various news stories on Pakistan and Afghanistan, I realized that all reporters and news journalists paid for translators and armed protection when crossing into Afghanistan. I wondered if this was a requirement. Whatever the case, all of our men were very comfortable with their weapons. They were warriors from the Soviet war and from their own civil war.

"What did you make of the scenes at the border?" We were, one weekend, hiking in the Margalla Hills at the base of the Himalayas still rehashing our implausible time in Afghanistan.

"That was intimidating going in," Daryle said looking across the blue ridge of mountains.

"It was like crossing some African border by car.

"It was like one of those dusty shacks in the middle of nowhere.

"You fill out reams of paper that no one ever reads.

"It was like shuffling from the car to the mucky shacks;

"Sometimes walking through tsetse fly chemicals before proceeding.

"But unlike the African border crossings, we weren't in control," he observed.

"Who has any control in Africa?" I confirmed.

"What you mean is we didn't have our passports.

"We were shoved across the border. I guess it was legal. Did you question it?"

"Of course.

"I was wondering what you got us into," he turned around again to make his point.

"I bet. Wasn't much better when we tried to get out," I acknowledged.

"What was that about, anyway?

"Why was it so traumatic getting out of there?" I tried to think through my emotions.

"I don't think it was us," he said.

"Maybe we thought it should have been about us, as a privileged minority?

"We were shoved, pushed along as locals. Maybe that was a good thing.

"You barely made it."

"It was frightening. I felt like I was in trouble for something. Like maybe we were illegal."

"I was glad to get out of there. Safe," I finally confessed.

"The challenge is mob mentality. It's how kids die at rock concerts.

"It's how crowds die in disco fires; how individuals are trampled in riots."

"Yeah; it was scary."

Networking

Our trip to Afghanistan was about networking in the villages. The timely trip was part of the information hunting and gathering. As tourists, visitors, guests, we provided the cover for our companions.

Is this all speculation? If it wasn't Ramzi Yousef, or Khalid Sheikh Mohammed it might have been someone else. We were used. The Goddess of the Serpent was the great decoy. Used? Covert operative? Clandestine undercover agent? That's what my American neighbours think. Well, it makes a good story. It was something like that.

Now when I watch the news, I watch for my Freedom Fighters, hoping Mirwaz used this trip for information gathering. Hoping they are not today's terrorists, hoping their cause is going well. I'm still reflecting on the trip to Afghanistan. The daily news reinforces the relevance and lends perspective. It took some time to sort and understand. We didn't get it until much later. Would I do it again? I would. I will go back as soon as it is feasible; any excuse.

In the end, there was no shopping. What was it all about? We provided the diversion. Would I go back? Of course I will go back. I didn't buy a thing.

Post Script

There seems an al Qaeda pattern of rectifying mistakes made. When the first Trade Centre bombing failed to topple both towers in 1993, Khalid Sheikh Mohammed followed through in 2001, with total success. Both towers collapsed, though the plane directed toward the Capitol was diverted before it crashed in a field.

Again in 1993 Ramzi Yousef planned and attempted to assassinate Prime Minister Benazir Bhutto. The hiccup in the plan caused him to abort as he fled the scene. She was later assassinated in December of 2007. That crime is still under investigation.

Although the original Bojinka Plot failed in Manila, the Pope was not assassinated and the multiple flight bombings did not pan out, the plan was reincorporated into the September 11 plot and was carried out successfully.

Richard Reid, the shoe-bomber, was unsuccessful in his attempt to bring down a Christmas flight with an explosive in his shoe in 2001. Again in 2009 on Christmas day, another attempt was made by Umar Farouk Abdul Mutallab the 'fruit-of-the-boom' bomber, however this plot also failed. At the time of this writing, Mutallab is defending himself in court. Osama Bin Laden is dead by a US drone.

In the end, scruffy old men were revealed and unveiled as flabby and sweaty without their flowing gowns and robes and turbans, without props to support the mystic. Washed away. They ended their reign in humility. Captured, killed a dictators' death.

When will the rage subside? The story goes on. Only the characters change.

Acknowledgements

For over 50 years I have lived and worked in exotic countries unlike and very different from my own. I owe my writing groups enormous thanks for keeping me on task and word-smithing my documents, for telling me when the narrative was flat and for encouraging me when the dialogue was alive. I owe special gratitude to my online international readers who persisted in reading and critiquing my work as I continued to move around the globe: **Haidee Dehner** who read my pages while writing her own memoirs, Joan Petiti who read faithfully while writing her own plays, **Alice Moerk** who read and reread forcing, pushing me forward, I express my appreciation.

My Dubai Writers' Group patiently critiqued numerous drafts as I tried to find my style, my voice. Thank you **Jessica, Jeanne, Melissa, Sarala** and **Susan**. Then we published *The Write Brained Woman and Women's Writes*. My Sarasota, **Pen Women Writers' Group**, Alice, Amy and Aina who came during the year to Paris; **Elizabeth Waterston**, whose insight helped me through several sections, Maddy, Ellen, thank you for helping me sort out the chapters and thank you for including me through cyberspace when I lived in other worlds. My **Paris Writers' Group** Susan, Joan, Mei Chee, Tehari, and Lili who came to Kampala and met incredulously every week to tweak each other's work. My two **Kampala Writers' Groups** including Hollie, Lucy, Carol, Sarah, Viv, Sheree, Monique shaped me into reality with merciless good humour.

Steven King, *On Writing* taught me to eliminate the ly words, to use no modifiers, and to eliminate all ing words, no passive voice. **Barbara Kingsolver**, *Poisonwood Bible* taught me it is okay to take 15 years to complete a work. It's okay to spend 12 years on research and rewriting. It's okay to wait thirty years for wisdom and maturity to write the story, though she denies those attributes, and credits the writing to the encouragement of others. When Kingsolver explained that she rewrote the complete manuscript of the *Poisonwood Bible* five times from five perspectives, to learn how each character envisioned the story events, I felt validated. I wrote another draft. **James Michener**, *The Novel*, taught me the value of a writers group. **Pico Ayer,** "Travel writing is much more a matter of writing than of traveling- the hard part of the journey takes place at the desk...... Travel writing is something everyone seems to do, when emailing a friend or writing the obligatory assignment, 'what I did on my summer vacation.' It is hard to do well precisely because it is so easy to do passably," from The Travel Writer 2004. **JK Rowling** is not satisfied with the quality of her work. She plans to rewrite *Harry Potter*, the first book; says she could do a much better job with it. Lesson: don't settle for mediocre.

Vivian Gornick, *The Situation and the Story* taught me the relevance of reflection. She quotes V.S. Pritchett about writing memoir, "It's all in the art. You get no credit for living." It's not about places and events; it's about reflection; distanced reflection. I found **Tristine Rainer's** *Your Life as Story* enormous(ly) helpful at the time I started to read it. Building the 'goina' challenged me in nonfiction. She taught me to build my scenes like a work of fiction, causing the reader to wonder what's goina happen next. **William Zinzer**, *Inventing the Truth* helped sort out what is permissible in nonfiction.

Linda Hunt, Whitworth College, taught me that passive is boring. She also gave me the quote for a sticky note on my computer: *Because it is due, this is what I will write.* **Meg Peterson** at Plymouth State made me write my first-ever drafts of Kampuchea, Khow I Dung, and Afghanistan. I was very nervous at the first reading. My voice cracked and my hand shook as I came to grips with those emotional events.

My Florida neighbours taught me, **David Napoliello, MD, EACS** saved my life in March 2005. This book could not have been written without the nationals I met along the way; those whose lives feature in these pages. Without them, I would be incomplete and there would be no story.

I am deeply grateful to daughter **Jessica**, who somehow managed to read my bits while writing her doctoral dissertation and son **Ian**, who has just completed his first martial arts action novel, both of whom tell their own stories, some of them the same, from their own perspectives. To my parents I express abundant gratitude; to my mother, the one who wanted to travel, and to my father who sponsored my work.

Most especially, this book would not have happened without the 'ticket to ride' provided by my husband of over 50 years **Daryle**; the fisher who took me 'round the world happily traipsing in and out of counseling jobs and classrooms. His gentle kindness, unwavering love, controlled patience and compassionate comprehension of my desperate need to transcribe these wanderings never faltered. He stuck with me through three Alpha Smart notebooks balanced on my knees in game parks, during the trauma of a stolen computer at the Copenhagen airport, a bashed laptop in the shipment from Mumbai, a stolen memory stick in Bandung and in the end pushed me to completion.

Ms Russell, by Katrya Bolger, age 4, Islamabad

Appendix 1

Glossary of Non-English Words Ethiopia

The author has attempted to make uncomplicated basic translations of non-English vocabulary. Any discrepancies are the sole responsibility of the author.

Adobe	Mud brick used for housing. *Spanish*
Ameseghinallehu	Thank you.
Azmari	Ethiopian music often played by itinerate musicians.
Beit	House.
Bene	Good. *Italian.*
Berbere	A blend of spices including chili, cardamom, cinnamon, cloves, garlic, ginger, basil, fenugreek. Very spicy. Included in many Ethiopian dishes.
Betam tiru new	It's very good.
Bidet	Stizbath. *French* (with German definition)
Bira	Beer.
Birr	Ethiopian currency.
Bravo	Great! Well done. *Italian.*
Bunna	Coffee.
Cappuccino	Italian coffee whipped with cream.
Carmella	Candy. *Italian.*
Chat	Narcotic leaf, chewed for relaxation.
Cinquecento	Italian Fiat 500 used as taxis in Addis.
Croissant	Bread of French origin shaped in crescent form.
Dehna hunu	Good bye.
Doro wot	Chicken stew prepared with bebere.
Eskista	Ethiopian dance utilizing lots of shoulder movement.
Esposo	Husband, *Spanish.*
Farenj	Foreigner.
Formaggio	Cheese, *Italian.*
Imposible	Impossible, *Spanish.*
Injera	Flatbread, crepe-like in size, made from teff flour and very bitter from fermented yeast.
Konjo new	It's beautiful.
Lijjoch	Children, kids.
Loo.	Toilet, slang Australia.
Masengo, masinko	One stringed instrument.

Mercado	Market in Addis Ababa said to be Africa's largest open air market.
Mescal/Mascal	Celebrating the finding of the true cross, believed to be the one Jesus was crucified on; also marks the end of the rainy season.
Mit'mita	Spice mixture of cayenne, paprika, ginger, garlic, fenugreek, cardamom, nutmeg, cloves, allspice. Used with raw red beef, kitfo.
Piazza	Central plaza, *Italian*.
Shamma	Ethiopian traditional dress for men and women.
Shai	Tea.
Shai, yifelegalu?	You want tea?
Shinte beit	Toilet.
Siga wot	Beef stew.
Sint new	How much?
T'ej	Wine
T'ej beit	Wine house, bar.
T'ejery	Winery.
Tella	Beer.
Tenaisteleen	Hello.
Tere siga	Raw meat.
Tinish, tinish betam ameseghinalleuh, kilil new.	
	Just a little. Thank you very much.
Todo es imposible escribir a usted	
	"*It's* impossible to write everything to you."
Tsjika Chika	Mud used for making bricks for houses and buildings.
Wishsha	Dog
Wot	Stew.
Xabier, lgziabiher	Savior.
Yelem	No.
Yeselm Guad	Peace Corps
Yifelegalu?	You want?
Zabana	Guard.

Appendix 2

Glossary of Non-English Words Philippines

Amok	Crazy, haywire. To run amok, to lose it; to lose control.
Baho naman	Smelly.

Bangka	Small wooden boat primarily used for fishing or transport.
Bangkero	Driver of small boat.
Barong tagalog	Philippine shirt for men.
Barrio	Village.
Bibi	Baby
Bolo	Knife.
Calamansi	Citrus fruit, cross between orange and lemon.
Calesa	Cart pulled by horses or oxen.
Centavos	Coins.
Chinellas	Rubber flip-flop sandals.
Chismis	Tsismis. Gossip.
Coup d'état	Overthrow the government.
Despedida	Farewell party.
Esposo	Husband. Spanish.
Frappe	Whipped. French.
Jeepney	War-time jeep converted into colourful taxi transportation.
Kim chee	Spicy cabbage. Korean.
Khmer Rouge	Red Khmer; Communist Red party in Cambodia/Kampuchea. French.
Lavendera	Laundry maid.
Leba	Thief.
Limonada	Lemonade.
Lola.	Grandmother.
Lumpia	Uncooked raps for fresh veggies or deep fried wraps filled with diced meats and spices.
Maitre d'maison	Head of restaurant or hotel
Majlis	Assembly, meeting place
Major domo	Steward. Latin.
Mariachi	Traditional Mexican music. Mexican group of musicians.
Merienda	Mid day snack.
Mezcal	Mexican distilled alcohol.
Miso	Japanese breakfast soup made of seaweed, fish base. May include vegetables.
Mga	Filler word.
Naku naman!	Oh my goodness!
Naman	Filler word, meaning again.
Nipa	Palm fronds used for thatch roof of bahay kubo.

Note on the use of P, F and Ph. Spelling variations occur due to the history of Spanish, English and Filipino languages within the country. "The people are called Filipinos in English, Spanish and Filipino, but many Filipinos prefer to call themselves Pilipino... The national language is based on Tagalog....It was called Pilipino but the official name in all three languages is Filipino."* In these pages I have used a variety of spellings.

Pandesal	Bread of salt. Popular rolls served all day.
Pangit	Ugly.
Persona non grata	Not welcome. Latin
Pina	Pineapple.
Plaza	Square.
Salamat po	Thank you.
Shifta	Thief.
Tao	Common man.
Tiara	Head piece.
Tres chic	Very cool. Very smart; stylish. French.
Xie-xie	Thank you. Chinese.

*Paul Morrow. *In Other Words,* **Pilipino Express**. November 2011

Appendix 3

Glossary of Non-English WordsSaudi Arabia

Abaya	Black robe for Saudi women.
Adobo	Philippine stew, usually chicken or pork with garlic.
Agora	Open spaces for oration in Greece.
Aiwa	Yes.
Al humdulilah	Thanks be to god.
Alluh Akbar	God is great.
Ana	I (I am).
Assalam alaykum	Arabic greeting meaning 'peace be with you.'
Baba ghanoush	Eggplant dip.
Baklava	Sweet dessert, Middle East.
Basura	Trash, garbage. Tagalog/Spanish
Bindi	Forehead decoration; a dot between the eyes of Indian women.
Buona sera	Good evening. Italian
Burqa	Full body covering, cloak, for women.
Capsa	Special meal of lamb, rice, onion, garlic, and spices.
Chai	Tea.
Ciao	Hello/ Goodbye, general greeting. Italian
Eid	Holiday to mark the end of Ramadan.
Eid/Id Mubarak!	Blessed festival.
Fatwa	Religious ruling. A legal opinion or ruling on Islamic law, issued by an Islamic scholar.
Ghutra	Head covering for Arab men, red/white check, white or black/white check.
Glasnost	Openness, transparency in Russia.

Hajj	The Islamic month of travel to Mecca; a pilgrimage.
Iftar	Evening meal for Muslims during the month of Ramadan fasting. Break fast.
Igal	Black coil to hold gutra in place.
Imam	Leader of prayers. Leader of the mosque. Varies in Islamic communities.
Iqama	Identification card for Saudi residents.
Jambia	Short, curved knife or dagger.
Kim chee	Korean spicy cabbage.
Ma' as-salaama	Goodbye.
L'macchina	Car. The machine. Italian.
Ma fii	There is not. There are not.
Ma fii mushkala	No problem.
Ma ismak minfudlak?	What's your name please?
Majlis	Meeting, session
Mezze	Sharing. Arabic. A combination of small servings presented at the start of the meal, or as a complete meal. A sampler plate or starter course.
Minfudluk	Please
Moya	Water.
Muezzin	Person at mosque who calls Muslims to prayer five times a day.
Mutawwa	Mutawwa'in. Volunteer. Used as a term for government-recognized religious police.
Naan	Flat bread prepared in an oven.
Pakidala mo ang cappuccino?	Please bring cappuccino? Tagalog.
Pancit	Noodles. Tagalog.
Perestroika	Restructuring. Russian.
Per favore	Please. Italian.
Qhawah, qahwah	Coffee.
Quran	Koran. Holy book for Muslims.
Ramadan	The Islamic month of fasting.
Sadiq Asdiqaa'	Friend.
Sadiqi	My friend.
Scusa	Excuse me. Italian
Shamal	Wind current/storm. Hot, dry, dusty and sandy. Desert sand storm.
Shawarma	Arab sandwich wrap usually of lamb or chicken.
Shukran	Thank you.
Shura	Consultative council. Majlis.
Sushi	Japanese finger rolls of rice and fish. Many variations.
Suq	Market
Tabbouleh	Salad made of bulgur, parsley, tomato, spices.
Thobe	Floor length robe for men, white in summer, possibly beige or grey in winter.
Umm	Mother.

Wa	And.
Wa alaikum assalaam	And upon you peace.
Wadi	Valley. Dry riverbed.
Yellah!	Let's go! Move it! Hurry up!

Appendix 4
Glossary of Non-English Words Pakistan

Burka	Full covering for women especially Afghanistan.
Dupatta	Long head scarf.
Shalwar kameez	Loose pajama pants, long shirt or tunic.
Suqi	Merchant used regularly. Personal helper at market, inclined to give discounts, freshest produce.

Appendix 5
Glossary of Non-English Words Afghanistan

Afghani	Afghan currency.
Chapatis	Flat bread made on the stove usually one at a time. Hindi, Urdu.
Charpoy	Four legs. A frame strung with woven fiber or rope for a bed.
Hadith	A book of anecdotes and sayings by or about the prophet Muhammad, PBUH.
Jihad	Struggle to become a good Muslim. Holy war to defend Islam.
Jihadists	One who struggles or fights a jihad.
Kilim	Hand woven, wool carpet.
Loya Jurga	Grand assembly, lawmaking body. Pashto.
Madrassa	Islamic seminary in Pakistan that teaches the Koran and Islamic subjects.
Mujaheddin	Holy warrior fighting jihad.
Mullah	Shia leader of prayers at mosque. Imam is Sunni leader of prayer.
Pakol	Woolen hat typical of the Chitral, Gilgit and Hunza

	areas, especially worn by Pashtun and mujahideen.
Pakora	Vegetables dipped in flour batter and deep fried, served as snacks.
Pashtunwali	Pashtun tribal code of honour, code of conduct, social code of behavior.
Qaaba. also Kaaba	Cube. The cube shape building in Mecca constructed by Ibraheem and Ishmaeel and contains the Black Stone, said to have fallen from heaven. It is thought to be the oldest mosque in history.
Talib	Afghan student attending the religious seminaries in Pakistan.
Taliban	Students. Now an Islamist militant and political group that ruled large parts of Afghanistan and its capital Kabul from September 1996 until October 2001. Mulla Mohammed Omar was the first leader of the group.

Survivor, 2006, with Jessica